The Toronto School of Communication Theory
Interpretations, Extensions, Applications

D1521247

The Toronto School
of Communication Theory
Interpretations, Extensions, Applications

Edited by

Rita Watson and Menahem Blondheim

UNIVERSITY OF TORONTO PRESS
THE HEBREW UNIVERSITY MAGNES PRESS, JERUSALEM

This book is published under the auspices
of the Halbert Centre for Canadian Studies
of the Hebrew University of Jerusalem
and the Israel Association for Canadian Studies

Library and Archives Canada Cataloguing in Publication Data
A record for this title is available from Library and Archives Canada

ISBN 978-965-493-292-9 (magnes)
ISBN 978-0-8020-9775-0 (cloth)
ISBN 978-0-8020-9529-9 (paper)

Table of Contents

Part II
Extensions

Part III
Applications

Acknowledgements

This volume has seventeen authors, two editors, and many parents. Intellectually, it reflects the influence and inspiration of two great scholars: Elihu Katz and David Olson, who also contributed, respectively, a foreword and an afterword. It is also a direct consequence of the efforts of a number of scholars and public leaders dedicated to furthering understanding and cooperation between Canada and Israel. Foremost among the individuals who made this volume possible are Daniel Ben-Natan, President of the Israel Association of Canadian Studies; the late Arie Shachar, and Joseph Glass, both formerly of the Halbert Center at The Hebrew University of Jerusalem. Steven Kotowych of the University of Toronto Press guided the project through the manuscript review process; the Manuscript Review Committee at University of Toronto Press and two anonymous reviewers offered detailed, insightful criticisms and suggestions that were invaluable for each chapter and the volume as a whole. Hai Tsabar and the Hebrew University Magnes Press provided editorial guidance and support in the final stages of production. The Halbert Centre and the Israel Association of Canadian Studies were instrumental in accommodating this project, beginning with the opportunity to organize the Toronto School Focus Sessions at the 2002 Biennial Conference, and throughout the process of editing and publishing this volume. Roz and Ralph Halbert of Toronto have fostered and materially encouraged academic and cultural cooperation between Canada and Israel over many years, and this book would not have been possible without their support. To all of the above, we express our sincere gratitude.

Menahem Blondheim and Rita Watson

Foreword

ELIHU KATZ

The Toronto School and Communication Research

The "Toronto School" insists that the technologies of the media of communication are far more influential than their content. Harold Adams Innis and Marshall McLuhan are not alone in making this claim, and not the earliest, but they have done so more provocatively and more persistently than others. What's more they argue that media technologies have a dominant influence not just on individuals but on social structure and culture, and not just in modern times but from the beginning. Their writings have attracted much interest – and fierce debate – but only little systematic research. If they are right, communications media deserve a central place in the history of civilizations, and communication research ought to rise to the challenge.

But it hasn't. The bigness of these claims – and the pride of place which they offer to the media – contrasts sharply with the conclusion of "limited effects" echoed repeatedly in studies of mass persuasion. These studies of media "campaigns" can be traced to the theory of mass society, suggesting that the atomized individuals of the early 20th century would be vulnerable – as if by remote control – to the ostensibly powerful appeals of broadcasters. However, the empirical research that set out to test this assumption – at Columbia (Klapper, 1960) and at Yale (Hovland, 1959) – found that it is far from easy to change opinions, attitudes and actions, and, moreover, that modern individuals are less isolated or alienated than was assumed. The claims of mainstream communications research became much more modest as a result.

The doctrine of limited effects has been challenged by various groups, especially by so-called "critical theorists" – best known among whom are the members of the Frankfurt School. They argue (1) that media effects are better conceptualized as protracted, rather than short run, processes; (2) that the media are more effective in the "cultivation" of values and images rather than in campaigns of "persuasion" aimed at entrenched attitudes and habits, a position with which cognitive theorists would agree; (3) that the primary effect of the media is to be sought in reinforcement of the status quo – that is, in non-change or the slowing of change rather than in accelerating change; and (4) that the message of the media derives from the interests of their owners and controllers, a position that parallels that of certain political economists. Even this call for a return to a conception of "powerful effects," however, assigns paramount influence to the content of the media. With certain important exceptions (Benjamin, 1968, for example), they are only marginally interested in other attributes of the media – their technologies, for example, or the locus in which they are consumed (Freidson, 1953; Katz & Popescu, 2004).

Technological theorists agree that the influence of the media is a long-run affair, so much so that the predominant medium of a given time and place leaves its indelible mark on personality and culture and social organization. Thus, McLuhan thinks of the linearity of print as having created linear personalities, inner-directed, formalistic and ascetic. He thinks of print as an unambiguously "hot" medium, delivering messages that add intensity and drive to culture, while television is ambiguous and "cool," inviting more meaning-making, more relaxed participation (in the subconscious activity of connecting the pixels) and offering immediate gratification. Unlike mainstream researchers who consider the abstractness of print more involving than the literalness of television, when McLuhan says "the medium is the message" he means that the technology of each new medium habituates the mind to a particular kind of decoding that shapes personality and culture.

For McLuhan, these predominant habits of mind also affect social organization. He associates the linearity of railroads and assembly lines with print, and sees the decentralization of the working place as a function of the diffuseness of electronic technology. Drawing on ancient history, Innis, too, links the bureaucratic centralization of Egypt with the invention of portable papyrus and written script so that orders from the Pharaoh at the center could be speedily transported up and down the Nile. For his part, Innis characterizes the media as space-biased and time-biased. Space-biased media expand the influence of empires and civilizations, while time-biased media – such as pyramids – are transmitted over time, from generation to generation. He believed that the two orientations needed to be continually equilibrated in order for a society to survive.

This radical breakthrough in thinking about media effects was made, not surprisingly, by "outsiders" – in both nationality and discipline. The technological theories of McLuhan, Innis and their associates hail from Canada, a land dependent on its innovative media technology for spanning vast territory and outlying settlements, and for differentiating itself from its southern neighbor. Meanwhile, private enterprise in the United States was creating a "culture industry" along with its technology.

Neither McLuhan nor Innis came from the social psychological tradition that reigned in mainstream (that is, American) communication research. McLuhan entered media studies through a side door and stormed onto center stage. A scholar trained in English literature, he shifted from an initial interest in media content to put all his weight on form (which would have won the approval of his Cambridge mentors) and on technology (Katz & Katz, in this volume). McLuhan was a great hit among executives of the culture industry, and attracted considerable attention from humanists (though not from social scientists), who initially warmed to his poetic provocations and then cooled down. His renown has also had ups and downs – and ups. In the process, Toronto became known as the center for the study of the social effects of media technologies.

Harold Innis, the economist, also entered through a side door, but his interest in the economics of nation building pointed him to the role of media and to close affiliation with McLuhan, more as mentor than collaborator. Nevertheless, there remains a significant territory of concurrence between the two. McLuhan agreed with Innis that word of mouth is a medium of "heart," favoring the communication of practical wisdom across generations – hence tradition and religion, as in Innis' notion of time-binding media. Print, on the other hand – an extension of the eye for McLuhan – is a medium of "mind." It favors the communication of specialized knowledge, hence nationalism and empire – reaffirming Innis' analysis of space-binding media. McLuhan's "global village" is a prophecy that sees the revival of oral culture in television and a welcome liberation from the tribalism of radio and the imperialism of print. McLuhan was not in love with television, however; he only hated it less than print.

Untimely death spared Innis from having to analytically confront television. He most likely would have seen it as the overextension of media of space, at the expense of the necessary balance with media of time. Given his pessimism, Innis might well have seen television as a force leading to a catastrophic growth of the spell of space, destined to bring down the over-biased civilizations snared by its charms.

Both Toronto scholars have left the effects of the avalanche of new media technologies in the latter 20th century to be studied by successors. But the early ripples they made indicate the productivity of their approach to media research. More in the spirit of Innis than McLuhan, technological theory has enlisted many first rank researchers: Goody and Watt (1968) have spelled out the effects of transition from orality to literacy; Eisenstein (1979) has explored the effect of the printing press on religion, science, and scholarship; Tarde (1901) credits the newspaper with the rise of the public; Carey (1989) has shown how the telegraph affected the economic integration of the United States; Gouldner (1976) suggests that the proliferation of paper created a need for ideology; Meyrowitz (1985) argues that television's accessibility has lowered the boundaries that separate generations, genders, classes, etc. Rather than wild speculation, each of these theories is specific about the particular attribute of media technology (the fixedness of print, the accessibility of television, the simultaneity of the telegraph) that is responsible for the hypothesized effect.

As a group, technological theories can be mapped in two related ways. McLuhan and his later adherents proposed to understand media as vehicles/engines of (a) change (b) in the mental processing (c) of individuals (d) in the long-run (e) as a result of unique technological attributes of the different media. This combines with the emphasis laid by Innis and developed by his followers on conceptualizing media's ultimate effects as (a) change (b) in social organization (c) of societies and institutions (d) in the long-run (e) in response to shifting media ecologies. Either of these approaches thus posits that the introduction of new media technologies is destined to bring about thoroughgoing and long-lasting change. The interpretation, extension, and application of these proposition – the three parts of this present volume – is surely called for as contemporary society is coming to grips with an avalanche of new media technologies introduced at the turn of the second millennium.

References

Benjamin, W. 1968. The work of art in the age of mechanical reproduction. In Hannah Arendt, ed., *Illuminations*. New York: Harcourt, Brace Jovanovich.

Carey, J. W. 1989. Technology and ideology: The case of the telegraph. In id., *Communication as Culture: Essays on Media and Society*. Boston: Unwin Hyman.

Eisenstein, E. 1979. *The Printing Press as an Agent of Change: Communications and Cultural Transformations in Early-Modern Europe*. 2 vols. New York: Cambridge University Press.

Freidson, E. 1953. The relation of the social situation of contact to the media in mass communication. *Public Opinion Quarterly*, 17(2): 230–238.

Goody, J., & Watt, I. 1968. The consequences of literacy. In Jack Goody, ed., *Literacy in Traditional Societies*. Cambridge: Cambridge University Press.

Gouldner, A. M. 1976. *The Dialectics of Ideology and Technology*. London: Macmillan.

Hovland, C. I. 1959. Reconciling conflicting results from experimental and survey studies of attitude change. *American Psychologist* 14, pp. 8–17.

Katz, E., & Popescu, M. 2004. Narrowcasting: On communicator control of the conditions of reception. In P. Golding & Ib. Bondjberg, eds., *New Media-New Europe*.

Klapper, J. T. 1960. *The Effects of Mass Communication*. Glencoe, Ill.: Free Press.

Meyrowitz, J. 1985. *No Sense of Place: The Impact of Electronic Media on Social Behavior*. New York: Oxford University Press.

Tarde, G. 1901. *L'opinion et la Foule*. Paris: Presses Universitaires de France.

Introduction

MENAHEM BLONDHEIM AND RITA WATSON

Innis, McLuhan and the Toronto School

> *Neither hand nor mind alone can long prevail*
> *without the instruments and tools that perfect*
> *them.*
>
> Francis Bacon

The articles selected for this volume are linked by a common debt to the ideas of a set of scholars commonly identified as the Toronto School. They explore communications and media in human cultures from oral traditions, through early and later forms of writing, to modern electrical and digital media. Many backgrounds and academic orientations are represented by these articles – media and political studies, law, history, sociology, psychology, pragmatics, as well as cultural studies and literary criticism. They also range from the theoretical to the empirical. Such a varied group of works in a single edited volume might appear awkward were it not for the fact that this same diversity characterizes the Toronto School itself.

Consider the founding fathers of the school, Harold Adams Innis and Herbert Marshal McLuhan. One was a hard-nosed political economist, an introvert, a former Ontario farm boy, once irreverently tagged by McLuhan a "Baptist hick." The other was a flamboyant literary critic, an extrovert, a cosmopolitan, Catholic savant and a professor of English. What could these two very different men have in common that would lead them to be identified as belonging to the same school of thought? The link is their great common breakthrough: the notion of communications as a distinct phenomenon, an idea that they abstracted out of the broader disciplinary concerns within which it had been embedded. They joined in focusing on communication as the key to understanding the co-development of mind, culture and society.

In our own times, the 21st century, the prominence of communications as an aspect of human culture may seem like an obvious, even commonplace, observation. However, this was hardly the case in the middle of the 20th century. By that time, scholars at the University of Chicago, such as Dewey, Mead and Park, had only taken the first steps in pondering the "significance of communication," and New York's prominent Frankfurt emigrés had yet to launch their influential quest to consider the institutional and cultural meaning of mass broadcast media. Paul Lazarsfeld and his colleagues at the Bureau of Applied Social Research began their attempts to measure the effects of mass mediated messages only after the Second World War. It was around this time that Innis, and subsequently McLuhan, were formulating their own original attempts to conceptualize communication as an object of academic inquiry, and beginning their radical and innovative conjectures about its consequences.

Themes: Process, Effects, Technology

While the theories of Innis and McLuhan are notoriously resistant to neat encapsulation, some general themes have emerged in scholarly attempts to situate them within the emerging discipline of communication studies that they helped to define. Three such themes can be seen as the most fundamental in characterizing the unique perspective of the Toronto School.

The first major theme that can be identified in the work of Innis and McLuhan is their common interest in communications as a *process*, rather than as structure. Unlike their Chicago predecessors, and much like their contemporaries Shannon and Weaver,[1] both Innis and McLuhan saw communication as a seamless circuit linking people through media and their messages. Their scope, however, was much larger and richer than Shannon and Weaver's reductionist approach. Their units of analysis spanned individuals, groups, societies and civilizations; spatially their outlook was ecumenical; and temporally they were oriented to seeing the world as developing through processes of communication.

---

1   Claude Shannon & Warren Weaver, *The Mathematical Theory of Communication* (Urbana: University of Illinois Press, 1963 [originally published 1949]).

The second theme is the focus on the *effects*, or consequences of communications. Although this concern was widely shared by early communication theorists, a hallmark of the Toronto School in pursuing it was their broad conceptualization of media effects. It ranged from economic, social and cultural change to cognitive consequences and even to influences on personality. This can be contrasted with the more narrowly conceived quest of the Columbia School to identify short-term, measurable effects of mass mediated messages on opinions, attitudes, and behaviors of individuals. Indeed, fascination with change itself may be seen as a defining characteristic of Innis' and McLuhan's approach. Accordingly, the Toronto School was unique in its orientation toward history – the study of change. Both the history of communications and the role of communications in history were central to their theorizing.

Among scholars who have explored differences between oral and written communication, particularly its significance in relation to cognition, a certain caution prevailed regarding the use of the term *effects* – probably because cognitive scientists tend to use the word *effect* only with respect to an isolable and empirically-verifiable *cause*, and it is notoriously difficult to identify clear cause-effect relations in this kind of inquiry. Some scholars commonly associated with the Toronto School, such as Havelock, Goody and Watt, and Olson, refer to a literate *bias* (following Innis) or to the *consequences* of literacy (see Chapter 9, in this volume, for a fuller discussion of this issue). However, in the literary tradition of the New Criticism, to which McLuhan was exposed at Cambridge, *effects* was the preferred term to refer to the subjective reactions of readers and listeners to poetry and prose, and it was the term that McLuhan used in his work on media, a usage which is also common in mainstream communication research.[2]

The third and distinctive theme of the Toronto scholars was the sharp focus on the *technology* of communication, or the medium. This focus on medium has been used to characterize the Toronto School, and by some scholars to dismiss it, under the rubric of "technological determinism." Such a dismissal would be unfortunate: after all, the role technology plays in communications is different from its role in any

---

2   Others have argued for *effects* in mapping communications, cf. Elihu Katz, "Media Effects," *International Encyclopedia of the Social and Behavioral Sciences* (Elsevier, 2001), pp. 9472–9479.

other field. Communication, thought of as a process, is the active linking of participants by messages which are conveyed by some technological apparatus – clay tablet, printed page, film, voice- or e-mail, – one may go on and on. In communications, the technology is ever present and salient because it is the substrate of the act. To illustrate: a slice of bread that reaches our table may be a consequence of cutting edge agricultural technology, such as genetic engineering, yet that technology does not impact in any direct way on the eating of the bread. In contrast, a *telephone* conversation, reading a *book* or watching *television* are activities that are inextricable from the technologies that support them. Even naming or describing these activities entails mention of the technology. This is precisely because communication is the *process* by which all constitutive elements: sender, message, coding, receiver, and channel – the locus of technology – become linked as active, integral parts.

Thus, when Innis and McLuhan began mapping out the new field of communications, with an emphasis on process, it was inevitable that technology would figure as central in the cluster of elements that constitute it. And given their quest to identify and understand media effects, technologies would be seen as elements molding the overall consequences of communicating. The quote from Bacon that opens this introduction illustrates the central role that technology may assume in extending human abilities.

Yet not all channels conveying meaning between communicators require technological gadgetry. Voice and gesture are certainly pre-technological. More importantly, language – not necessarily defined as a technology – is a basic mediation channel. Not surprisingly, therefore, both Innis and McLuhan pay considerable attention to what Walter J. Ong subsequently identified as "primary orality" – the oral culture of communication that preceded technological developments, such as writing. In this context, it is worth noting that Vygotsky used Bacon's paean to instruments and tools to characterize language, which he argued to be the most basic tool by which thought is perfected.[3]

By taking non-technological communication processes into account, Innis and McLuhan paradoxically enrich the understanding of technology

---

3   Lev Vygotsky, *Thought and Language* (Cambridge, Mass.: MIT Press, 1962).

and its role in communications. The routine coexistence of ordinary oral language alongside technologically-mediated communication can serve as the ultimate benchmark for understanding the role of technology, and as a baseline for considering its significance and consequences. Just as the consequences of language on mind are pervasive but transparent, so too are the effects of communication technologies: their users are unaware of their effects (see Chapter 9 for a fuller discussion).[4] Ultimately, any technology of communication, as a prosthesis or extension of primary orality, is an attempt to perfect the performance of hand and mind. McLuhan and Innis were inventive, each in his own way, in showing how broadly the ripples of these consequences or effects may reach, and both ultimately understood that the expanse and power of these effects were traceable to their origins in primary oral environments.

That Innis and McLuhan concurred on the fundamental unifying themes of process, effects and technology is as remarkable as it is unexpected. That an economist would ponder process rather than structure, and that both an economist and a literary scholar should focus on the centrality of effects and technology, appears odd on first glance. Yet the points of agreement between this odd couple become plausible when one considers their common breakthrough: the notion of communication as a distinct phenomenon to which process and technology are both elemental and inextricable.

Nevertheless, the ideas of these two scholars diverged greatly, retaining residual imprints of both the distinct general scholarly domains from which they were derived, and also the great differences in personality, temperament and social background of the two men. To an extent, Innis and McLuhan may be seen as the products of two very different generations.

4   Daniel Dennett, Language and Intelligence. In Jean Khalfa, *What is Intelligence?* (Cambridge: CUP, 1994), discusses the ubiquitous and transparent influence of language on thought; Paul Levinson, *Digital McLuhan: A guide to the Information Millenium* (New York: Routledge, 1999), discusses the extension of McLuhan's notions of the influence of media on forms of mental and cultural representations to multi-modal electronic communications.

Harold Adams Innis

Harold Adams Innis, a Canadian nationalist, would probably have been gratified to see his work featured at the center of a volume with "Toronto" in its title. His scholarly career was distinctively Canadian, and Toronto stood at its center. Innis, who was born in 1894 and raised on a relatively isolated farm near Otterville, Ontario, had never imagined or planned an academic career. With the calling of a Baptist minister in mind, he chose McMaster University, then in Toronto, for his undergraduate studies, eventually completing a Master's degree there. He would spend his entire teaching career at the University of Toronto, where he held the positions of Head of the Department of Political Economy and Dean of the Graduate School until the day of his untimely death at the age of 58, in 1952.

The one non-Canadian stint of his scholarly career was the period of his doctoral studies in economics at the University of Chicago, between 1918 and 1920. However, as he informed his Chicago advisor, he wished to work on a theme in Canadian economic development for his thesis. The topic suggested to him was a history of the Canadian Pacific Railroad, and the student who had spent hours every day traveling by railroad to his high school took up the topic with enthusiasm. Needless to say, the dissertation was researched mainly in Canadian archives. On the commencement of his academic career, Innis turned down a lucrative position at Beloit University, "on the chance," he explained, "that a Canadian university will send in an application."[5] He seized the chance presented to him by the University of Toronto, his first choice from among Canadian universities. He would remain there throughout his academic career, and when offered, at its prime, a professorship at the University of Chicago, he turned it down.

Innis did leave Toronto for two other extended periods, but both sojourns underscored his Canadian nationalism. The first took him via England to the First World War battlefields of France. Serving in the artillery of the First Division of the Canadian Expeditionary Force (significantly, perhaps, as a signaler), he was injured in Lens-Arras near

---

5   Quoted in Donald Creighton, *Harold Adams Innis: Portrait of a Scholar* (Toronto: University of Toronto Press, 1957), p. 46.

Vimy Ridge. Only after many months of convalescence in England he returned to Canada and was discharged. His other major absence from Toronto was his service, as Canada's premier political economist, on the Royal Commission on transportation. The issues involved in the Commission's work touched on the core of his entire research career: In his doctoral dissertation Innis had argued that transportation represented a crucial aspect not only of Canada's economic development, but of nation-building. By the time he served on the Royal Commission, his views of the causal relation of transportation to national development had changed; yet his rating of its significance had, if anything, increased. The work of the Commission focused on Ottawa, and Innis spent many months there in the course of his service, from 1948 to 1951.

Thus, the Toronto affiliation as highlighted in the title of this volume would appear to locate Innis appropriately in both body and mind – in geography as well as in identity and ideology. Less immediately obvious is associating the work of Canada's leading political economist with communication theory. After all, Innis turned to the study of the history of communication only late in his career; and while his seminal contributions to Canadian economic history were widely appreciated in his lifetime, he did not live to see comparable recognition of his work on communication. Nevertheless, Innis would probably have been particularly gratified to see his achievements in theorizing about communications celebrated, for they can properly be seen as the culmination of his entire scholarly journey, subsuming all his previous scholarship.

Innis' seminal works in Canadian economic history can be deceptive in their descriptiveness. His exhaustive accounts of Canada's main staples – first the fur industry, then the cod fisheries, later yet grain and dairy, and finally paper production – may appear as a rigorous exercise in documenting and analyzing the successive major players in the Canadian economy. Yet Innis' thrust in these definitive, detailed studies went beyond setting the record straight on the production and bringing to market of Canada's main products. He was seeking the role of these staples – and by extension, of Canada – in the broader picture of the intercontinental economy, and in the political and social implications of the flow of the products he studied. Thus, the intra-Canadian process of establishing and developing the staple economy could be seen to both reflect and effect relations to a broader field of economies and nations; and the flow of furs and cod fish could serve to chart political, social, and cultural links and identities. The staples and their workings were thus a parable, in concrete physical disguise, for imaginations, sensibilities, and identities.

The paper industry made this connection between the physical staple and the life of the mind much more obvious and concrete. The main use of the commodity was in printing – the process of recording and diffusing knowledge and ideas. The traffic of the commodity thus underscored the economy and flow of ideas, opinions, and interaction, making the implicit political and social story of the staples economy explicit. From this point on, Innis no longer told the story of generating and transporting staples, and the political and social networks their journey implied. Instead, he ventured into the process of generating and communicating knowledge and ideas directly. Rather than observing the political and social networks the conveyance of staples underscored, he zeroed in on the interfaces themselves: the nexus became the center of the story. In this way, Innis' later work on communications can be seen as a finale of his lifelong study of Canadian political economy.

The grand move from economic history to communication theory inevitably left its traces: some of the distinguishing features of Innis' thinking about communication reflect the process of their emergence. The most distinctive perhaps is the residual presence of the staple – the concrete, physical element – in his theorizing about communications. Innis, and following him and his disciples, and then the rest of the world call it the medium.[6] Whether a pyramid, a papyrus, or a cellular handset, the process of communicating is anchored in a staple – just as staples are moved in a field mapped by communications. And most naturally, according to Innis, the communication staples – the media – inevitably obey economic principles, in scarcity or plenty, monopoly or free market.

Another carryover from staple theory to communication theory is the level of analysis. Innis addressed communications on the level of nation, empire, and civilization, just as he had formerly analyzed the role of staples in a super-macro matrix. Innis studied in Chicago at

6   Lance Strate, "A Media Ecology Review," *Communication Research Trends*, 23:2 (2004), p. 8.

the time its social thinkers were coming to confront issues of social communication. The project of Park and Dewey, Mead and Cooley focused on communications in and across social groups within national society. Although McLuhan identified Innis with the Chicago group, there is no actual evidence that Innis meaningfully engaged with or had even been influenced by the ideas of these thinkers.[7] Be that as it may, they surely would not fit the grand ecumenical scale of his theorizing. Even most of Innis' partners and successors in thinking about communications – to include Marshall McLuhan – would decline working on Innis' expansive level of analysis. Moreover, Innis, who throughout his academic career was identified as a political economist, focused on the political and social consequences of communication media, as well as their cultural implications. His colleagues and followers, however, would not necessarily concur in that interest. Most notably, McLuhan would consider cognitive and behavioral implications of media, to the neglect of their political effects and their impact on social organization.

Finally, Innis thought about media and researched them from a historical perspective, just as his economic work focused on the development and change of Canada's products and markets over the ages. Yet while there was continuity in his general historical outlook, his strategy of historical research shifted markedly when he moved from economic research to communication studies. Rather than collecting and studying primary sources, Innis' histories of communication depended exclusively on secondary sources, apparently believing that such were the appropriate sources for what he was attempting: philosophical history. This neglect of primary sources may explain the regrettably meager impact of Innis' work in historical studies. Nor did his historical approach find a meaningful following among social scientists interested in communications. They did, however, find imaginative ways to utilize Innis' pioneering historical work, and reorient it, from looking backwards at the past to understanding the present and projecting the future.

---

7   McLuhan, in his introduction to Innis' *The Bias of Communication* (Toronto: University of Toronto Press, 1964), p. xvi, considered Innis "the most eminent of the Chicago group headed by Park."

Herbert Marshall McLuhan

Marshal McLuhan was an enigma, even to those who knew him well. Three parts genius and one part madman, he was once described at the height of his fame.[8] That ratio would come to be disputed among his academic colleagues. His enduring impact on communication theory, however, is beyond question. Far from fading into obscurity, his work is assuming new relevance in the face of the transformative growth of communication technologies in the 21st century.[9]

The eldest son of Herbert and Elsie McLuhan was born on July 21, 1911, in Edmonton, Alberta, and was to live in seven different homes before his parents finally settled in Winnipeg eleven years later. Young Marshall absorbed his legendary gift of the gab from Herbert senior's genial Irish narratives and Elsie's fierce, dramatic declamations. In explosive debates over the kitchen table, she imbued her son with her formidable verbal skills and a burning ambition to achieve in the larger world, a drive that would eventually push him to the limits of his body's ability to cope.

He won the gold medal for achievement at the University of Manitoba in 1934, but the major intellectual influences that would shape his professional life date from his arrival at Cambridge that same year. The groundbreaking New Criticism of I. A. Richards and William Empson and the influence of the moderns – notably Eliot, Pound and Joyce – created a heady milieu for a young man from the Canadian prairie. He absorbed it ravenously. Teaching stints at Madison and St. Louis followed his two years at Cambridge, as did a conversion to Catholicism, under the intellectual influence of G. K. Chesterton and Jacques Mauritain and a personal dialogue with Father Gerald Phelan, a priest at the University of Toronto's St. Michael's College, where he would eventually spend the greater part of his career. The onset of the Second World War found McLuhan back at Cambridge, newly wed to Corinne (to whom Elsie had introduced him). Corinne's choice of the penurious young academic was apparently the right one: it was an enduring marriage that produced six children.

---

8   Philip Marchand, *Marshall McLuhan: The Medium and the Messenger* (Toronto: Vintage, 1989).
9   Levinson, *Digital McLuhan*.

After returning to St. Louis, McLuhan was asked to teach at the University of Windsor and from there was invited to St. Michael's College at the University of Toronto in 1946, both of these recruitments influenced to no small degree by the force of his personality and his verbal virtuosity. He was a stimulating colleague, a great conversationalist and an astonishingly original and prolific generator of ideas, which succeeded in winning him the enmity of some of his more conservative colleagues. Although his Cambridge PhD, natural arrogance and rhetorical skills were usually enough to quell any active opposition, he realized early on the necessity of reaching beyond the conventional confines of his profession to find intellectual companionship. McLuhan became a master at the recruitment of other minds in the service of his great quest, one that far surpassed the usual ambitions of a professor of English literature: no less than a coherent vision of the great achievements of civilized man. He cultivated relationships with a broad range of prominent individuals in the arts, business and government as well as academia.

Two critical events that occurred within seven years of his arrival at the University of Toronto put him on the path to renown. The first was his meeting with colleague Harold Innis. McLuhan found a resonance between Innis' theories of the effects of the commodities trade on its participants, and the ideas of his Cambridge mentors regarding the effects of poetry and literature on readers and listeners. It led McLuhan, in his theory-building, to locate the impact – or *effect* – of communication media in the minds of individuals. This innovative insight was given a high-octane boost by another event: the awarding of a highly competitive Ford Foundation Research Grant to McLuhan and his colleague Ted Carpenter in 1953. The prestige of the award was a tonic and a vindication, and the money enabled him to apply an insight he had absorbed in his student days from F. R. Leavis at Cambridge: the principles of the New Criticism could be applied not only to literature, but to culture at large. McLuhan lost no time in applying this to the domain that had opened up to him through his fruitful contact with Innis: the technologies of communication. His short-lived journal, *Explorations*, in nine issues published between 1953 and 1959 with the help of funds from the grant, contains early versions of most of the ideas that were to form the basis of his later celebrity.

Carey (Chapter 3, in this volume) gives a personal account of the next milestone in McLuhan's career. The National Association of Educational Broadcasters invited him, in 1959, to design a syllabus for teachers and students to come to grips with the consequences of the new media. This project, and the subsequent notice it brought McLuhan, was arguably the catalyst that launched "Canada's intellectual comet"[10] into the stratosphere of international recognition. The publication of *The Mechanical Bride* in 1951 had passed almost without notice. The *Gutenberg Galaxy* in 1962 won him the Canadian Governor General's award for non-fiction, a review in the *New Statesman* and an invitation to write an article on the effects of print for the *Times Literary Supplement*. *Understanding Media* in 1964, for which the NAEB report had formed the basis, was reviewed in *The New Yorker* and was followed by a string of high profile interviews, speaking engagements and consultations in the worlds of television, publishing, business, government and the arts. The book's popularity – it sold 100,000 copies – together with its scathing critical reviews, presaged both the adulation and the abuse that were to dog him over the coming years.

In the tumultuous sixties, when no one knew what the world was coming to, McLuhan seemed to appear *deus ex machina* to explain it all. His insights were universally in demand, by intellectual luminaries and figures in the business and entertainment worlds alike. While his interviews were celebrated, his prose remained consciously aphoristic and logic-defying. Although wounded by his critics, he refused to alter it, and had little patience for systematic revision or extended academic explanations. He preferred the one-liner, and for these he is most remembered. "The Medium is the Message" was the catchphrase that distilled the complex notion of "effects," the germ of which he had imbibed at Cambridge and that had taken a quantum leap after meeting Innis in 1949: the technologies of communication – manuscript literacy, print, radio, television, and so forth – had effects on their users that were far more powerful than the ostensible content being transmitted. Print was linear, logical, highly defined and information intensive. Television, on the other hand, bypassed the rational, invoked primary sensory responses and was low-definition, requiring the viewer to "fill in the gaps."

10 Marchand, *Mcluhan*, p. 171.

The era of instantaneous electronic communications, McLuhan claimed, would engender a "discarnate man" whose identity was no longer contained in a physical body but extended outward in the bits of information coursing through wires or broadcast through space. McLuhan predicted a resulting loss of both identity and privacy in the era of electronic communications (see Chapter 12, in this volume, for an extended discussion of the issue of privacy in modern, media-intensive environments). Another aphorism he coined, influenced by his dialogues with Wyndham Lewis, was the "Global Village" (see Chapter 10, in this volume). The borders of a nation-state would no more define us than our physical bodies. Nations were a consequence of the linear, rational, hierarchical culture built up over centuries by a literate society. "Discarnate man" would undergo a return to the primary, sensory-driven reality of a pre-literate world, one that pulsed with drumbeat of the oral.

In order to keep a now-famous Marshall McLuhan on board as a member of the University faculty, Father John Kelley, the head of St. Michael's College, and Claude Bissell, then president of the University of Toronto, gave him the resources in 1963 to establish the Center for Culture and Technology, housed initially in a rambling Victorian structure on the St. Michael's campus, from which he could hold forth. McLuhan was delighted at this show of support, and filled it with the beloved books that he read so prodigiously and with personal treasures, such as his Cambridge oar. Most importantly, he filled it with people. Like his home, the Center was regularly filled with students, colleagues and visitors who flocked to seminars and social events with the man popularly hailed as a media guru, "The Prophet of the Electronic Age." McLuhan always held center stage at such events. Other than a stressful year at Fordham in 1967–68, where he was invited by John Culkin, McLuhan spent the remainder of his academic career at Toronto, where he felt most at home.

Talking, for McLuhan, was an epistemic process. By his own account, it was in dialogue that he did his best work. Writing, in contrast, was an ordeal. He was plagued by an ever-increasing gap between a prolific wellspring of ideas and their expression on paper in something approaching a comprehensible form. His critics demanded proof, or at the very least a coherent argument, but even as McLuhan's ideas kept spilling forth in multiple public forums he labored against the feeling that there was never enough time to keep up with the written version of things. His office was littered with unfinished projects that would never be published. Even so, Phillipe Marchand, one of his biographers, lists seventeen books that McLuhan published from 1951 to 1977, as well as the posthumously published *Laws of Media* in 1988, and over one hundred articles. Much of McLuhan's prose remains impenetrable. It was this, along with his increasingly difficult personality – short-tempered, unpredictable and impatient with detail – that led to an increasing disaffection and alienation from the public and outright dismissal by academic colleagues, some of whom claimed that his thinking was both erratic and unsound.

What goes up must come down, and the bubble eventually burst. Formerly ardent supporters became his harshest critics,[11] colleagues discouraged students from taking his seminar, attendance dwindled, potential projects were stillborn and manuscripts were left unpublished. From the early seventies until his death in 1980, McLuhan suffered an ignominious loss of celebrity and influence, to the point of being described as a Canadian "eccentric."[12] This change in fortunes was as abrupt as it was complex, and it was not unrelated to McLuhan's declining physical condition. As early as 1960, during the strain of preparing the NAEB final report (referred to above and in Chapter 3 of this volume), he suffered the first in a series of strokes, and was subsequently plagued by blackouts through the sixties. Eventually diagnosed with a massive brain tumor in 1968, he underwent major surgery from which he never fully rebounded. The quick wit and rhetorical agility that had served him so well early in his academic career and in the public arena began to fail. His optimism and boundless energy were gradually supplanted by anxiety and irritability. He maintained a wry sense of humor and never admitted to infirmity, but continued to suffer minor strokes over the next decade, quietly plagued not only by the loss of his mental agility, but by the anxiety engendered in an awareness of their loss. A massive stroke in 1979 finally robbed him of the power of speech, and the man who had lived for dialogue endured a year of mute agony before passing away in 1980.

11 Jonathan Miller, *McLuhan* (London: William Collins, 1971).
12 Marchand, *McLuhan*, p. 247.

The Toronto School

The kind of discovery Innis and McLuhan converged on, from their distinctive backgrounds, has proved inspiring. It was innovative enough to generate interest, broad enough to be relevant for scholars from a variety of fields, and distinctive enough to remain clearly identified with those who revealed it. No less important, it was an idea and an approach that had the potential of growth, by way of intellectual expansion and original applications. These are precisely the attributes of a school of thought, and ironically, while invisible colleges[13] can exist through communications and need not have any particular geographical focus, this one did, and it was Toronto.

The first to realize the potential of Innis' breakthrough in thinking about communication to form the foundation of a school was appropriately McLuhan. He found in Innis' work "lines... which suggest the possibility of organizing an entire school of studies." Proceeding literally, and administratively – neither of which was his forte – he suggested that "Bloor Street is the one point in this University where one might establish a focus of the arts and sciences," organized around "communication theory and practice." Bloor Street was, of course, the address of Innis' Department of Political Economy, since the early 1930s.[14]

If McLuhan thought of organizing a school around Innis' ideas a priori, many scholars from diverse subfields of communication have identified a "Toronto School" of communications in retrospect. Jack Goody, in 1968, was among the first to frame the concept and use the term, and many others, including Carey and Katz (both contributors to

13 D. J. Price & D. de B. Beaver, "Collaboration in an Invisible College," *American Psychologist*, XXI (1966), 1011–1018; Diana Crane, "Social Structure in a Group of Scientists: A Test of the 'Invisible College' Hypothesis," *American Sociological Review*, XXXIV (1969), 335–352; N.C. Mullins, "Social Networks among Biological Scientists" (PhD diss. Harvard University, 1966) and "The Microstructure of an Invisible College: The Phage Group," paper delivered to the American Sociological Association Annual Meeting, Boston, 1968.

14 McLuhan to Innis, 14 March 1951, in Matie Molinaro, Corinne McLuhan, and William Toye, *Letters of Marshall McLuhan Complete Correspondence* (New York: Oxford University Press, 1987).

this volume), Theal and Meyrowitz would interpret its significance.[15] Dreyer Berg and Derrick de Kerckhove have published significant analyses of the concept of the Toronto School and, more recently, Lance Strate sees the notion of a Toronto School being subsumed by the broader concept of "media ecology." [16]

Although identified geographically with Toronto, a school remains an invisible theoretical construct, charting an imagined network of intellectuals and their ideas. Each of the scholars who has developed, commented on, or thought of the concept of the Toronto School, had a different network of scholars in mind, save the two anchoring thinkers – Innis and McLuhan, and their corresponding ideas.

While identifying two scholars as the core of a school of thought would tend to highlight the fundamental compatibility of their ideas, as we have seen, those of Innis and McLuhan diverged greatly. It may be precisely this kaleidoscopic variety of their combined interests – spanning literature and macroeconomics, cognition and social organization, personality and politics – that helps to explain the staying power of the Toronto School and its continuing appeal to scholars from a variety of disciplines.

Interpretations, Extensions, Applications

The articles in this volume underscore the enduring engagement of the humanities and social science disciplines in common discourse and concerns with the Toronto School. In the first section, *Interpretations*, the chapters highlight the diverse disciplinary perspectives of Innis and McLuhan: when one interprets these scholars one invariably talks about

---

15 See Robert Babe, *Canadian Communication Thought* (Toronto, Ontario: University of Toronto Press, 2000), an edited volume that focuses on Innis and McLuhan.
16 Dreyer Berg, "Cambridge and Toronto: The Twentieth Century Schools of Communication," *Canadian Journal of Communication*, 11:3 (1985): 251–267. Jack Goody, ed., *Literacy in Traditional Societies* (Cambridge: Cambridge University Press, 1968); Derrick de Kerkhove, "McLuhan and the 'Toronto School of Communication,'" *Canadian Journal of Communication*, 14:4 (1989): 73–79; Lance Strate, "A Media Ecology Review," *Communication Research Trends*, 23:2 (2004): 3–48.

what they brought with them to the field of communications from their previous fields of inquiry. Thus, in Chapter 1, Deibert examines media and international relations and world order transformations, which were one of Innis' primary concerns. Innis' historicity is highlighted in Chapter 2 by Blondheim; in Chapter 3, Carey articulates McLuhan's unique contributions to the field of media studies, and links them both to personal recollections and to McLuhan's social and political sympathies; and in Chapter 4, Katz and Katz discuss the intellectual traditions that preceded and influenced McLuhan's understanding of media. In Chapter 5, Siegel presents a unique perspective on Innis by one of his contemporaries and colleagues at the University of Toronto, Northrop Frye, and discusses the role Frye subsequently played in Canadian media institutions.

The second section, *Extensions*, illustrates the integration and extension of the concerns of the Toronto School in different thematic and disciplinary directions. In Chapter 6, Frosh offers an expansive exploration of Innis' notion of space, leading to a broad canvas of image and connectivity in Western thought. In Chapter 7, Allen's historically oriented exploration juxtaposes Innis' ideas about media development with the historical development of electronic communications in Canada in the 19th century and their institutional underpinnings. In Chapter 8, Zhao extends Innis' concerns forward in time to address the meaning of the Internet and other recent media technology developments; and in Chapter 9, Watson locates and expands the notion of cognitive consequences touched on by McLuhan within the recently-emerging theoretical framework of cognitive pragmatics.

The third section, *Applications*, is possibly the most innovative section of this book, illustrating the implications of insights developed in the Toronto School to contemporary practical dilemmas. In Chapter 10, Adoni and Nosseck operationalize and develop McLuhan's concepts into an explanatory framework for the interpretation of new media consumption patterns, reflecting the contemporary map of social relations; in Chapter 11, Cohen-Avigdor and Lehman-Wilzig zero in on the power of McLuhan's ideas to define and interpret the new medium of e-magazines; in Chapter 12, Cohen-Almagor gives a thorough and extensive comparative analysis of professional, ethical and legal issues in Canadian media; and in Chapter 13, Shifman and Blondheim test the idea of ecology, extrapolated from Innis and constructed as a paradigm of media development, against the historical process of media evolution, down to the Internet.

Commensurate with the variety and multiplicity of the ideological and disciplinary approaches represented by the articles in this volume are their multiple formats and styles. We thought that rather than forcing them into a common stylistic mold, preserving this diversity of form was one way of illustrating the breadth and variety of the legacy of the Toronto School.

Notwithstanding this variety, readers will notice a preponderance of contributions from Canada and Israel. This is a consequence of the event that was the genesis of this volume: the 9th Biennial Jerusalem Conference of the Israeli Association for Canadian Studies, held at the Hebrew University in July, 2002. In addition to selected papers that were presented at the conference, a number of significant contributions were subsequently invited, some of which were original contributions and others published previously, in an attempt to round out the volume and make it more fully representative.

Beyond the scholarly link formed between Canadian and Israeli scholars on the occasion of this conference, a case can also be made for a substantive similarity of interests. For both Canada and Israel are uniquely challenged by communications, in some similar but other radically different ways. Both are multi-ethnic, polyglot societies highly aware of the importance of national media in cementing national cohesion. In Canada's case, the obvious challenge to national communications is *space* – and lots of it. On first glance, Canada may appear as a nation divided, rather than united, by the sheer physical expanse of its shared territory. The national experience of Canada, the only polity to have written railroads into its Constitution, is marked by the constant struggle to link, via communications, a population thinly scattered over the breadth of a gigantic continent.

In this respect, Israel represents a polar opposite to Canada. Space is not the source of the communicative challenge in this extremely compact country – one of the most densely populated geographies in the western world. In communications, Israel is challenged by *time* – and lots of it. As a Jewish state understood as the modern restoration of an ancient nation marked by continuous territory, shared institutions, and a common language, the young state of modern Israel must bridge a gap of nearly two millennia of diasporic existence.

Looking outwards, beyond their national borders, both Canada and Israel can also be seen to face significant, but opposite, communicative challenges. Canada's proximity to a dominating "big brother," the United States, has traditionally bred a distinct case of "anxiety of influence." It gave urgency to Canada's efforts to assert and maintain its distinctiveness from its imposing neighbor, with which it shares fundamental human values, political philosophy, elements of a continental economy and a dominant spoken language. In contrast, Israel's distinctiveness from its close neighbors is marked by differences in ideology and values, economy and language. It feels a commonality and seeks affiliation with the geographically-distant United States – Canada's identity-absorbing neighbor – with which it shares ideas and cultural values, economic and strategic alliances.

Nevertheless, when it comes to these differences between Canada and Israel, Innis' Canadian theory of communication and its biases would tend to underscore the unity of such opposites – in this case, the unity of communication-challenged polyglot nations, albeit challenged in different ways. Innis assumed that healthy societies, aware of their bias in either space or time, would try to balance their communication act (Chapters 2 and 9 in this volume). In such cases societies would consciously exert considerable effort – political, economic, and intellectual – in an attempt to counteract deficiencies in continuity by developing time-binding communications, and deficiencies in reach by enhancing space-binding media. They would build bridges across space to enhance international alliance and cooperation with distant friends, and build barriers to distance them from neighbors who seem too close for comfort.

Perhaps one way in which Israel and Canada demonstrate their wrestling with parallel formidable communicative challenges is their outstanding involvement in efforts to understand, shape, and change the media environment. Thus, in both Canada and Israel issues of media and their regulation – in their relation to national development – are prominent on the political and public agenda. Similarly, the salience and disproportionate presence of both Canadian and Israeli scholars in international forums of media research may point to the same kind of dynamic. And it may be no accident that both countries are hotbeds of new technology R&D, the origins of business enterprises that aim to effect change in prevalent modes of communication. Ultimately, the

congruence of sensibilities suggested here highlights a commonality of
relevance that the ideas explored by the Toronto School have for both
Canada and Israel.

PART I

INTERPRETATIONS

RONALD J. DEIBERT

1. Between Essentialism and Constructivism: Harold Innis and World Order Transformations

Although his work is much too diverse to pigeonhole, it is probably fair to say that one of Harold Adams Innis' overarching concerns was with the dynamics of large-scale social and political change.[1] Such a focus is particularly appropriate today in light of the forces of globalization, the planetary reach of the United States, the prevalence of social and political networks, and the implications of all of these for the modern system of sovereign states. Unlike many of the world political theorists John Ruggie recently chastised for failing to conceptualize change, Innis' work provides a rich vocabulary of fundamental transformation.[2] Innis would be well at home in contemporary discussions of the collapse of the Soviet Union and the end of the Cold War, the "unbundling" of sovereignty, and the significance of globalization.

Innis' work covers a broad range, historically, geographically, and philosophically. Innis had a special dislike of academic specialization, and often pronounced against the artificial separation of the social sciences.[3] Writing in the 1930s, 1940s, and 1950s, Innis was an advocate of inter-disciplinarity. Such anti-compartmentalization was fundamental to Innis' approach, which falls into a genre that is perhaps best captured by what Charles Tilly calls "world-historical" research.[4] In probably his most well known study, *Empire and Communications*, for example, Innis moves from Ancient Sumer and Egypt to the Middle

---

1 This chapter is based on Ronald J. Deibert, Harold Innis and the Empire of Speed, *Review of International Studies* (1999), 25, 273–289.
2 See John Gerard Ruggie, Territoriality and Beyond: Problematizing Modernity in World Politics, *International Organization*, 47 (1993), pp. 139–174.
3 See Harold Innis, *The Bias of Communications* (Toronto, 1952), pp. 203–214, among other sections.
4 Charles Tilly, *Big Structures, Large Processes, Huge Comparisons* (New York, 1984).

Ages, from the Greece of Plato to the Germany of Hitler. Earlier works that focused on the explorations of the "New World" cover in detail the events of centuries. For Innis, as for Fernand Braudel, the *longue durée* was his preferred level-of-analysis.[5] Such a broad historical sweep and inter-disciplinary approach is crucial for putting into perspective the significance and character of contemporary world order transformation.

In what follows I will excavate three "meta-theoretical" traits running through Innis' writings, linking them to contemporary debates among those scholars who theorize about world political economy and international relations – the primary level of analysis in which Innis worked in his day. Specifically, these are his thorough historicism, his skillful combination of material and ideational factors, and the importance he attaches to the biases of space and time in understanding empires and civilizations. This will help hopefully to offer some new and interesting ways of thinking about the study and practice of world politics. As I will argue below, Innis does not fall comfortably into any of the standard typologies of theories of large-scale political and social change. Critical of the type of ahistorical theorizing that characterizes the rationalist mainstream, yet too materialist to be fully aligned with social constructivism and postmodernism, Innis provides an interesting and novel bridgehead to what I call an "ecological holist" perspective on world politics.

Bridging the "early" and "late" Innis

Born near Toronto, Canada in 1894, Harold Innis' route to academia began with undergraduate work at McMaster University, followed by a Ph.D. in economic history at the University of Chicago, and then a return to Canada with an appointment to the Department of Political Economy at the University of Toronto. Remaining at the University of Toronto for his entire academic career until his death in 1952, Harold Innis produced numerous articles and several books, including *The Fur Trade in Canada, The Cod Fisheries: The History of an International*

5   Fernand Braudel, *On History* (Chicago, 1980).

Economy, Empire and Communications, The Bias of Communications, and *Changing Concepts of Time.*[6] Most commentators divide Innis' body of work into two distinct phases: the "early" phase comprises books and articles that focus on trade in staples, primarily in Canada, while the "later" phase is characterized by Innis' forays into communications in *Empire and Communications* and *The Bias of Communications.*[7] However, such a neat division is probably more a reflection of the different ways Innis has been appropriated by later scholars than by anything inherent in Innis' writings. Those who have concentrated on Innis' so-called "early" phase have tended to read him as a proto-dependency theorist whose "staples-thesis" shows how the economic and political development of raw-material exporting countries like Canada was shaped by dependence on large importing countries such as Great Britain and the United States.[8] Those who have concentrated on Innis' later writings on communications, on the other hand, have usually come to Innis via the writings of his student Marshall McLuhan, and have largely ignored his earlier works on staple production.

The artificial division between the "early" and "late" Innis also obscures important continuities that weave their way through all of Innis' writings. For example, through both "phases" one can read in Innis a very pessimistic view of technology, particularly regarding the inventions of 20th century mass media, which Innis said, "have produced a state of numbness, pleasure, and self-complacency perhaps only

6 Harold Innis, *The Fur Trade in Canada: An Introduction to Canadian Economic History* (New Haven, 1930); Harold Innis, *The Cod Fisheries: The History of an International Economy* (New Haven, 1940); Harold Innis, *Changing Concepts of Time* (Toronto, 1952).

7 See Paul Heyer, *Communications and History: Theories of Media, Knowledge, and Civilization* (New York, 1988). See also Leonard Dudley, Space, Time, and Number: Harold A. Innis as Evolutionary Theorist, *Canadian Journal of Economics* (November 1995), pp. 754–767. See also Paul Heyer, *Harold Innis* (Lanham, 2003).

8 For dependency theory, see Fernando Henrique Cardoso and Enzo Faletto, *Dependency and Development in Latin America* (Berkeley, 1979). Although Innis shared the view that Canada's economy was shaped by its dependence on the British Empire and the United States, he did not communicate this view in the language of Marxism, world-systems, or unequal development that characterizes the dependency theorists of Latin America and elsewhere.

equaled by laughing gas."[9] His admitted bias was with the oral culture of ancient Greece. As the quotation above suggests, Innis' writings also exhibit a disarming, dry sense of humor that often reveals itself in odd juxtapositions and playful aphorisms. He was fiercely protective of Canadian culture in the face of what he saw as the overwhelming threat of American commercialism, especially in his later years.[10] Indeed, it is possible that the fate of Canada positioned precariously next to the empire of the United States was *the* backdrop for all of Innis' scholarship. Perhaps this also explains why Innis has been "canonized in Canada but largely ignored in the US."[11] Beyond these very general and stylistic continuities, however, is a more substantive set that characterizes Innis' scholarship. It is to these more fundamental traits that I now turn my attention.

Historicism

Perhaps the best place to start with an excavation of Innis' thought is "at the bottom," so to speak, with his outlook on how we go about acquiring knowledge. To do so, however, we need first to make a brief detour into general questions of epistemology. It is often said that two fundamentally different "modes of thought" or epistemologies can be discerned in Western philosophy and science.[12] The first, which

9 Harold Innis, The Church in Canada, in *Essays in Canadian Economic History* (Toronto, 1956), p. 383.
10 See especially Innis, *Changing Concepts of Time*, pp. 19–20 where Innis remarked that "The jackals of communication systems are constantly on the alert to destroy every vestige of sentiment toward Great Britain holding it of no advantage if it threatens the omnipotence of American commercialism." Innis would have been dismayed, to say the least, at recent World Trade Organization rulings on "split-run" magazines and other deteriorations of the regulatory mechanisms that preserve Canadian culture.
11 Ian Angus and Brian Shoesmith, Dependency/Space/Policy: An Introduction to a Dialogue with Harold Innis, *Continuum: The Australian Journal of Media and Culture*, 7 (1993), p. 5.
12 See Robert Cox. Social Forces, States and World Order: Beyond International Relations Theory, in Robert O. Keohane (ed.), *Neorealism and its Critics* (New York, 1986), pp. 239–249; and Charles Taylor, Philosophy and its History, in

we might call the "essentialist" mode, is concerned with uncovering fundamental laws and universal truths about nature and society.[13] This mode of thought is called "essentialist" or "foundationalist" because it seeks to build knowledge on stable, unchanging foundations. It seeks to explain particular events as part of a more general pattern or law that is both timeless and contextless (i.e., applicable across both time and space). It is for this reason that essentialists are referred to by their critics as *ahistorical*, not because they ignore or are not learned in history, but rather because they search for foundations or essences that stand apart from history.[14] From the essentialist point of view, history is seen as a repository of data, a "quarry providing materials with which to illustrate variations on always recurrent themes."[15] Hence, orthodox Marxism and most mainstream theories of large-scale political and social change – i.e., those that fall within the neorealist or neoliberal camps – are essentialist and ahistorical by their stress on the timeless constraints of the mode of production, anarchy, or the rationality of actors.[16] Even among those theories that account for change through history in the rise and fall of great powers, there is still a "static image of historical necessity" in the laws or dynamics that are identified as the generators of such change.[17] Each shares the view that scientific theories should strive to have a transtemporal duality – in other words, have an applicability "regardless of different historical and cultural settings."[18]

Richard Rorty, J. B. Schneewind and Quentin Skinner (eds.) *Philosophy in History: Essays on the Historiography of Philosophy* (Cambridge, 1984), pp. 17–30.

13 On "essentialism," see Daniel Dennett, *Darwin's Dangerous Idea: Evolution and the Meanings of Life* (New York, 1995), pp. 35–39; see also Richard Rorty, *Philosophy and the Mirror of Nature* (Princeton, 1979), pp. 361–365.

14 Cox, Social Forces, States, and World Order, p. 243.

15 Ibid., p. 212.

16 For discussion, see Emanuel Adler, Cognitive Evolution: A Dynamic Approach for the Study of International Relations and their Progress, in Emanuel Adler and Beverly Crawford (eds.), *Progress in Postwar International Relations* (Columbia, 1993), pp. 43–88; see also Richard K. Ashley, Three Modes of Economism, *International Studies Quarterly*, 27 (1993); and R. B. J. Walker, *Inside/Outside: International Relations as Political Theory* (Cambridge, 1993).

17 See Robert Gilpin, *War and Change in World Politics* (Cambridge, 1981). The quotation is from Jim George, *Discourses of Global Politics: A Critical (Re) Introduction to International Relations* (Boulder, Col., 1994), p. 4.

18 Erik Ringmar, Alexander Wendt: A Social Scientist Struggling with History, in Iver

Essentialism has been the dominant mode of thought in Western philosophy having roots that reach back to ancient Greece.[19] It was there that the biases in favor of the fixed and permanent over the changing and mutable were first formed and articulated. Since then, with minor exceptions, "to know is to grasp a permanent end that realizes itself through changes, holding them thereby within the metes and bounds of fixed truth."[20] Such an orientation to knowledge seems like common sense today not only because it is deeply engrained in our culture through the past, but also because it satisfies deep spiritual yearnings. As Dewey explains:

It was not then for metaphysical reasons that classic philosophy maintained that change, and consequently time, are marks of inferior reality, holding that true and ultimate reality is immutable and eternal. Human reasons, all too human, have given birth to the idea that over and beyond the lower realm of things that shift like the sands on the seashore there is the kingdom of the unchanging, of the complete, the perfect. The grounds for the belief are couched in technical language of philosophy, but the cause for the grounds is the heart's desire for surcease from change, struggle, and uncertainty.[21]

The alternative to essentialist modes of thought sees history not in terms of "unchanging substances but rather as a continuing creation of new forms."[22] From this *historicist* perspective, rationalities, nations, and states – though potentially stable in their basic characteristics over long periods of time – are nonetheless products of historical contingencies and thus subject to change as nature and society evolve.[23] Unlike the

---

B. Neumann and Ole Waever (eds.), *The Future of International Relations* (New York, 1997), p. 284.

19 See R. G. Collingwood, *The Idea of History* (New York, 1956), pp. 14–45.

20 John Dewey, The Influence of Darwinism on Philosophy, in James Gouinlock (ed.), *The Moral Writings of John Dewey* (New York, 1994), p. 26.

21 Ibid., p. 33.

22 Cox, Social Forces, States, and World Order, p. 213.

23 Like Cox, the sense in which I use the word "historicism" here is exactly in opposition to the sense it was used by Karl Popper in *The Poverty of Historicism* (Boston, 1957). Popper had in mind what I would call "essentialist" theories of history, such as those of Plato and Marx.

essentialist mode of thought, the historicist privileges change over continuity, flux over permanence. It is informed by a "Darwinist" view of history – that is, one that sees no unfolding logic to history, but only "descent with modification."[24] While essentialism is animated by a desire to escape from the world of time, appearance, and circumstance into a world of enduring truth and permanence, historicism is content to be one among many of Nature's experiments.[25] For the historicist, contingency reigns supreme.

Such an orientation to history has some specific consequences for epistemology.

The idea of framing knowledge as the search for a fixed truth standing apart from history is inapposite to the historicist approach. As Cox points out, "one cannot therefore speak of 'laws' in any generally valid sense transcending historical eras, nor of structures as outside of or prior to history."[26] What regularities can be discerned are the products of a particular historical context. Nor can knowledge be grounded on a fixed human "nature" or a kind of inverted Platonism that characterizes rational-actor approaches.[27] Historicists insist that socialization, and thus historical circumstance, goes all the way down – that there is nothing "beneath socialization or prior to history which is definatory of the human."[28]

Where Innis falls on this divide between essentialism and historicism is somewhat ambiguous, with many reading into his aphoristic style of writing a latent technological determinism or crude reductionism. Certainly phrases can be gleaned from Innis' writings superficially that might suggest as much: "The monarchies of Egypt and Persia, the Roman Empire, and the city-states were essentially products of writing."[29] "Greek science and paper with encouragement of writing in the vernacular provided the wedge between the temporal and the spiritual power and destroyed the Holy Roman Empire."[30] "Sumerian

24 See Richard Rorty, *Contingency, Irony, and Solidarity* (Cambridge, 1989); see also Dennett, *Darwin's Dangerous Idea*.

25 Rorty, *Contingency, Irony, and Solidarity*, p. 45.

26 Cox, Social Forces, States, and World Order, p. 244.

27 On "inverted Platonism," see Rorty, *Philosophy and the Mirror of Nature*.

28 Rorty, *Contingency, Irony, and Solidarity*, p. xiii.

29 Harold Innis, *Empire and Communications* (Oxford, 1950), p. 8.

30 Harold Innis, *The Bias of Communications* (Toronto, 1952), p. 31.

culture based on the medium of clay was fused with Semitic culture based on the medium of stone to produce the Babylonian empire."[31] My own impression is in accord with Robert Cox's, however, who regards such phrases as "devices to set you thinking" as not suggestive of any kind of essentialism.[32] A closer inspection reveals that of the two modes of thought, Innis was fully in tune with the historicist approach.

One indication of Innis' sympathies towards historicism is his consistent critiques of the predominant essentialism that characterized the study of political economy in his day, whose ahistorical tendencies he referred to derisively as "present-mindedness."[33] An even more telling indication of his historicism, however, can be found in his own approach to history. Although not articulated explicitly as such, *radical contingency* features prominently in Innis' writings.[34] Using the narrative mode of explanation, Innis unearths the historical coincidences and conjunctions that take the evolutionary path down one road as opposed to the other. In this respect, he was clearly writing against the grain of the then emerging modernization paradigm, which assumed a single, linear path of development for all societies.[35] For Innis, the political and cultural development of particular societies is always contingent on the peculiarities of historical circumstance.

Examples abound of Innis' skillful attention to the interaction of contingent variables in the course of human history. In his studies of both the cod fisheries and the fur trade in early modern Canada, for example, Innis details how the exploitation of particular staples by Europeans

---

31 Innis, *Empire and Communications*, p. 166.

32 Robert Cox, Civilizations: Encounters and Transformations, *Studies in Political Economy*, 47 (1995), p. 20.

33 Harold Innis, *The Bias of Communications* (Toronto, 1952), p. 61. Innis believed that the neo-classical paradigm, with its pretensions to universality, was a "form of exploitation with dangerous consequences." See Trevor Barnes, *Logics of Dislocation: Models, Metaphors, and Meanings of Space* (New York, 1996), p. 212. Barnes is also of the view that Innis was fundamentally anti-essentialist.

34 I have found Innis' essays to be similar in this respect to those of the popular writer on evolution, Stephen Gould. See Stephen Jay Gould, *Ever Since Darwin: Reflections in Natural History* (New York, 1977) and other books that have followed in that series.

35 W. W. Rostow, *The Stages of Economic Growth: A Non-Communist Manifesto* (Cambridge, 1960).

had indirect ramifications for later political and social developments in Canada depending on the type of cargo in outbound and return vessels. In the case of the fur trade, for example, outbound ships from France were loaded down with material goods used for bartering with the natives in exchange for furs. This had the effect of restricting personnel and immigration from France to Canada because of the lack of space on outbound vessels. With Great Britain, however, the exploitation of resources was concentrated on timber, where the situation was reversed: return vessels were heavy with cargo, while outbound vessels were light, thus encouraging immigration. Hence in concluding *The Fur Trade in Canada*, Innis noted that "Canada emerged as a political entity with boundaries largely determined by the fur trade." That it did so was at least in part because of the political implications of "unused capacity" in ships.[36]

Similarly, *The Bias of Communication* could be read as an extended essay on how historical circumstances and the constraints and opportunities of local context take history in particular directions. Consider in the following passage the unique set of environmental, technological, and cultural factors to which Innis attributes the extraordinary development of ancient Greece, particularly its subordination of religion in the conduct of civic life that set it apart from previous civilizations of the time:

> The Phoenician Semitic consonantal alphabet was taken over by the Greeks on the north shore of the Mediterranean. Unlike the peoples of Aryan speech in Asia Minor the Greeks escaped the full effect of contact with the civilizations of Egypt and Babylonia. The necessity of crossing water enabled the Greeks to select cultural traits of significance to themselves and to reject others. Without a script they had built up a strong oral tradition centering about the courts of conquering people from the north. The Homeric poems were the work of generations of reciters and minstrels and reflected the demands of generations of audiences to whom they were recited. This powerful oral tradition bent the consonantal alphabet to its demands and used five of the twenty-

---

36 Innis, *The Fur Trade in Canada*, p. 393. See also Harold Innis, *Essays in Canadian Economic History* (Toronto, 1956), p. 141 *passim*.

four letters as vowels. . . . The written language was made into an instrument responsive to the demands of the oral tradition. . . . The delay in the introduction of writing until possibly as late as the beginning of the seventh century, the difficulties of securing large and regular supplies of papyrus from Egypt, and the limitations of stone as a medium combined to protect the oral tradition. No energy was lost in learning a second language and monopolies of knowledge could not be built around a complex script.[37]

In a remarkable passage in *Empire and Communications*, Innis explains how the use of the parchment codex by Christian monks, the cut-off of supplies of papyrus to the West as a result of the rise of Islam in the seventh century, the favorable ecological circumstances of western Europe for the production of parchment, and the relatively low level of lay literacy at the time, all combined to create circumstances advantageous to the rise of the Roman Catholic Church in the early Middle Ages.[38] In the face of passage after passage such as these, one cannot help but question the idea of "laws" or "regularities" standing outside of human history.

Innis' historicism did not stop with his interpretation of historical processes, however. One of the difficult conundrums of historicism is that, when carried to its logical conclusion, it leads ultimately to recognition of the limitations of knowledge itself. Historicism, as Robert D'Amico puts it, is also a thesis of "how human understanding is always a 'captive' of its historical situation."[39] Innis did not shy away from this recognition that the lives of all human beings – including scholars such as himself – are lived within "horizons."[40] To the contrary,

---

37 Innis, *The Bias of Communication*, p. 41.

38 Innis, *Empire and Communications*, pp. 117–119. Innis used the term "cyclonic" to refer to the process whereby several contingent variables come together in a kind of symbiosis to generate large-scale social changes of the sort noted above. For discussion, see Barnes, *Logics of Dislocation*, p. 219. The meteorological metaphor is, in my mind, another indication of Innis' appreciation of contingency.

39 Robert D'Amico, *Historicism and Knowledge* (New York, 1989), p. x.

40 The metaphorical use of "horizons" to refer to constraints on knowledge is associated with the thought of Friedrich Nietzsche. On Nietzsche's horizonism, see George Grant, *Time as History* (Toronto, 1969). As Nietzsche remarks in the preface to *The Genealogy of Morals*, "The sad truth is that we remain necessarily strangers to ourselves, we don't understand our own substance, we *must* mistake

he incorporated it reflexively, consistently, and ironically into his own interpretation of history:

> Immediately we venture on this inquiry we are compelled to recognize the bias of the period in which we work. An interest in the bias of other civilizations may in itself suggest a bias of our own. Our knowledge of other civilizations depends in large part on the character of the media used by each civilization in so far as it is capable of being preserved or of being made accessible by discovery . . . Writing on clay and on stone has been preserved more effectively than that on papyrus. Since durable commodities emphasize time and continuity, studies of civilization such as Toynbee's tend to have a bias toward religion and to show a neglect of problems of space, notably administration and law. The bias of modern civilization incidental to the newspaper and the radio will presume a perspective in consideration of civilizations dominated by other media. We can do little more than urge that we must be continually alert to the implications of this bias and perhaps hope that consideration of the implications of other media to various civilizations may enable us to see more clearly the bias of our own.[41]

Given this thoroughgoing historicism, it should come as no surprise that law-like generalizations are notably absent from Innis' writings. Whatever future commentators of essentialist persuasions may read into Innis' aphorisms and rhetorical flourishes, it is clear that Innis saw history as open-ended, contingent, and without overarching purpose save for that created in local contexts under the constraints of particular historical circumstances.

---

ourselves." In Friedrich Nietzsche, *The Birth of Tragedy* and *The Genealogy of Morals* (New York, 1956), p. 149. Although there are some scattered allusions to Nietzsche in Innis' work, his historicism is probably more attributable to the influence of Veblen and the Institutionalist school of thought, which, along with the American Pragmatic school of John Dewey and William James, was a strong presence during Innis' graduate training at the University of Chicago. For a similar view, see Barnes, *Logics of Dislocation*.

41 Innis, *The Bias of Communications*, pp. 33–34.

Ecological holism

Translating Innis' historicism into today's language, most would see an affinity between his approach and that developed by so-called social constructivists.[42] Both are skeptical of timeless constraints, whether in the order of things or the nature of being. Both consider values and interests as intersubjectively generated in particular historical and cultural contexts. Both emphasize discontinuities in history, and see institutions and orders as emerging and being sustained by social practices, rather than as "givens."

But in their indictment of the crude, static materialism of neorealism, constructivists have perhaps swung too far in the direction of an airy "idealism," not in the utopian head-in-the-clouds sense of the term, but rather in their slighting of the importance of material factors as constitutive forces in society and politics. Social constructivism, in the words of Dan Deudney, is "de-natured" social science:

> In correcting for the reification of social structures, constructivism risks its own blindness in failing to distinguish between social structures constituted by social practice, and material or deep structural realities that are not socially constructed. Natural and material realities structure human action, and such structures are subject to various socially constructed interpretations, but they are not generated by social practices.[43]

The problem with most materialist theories in recent times is that they have been either prone to the type of ahistorical reification that constructivists so skillfully expose in, for example, the structural realism of Kenneth Waltz, or they have slighted the importance of ideas, norms, and culture altogether, as in orthodox Marxism.[44] A sophisticated

---

42 On social constructivism in the social sciences, see especially Peter L. Berger and Thomas Luckmann, *The Social Construction of Reality* (New York, 1967).

43 Daniel Deudney, Binding Sovereigns: Authorities, Structures, and Geopolitics in Philadelphian Systems, in Biersteker and Weber (eds.), *State Sovereignty as Social Construct*, p. 193. See also, Daniel Deudney, "Bringing Nature Back In: Geopolitical Theory from the Greeks to the Greenhouse" (Paper delivered to the American Political Science Association annual meeting, September 1993, Washington DC).

44 Kenneth Waltz, *Theory of International Politics* (New York, 1979).

materialist alternative has, for the most part, been either lacking or ignored. Rediscovering Innis' elaborate combination of "natural" and "social" factors suggests just such a sophisticated materialist alternative – one that might help to "bring nature back in."[45]

Innis was naturalistic without being reductionist. His writing demonstrates a kind of "non-reductive physicalism," or what I have elsewhere called "ecological holism" in its incorporation of natural, technological and ideational factors in the constitution of civilizations or societies.[46] In this respect, Innis is perhaps best situated as part of a now largely overlooked tradition of naturalistic or physio-political theorizing of the late 19th/early 20th century that includes such figures as John Dewey, Lewis Mumford, or Fernand Braudel.[47] As with these writers, Innis rejected the long-standing binary opposition in Western metaphysics between material and ideational factors. Instead, he weaves elements of both together into a coherent holistic explanation.

As with Braudel, the starting point for Innis in any analysis was the deep material context of the civilization or empire in question. As Innis put it, "geography provides the grooves which determine the course and to a large extent the character of economic life."[48] Hence in his study of "Transportation as a Factor in Canadian Economic History," Innis first traces the distinctive waterways of the "Precambrian formation" whose "resistant character" and "relatively level surface have been responsible for a network of lakes and rivers." Likewise, in both *The Fur Trade* and *The Cod Fisheries*, Innis begins his analysis by focusing on the way the material context of North America – particularly its wildlife – influenced both European explorations and later political and social developments. *The Fur Trade* opens with a careful scrutiny of the habits of the beaver, and how its mating and migration patterns, its habitat, and its fur shaped the character of European exploration, immigration, and trade. In *The Cod Fisheries*, Innis' narrative begins with a close examination of the

45 See Deudney, Bringing Nature Back In, for an informative overview of sophisticated materialist theories of world politics.
46 On "non-reductive physicalism," see Richard Rorty, *Objectivism, Relativism, and Truth* (Cambridge, 1991), pp. 113–125. On "ecological holism," see Ronald J. Deibert, *Parchment, Printing, and Hypermedia: Communication in World Order Transformation* (New York, 1997), ch. 1.
47 For an overview, see Deudney, Bringing Nature Back In.
48 Innis, *Political Economy of the Modern State*, p. 87.

water temperature and salinity level of the Grand Banks, the gravity of cod's eggs, and the feeding habits of newly-hatched fry, all of which restricted the fishing industry "to areas and seasons."

Innis' most impressive combination of material factors and ideas, however, can be found in his discussions of communication technology. Here, natural, technological and cultural factors are strung together into a seamless explanatory web. Consider, in the following example, how Innis combines communication technology, institutional inertia, and prevailing values in his explanation of the rise of the Roman Catholic Church over elite culture in the early Middle Ages:

> The spread of Mohammedanism cut off exports of papyrus to the east and to the west . . . Papyrus was produced in a restricted area and met the demands of a centralized administration whereas parchment as the product of an agricultural economy was suited to a decentralized system. The durability of parchment and the convenience of the codex for reference made it particularly suitable for the large books typical of scriptures and legal works. In turn, the difficulties of copying a large book limited the numbers produced. Small libraries with a small number of books could be established over large areas. Since the material of a civilization dominated by the papyrus roll had to be recopied into the parchment codex, a thorough system of censorship was involved. Pagan writing was neglected and Christian writing emphasized.[49]

An account of an earlier period is equally adept in drawing out the peculiarities of the mode of communication for social and cultural developments:

> Dependence on clay in the valleys of the Euphrates and the Tigris involved a special technique in writing and a special type of instrument, the reed stylus. Cuneiform writing on clay involved an elaborate skill, intensive training, and concentration of durable records. The temples with their priesthoods became the centers of cities. Invasions of force based on new techniques chiefly centering around the horse, first in the chariot and later in cavalry, brought union of city states, but a culture based on intensive

49 Innis, *The Bias of Communications*, p. 48.

training in writing rendered centralized control unstable and gave organized religion an enormous influence. . . . The influence of religion in the Babylonian and Assyrian empires was evident . . . in the development of astronomy, astrology, and a belief in fate . . .[50]

At other times in Innis' analysis, the balance shifts from material factors to "ideas" or "culture." Consider the following account of the influence of Stoic philosophy on the Roman state:

> Through Cicero . . . Stoicism received fresh support in its influence on Roman law, bringing to it the ideas of the world state, natural justice, and universal citizenship in an ethical sense, which were independent and superior to the enactment of kings. The conception of natural law brought enlightened criticism to bear on custom, helped to destroy the religious and ceremonial character of law, promoted equality before the law, emphasized the factor of intent, and mitigated unreasoning harshness . . . The *jus gentium* began to be conceived as a law common to all mankind and equivalent to the law of nature.[51]

For Innis, the important point is not whether "material" context or intersubjective "ideas" matter the most. The question itself bespeaks a duality alien to Innis' ecological holism. Innis saw a seamless connection – an inclusive functional system – between human beings as living organisms, the intersubjective web-of-beliefs into which they are acculturated, and the natural environment around them. Such a sophisticated materialism seems especially appropriate today when nature is being "brought back in" involuntarily – from global warming to infectious diseases. A reconsideration of Innis' ecological holism might help deepen social constructivism without the reifications of crude structuralist-materialism and thus help to see the intimate connections between changing material context, technology, and culture.

---

50 Ibid., p. 6.
51 Innis, *Empire and Communications*, p. 98.

Time-space biases

One of the more novel and potentially valuable aspects of Innis' work is his concentration on the way different civilizations or societies apprehend the categories of space and time. For Innis, these categories are not fixed and transparent, but variable from culture to culture and epoch to epoch. "[H]istory is not a seamless web but rather a web of which the warp and the woof are space and time woven in a very uneven fashion and producing distorted patterns."[52] In *Empire and Communications* and *The Bias of Communications*, and in scattered essays, Innis chronicled how civilizations throughout history have demonstrated a remarkable variety in the ways they have extended their control over space or have conceived of temporality.

> It has been pointed out that astronomical time is only one of several concepts. Social time, for example, has been described as qualitatively differentiated according to the beliefs and customs common to a group and as not continuous but subject to interruptions of actual dates. It is influenced by language which constrains and fixes prevalent concepts and modes of thought.[53]

Innis argued that control over predominant ways of ordering space or apprehending time have been important sources of social power in history, and struggles between social groups have often centered on competing conceptions of these categories. In ancient Sumer, for example, where the system of agriculture was dependent on irrigation, the prediction of harvests, seed-times, and floods provided political leverage:

> The selection of holy days necessitated devices by which they could be indicated and violation of them could be avoided. Dependence on the moon for the measurement of time meant exposure to irregularities such as have persisted in the means of determining the dates for Easter. Sumerian priesthoods apparently worked out a system for correcting the year by the adjustment of lunar months but the difficulties may have contributed to the success of Semitic

52 Innis, *The Bias of Communications*, p. xvii.
53 Ibid., p. 62.

kings with an interest in the sun, and enabled them to acquire control over the calendar and to make necessary adjustments of time over the extended territory under their control.[54]

In Egypt, according to Innis, "It is possible that the absolutism of Egyptian dynasties was dependent on the ability of kings to determine the sidereal year in relation to the appearance of the star Sirius."[55] Likewise, the reform of the Roman calendar by Julius Caesar not only had significant political and economic consequences but it also reflected the character of Roman culture. "A fixed date of reckoning, that of the founding of the city, reflected the interest of Rome in the unique character of a single day or hour and the belief that continuity was a sequence of single moments. An emphasis on specific single acts at a unique time contributed to the growth of Roman law notably in contracts in which time is of the essence."[56]

Although struggles over competing conceptions of space and time are important, more often space/time biases creep glacially and surreptitiously into a culture through a combination of historically contingent factors. For example, as with his contemporary Lewis Mumford, Innis emphasized a connection between technology, time, and the rise of modern industrialism:

> Spread of monasticism and the use of bells to mark the periods of the day and the place of religious services introduced regularity in the life of the West. Sun-dials, whose usefulness was limited in the more cloudy skies of the north, gave way to water clocks and finally to devices for measuring time with greater precision. The modern hour came into general use with the striking clocks of the fourteenth century. . . . Regularity of work brought administration, increase in production, trade, and the growth of cities. The spread of mathematics from India to Baghdad and the Moorish universities of Spain implied the gradual substitution of Arabic for Roman numerals and an enormous increase in the efficiency of calculation. Measurement of time facilitated the use of credit,

54 Ibid., p. 65.
55 Ibid., p. 66.
56 Ibid., p. 69.

the rise of exchanges, and calculations of the predictable future essential to the development of insurance.[57]

In a passage strikingly similar to John Ruggie's recent overview of the rise of early modern notions of space and territoriality, Innis isolates several coincident touchstones that shifted the time bias of the Middle Ages towards the spatial bias of the modern period:

> A new interest in space was evident in the development of the mariner's compass and the lens. Columbus discovered the New World, Magellan proved the earth a sphere, and in astronomy the Ptolemaic system was undermined especially after the invention and the improvement of the telescope. The architect Brunelleschi has been credited with first constructing a scene according to a focused system of perspective. Durer advanced from the empirical to mathematical construction. In Florence the new conception of space was translated into artistic terms as a counterpart of the modern notion of individualism. Its immediate effect on architecture was evident in the baroque. In philosophy, Leibniz was the first to explain space as pure form, an order of existence, and time as an order of succession.[58]

Although Innis' concrete examples of space/time biases in history emphasized variability, contingency, and idiosyncrasy, he did make some overarching generalizations. It has been these generalizations, often articulated by Innis in ways suggestive of testable hypotheses that have provided the grounds for those inclined to a more scientific-positivistic reading of Innis. Innis felt that most civilizations tend to have a bias in cultural orientation towards either space or time, and that rarely is a delicate balance achieved. Imbalances in one direction or the other create instability, and often invite challenges from the margins, which in the past have contributed to the collapse of empires or to epochal transformation.[59] Innis also believed that there was a close connection between the communication media available to a civilization and its bias towards either time or space. As he put it:

57 Ibid., p. 72; for Mumford's discussion, see Lewis Mumford, *Technics and Civilization* (New York, 1934).
58 Ibid., pp. 128–129. Compare with Ruggie, Territoriality, pp. 158–159.
59 See Innis, *Empire and Communications*, p. 5.

Media that emphasize time are those that are durable in character, such as parchment, clay, and stone. . . . Media that emphasize space are apt to be less durable and light in character, such as papyrus and paper. The latter are suited to wide areas in administration and trade.[60]

One way to see Innis' formulations outlined above is in programmatic terms, as rigid theses on the rise and fall of empires or the invariable link between certain types of media and certain ways of apprehending space and time.[61] I think this would be to cast Innis mistakenly in an essentialist light. My impression is that Innis' space/time biases are better conceived of as shorthand designates for the supports and constraints presented by different communication media to prevailing *mentalités* and institutions through history. For example, to say, as Innis did, that a communications medium such as clay during the period of the Sumerian city-states had a bias towards time is not to reduce Sumerian culture solely to that mode of communication. Rather, it is to reveal the way the material context and available technology of the time constrained or supported existing institutions, social groups, and *mentalités*.[62] Treated this way, they provide a lens or window on to how different cultures at different times apprehend the categories of space and time, thus demonstrating their historical variability. Likewise Innis' comments about imbalances towards space or time inviting reactions from the margins can either be treated as a full-blown dialectical theory of history, or as a limited statement on forms of human struggle and the tendencies of opposing forces. My sense is that the latter is both the most fruitful and consistent with Innis' overall views on history.

In what ways does an Innisian approach help illuminate the space-time biases in circulation today? At the time of his death in the early 1950s, Innis believed that there was an imbalance in Western civilizations towards the bias of space with a corresponding neglect of time:

60 Ibid.

61 See, for example, Dudley, "Space, Time, and Number" for such an extrapolation.

62 Certainly a glance at Innis' discussion of the relationship between clay, writing, and Sumerian culture on pp. 29–30 of *Empire and Communications* would bear out the subtlety of Innis' interpretation and rule out any attribution of determinism or reductionism to Innis.

Lack of interest in problems of duration in Western civilization suggests that the bias of paper and printing has persisted in a concern with space. The state has been interested in the enlargement of territories and the imposition of cultural uniformity on its peoples, and, losing touch with the problems of time, has been willing to engage in wars to carry out immediate objectives. Printing has emphasized vernaculars and divisions between states based on language without implying a concern with time.[63]

In these words can be discerned a picture of what might be called "High Westphalia" – a condition of territorial exclusivity and spatial differentiation that marks the modern period.[64] In his essay, "A Plea for Time," Innis urged a correction to this imbalance, believing that the time dimension had been reduced to a superficial "present-mindedness" reflected in an obsession with statistics in the social sciences, and the fetish of newspapers with current events and catastrophes.[65]

Since Innis made these observations, however, profound changes in communication technologies have occurred in such areas as digitization, fiber optics, computer processing, and satellite transmissions. From an Innisian perspective, we would expect space-time biases to be reconfigured and transformed accordingly, forming a new horizon of power on the world political landscape. Although the preoccupation with space that Innis describes still persists, many have pointed to a new *temporal* bias superceding it, supplanting itself into the sinews of power and culture of post-industrial societies.[66] Indeed, Innis himself may have located some of the roots of this bias long before it was unleashed on a real-time planetary scale by digital electronic-telecommunications:

The newspaper has been a pioneer in the development of speed in communication and transportation. Extension of railroads and telegraphs brought more rapid transmission of news and

63 Innis, *The Bias of Communications*, p. 76.
64 In his description of the spatial biases of the modern state, Innis' analysis evokes the more recent conceptualization of, for example, Rob Walker. See Walker, *Inside/Outside*, ch. six.
65 Ibid., pp. 61–91.
66 See, in particular, James Der Derian, *Anti-Diplomacy: Spies, Terror, Speed, and War* (Cambridge, 1992) and Paul Virilio, *The Art of the Motor* [translated by Julie Rose], (Minneapolis, 1995).

wider and faster circulation of newspapers; and newspapers, in turn, demanded further extension of railroads and telegraph lines. Cables, postal systems, express systems, aviation lines and radio have been fostered and utilized by newspapers. The concentration of the natural sciences on the problems of physics and chemistry concerned with speed reflects the influence of the newspapers. Educational systems and literacy have been subject to their influence directly and indirectly. Speed in the collection, production, and dissemination of information has been the essence of newspaper development.[67]

Moving from the newspaper and the telegraph to today's hypermedia environment, an *Empire of Speed* has emerged working in the direction of unleashing the velocity and flow of information across borders and around the world. At its heart are the swift currents of capital that circuit the globe twenty-four hours a day, shifting astronomical sums in a "cyclonic" swarm of electrical impulses. It is manifested in the dream of "friction-free" capitalism over the Internet, and the rise of "E-commerce" and "digital cash." It is formed in and around the space-of-flows that define the just-in-time production networks of so-called *Kanban* capitalism. It is driven by the mass obsession for ever faster computing and communication technics, which has ripped through governments and consumer culture – greater bandwidth, more baud-rate, faster Ethernet connections, speedier processors. "The power complex today is preoccupied only with acceleration."[68]

This temporal bias is, in turn, transforming the basic character of power, security, and authority in world politics. In the *Empire of Speed*, "having open and unconstrained access to flows, not closed domination of places, becomes a crucial attribute of power, perhaps as vital as juridico-legal sovereignty, in informationalized societies."[69]

---

67 Harold Innis, The Newspaper in Economic Development, in Harold Innis (ed.) *Political Economy in the Modern State* (Toronto, 1946), p. 32.
68 Lewis Mumford, *The Pentagon of Power: The Myth of the Machine*, vol. 2 (New York, 1970), p. 148, plate 4.
69 Timothy Luke, "Sovereignty, States, and Security: New World Order or Neo-World Orders?" (Working Paper 95–1, Adlai Stevenson Program on Global Security, University of California, Santa Cruz), p. 19.

Control of tempo and pace rather than territory and space, in other
words, increasingly determines who gets what, when, and how.[70] In
turn, the circuit "crash" is becoming the predominant "threat" – the
network itself the primary referent of security. Guarding borders from
possible penetration is becoming less important than protecting circuits
from illegitimate violation.[71] *National* security is being transformed
into *network* security, and the "nerves of government" bristle in an
accordingly new way.[72]

The affinity between an Innisian perspective on speed and power and
those of postmodern theorists, such as Paul Virilio, is readily apparent.
Both share the view that, in Innis' words, "The concepts of space and
time must be made relative and elastic and the attention given by the
social scientists to problems of space should be paralleled by attention to
problems of time."[73] However, some important differences remain that
distinguish an Innisian from a postmodern perspective. For example,
rather than treating the *Empire of Speed* as a purely discursive construct,
an Innisian approach locates it firmly in the material and technological
context of post-industrialization and the hypermedia environment. This
not only reveals the depth and extent of the constraints imposed but also
suggests potential avenues by which counter-movements might begin
– something postmodernists are reluctant to do. For Innis, concerned
as he was with balance, a recovery of a deeper sense of time than the
"eternal present" of the *Empire of Speed* – perhaps in some form of
spirituality – remains a critical issue.

Conclusions

At the end of his recent essay on "Territoriality," John Ruggie suggested
that understanding contemporary transformations requires a different
analytical and epistemological posture. To illustrate the type of posture

---

70 Der Derian, *Anti-Diplomacy,* pp. 129–130.
71 See David Mussington, Throwing the Switch in Cyberspace, *Jane's Intelligence Review* (July 1996), pp. 331–334.
72 Karl Deutsch, *The Nerves of Government: Models of Political Communication and Control* (New York, 1966).
73 Ibid., p. 34.

he thought would be appropriate, he quoted Quentin Skinner to the effect that it must embody "a willingness to emphasize the local and the contingent, a desire to underline the extent to which our own concepts and attitude have been shaped by particular historical circumstances, and a correspondingly strong dislike . . . of all overarching theories and singular schemes of explanation."[74] In this article, I have attempted to show how an excavation of the work of Harold Innis might help point the way to just such an approach. Although it is often a cliché to say so, Innis was a theorist very much out of his time. He emphasized contingency and historicity at a time when the momentum of the social sciences was in the direction of modernization and teleology. His sophisticated incorporation of natural and material factors was written at a time when "the expulsion of nature from social science" was the dominant trend.[75] His attentiveness to symbolic forms and the social constructs of space and time in different cultures and epochs presaged the writings of postmodern theorists, such as Michel Foucault and Paul Virilio. In these respects, re-visiting Innis is not a stale resuscitation of an old-fashioned theorist but a revival of a vital and imaginative thinker who had much to say on world politics and human history.

While Innis' scholarship concentrated on empires through history, his approach was entirely different from those who have done so from a realist or neo-realist perspective now predominant in the study of world politics. He would have considered the search for timeless causes of the rise and fall of great powers or empires to be misguided. The lesson of Innis' historicism is that while regularities can be discerned in particular historical contexts, general explanations that stand apart from history are unattainable. Likewise, Innis would have regarded the examination of imperial systems of rule as specific models or world ordering principles standing between anarchy and hierarchy as spurious throwbacks to a kind of Aristotelian essentialism. For Innis, the character of individual empires – though perhaps sharing some very general orientations towards space or time – are always shaped idiosyncratically depending on the specific material, technological, and cultural context of the time in question.

---

74 Ruggie, Territoriality, pp. 169–170. The original quotation is from Quentin Skinner, *The Return of Grand Theory in the Human Sciences* (New York, 1985), p. 12.
75 Deudney, Bringing Nature Back In, p. 11.

Although his thoroughgoing historicism in this respect, and his skillful attention to the social construction of time and space, aligns him with social constructivists, postmodernists, and others in the so-called "reflectivist" camp, Innis' incorporation of natural or material factors into his analysis would set him apart here as well. Yet even here, Innis' broad encompassing of natural, technological, and cultural factors would distinguish his analysis from those employing the economistic categories of Marxist thought. Such a sophisticated materialist approach – one that privileges neither material, technological, or cultural factors – seems especially *apropos* at a time when the unintended consequences of modern industrialism are materializing in ozone depletion and global warming, and when earth-circling satellites and webs of fiber optic cable bind the planet together in a hypermedia environment. While Innis did not live long enough to provide his views on these developments, his approach at least suggests a lens or framework with which to investigate them.

MENAHEM BLONDHEIM

2. "The Significance of Communication" According to Harold Adams Innis

Communication technologies represent an interface of mind and matter: They are the physical means for representing, manipulating, conveying, and storing knowledge and ideas.[1] A reasonable proposition would therefore suggest that significant change in media technologies, and in the communication environments they shape, would be related to transformations in the life of the mind and to changes in collective *mentalité*. Further, should we happen to hold that ideas drive behavior and action, that same proposition would imply, by extension, that changes in communication technology may relate to significant change in society and culture, even in the human condition generally. This simple proposition was the focus of a body of scholarly work produced by Canadian scholar Harold Adams Innis in the middle of the previous century.

Innis had been Canada's foremost economic historian and political economist, a leader of Canadian academe who exerted an important influence on the shaping of national economic policy. In his later years Innis shifted his scholarly focus from the production and distribution of North American staples and the institutions governing the nexus of these products and their markets, to the ecumenical historical study of the production and dissemination of knowledge and the shaping of cultures, as they related to technological media and their institutional environments. Innis' odyssey to the universe of communications was abruptly discontinued by his death at the age of 58, in 1952.

The 50th anniversary of Innis' passing came in a period uniquely aware of, and perplexed by, thoroughgoing change in communications and the technologies underpinning them. True enough, throughout

---

1 This chapter is based on Menahem Blondheim, "Discovering 'The Significance of Communication': Harold Adams Innis as Social Constructivist," *Canadian Journal of Communication*, 29 (2004): 119–143.

the modern era (and possibly in prior epochs too), people had been uniformly impressed by what they thought was the unprecedented degree to which new technologies were transforming their daily lives. Indeed, it is questionable whether our generation has a better claim than any previous one to revolutionary technological change as applied to everyday life. Yet the past decade or two have a marked distinction in the historical evolution of technological gadgetry: For in perhaps no former period in history has technological progress as applied to daily life focused so sharply on a single aspect of human activity as it has focused recently on processes of communication.

The radical change in the practice of mediated communications in our times has spurred considerable efforts to understand the relation of communication technologies to other aspects of the human experience. Surprisingly perhaps, Innis' legacy has been largely overlooked in this project of re-understanding media environments as transformed by technology. Even his successors in what some call the "Toronto School" of medium-focused analysis of communication, most notably his junior colleague Marshall McLuhan, have fared better than the pathfinder.[2] This neglect of one of the richest bodies of thinking on the meaning of media and technology, and one of the most broadly construed attempts at understanding the dynamics of their historical co-evolution, is both unfortunate and curious.

One reason for the marginalization of Innis in our contemporary media debate may be related to the unique nature of his written legacy. For if Innis' works on Canadian economic development are complex but coherent, the subsequent corpus of communication texts appears more like a bag of tricks Innis played on his fellow scholars: his communication scholarship is opaque, contradictory, occasionally even tantalizing. And indeed, while his economic histories are considered definitive, his communication works, highly suggestive but glaringly

---

2   McLuhan himself had described his own work as a "mere footnote" to Innis'; even more significantly, perhaps, McLuhan who cultivated the image of a whimsy iconoclast conceded that his outwardly conservative senior colleague was "the real freak." Marshall McLuhan, "Introduction," *The Bias of Communication* (Toronto: University of Toronto Press, 1951); McLuhan quoted in Philip Marchand, *Marshall McLuhan: The Medium and the Messenger* (Toronto: Random House, 1989), p.113.

incomplete, are more of an inspiration and a challenge. Innis' ideas about communication in its relation to culture, society, and world order, are supposed to emerge, somehow, from surveys of communication in history, and lots of it. His texts are essentially a parade of historical experiences in their relation to media, marched over and over again in lectures, articles and monographs about communication. This recurring historical parade usually proceeds along a chronological axis, though lapses and errors occur quite frequently. Innis, as if viewing the parade from a grandstand, occasionally seizes on a fact or a relationship to make an editorial point.[3]

The readers of these historical surveys, patterned as a historical play-by-play interlaced with expert analysis, are engaged by a problem of coherence on at least two levels. First they encounter the problem of contradictions and inconsistencies that emerge from a close reading of the texts. Seeking a dialectic that would clarify them, readers are challenged by the more general problem of the chaotic nature of Innis' comments, observations, and arguments – their tendency to go "backwards and forward and sideways all at the same time." Readers must ask whether a real theory or even a consistent point of view may be found in these texts, whether there really is a demiurge somewhere. Then the reader discovers that she herself must be that demiurge, and provide coherence to the author's elusive inconclusiveness. Not many students of communication in contemporary society are open to this journey into history and to the edge of chaos.

Nevertheless, over the past half century a series of perceptive scholars have responded to the challenge of deciphering Innis, systematizing his observations, and crystallizing a coherent theory from them. The effect of this hermeneutic process, at least in communication theory, has been the compromising of Innis' dizzying openness and his freezing into a comfortably closed and unambiguous mold. This present essay represents an updated chapter in the cumulative project of domesticating

---

3   This plan of composition is demonstrated most strikingly in Innis' draft of "History of Communication," a 1,000 page manuscript left among his papers: it represents an impressive, if disorganized, collection of fragments of historical information, from an eclectic array of sources, in a more or less chronological order. The manuscript is located in the Innis collection, University of Toronto Archives, Thomas Fisher Library, University of Toronto. It is also available in microform.

Innis. First it attempts a summary of the received wisdom on the meaning
of his communication texts and theorems. Then, aspects of that schema
are critically reviewed through following two parallel thrusts. One
cross-checks the abstract of Innis' work as canonized in communication
studies against the genuine item. The other seeks the sources of Innis'
approach, by tracing the origins and the development of his thinking
about communication.

This revisiting of Innis' texts and their development inevitably
reflects contemporary experiences and concerns. It highlights,
nevertheless, the essentially historicist dimension of Innis' project,
leveraging his historism to point out the relevance of his approach
toward an interpretation of our contemporary media dynamic. Although
this update does not attempt to draw any relevant morals, it expects
to underscore elements of Innis' heritage that may prove useful in
understanding communications today.

The Accepted Innis

In contrast to the contradictory and open-ended nature of the original,
the conventional sketch of Innis available to students of communication
theory in textbooks and overviews is refreshingly coherent, and
includes a number of consensual components. The first concerns Innis'
methodological approach and points out the fundamental historicity
of his scholarship and theory. His ideas about communication, it is
acknowledged, emerge from, and are sustained by, the study of the
history of communication and of communication in history. Not much,
however, is made of this historism, either in analyses of Innis in the
communication studies tradition or in intellectual histories of the
evolution of thinking about communication in his times.

Further, it is widely held that for Innis, communication technology,
to an important extent drives history. And indeed, a second element
of the accepted Innis is his focus on the medium – a technological
artifact – in analyzing processes of communication and their social
significance. The particular technological attributes of a medium, or
a mix of media prevalent in a given society, condition the practice
of communication in that society, the institutions and socio-cultural
arrangements associated with those practices, and through them more

general societal arrangements and cultural climates. Given the emphasis on the role of media in determining the institutions and systems of social communication, the technological determinism label is commonly applied to Innis' approach.[4] Marshall McLuhan, in introducing *The Bias of Communication* – an introduction toned as a ceremonial induction of Innis into a communication theory hall-of-fame – enunciated these two cornerstones of the accepted Innis – historism and technological determinism – in a single sentence: "He had discovered a means of using historical situations as a lab in which to test the character of technology in the shaping of cultures."[5]

A third, and one of the most broadly applied elements of Innis' legacy was his notion of monopoly of knowledge.[6] By transplanting the economic concept of monopoly to the field of communications – to knowledge artifacts and skills – Innis elegantly buttressed his media determinism. When certain media or their knowledge products dominate society's communication environment, the peculiar dynamics of oligopoly make for amplifying and perpetuating the hold of those media and the bodies of knowledge associated with them. They block the emergence of alternatives, and ultimately enhance the effects of the monopolistic medium and skills on society and on its political, social and cultural profile.

Finally, communication scholars aver that Innis proposed an extremely effective criterion for organizing and analyzing the plethora of communication media which bowed in and bowed out in the course

---

4   A good example of this conventional casting of Innis is the summary of his work in one of the most respected standard textbooks on mass communication theory: Denis McQuail, *Mass Communication Theory* (London: Sage Publications, 1994), pp. 97–98. Arthur Kroker's discussion of Innis' emphasis on technology side-steps the question of determinism and considers Innis' focus on technology as a heuristic devise: *Technology and the Canadian Mind: Innis, McLuhan, Grant* (New York: St. Martin's Press, 1984), pp. 87–122.

5   Marshall McLuhan, "Introduction," *The Bias*, p. xi. On the vicissitudes of this introduction see William J. Buxton and Charles R. Acland, "Harold Innis: A Genealogy of Contrasting Portraits," in: *Harold Innis in the New Century: Reflections and Refractions* (Montreal: McGill-Queen's University Press, 1999), pp. 7–9.

6   A short, representative discussion of monopoly of knowledge, oriented to students is: Marshall Soules, "Harold Adams Innis: The Bias of Communication and Monopoly of Power," http://www.mala.bc.ca/~soules/media212/Innis/Innis.htm

of history, affecting communication systems, societies, and their culture in the process. This criterion is the time-space divide as applied to the performance of media and their underlying technologies. In this view, some media are more effective in delivering knowledge over time – from past to present and from present to future – other media are more effective in delivering knowledge across space. And indeed, on this central point, Innis is unusually clear. On page one, paragraph one of his *The Bias of Communication*, he suggests that any medium of communication

> has an important influence on the dissemination of knowledge over space and over time... According to its characteristics [it] may be better suited to the dissemination of knowledge over time than over space, particularly if the medium is heavy and durable and not suited to transportation [e.g., tablets, pyramids], or to the dissemination of knowledge over space than over time, particularly if the medium is light and easily transported [e.g., papyri, electrons].[7]

The divergence of orality and literacy can be seen as the fundamental model, as well as the historical origin, of the time-media / space-media polarity.[8]

The proposition that individual media, and ultimately media-mixes, diverge on a time-space axis has been solidly entrenched in the canonized version of Innis. Following Innis' lead subsequent scholars crystallized elaborate series of variables determining the portrait of society: political, economic, religious, legal, administrative, managerial – one could go on and on – that parallel the time-space polarity. These variables intersect into exquisite sets of coherent and congruent overall portraits of societies and their biases as determined by the media they employ. Not least among the factors converging into the conflicting time and space sets were the nature of knowledge and of knowing, even states of consciousness.[9]

7   Innis, *The Bias*, p. 33.
8   Chapter 13 in this volume discusses this observation.
9   See, e.g., William Christian, "The Inquisition of Nationalism," *Journal of Canadian Studies* 12:5 (Winter 1977): 62–72;   Nick Stevenson, *Understanding Media Cultures: Social Theory and Mass Communication* (London: Sage Publications

There is a considerable consensus among communication scholars on the validity and usefulness of this basic observation. In fact, there appears to be only one conspicuous dissenting voice which challenges the relation of the media durability-ephemerality continuum to the social biases of time and space. In discussing the metabolé of the old kingdom in Egypt into the middle kingdom, this scholar states: "A decline of centralized bureaucratic power and a shift from an emphasis on control over space reflected in the pyramid to a decentralized bureaucratic power with an emphasis on continuity and religion [namely time] to be seen in the spread of writing and the use of papyrus.... weakened control over space..." This argument appears to put on its head Innis' proposition that durable media such as the pyramids are associated with a time-bias, and that light-weighted, short-lived, and easily transportable media such as papyri are to be associated with society biased toward space. This proposition, contradicting Innis, was made by no other than Innis himself, in "The Problem of Space."[10]

In trying to reconcile these two contradictory statements, it may be well to first consider a preliminary, and much more fundamental, challenge to Innis' time- and space-media theorem. The source of the problem is the nature of orality itself. As noted, a central insight Innis had developed, conspicuously presented in *The Bias of Communication*, traceable throughout *Empire and Communication*, and elaborated on in "Minerva's Owl" and in "A Plea for Time," concerned the social

---

Ltd., 1994), pp. 115–116. James W. Carey's construction of these time and space sets are particularly illuminating: "Canadian Communication Theory: Extensions and Interpretations of Harold Innis," in: Gertrude J. Robinson and Donald F. Theal, eds., *Studies in Canadian Communications* (Montreal: 1975); "Harold Adams Innis and Marshall McLuhan," in: Raymond Rosenthal, ed., *McLuhan Pro & Con* (Baltimore: Penguin Books, Inc., 1968), pp. 270–308; "Culture, Geography and Communications: The Work of Harold Innis in an American Context," in: William H. Melody, Liora Sleiter, and Paul Heyer, eds. *Culture, Communication, and Dependency: The Tradition of H. A. Innis.* (Norwood, NJ: Ablex, 1981), pp. 73–91; a revised version of the latter was published as "Space, Time and Communications: A Tribute to Harold Innis," in: James W. Carey, *Communication as Culture: Essays in Media and Society* (New York: Routledge, 1992), pp. 142–172. See also: Carey, with John J. Quirk, "The Mythos of the Electronic Revolution," ibid., pp. 113–141.

10 Innis, *The Bias*, p. 95.

implications of orality as opposed to script. Orality, according to Innis, is not space-binding but time-binding. Now, the space side of the equation appears to work well enough. After all, there are severe physical limitations on the reach of the human voice in space, and the corruption of oral knowledge as it is relayed from place to place and from person to person makes the oral medium ineffective in binding space. However, the fact that orality is not effective in binding space does not necessarily yield a fit between the oral medium and time – on the durability of messages. The opposite would appear to be the case: the oral medium is anything but heavy, resilient, and durable as are pyramids, stellae, or clay tablets; it is effervescent and ephemeral. Innis, however, clearly considered orality to be the model, the cornerstone, of time-biased communications.

The solution to this theoretical non-sequiter would appear to be built into human adjustment to the peculiar limitations of the medium. Given the fleeting nature of oral knowledge, it can be preserved only through digesting, internalizing and repeating the message time and again, to oneself but more effectively to others. Thus, if orally-transmitted knowledge is to exist at all, it must be received from a predecessor, internalized, and made part of living consciousness. It is in this sense that orality is time-binding. It creates a concern with preserving useful knowledge from the past, demands continuity, and requires the keeping of that knowledge, and through it the past, alive. For knowledge of the past and from the past to exist, in an environment lacking durable media, it must exist through continuity, and as living knowledge it binds the present to the past. Thus, precisely the limitations on the durability of oral knowledge bind and bias an oral society to its past.

Armed with this dialectic module, which appears time and again in his reasoning, the conflict between the Innis of *The Bias* and the Innis of "The Problem of Space" can be resolved quite simply. In line with the structure of orality's time-binding dynamic, Innis is telling us that if a socio-political system is shaped to be effective in its control over, say, space, its problem becomes time; it is threatened by discontinuity in time. Once it becomes conscious of, and concerned about, this deficiency and its dangers, it will invest considerable efforts in developing time-binding media: it will develop a concern, or a bias toward time. And by the same token, a socio-cultural system with effective time-binding media in place may naturally become concerned about its space-binding powers and necessarily focus on them. More generally, a bias, if recognized, will generate a counter bias as a corrective, in the cause of equilibrium.

Innis presented this dynamic of inverted-determinism most simply and straightforwardly in his *The Bias of Communication*, one page after having pointed out the basic polarity of media of time and media of space quoted above. In describing the rise of the early monarchy in Egypt to power, he suggests that the "success of the monarchy in acquiring control over Egypt in terms of space necessitated a concern with the problem of continuity or time." This concern translated into mummification and the construction of the pyramids "as a device for emphasizing control over time."[11] Similarly, after recovering from the Hyksos occupation in the middle of the second millennium BC and building an empire over a vast expanse, it was precisely the "solution to the problem of space" that "compelled the king to attempt a solution of problems of continuity."[12]

It is in the context of this inverted-determinism dialectic that Innis' concept of, or concern with, monopoly of knowledge assumes its greatest significance. As noted, media are essentially a technological apparatus that provides for the interface of mind and matter – a technical resource that sustains the lifeworld of ideas. Through achieving a monopolistic position, a certain communication apparatus may become the sole provider of the physical infrastructure for communications and thus dominate the nature and the spread of knowledge. This monopoly of matter, however, since it serves the mind, can perpetuate and fixate not only itself but also the interests and concerns of society, shaping them in its own image. The dynamics of oligopoly operate even more directly when beyond the technical resources that sustain it, knowledge itself is monopolized. And all the more so when the party in possession of this knowledge is compact and effectively organized. Either way, the most dangerous aspect of monopoly of knowledge is in barring mental and ideological change. By virtue of their uncontested power, monopolies of knowledge and consciousness may blind individuals and societies even to the mere fact of imbalance between time and space media, let alone to its dangers and to the feasibility of alternatives. The consequent

11 Innis, *The Bias*, p. 34.
12 Innis, *The Bias*, p. 35.

fixation on either trajectory – that of time or that of space – precludes correction and readjustment. It makes the inverted-deterministic thrust towards balance impossible.

The far-reaching implication of monopoly on the dynamic play of determinism and counter-determinism may be illustrated by applying it to the case of the modern state. Like empires – Innis' basic unit of analysis – the now beleaguered entity of the state depends on a balance of time- and space-binding powers. After all, it is founded on a mix of time and space orientations: on the one hand it is a creature of space – it is defined territorially and manages very many individuals and communities, scattered over its space, networking them into a coherent entity. On the other hand, the state is the creature of time: its self-defining rationale is founded on genealogy, history and memory. [13] Ideally for the state, the play of determinism and inverted determinism would balance the conflicting orientations of time and of space and ensure stability. The common roots in time, according to Innis, would demand awareness of and efforts toward the development of its space-binding communications. The state's territorial coherence would direct it to develop its media for time-binding. The convergence of these opposites would yield balance and stability.

However, should the options for developing either of these thrusts close down, should either time or space monopolize society's concerns, the state is doomed. The shaky condition of the contemporary state demonstrates both dangers. When what was once Yugoslavia relents in its efforts to bind its space, a monopoly of genealogy and history will prevail, shattering its territorial coherence into separate and hostile, then belligerent and ultimately warring, historically defined ethnic and religious entities. Should countries in western Europe, weary of centuries of the tyranny of time, relent on their efforts to keep the past alive and focus instead on markets and amusements – on space – time will be forgotten, space will take over unifying vast territories, on a continental scale, in their economy, currency and bureaucracy, featuring a NATO, an EC, and ultimately a European Union. Either of these imbalances, let alone both, leave the state dwarfed and doomed to irrelevance.

13 For a short consideration of nationalism in the context of time and space biases see Stevenson, *Media Cultures*, pp. 116–117.

Canada would also face significant challenges should either time or space monopolize its concerns. Canada represents a mirror image of the "normal" national state. Given its vast and fragmented expanse it is a country divided by a common geography. Given its novelty and demographic heterogeneity, its unity is threatened rather than sustained by memory and history. Canada's coherence is therefore contingent on purposefully and actively cultivating both time and space orientations. To survive as a state, Canada would have to develop space-binding media, such as the transcontinental railroad written into its constitution, and it would also have to actively develop its own culture and traditions, rather than have that option frozen into an American and a British monopoly of knowledge. A failure on either account would compromise both Canadian nationalism and Canada's geographical integrity.[14]

Yet if this understanding of Innis' theory of dynamic equilibrium of time and space concerns is valid, it undermines one of the most prevalent assumptions about his approach, namely, his being a technological determinist. Possibly a straw man, a technological deterministic approach is usually construed to include three elements. First, that technology, as the bastard offspring of pure science – the source of novel ideas presumably developed independently of social expectations – is an autonomous force. Further, that given social equilibrium, technology is the primary source of change in the human condition. Finally, that given social equilibrium, changes effected by new technology are prone to have major effects that reverberate throughout society and transform it.[15]

Innis himself indeed appears to claim the questionable distinction of being a technological determinist. "A medium of communication," he writes, "has an important influence on the dissemination of knowledge… and it becomes necessary to study its characteristics in order to appraise its influence in its cultural setting." Such an examination of the

---

14 The numerous discussions of Canadian nationalism in its relation to communication have been strongly influenced by Karl Deutsch, *Nationalism and Social Communication* (Cambridge: Harvard University Press, 1966).

15 A variety of perspectives on the meaning of technological determinism and of social constructivism is available in Merritt Roe Smith and Leo Marx, eds., *Does Technology Drive History? The Dilemma of Technological Determinism* (Cambridge: The MIT Press, 1996).

characteristics of a technological medium may indeed yield dramatic results:

> The use of a medium of communication over a long period will to some extent determine the character of knowledge to be communicated and suggest that its pervasive influence will eventually create a civilization in which life and flexibility will become exceedingly difficult to maintain and that the advantages of a new medium will become such as to lead to the emergence of a new civilization.

The character of this new civilization, in turn, would also be determined by the nature of its media and so turns the wheel.

Inverted determinism, however, could prevent such a sorry state of affairs, and also redeem Innis from the onus of being a technological determinist. If Innis maintains that societies are capable of balancing their time-space act through encouraging and appropriating communication technologies that would counter the monopolizing tendencies of entrenched media, and ultimately their freezing into an un-adaptive, inflexible state, he is not much of a technological determinist. Rather, he emerges as a through and through social constructivist, holding that technological change is engineered and affected by society's strategies and choices.[16] It is society that decides how much literacy it wants to mix into its orality, whether it wants to journey in space or in time, whether it prefers Xerox machines or Pravdas, satellite feeds of Seinfeld or sermons preached in a local Mosque, Synagogue, or Church. Media determinism, as disinfected by the prospect of inverted-determinism, posits that the social dog wags its technological tail rather than being wagged by it.

Nor is communication technology, however introduced into society, the primary source of change for Innis. In his parade of historical datum after historical datum, marched over and over again in his communication

---

16 William Westfall has suggested that Innis, always intrigued by theological questions, applied the tension between free will and God's plan of history to the concept of bias. This present tension between determinism and inverted-determinism would surely represent a tension congruent to the theological archetype. William Westfall, "The Ambivalent Verdict: Harold Innis and Canadian History," in Melody et al., *Culture Communication*, p. 43.

texts, the sources and origins of social change vary considerably. It could be the pattern of the Nile's flooding, foreign invasion, military victory or defeat, the invention of new gods and new ideas, and numerous other novelties that both reflect and affect change in societies. Technology as the source of social change is the exception, not the rule.

Only in one feature of Innis' portrayal of the dynamics of change can one hear an echo of technological determinism. As noted, a technological deterministic approach expects the introduction of new technologies to a homeostatic society to yield effects of the greatest magnitude. For even if it is society that drives technology, even if technology is deployed to react to change which was enacted by other factors, once selected and deployed by society, communication technologies may be expected to have very powerful and highly significant consequences, since they touch on the nexus of mind and matter. In this respect at least, Innis would fit the bill of a communication-technology determinist.

But there is a nuance in emphasis to be noticed at this point. When Innis parades human history he indeed does pay considerable attention to communication technologies, and moreover does point out the revolutionary transformations they were capable of bringing about, even if as agents, not the sources of change. However, the accent in the communication-technology composite is placed emphatically on the communication, not the technology side of the compound. In other words, Innis was a communication determinist. He considered processes of communication and the institutions associated with them to have tremendous effects on the nature of society and culture and on the course of their history.

What determines what?

In looking back at Innis' communication scholarship after fifty years, communication determinism emerges as its towering revelation. Innis uncovered "the significance of communication" – the fact that civilizations are "profoundly influenced by communication and that marked changes in communication have had important implications."[17]

17 Innis, *The Bias*, p. 3.

The economic historians found that communication, rather than money, makes the world go around. And since he believed that communication history was the key to world history, he went on to read the history of the world as a history of communication, just as a former Innis wrote the national history of Canada as a history of political economy. Thus, in a sense, his great revelation in communication theory was suggesting that there should be such a thing, his revolution as a communication theorist was being one.[18] Upon embarking on his exploration into communications, Innis assembled a comprehensive and imposing bibliography of some 2,000 potentially relevant titles. Exercising his fabled work ethic, the former Ontario farmboy managed to consume and digest them. A generous selection from that formidable bibliography found its way, in the form of quotations and references, into the essays comprising *The Bias of Communication*. Not a single one of the works cited therein includes the word "communication" or "media" in its title or subtitle. It was indeed in isolating communications as an aspect of history and culture, and further positing its development as a key to unlocking the vicissitudes of mind, matter and their interface, that Innis' work was revolutionary.

Given the bias of social and academic life in the late 20th and early 21st century, Innis' revelation of the "significance of communication" may appear commonplace. As communication developed into a legitimate field of academic inquiry, featuring university departments and professional associations, scholarly periodicals and textbooks, the proposition of thinking about communication as a distinct field of the social experience, one which moreover may serve as a key to understanding other fields, realized itself and to an extent depleted itself. Moreover, and as noted on top, the characteristic rhetoric of the past generation celebrated a "communication revolution" that was supposed to usher in an "Information Age." Thus, the professional bias of contemporary communication scholars and the bias of the period they live in would tend to make Innis' discovery a trivial truism rather than a breakthrough.

---

18 "There is good reason to regard Innis as the first writer to create a distinct field of inquiry using the social and economic consequence of developments in communication as subject matter." Paul Heyer, "Innis and the History of Communication," in Melody et al., *Culture Communication*, p. 250.

Innis presented his discovery in the beginning of *The Bias of Communication*. However confusing the texts of his essays could become, he usually commenced them by succinctly exposing their purpose as part of an overall agenda; and *The Bias of Communication*, originally presented as a paper at the University of Michigan in 1949, was no exception. In its opening paragraph Innis' cause was put in the form of a proposition:

> The appearance of a wide range of cultural phenomena at different periods in the history of Western civilization has been described by Professor A. L. Kroeber in *Configuration of Cultural Growth*. He makes comments at various points to explain the relative strength or weakness of cultural elements, but refrains from extended discussion. I do not propose to do more than add a footnote to these comments and in this to discuss the possible *significance of communication* to the rise and decline of cultural traits. (Italics mine.)

It is indeed in relation to Kroeber's argument that the revolutionary nature of Innis' suggestion emerges. Kroeber, like other prominent scholars of the 20th century's Era of the World Wars, focused on civilizations as their unit of analysis.[19] Kroeber's project was to first establish, then account for, the pattern of simultaneous, rapid advances in the major branches of cultural endeavor in the course of the rise of civilizations. He categorized the key branches of cultural development as philosophy, science, literature, fine arts and the performing arts. Innis, in humbly "adding a footnote" to Kroeber's project, was proposing much more than adding communication as the sixth item on the list of cultural traits alongside science, philosophy, and their likes; he was proposing communication as a meta-category which would not only co-change as part of the pattern of congruent acceleration of cultural development, but to an important extent condition the entire process.[20]

---

19 See, e.g., Stephen K. Sanderson, ed., *Civilizations and World Systems: Studying World-Historical Change* (London: Altimira, 1995).

20 In this context, "footnote" should be expansively construed as taking a further step, piggy-backing on the validity of Kroeber's findings and subsuming them. Innis employs a similar usage in the opening of *The Press: A Neglected Factor in the Economic History of the 20th Century* (London: Oxford University Press, 1949):

By aligning himself with Kroeber, Innis was doing more than economizing on scholarly energy by taking a ride on giants' shoulders. He was also indicating a dramatic shift in his outlook and method, even in his scholarly identity. Kroeber, in his *Configurations,* was venturing into history from anthropology, expecting that history might validate his grand hypothesis about the structures of cultural development. Innis found himself in the same methodological juncture as Kroeber, but he had reached it by taking the opposite tack – from history to general theory. In taking this path Innis was apparently acting on his notion of a Hegelian idea. Hegel differentiated a number of levels of historical inquiry, spanning the "original" history of the primary source, through "reflective" history that represents attempts by later historians to record and make sense of the past – inevitably in terms of their own experiences – and finally "philosophical history" which is an interpretation of history yielding a general understanding of human development. Philosophical history, according to Hegel, uses the findings of reflective history in its quest for a general understanding of the world. Most importantly, Hegel sees histories of specific fields such as art or religion, which take a "universal point of view," to be a bridge between reflective and philosophical history. Innis, in moving from Canadian economic history to the ecumenical study of communication, was consciously crossing over from the reflective to the philosophical, from history to theory.[21]

Innis' redefinition of himself as a philosopher of history has important implications in understanding his legacy, not least among them the textual problems of his communication scholarship. One such problem is the radical and otherwise inexplicable shift in his sources, from the use of primary materials when studying Canadian economic history, to the practically exclusive use of secondary sources in his studies of

---

"I am aware that I am only presenting a footnote on the work of Graham Wallace." There, too, Innis' footnote was a radical extension of Wallace's work.

21 Hegelian ideas permeate Innis' thinking and work. For a most expansive statement of Hegelian influences, particularly his language theory as received in Canada: Judith Stamps, "Innis in the Canadian Dialectical Tradition." For other references to Innis' incorporation of Hegelian models and concerns see: Donald F. Theall, "Exploration in Communication Since Innis," in: Melody et al., *Culture Communication*, pp. 225–234; and my own "Harold Adams Innis and his Bias of Communication." Cf. Judith Stamps, *Unthinking Modernity: Innis, McLuhan, and the Frankfurt School* (Montreal: McGill-Queen's University Press, 1995), p. 68.

communication. Assuming that on this, as in other issues, Innis was following Hegel, his choice of sources is fully understandable. Since Hegel taught that the universal history of an isolated field – such as communication – is philosophical history, and since he prescribed reflective histories as the material for writing philosophical history, Innis' change of methodology is accounted for. More generally, the particular mode of presentation characteristic of his communication studies, described above as a historic play-by-play interlaced with analytic comments, reflects a self-conscious adaptation of form and structure to the rationale and method of philosophical history. Facts of history are marched chronologically, one by one, and Innis, the philosopher in the grandstand, gains insight and contributes comments on them, as they relate to his philosophical focus: the determining influence of communication on society and culture.

Similarly, Innis' self-perception as a philosopher of history puts a new face on the problem of internal contradictions in his work: the source of contradictions as well as their toleration. Many explicit contradictions in and between his essays, even the systematic ones in *Empire and Communication*, reflected disagreements between Innis' sources. Since it was no longer his task to establish an accurate historical record and ascertain the facts, these conflicts could only be documented and acknowledged, not resolved. Moreover, both sides to the contradiction were just as pertinent to his main thrust, since either and all possibilities ultimately demonstrated the "significance of communication." On points of interpretation too the new Innis could afford great leeway: his varying, even conflicting interpretations of affects and consequences of communication technologies were essentially equivalent since his purpose was to demonstrate that they did indeed have effects, and significant ones.

The Origins of Innis' Discovery

The origins of Innis' discovery and the process through which he came to realize the "significance of communication" to human development are surprisingly vague. One way of approaching the problem is through a close scrutiny of the internal evolution of Innis' works and tracing the theme of communication within them. This approach assumes that Innis developed his revolutionary perspective *sui generis*, through a complex process of intellectual growth. An alternative approach is to scan the intellectual horizon of his times, seeking external influences. In such a canvass a particular focus on a southern vista, from Toronto to Chicago and its university, is of particular importance given the ferment in social thinking at the University of Chicago of Innis' time, and the interest of its luminaries in problems of communication. Innis' affiliation with the University of Chicago, first as student then as prospective teacher, make a Chicago connection particularly plausible.

In pursuing the first approach, which posits a self-discovery, the question of continuity from the early Innis of Canadian staples to the later Innis of world communications becomes important.[22] The radical shift in the nature of his research upon moving from economic history to communication history – his move from history proper to philosophy of history – would appear to support the notion of discontinuity. Yet the fundamental hypothesis of Innis' philosophy of history – "the

22 This issue is the subject of extensive debate. Creighton, in "Innis: An Appraisal," presents perhaps the most extreme position of discontinuity. Interestingly, attempts at interpreting the shift in Innis' work from staple economics to communications, such as the early convention that through his study of the Canadian wood and pulp industry as a staple feeding the US production of finished knowledge goods Innis became interested in the political economy of the latter, in effect highlight the chasm between the two phases of his scholarly career (e.g., Carl Berger, *The Writing of Canadian History: Aspects of English-Canadian Historical Writing, 1900–1970* (New York: Oxford University Press, 1976); and, to an extent, Leslie A. Pal, "Scholarship and the Later Innis," *Journal of Canadian Studies*, 12:5 (Winter 1977): 33–44, who emphasizes Innis' thinking about scholarship and academia as the contingency for the shift between the two. One of the most insightful discussions of the shift, but also the thematic links between the two phases is A. John Watson, "Harold Innis and Classical Scholarship," *Journal of Canadian Studies*, 12:5 (Winter 1977): 45–61. Neill, *Theory of Value*, provides a broad basis for the continuity perspective. Ian Parker, in "Innis, Marx, and the Economics of Communication: A Theoretical Aspect of Canadian Political Economy," in: Melody et al., *Culture Communication*, demonstrates the relevance of the staple studies to the political economy of communications, and in "Harold Innis: Staples, Communications, and the Economics of Capacity, Overhead Costs, Rigidity, and Bias," in: *Explorations in Canadian Economic History: Essays in Honor of Irene M. Spry* (Ottawa: University of Ottawa Press, 1985), pp. 73–93, points out the implications of Innis' findings in his communication studies to fundamental problems of economic theory.

significance of communication" – appears to span both phases of his scholarly career, representing a stable core. The inverted-determinism dialectic may present itself as a key to bridging these two phases of Innis' scholarship.

Communication was on Innis' mind from the earliest stages of his scholarly career. His first major work, a reflective history of the Canadian Pacific Railroad (CPR), was essentially a study of a medium of communication in a particular time and place. A two-volume critical sourcebook of documents in Canadian economic history which Innis prepared together with A.R.M. Lower is particularly revealing of this early focus on communications. The first volume of the sourcebook, which was mainly Lower's production, treats communication issues sparingly and sporadically. In contrast, the second volume, that was mainly Innis' handiwork, was divided into four sections each covering a region of Canada. In each of these sections the very first subsection, and one of the most substantial, was devoted to "Transportation and Communication."[23] Clearly, Innis recognized the significance of communication, in this case as a key to economic history, from early on.

The place of the communication theme in Innis' staple studies is less obvious, but at least as important. In one of its broader meanings, the staple theory represented a critical response to Frederick Jackson Turner's frontier thesis. This is made clear in the concluding chapter of *The Fur Trade in Canada* which serves as an analytical conspectus of the work as a whole. Though Turner's name is not mentioned, Innis was directly responding to his frontier thesis and challenging it.[24] Turner, in asserting American exceptionalism, maintained that a fact

23 Harold Adams Innis and A. R. M. Lower, *Selected Documents in Canadian Economic History*, vol. 1 (Toronto: University of Toronto Press, 1929), vol. 2 (Toronto: University of Toronto Press, 1933).

24 James Carey has perceptively pointed out relations between Innis' thinking on communication and Turner's frontier thesis, most recently in: "Innis 'in' Chicago: Hope as the Sire of Discovery," in: Buxton and Acland, *Harold Innis*, pp. 81–104. See also Carey, "Culture Geography and Communications," pp. 80–84, and in his other discussions of Innis, note 7 above. A important recent discussion of Innis' intellectual roots, highlighting both the Hegelian and the Scottish Common Sense Tradition is provided by Judith Stamps, "Innis in the Canadian Dialectic Tradition," in Buxton and Acland, *Harold Innis*, pp. 46–66.

of geography had a determining influence on individual *mentalité*, on social institutions, and on national culture and ideology. In his view the physical distance of North American settlers from their European origins, later the distance of frontiersmen from centers of North American population, made for the decay of received and unadaptive elements of old-country, later eastern-American standards and traditions. Moreover, the transformative experience of living in a wilderness world of nature, beyond the frontiers of established society, produced a characteristic new-world outlook and new institutions, and ultimately a fresh culture bred of coping with the challenges of the wilderness. The new ideas and institutions, as developed on the frontier, radiated back to the established centers of North American society, transforming them too in the process. In this way, the frontier, a fact of space, had a major transformative influence in the dimension of time – it made for dramatic discontinuities in the received, traditional heritage of individual, community, and society.[25]

Innis proposed a reverse perspective on the frontier experience and its implications for the connectedness of east and west, Europe and North America, past and present. Rather than how the frontier shaped Europeans, Innis was more impressed by how European, later eastern American institutions, challenged by the frontier, shaped a response. What he was finding, through his detailed studies of geography, transportation, business arrangements, and economic enterprise, as conditioned by political and social institutions, was that distance and isolation, precisely by representing potential wedges of discontinuity and separation, generated a reactive response tending toward connection and continuity.[26] The challenge space posed to time – namely to tradition and social connectedness – generated a response through which traditional institutions were mobilized to extend their binding force over space.

---

25 The literature on the Frontier Thesis is vast. Good introductions include: Ray A. Billington, *Frederick Jackson Turner: Historian, Scholar, Teacher* (New York: Oxford University Press, 1973); Allan G. Bogue, *Frederick Jackson Turner: Strange Roads Going Down* (Norman: University of Oklahoma Press, 1998); and the essays in George R. Taylor, ed., *The Turner Thesis* (Boston: Heathe, 1972).

26 This theme may be traced to Innis' study of the Canadian Pacific Railroad. There too he might have been indirectly engaging Turner, see, e.g. *Canadian Pacific Railroad*, p. 287.

By establishing and perfecting effective means of transportation and communication, a veteran mercantilist system could expand westward, from Europe over the Atlantic and on across the new continent all the way to the Pacific. The potentially deterministic influence of the frontier generated a response that was the staple economy.

This interpretation of the significance of the frontier amounted to a theory about communications, social and economic organization, and determinism. It was society's will to extend itself across space that ultimately determined the implications the frontier would have. This social desire to overcome space was realized through the establishment of a grand space-binding economic and social system, founded on powerful media of transportation and communication. In this inverted-deterministic perspective, Canadian nationalism emerged as a centripetal response to the centrifugal challenge posed by tremendous geographical expanse and the physical barriers and discontinuities within it. Its core was a coherent system of communication and transportation. Innis' direct and unequivocal response to Turner's revolutionary 1897 essay, "The Significance of the Frontier in American History," was "the significance of communication," in North American history. Ultimately he came to believe that the significance of communication transcended the Atlantic theater and the eras of transatlantic migration and settlement; it was a key to all of history. Innis' communication studies can thus be seen as a hefty footnote, a radical extension of his North American economic, institutional, and national history.

According to the foregoing, Innis had a bias of communication from the commencement of his research into Canadian economic history. He acted on it through tracing the role communication and transportation played in shaping economic development in Canada, in its relation to the broader Atlantic theater of economic institutions. This outlook broadened in space and in time to become an ecumenical panorama of institutions as creatures of communication, yielding a unique and original theory of the role of communication in the development of civilizations. This understanding of historical development as anchored in changing processes of communication was thus very much Innis' own, the product of a career-long investigation into the flow of goods and ideas.

But his casting of Innis' scholarly development makes external influences quite possible. For if an interest in communication was a stable core in his intellectual career, a preliminary orientation in that direction or a reinforcement of the focus on communication is certainly reasonable. A most probable source of such influences were indeed members of what is known as the Chicago School. Prior to Innis' discovery of communication determinism, John Dewey and Robert Park, Herbert Mead and Charles Horton Cooley had developed a body of theory which took processes of communication to be a significant source and an important instrument of social organization. "The Significance of Communication," a short programmatic essay by Cooley, predated and pre-phrased Innis' proposition in that communication was the ultimate key to understanding social and cultural development.

Authorities on Innis differ in evaluating the influence of these Chicago predecessors on his thinking and scholarship. While McLuhan thought of Innis' work as an extension of the Chicago tradition, and went as far as considering Innis "the most eminent of the Chicago group headed by Robert Park," James Carey found only a limited carry-over from Chicago to Toronto. Other scholars take intermediate positions between the poles of a dominant and a marginal Chicago influence. [27] The evidence as to direct contact between Innis and the Chicago masters is limited, and not very revealing. Innis pursued his doctoral studies at Chicago at the same time Cooley and Park, Dewey, Mead and Mills were most active in developing their thinking about communication. However, Innis' transcripts demonstrate that he had not studied with any of them. Moreover, the bibliography to his Chicago dissertation on the Canadian Pacific Railroad does not include Cooley's seminal works on American railroads, nor did I notice a direct reference by Innis to other of the Chicago group's writings about communication. It may well be, however, that just as in the case of his dialogue with Turner and his thesis, Innis only referenced works he used as his authorities – those which provided him with facts or ideas which sustained his own arguments. He may have not cited works that did not serve as foundations for his own arguments or with which he disagreed.

In the case of Cooley's thinking about the significance of communication, the disagreement is patent enough, and is underscored by precisely the high degree of correspondence between their

27 McLuhan, "Introduction," *The Bias*, p. xvi; Carey, "Space, Time," pp. 143–146. Stamps, *Unthinking Modernity*, 51–56; Neill, *Theory of Value*, pp. 25–34.

perspectives.[28] Cooley had an expansive grasp of communication, he thought it to include all expressions of, and exposure to, human meaning; and as such it was the cause and effect of human consciousness. He too found media significant: meaning, the cause and effect of consciousness, was channeled by media. Cooley had offered an illustration for this relation of media and human consciousness: one could get at mental processes by studying the communication environment "just as one who wishes to grasp the organic character of industry and commerce might well begin with the study of the railway system and of the amount and kind of commodities it carries, proceeding thence to the more abstract transactions of finance." Cooley's allegorical move from communication to economics was precisely the road Innis took, albeit in the opposite direction, in his scholarly evolution from economics to communication. Indeed, both Cooley – son of an eminent railroad scholar – and Innis had studied the railroad as a key to understanding North American economic development. Furthermore, Cooley had identified four fundamental factors determining the nature of processes of communication, and they highlighted the dimensions of time and space. They included, besides *expressiveness*, also *permanence* – "the overcoming of time," *swiftness* – "the overcoming of space," and *diffusion* – a space-oriented measure of the size of the audience. Here, then, were time and space as fundamental variables of the communication matrix.

At this juncture, with both scholars understanding communications as bridges in time and space, their paths parted. Cooley was locked on the idea of progress as a sweeping, inevitable, course of human history; he considered it an accelerated conquest of human happiness evolving in time and spreading in space. This was also the course of the evolution of communication: no contradiction hindered the parallel, onward, march of "swiftness," "diffusion," and "permanence," and indeed, he found no fault with the globalizing, unifying thrust of communication over space. Even had Cooley understood that there was a trade-off between space and time, it probably would not have dampened his enthusiasm about the advent of powerful and rapid new media of space: progress, in

---

28 For a short and authoritative summary of Cooley's ideas see John D. Peters, *Speaking into the Air: A History of the Idea of Communication* (Chicago: The University of Chicago Press, 1999), pp. 184–188.

its future-orientedness, had nothing to gain from time – from memory, continuity, and history.

Innis disagreed sharply – he found that the expanding reach and accelerating swiftness of media came at the expense of "permanence," and ultimately of stability. Given the trade-off between time and space media, unbalanced progress was inevitably regressive. Most generally, Innis didn't buy into the Whig interpretation of human history and the utopian world anticipated by the idealist progressives. His historism compelled him to consider the decline and fall of civilizations as well as their rise, and his pessimism to consider potential dangers in the evolution of media. His credo was balance rather than progress, and his agenda its deliberate restoration. In opposition to Chicago's future-orientedness, Innis proposed an orientation toward historical consciousness, tradition and memory. Thus, his analysis of communication and social and political organization evolved along the same lines, but reached conclusions that were diametrically opposed to those of Chicago's enthusiastic progressives. To the extent that he was a disciple of Chicago's communication-minded scholars, he was an apostate, a new light spreading a new and revolutionary message. He preached the gospel of history and time, of looking back as a way of marching forward.

Innis: Past, Present, Future

Although conventional abstracts of Innis' communication theory duly acknowledge the fundamental historicity of his approach, its implications have not been meaningfully followed-up. Innis' historicity had two complementary planks: one was basing a philosophy, or theory, of communication on historical evidence, using history as the great laboratory which would generate and test ideas about communication. The other was understanding communication as a key to interpreting history. Neither of these prospects generated much methodological interest or practical emulation.

Yet historicity may ultimately represent one of Innis' most useful and inspiring messages. As historians have become more aware of communication as a significant factor in their own lives, communication has been emerging as a topical focus of an ever-increasing number of responsible specialized studies, based on primary sources. This research, over the past decade, has yielded a body of works which may effectively be applied to writing ecumenical histories of communication and which may serve as a sound basis for generating and testing theory in communication. Communication theory, in turn, is no longer as crude and as speculative as when Innis and his contemporaries were making their first steps in establishing it. It can conceivably serve to orient historical research and ultimately provide for a better understanding of human history. These prospects for serious studies of the history of communication and of communication in history are emerging just as academia is entering on a post-interdisciplinary thrust, razing walls separating disciplines rather than providing bridges for crossing them as in its inter-disciplinary phase. Innis' pioneering effort in this vein may yet serve as an inspiration and as a model for such a project.

But there is even more to gain from a revival of Innis' historicism. As noted, few if any observers resort to his ideas or make reference to his texts in attempting to interpret the rapid and radical changes in the communication environment over the past generation. It is precisely the neglect of the historical dimension of Innis' work – its orientation to the past – that accounts for its only limited usefulness in groping with the present and future. History, after all, is the study of change, and Innis, a historian, had methodically merged dynamic mechanisms with the structural and systemic thrust of his ideas. The play of determinism and inverted-determinism was the central dynamic element of the approach, and as we have seen, it was downplayed or even eliminated in the process of streamlining the icon of Innis in communication theory.

Innis, the scholar, taught us that media delivered a message that society and individuals could and would answer. At best they would react to an over-emphasis of time by deliberately and judiciously shifting their emphasis to space; and would highlight time if space was threatening to monopolize society's horizon. Optionally, peripheral players, not dominated by the monopolistic tendencies at society's center, would reintroduce the suppressed, opposite tendency. At worst, severely imbalanced entities would become dysfunctional and only a drastic correction, usually by unfriendly outside forces, would restore balance.

Innis, the involved public man, academia leader, and policy maker observed, with foreboding, that what he labeled as a space bias seemed to be threatening his society's well being. He feared that monopoly was driving Canada, and western civilization generally, into a dead-end of infinite space. As noted, one of the most marked differences between his perspective and that of members of the Chicago school concerned the nature of progress. Innis emphatically declined his predecessors' Whig interpretation of communication development, their belief that technical and institutional advances in communication inevitably made for improvements in social conditions. Innis saw no necessary relation between advances in the performance of social communication and social betterment. Granted, more effective communications would have great effects, but they could be for the worse as likely as for the better. Temperamentally a pessimist, Innis feared the worst; he envisioned a space bias marching triumphantly on, bound to ultimately devastate western society and culture. Having averred, time and again, that that unbalanced development would generate a backlash, Innis sounded an alarm.

Not that Innis was sounding a false alarm. At the time he was thinking through the biases of time and space, western society was indeed marching to the frontiers of space, space in the expansive, composite sense Innis had construed. In mid-century the Cold War was the stage on which two enormous empires played out their antagonistic game, supported by an ever-expanding cast of players merging into two globe-wide blocks. Experimental science was celebrating unparalleled triumphs, grounding the military might of the super powers and the economic power of business enterprises ballooning into global scope. As physical space was capturing imaginations which would ultimately launch man to the moon, an entertainment and culture industry was diverting minds, world over, from complexity and dialectic and from concern with religion, tradition, and history, to a celebration of present mindedness and consumerism. Giant corporate conglomerates footed the bill for the amusement extravaganza, realizing windfall profits in the process. Within a few decades it was only one empire – as Innis would have suspected, the American one – stretching its influence over the entire globe and setting a new political and economic order, imprinting the world with a common price and a common value system, to the beat of a globalizing amusement industry. Taken together, these processes were bringing about what one historian called "The End of History," or as Innis would have put it, an end of time.

Innis the theorist would expect a reaction to set in, a remedial resurgence of the time set. Innis the pessimistic public man would expect dangerous threats to his imbalanced, space monopolized, civilization by the conservators of time. And as we now know, with the benefit of hindsight, that is precisely what happened: both the theoretical scenario of correction and the political concern with aggressive challenge, from the inside as well as from the outside, began playing themselves out as the 20th century drew to its close. Paralleling the globalization trend there emerged a rainbow of counter movements, in numerous places of a variety of cultural expressions. Past-oriented loyalties flowered into a new emphasis on ethnic identity, multiculturalism and multilingualism, a revival of interest in, and commitment to, religion and mysticism, all underscoring a revived concern with the time-set. Environmental consciousness, and a new awareness of class implications of a global economy, generated powerful anti-globalization sentiments embracing localism and communal coherence. In the world of ideas an inward looking subjectivity came to hold the modernist notion of objective science irrelevant. In line with the emergence of these time-biased concerns, fundamentalism and tribalism began fragmenting and splintering political and administrative units to their bare and most fundamental elements in a quest oriented toward history and tradition.

Innis' concerns over the state of world and Canadian politics, economics and ideologies were inseparable from his concerns over the state of communication technologies. After all, he had discovered the "significance of communication" in the shaping of societies, cultures, and world order. And indeed, his pessimistic analysis of paralyzing imbalance was fully understandable when considering the shape of the media environment of his times. Throughout his lifetime media developed in a single direction – spaceward. Following the script/print model, the new media of his times made it possible to engage ever more people, less intimately, and with greater authority. The telephone had been the last technological improvement applied to oral, dyadic, two-way communications, and it had arrived three generations before he was writing about communication. Thereafter, the progress of media was the progress of scale, scope, and synchronicity, with fewer doing the talking, ever more listening, and no one questioning, answering, or talking back. First the mass circulating national magazines and the grand newspaper chains emerged. Then wireless, originally a two-way medium, was converted to broadcast radio; and by the time Innis was writing his communications essays, television was rising to become a major fact of western life. With the arrival of television the mix of available media had reached an unprecedented degree of imbalance on the time-space axis, tending decisively to the space pole. Single, uncontested messages were reaching unprecedented numbers of people, over an ever-expanding space, in real time. To invert McLuhan, the lecture superceded dialogue.

It was then that Innis sounded his alarm. His was the urgent message of the involved citizen combined with the wisdom of the theorist of inverted determinism, of correction and re-balance. And indeed, as his theory predicted and before long, the history of communications changed its course. On the heels of the steep upsurge in the space trajectory of media development, an opposite trajectory of media of time was emerging. Founded on the same powerful technologies which served the 20th century's media of space, alternative media which structurally paralleled orality were coming to the rescue. The audio cassette and CD, VCR and Camcorder, Minitel and PC, voice mail and electronic mail, were working against breathless synchronicity. Technical improvements enabling a dramatic increase in bandwidth and channels for voice, video and data transmission paved the way for narrowcasting, fragmenting in the process mass, even global audiences into compact communities. Satellite-mediated video conferences and computer-mediated discussion groups and chat rooms, ultimately interactive TV, emerged to counter the one-way plan of broadcast media. In short, just as the space-oriented thrust of media development was enabling a uniform global information environment, an opposite thrust was enhancing time-oriented communication plans. Innis would have been particularly amused by how the possibly most centralizing, space-minded bureaucracy of modern society – the national security establishment – would invert the centralized, hierarchic structure of its communication network through space, and seek a decentralized, non-hierarchic and periphery-focused medium of communications, which would mature into the Internet: an inverted-deterministic move if there ever was one.

In accord with Innis' proposition, there appears to have been a significant link between the emergence of these new media and of the new social and political movements and their ideologies. The new political forces that were not submerged in the onslaught of western civilization's radical orientation to space took hold of the new "little" and interactive media of time, countering the dominance of space-oriented media within western society and sustaining their time-bias in the process. Essentialist and fundamentalist movements organized and stood up to the dominance of the leaders, financers, and prophets of global culture, economy, and polity, sustained in their resistance by the universe of little media.[29]

The revival of the fruitful tension between time and space biases within western civilization has been underscored by external threats to it. A most salient and gory illustration of this emerging contest played itself out on September 11th, 2001. On that day, an attack was launched on the most cosmopolitan, multiethnic, and multiglot topos of the universe of space – its dominant center of global tastes, finances, and mass-culture – in the name of an ancient religion. Its perpetrators, in the time honored tradition of religious martyrs lured by the promise of eternal life, demonstrated the resilience of time-oriented culture and the threat it posed to amnesiac space-biased culture.

Innis' sweeping historism and his discovery of the significance of communication can inspire a symbolic analogy between the story of New York's twin towers to the ancient myth of the tower in Babel. Imperially imposing over a globalizing space and oblivious to time, both the new towers and the old one were shattered in the cause of a supposedly eternal message. And in both cases the erection and the shattering of the towers foregrounded the significance of communication. The towers' message was that "the whole earth was of one language and of one kind of words." The cause and the effect of their destruction was people "not understand[ing] one another's speech," people living "after their families, after their tongues, in their countries, in their nations." Exactly half a century ago Harold Adams Innis had proposed that only the re-balancing of these opposite orientations of mind, communications, and community would ensure stability and progress.

---

29 My paper "Communicating a Counter Culture: Israeli Mainstream Media and Amnon Yitzhak Alternative Media Empire," read at the 49th Annual Conference of the ICA and available upon request, includes a comprehensive bibliography documenting this process.

JAMES W. CAREY*

3. Marshall McLuhan: Genealogy and Legacy

I

In the summer of 1960 I was at the University of Illinois writing a dissertation in a field yet to be invented, the economics of communications.[1] Most of my intellectual training had been in economics, and I aspired to and sometimes practiced the craft of freelance journalism. As is well known, such journalists are paid by the word: a dollar a word on good days, a nickel a word on the bad ones. And every word, from the shortest to the longest, carried the same price. That led to a flirtation with an understanding of the peculiarities of the market for words, and the alienation inevitably involved when one sells one's soul at five cents a "bit." That led me to the work of the only economist who had remotely addressed this issue, the Canadian, Harold Innis. Innis provided a number of clues to the ways in which the telegraph – for that was the key innovation – created a market for words and the mechanism for pricing words in that market.

To state the obvious once again, Innis was the most important Canadian intellectual of his era: President of the Royal Society of Canada and the American Economic Association. He chaired or served on many of the most important Royal Commissions shaping policy in education, communications, and economics. His scholarship was devoted primarily to staples – codfish, timber, fur and wood pulp. These commodities shaped both the economy and culture of Canada – a colonial economy, an outlier country on the western margin whose fate was tied to the demand for fur hats or dried fish in European

* James Carey, profound scholar, inspiring teacher and beloved colleague, passed away on May 23, 2006, while this volume was in the process of publication. "The words of the righteous are their memory." *Jerusalem Talmud*, Shekalim, 11/9.

1 Prior to publication in this volume, this article appeared in the *Canadian Journal of Communication*, Vol. 23, No. 3, 1998 (reprinted with permission).

capitals. The analysis of wood pulp suggested the powerful role of communications in shaping the political and economic structure of nations and empires. To that study he devoted himself in the years after World War II, producing four books on the subject: *The Bias of Communication*, *Empire and Communications*, *Political Economy and the Modern State*, and *Changing Concepts of Time*. He was also Dean of the Graduate School as well as Head of the Department of Political Economy at the University of Toronto when, to at last get to the point, Marshall McLuhan arrived there in the autumn of 1946.

McLuhan had been trained in literary criticism at Cambridge University when F. R. Leavis dominated literary studies there and from Leavis had picked up an interest in the consequences of the industrialization of the popular arts for the traditions of high culture. McLuhan had taught at a number of North American universities – Wisconsin, St. Louis University, Assumption College – before he landed in Toronto. Actually he landed at the Catholic college within the University of Toronto, St. Michael's. McLuhan had undergone a conversion to Catholicism, influenced by another famous convert, G. K. Chesterton, while at Cambridge. Following his stint at Wisconsin, McLuhan taught in Catholic universities for the rest of his career. This is not an altogether insignificant fact for McLuhan's history of technology is in many ways a secularized version of the basic Christian story of Eden, the Fall and Redemption. Technology restored the intimate connection to the Godhead sundered in the moment of rational and sinful alienation. The metaphors which lace his work are religious ones as well, drawn, in particular, from a Catholic vocabulary of ritual and sacrament. Finally, though it is not something to be demonstrated here, his understanding of the oral tradition (an understanding quite at odds with that of Innis) is deeply informed by a liturgical sense of chant and memory rather than a political sense of discussion and debate. The preliterate world for which he yearned was a liturgical world rather than a political one.

As I worked on the problem of the economics of words in July 1960, Marshall McLuhan arrived in Urbana, Illinois, with a disordered, mimeographed manuscript entitled "Understanding Media" under his arm (McLuhan, 1960). It was the damnedest thing I had ever seen. The manuscript did not fit any of the established categories of academic writing I had encountered; it was an exercise in genre bending, indeed genre inventing, performed before we recognized the blurring of genres as one of the distinctive landmarks for navigating postmodern writing. The manuscript was destined for the United States Office of Education that had inadvertently commissioned it. A recurring fantasy of that summer was the bewilderment that would greet its arrival in Washington where it was to become the most unorthodox report ever to be submitted to that staid bureaucracy.[2] This was the first draft of the book, *Understanding Media: The Extensions of Man*, destined for publication as the herald of McLuhan's international celebrity in 1964. The manuscript contained the central ideas of the book, but with a much more limited focus. McLuhan was trying to convince the Office of Education that his developing ideas could be the lever of reform in the educational system, moving it from a dependence on classical literature to an engagement with the "new media," the media which formed and carried the real culture of students.

His study, if it can be called that, was commissioned by an organization now defunct, the National Association of Educational Broadcasters. Educational broadcasters, as those in public television were then known, provided the first receptive audience McLuhan found for his speculations concerning media. (The first appearance of McLuhan on television that has survived was on a program from Ohio State University's television station that featured a discussion McLuhan dominated, through a haze of smoke, among educational broadcasters.) Unlike commercial broadcasters, those in education sought an understanding of and a defense and legitimization of television – a medium they were pioneering in education while trying to preserve a portion of the television spectrum for, broadly, cultural uses. Television

2   The shorthand title of the undertaking was "Project 69" and McLuhan described it as follows in the statement of purpose: "Project 69 in Understanding Media proposed to provide an approach to media and a syllabus for teaching the nature and effects of media in secondary schools.... My objectives were: (a) to explain the character of a dozen media, illustrating the dynamic symmetries of their operation on man and society, (b) to do this in a syllabus usable in secondary schools. (Secondary schools were chosen as offering students who had not in their own lives become aware of any vested interest in acquired knowledge. They have very great experience of media, but no habits of observation or critical awareness. Yet they are the best teachers of media to teachers, who are otherwise unreachable)" (McLuhan, 1960, pp. l, 4).

was then an object of universal contempt (and secret viewing) among the educated classes. No one with intellectual pretensions took it seriously except as further evidence of the decline of high culture and Western civilization. The literature concerning television that existed during the 1960s was pretty dismal and of two sorts: either a blanket condemnation of the medium or aggressive promotional tracts aimed at exploiting the commercial possibilities of television. McLuhan was the first intellectual not only to take the medium seriously but to see possibilities in it for something more than transmitting high culture or debasing the popular arts.

In 1960 McLuhan was virtually unknown beyond a small coterie and certainly unread and unrecognized among scholars in the humanities and social sciences; there was no hint as yet of the international celebrity that awaited him and no one thought that he would give rise to an ideology – *mcluhanism*. His first book on media, *The Mechanical Bride: Folklore of Industrial Man* (1951), was unorthodox in form but, on the surface at least, reasonably conventional in content. The title referred to the intertwined images of violence, sexuality and death that dominated (and still dominates?) the popular arts, at least in North America. The book did not sell well (a few hundred copies) nor did it bring him much attention. McLuhan's important but short-lived journal, *Explorations*, in which he pursued his more unorthodox ideas had a tiny circulation and was influential among only a small group of academics. This was four years before the publication of the transmogrified and even more outrageous book version of *Understanding Media* and five years before Tom Wolfe's article in *New York* magazine – "What If He Is Right?" – that initiated his career as the first celebrity intellectual of the electronic age. During the "Urbana Summer" he was working on *The Gutenberg Galaxy: The Making of Typographic Man*, a project underway for a decade, though actually written in less than 40 days later that year.

My reaction to McLuhan's work was at first very admiring. I could see the impetus he had picked up from the pioneering scholarship of Harold Innis, though he naturally took that economic analysis in literary and cultural directions. Moreover, he was a wonderful conversationalist and companion, a raconteur with a bottomless well of jokes, stories and apothegms. As he became a more public figure later in the decade, I became rather more hostile. It must be remembered that his work reached the general public and he became the most important public intellectual in North America during the Civil Rights Movement and the anti-Vietnam War protests. These were the matters that were on *our* political/intellectual agenda. While he had some intelligent things to say about the role of television in the civil rights movement and the consequences of putting war on television, he took the politics out of these two issues and reduced them to mere matters of technology. (His 1968 book, *War and Peace in the Global Village,* did not refer in any detail to the Vietnam War, the first war of the Global Village.) Moreover, we believed – whomever we were – that his conservative politics made him indifferent to the outcomes of these two protest movements and that he was in secret sympathy with those resisting the civil rights movement and supporting the extension of the war. On all such matters McLuhan was silent, if not indifferent, and frequently contemptuous. His public style was often, deliberately or not, arrogant and supercilious with those with whom he disagreed. He regularly dismissed his critics as obsolete, as if only he had a purchase on the future. McLuhan was peculiarly disconnected from the politics of his time and was admired by and appealed to those who reduced politics to technology or who sought technological solutions to political dilemmas.

In the 1960s McLuhan's work drove one to face an intractable problem. For all the cultural creativity and innovation associated with the technology of printing, the medium had an inescapable dark side. Printing was indissolubly wed to the rise of the nation state, colonialism and empire; to the domination of the bourgeois class; and to the worldwide extension of capitalism. If that is true, then what about the institutional power and political implications of electronic communication? Did the growth of electrical communication from the telegraph through television, and the evolution of electronics from simple servomechanisms through advanced computer information utilities, reverse the general developments associated with printing or did they merely modify and intensify what Lewis Mumford called the "pentagon of power," the "gods" of modernity: political power, profit, property, productivity and publicity?

There is no easy answer to this question but around it have whirled virtually all the conceptual and ideological debates concerning the relations of communications technology to culture. Mumford, who was McLuhan's most immediate predecessor, argued from the mid-1940s forward that electronics intensified the most destructive and power-oriented tendencies of the "age of print," whereas McLuhan, who was, in a certain sense, the first postmodernist, prophesied a new postmodern, postindustrial age in which electronics would produce a qualitative change in the nature of social organization and cultural life. There were and still are large intellectual and political stakes in the resolution of this argument for its outcome will shape ideological discourse and social policy in the arena of communications in the decades ahead. Globalization, the Internet, and computer communications are all *underdetermined* by technology and history. The final destination of these new forms is one prepared by politics.

The ideological hinge of *Understanding Media* was recognized by some of the more acute of his earliest reviewers. Harold Rosenberg (1967) noted, for example, that "while McLuhan is an aesthete he is also an ideologue – one ready to spin out his metaphor of the 'extensions' until its web covers the universe.... [T]he drama of history is a crude pageant whose inner meaning is man's metamorphosis through the media" (p. 202). Actually, *Understanding Media* is a book very much in the American grain, one that explicitly and implicitly drew on some of the deeper political myths of the culture. The central term of that myth, the "communications revolution," was first used, as best I can determine, by the American historian Robert Albion (1933). He used it to describe the projects of communication and transportation (they were then taken to be identical processes) undertaken under the slogan of "internal improvements," planned by Jefferson's administration to unite the country north and south, east and west: an ambitious plan of road, canal, and, later, telegraph and railroad building – all instruments of communication in nineteenth-century terms. While such improvements greatly enhanced the scope, power and size of the country, they were hardly revolutionary; they merely extended the geography of the nation, while keeping in place its central principles of both politics and communication. But the notion of the United States as a permanent communications revolution is in fact the hardiest plant in the North American mental hothouse. The ideological side of *Understanding Media* replayed certain ideas that entered American life in the decades after the Civil War (1865 forward) when electricity as fact and symbol seized hold of the native imagination and envisioned a new form of communication as the architecture of a new form of civilization. This is the tradition of thought McLuhan seized upon in *Understanding Media* in projecting a technological utopia then aborning through the irresistible impulses of electrical communication. McLuhan lifted hyperbole to metaphor, transforming the body into a metaphor for technology, and assigning a characteristic quality to each of the senses; he assigned sound and participation to the ear, taste and discrimination to the tongue, vision and privatization to the eye. He gave a biological and technological root to T.S. Eliot's notion of the disassociation of sensibility. And, in the critical move, he assigned to electrical communication the capacity for the reassociation of sensibility: the restoration of psychic life in a balanced sensorium and of social life in a global village. By such metaphors, aesthetics, biology and technology were converted into ideology. There is a kind of liberation theology contained in his formulation, though it is rather different than what was encountered in Latin America.

As I said earlier, *Understanding Media* entered both a political and intellectual atmosphere and brought them together. McLuhan seemed to suggest that the spread of television would heal the racial animosities that had perennially scarred "the American dream." And he inspired and supported, however unwittingly, political policies playing out in Southeast Asia. There was no more obvious example of the errors reinforced by the ideology than the Vietnam conflict. In the Pentagon and the State Department, the technical approach – in complete contrast to the politics of diplomacy – could not perceive basic factors of nationalism, ethnic and regional differences, and historical forces that could not be overcome simply by computer planning, electronic surveillance of hostile elements, and electrification of rural areas and the Mekong basin. The "pacification" and "strategic hamlet" programs were evaluated by computers that could not simulate the entire Vietnamese experience. One Defense Department spokesman complained at the time that there was an "inundation" of data that actually operated against sensible decisions. Vietnam was also an attempt to test what General William Westmoreland called "the automation of war." The "electronic barrier" across the demilitarized zone projected by Robert McNamara to stop infiltration did not succeed, and military officers complained that it tied U.S. forces down during a mobile, shifting war. Further, Lyndon Johnson expected that his co-optation of a proposal to electrify the Mekong Valley like an Asian Tennessee Valley Authority and to install "security lights" in villages under the auspices of the Rural Electrification Commission would both win the sympathy of the Vietnamese masses and stop Vietcong night operations. Indeed, the rhetoric of Lyndon Johnson and his administration on these issues reveals a complete mesmerization by the mystique of computers, hydroelectric turbines and electronic eyes, which led to terrible and tragic commitments.

II

That was the downside of *Understanding Media*, the constellation of politics, ideology, and intellect that led me to react negatively to the project of the book. But there was an upside and thirty years later it is appropriate to recognize it. McLuhan's work represented a genuine and multifaceted intellectual advance that has become part of our inheritance and the more enduring legacy of his work. I cannot here give the full dimensions of that tribute but a place to begin a brief exposition is with the announcement of a recent conference on Medieval Studies at Pennsylvania State University. It read:

> Although still only in its initial stages, the current revolution in information and communication technologies has brought profound changes to the ways in which people live and interact in modern society. Understanding the complex political, social and cultural implications of this phenomenon requires that we place it in its proper historical perspective, particularly in terms of earlier, equally significant communications revolutions in Western history.

After briefly noting the bookends of the two dimensions of the revolution of the Middle Ages – Carolingian minuscule text in the sixth century and the Gutenberg printing press in the fifteenth – and parallel changes in the role of aural, iconographic, and numeric representation, the announcement continues that these medieval developments can be employed to "place the present-day revolution in information technologies within an historical context."

There are three aspects of that introduction that are deeply problematic but that could not have been lucidly stated as problems until McLuhan's scholarship created an intelligible context. First, one could not see a useful connection between Carolingian script and, say, the computerization of the social, between the expansion of satellite broadcasting and the "broadcasting" of messages facilitated by the invention of printing, until McLuhan generalized the term "media" in such a way as to call forth the intrinsic family resemblance of these technologies. Second, by placing printed, iconographic, aural, numeric and scribal representation in the same envelope, McLuhan led us to think not just of media but of media ecologies: the dense synchronic and diachronic relations among forms of representation. He suggested that we might understand the revolution in modern communications by comparing it with a similar revolution in the Middle Ages and, conversely and more radically, we might understand the revolution of the Middle Ages better by comparing it with changes in modern communications technology. Moreover, these diachronic slices could be better comprehended if we recognized the ways in which modalities of communication – words and numbers, sights and sounds, icons and ideographs – formed constellations of perceptive capacities which collectively defined the nature of subjectivity. In short, McLuhan taught us to see new relations between the medieval and the modern world and new relations among our apprehensive capacities and their extension in technological form.

Third, McLuhan taught us to see the "problem of communications" as a historical one, a problem that could not be understood simply by a universal and mathematical theory of communications such as proposed by Norbert Weiner (1948), Claude Shannon and Warren Weaver (1949), and others who pioneered cybernetics and information theory. The latter group understood communications solely as a problem of *transmission*. McLuhan's decisive advance, though he was not alone in this, was to argue that communication has three interlarded dimensions: transmission, creation and retention. The problem of communications was not to be analyzed solely as the speed and capacity with which a given medium can disseminate "bits" of information. Rather, McLuhan analyzed the varying but interrelated capacities of different media to transmit or disseminate, to retrieve or store, and to create or produce an entire culture. Media were not only things with which messages were sent but, in addition and more importantly, things with which to think and with which to shape collective memory. As was his playful manner, he often threw away this insight in a slogan: "the medium is the message" or it is "culture retrieved rather than received that counts." But by enlarging the generally accepted understanding of communication, he was able to direct attention away from the "revolutions" in materials (iron, copper, brass) or forms of economic organization (mercantilism, industrialism, capitalism, socialism) or politics (the divine right of kings, the social contract, the dictatorship of the proletariat) and onto revolutions in communications (from speech to script to print to electronics). Again, these latter "revolutions" were not merely extensions of the speed and distance of communications, as important as such variations were, but alterations in the apparatus through which the world could be "thought" and retrieved in "memory."

McLuhan's advance has led to a distinguished body of scholarship on literacy, printing, the evolution of mind and the nature of electronics. There is not space to review that work here, except to state a general outline and a few specifics of his own accomplishment. In the intervening years, there has developed a convention in historical writing about communications to partition time into three distinct phrases, each governed by a defining technology and master symbol: the oral tradition, the printing press and the television screen. This is the story of social evolution, Lamarckian or not, as the evolution of communication. The narrative is organized around a series of decisive breaks or revolutions: from the voice to the printing press to the television screen; from speech to print to electronics; from the performer or orator to the printer or typographer to the programmer or producer; from the forming of sounds to the casting of letters to the production of narrative images. Other words would do: Performance, Print and Program as objects; Speaking, Printing and Programming as actions; or Speaker, Typographer and Programmer as social types. While much work in recent years has concentrated on the transition from speech to print, from a society in which speaking and performing are primary to a society in which reading and writing are primary, the larger objective is to understand the presumed communications revolution of our own time: the movement beyond literacy, beyond the printed word, to something quite new and problematic – visual literacy, computer literacy, the information society – a world in which the computer is the master trope.

McLuhan, in making this advance, defined technology rather artlessly as "extensions of man," extensions which form a feedback loop. The instruments we use become extensions of our bodies. In order to operate these instruments skillfully, we must internalize aspects of them in the form of kinesthetic and perceptual habits. In that sense at least, such instruments become literally part of us, modify us and alter the basis of our relationship to ourselves. One would further expect us to more intensely cathect instruments that couple directly to our own intellectual, cognitive and emotive functions than to those machines that merely extend the power of our muscles. This point has been made forcefully by Lewis Mumford in a quote I stitch together from several different essays:

> ...the organic has become visible again even within the mechanical complex. Some of our most characteristic mechanical instruments – the telephone, the phonograph, the motion picture – have grown out of our interest in the human voice and human ear and out of knowledge of their physiology and anatomy.... In back of the development of tools and machines lies the attempt to modify the environment in such a way as to fortify and sustain the human organism: the effort is either to extend the powers of the otherwise unarmed organism or to manufacture outside the body a set of conditions more favorable toward manufacturing its equilibrium and ensuring its survival.... [T]he investigation of the world of life opened up new possibilities for the machine itself: vital interests, ancient human wishes influence the development of new inventions. Flight, telephonic communication, the phonograph, the motion picture all arose out of the more scientific study of living organisms.... [T]his interest in living organisms does not stop short with machines that stimulate eye and ear.... [T]he perfected forms begin to hold human interest even apart from practical performances: they tend to produce that inner composure and equilibrium, that sense of balance between the inner impulse and the outer environment, which is one of the marks of a work of art. The machines, even when they are not works of art, underlie our art – that is, our organized perceptions and feeling – in the way that Nature underlies them, extending the basis upon which we operate and confirming our own impulse to order.
>
> (Mumford, 1934, pp. 6, 10, 356)

Tools, then, are pedagogical instruments, part of the stuff with which we fashion our imaginative reconstructions of the world. Tools are not merely instruments nor only signs of human imagination and creative reach. They also symbolize the activities they enable and act as models for their own reproduction and as scripts for the re-enactment of the skills they represent. That is the sense in which media are pedagogic instruments, vehicles for instructing men and women in other times and places in culturally acquired modes of thought and action. The tool as symbol in all these respects thus transcends its role as a symbolic recreation of our world. It must inevitably enter into the imaginative calculus that constantly constructs the world (Weizenbaum, 1976). In that sense, then, the tool is much more than a mere device; it is an agent for change. This is the sense in which the medium is the message: the complex of habits, dispositions, extensions, metaphorical, and imaginative reproductions it creates and the secondary service background or industry it creates around it.

From his Renaissance studies McLuhan absorbed Bacon's dictum that nature was a book to be read, although for the pioneers of modern science it was a text composed in obscure mathematical characters. McLuhan argued that social life could also be viewed as a book, a text, something composed, though written in the far more accessible characters of sound, gesture, and word. Consequently, technology did not have to be treated as a purely physical force but could also be viewed as a text. Technology was both an extension and embodiment of mind and therefore contained and manifested meaning. It could be read, then, in an exegetical sense; its meaning could be unearthed from its material form in ways parallel to the treatment critics accorded literary texts. McLuhan's methodological advance, then, came through his attempt to break through the constraints of conventional North American social and communication theory with a new hermeneutic, a hermeneutic of technology and social life.

Intellectually, that advance was contained in two remarkable insights which McLuhan pressed with the outrageous daring necessary to arrest the attention of modern audiences. First, he argued that forms of communication such as writing, speech, printing and broadcasting should not be viewed as neutral vessels carrying given and independently determined meaning. Rather, he proposed that these forms be considered technologies of the intellect, active participants in the process by which the mind is formed and in turn forms ideas. To put the matter differently, he argued that all technical forms were extensions of mind and embodiments of meaning. Technologies of communication were principally things to think with, moulders of mind, shapers of thought: the medium was the message. In pressing this argument he opened a new avenue of historical scholarship and rephrased a large set of questions that had vexed scholars.

The second advance McLuhan pioneered and which set certain constraints upon his critics grew directly out of his literary studies. Students of the arts are likely to examine communication with quite a different bias than that advanced by social scientists. The question of the appeal of art is essentially a question of taste, broadly of aesthetics. McLuhan recognized, earlier than most, that the new means available for producing and reproducing art would demand and create an entirely new aesthetic. He sensed that cultural forms operated not at the level of cognition or information or even effect. The media of communication affect society principally by changing the dominant structures of taste and feeling, by altering the desired forms of experience.

The new and proliferating means of recording experience meant that the monopoly enjoyed by print was to be exploded and that no one means of experiencing the world would dominate as printing had among educated classes for centuries. The new means of reproducing reality also meant that the historic barriers between the arts and between the arts and other departments of life – art and science, work and leisure – would be driven down. Electronic communication would jumble experience and creatively juxtapose ideas, forms and experiences previously disseminated in different and isolated ways. In turn this would create new patterns of knowledge and awareness, a new hunger for experience, in much the same way that printing, by assembling the sacred and the profane, the new and the traditional, the exotic and the mundane, the practical and the fanciful in the same printer's workshop led to a decisive alteration in modern taste.

This erosion of barriers between the arts meant as well the erosion of barriers between the audiences. The division of culture into high and low; folk and popular; mass and elite; highbrow, lowbrow and middlebrow – barriers and distinctions that were themselves the product of printing – would have to be discarded under the impact of new forms of communication which simply did not recognize these distinctions. The high arts were now as often pirating mass and folk culture, and mass culture in turn was leaching the traditional arts. Thus, the ability to make things more widely available in graphic form, to reproduce at will sacred texts and treasured painting, to make reality itself in the drama of film and television, to record and freeze the most mundane of persons, scenes and slices of reality that were historically conveyed in different and isolated ways, signaled the existence of a new hunger for experience and a new means to realize it, and both of these demanded a new theory of aesthetics.

But what was critical in this argument is McLuhan's realization, a realization he shared with Walter Benjamin and derived from James Joyce and the symbolists, that the new desires realized in the impractical objects of art would be demanded as well in the practical objects of everyday life. McLuhan erased the distinction between art and utility, between aesthetic action and practical form. Everyday objects – cars, clothes and light bulbs – were governed less by utility than by aesthetics: their meaning was to be sought in a principle of taste rather than a principle of interest and action. Specifically, communications media were to be read less in terms of their potential to transmit information or to service the practical needs of persuasion and governance and more in terms of their insinuation of a desire to aesthetically realize experience in altered form.

Changes in technology, he came to conclude, offered the potential for redefining the aesthetic – that is, for altering taste and style and, through that alteration, for redesigning the basic structures of social life. Technology does this at the most abstract level by offering the potential for re-experiencing time and space. Differing technologies of communication have the capacity to expand or contract space and to expand or contract time, changing the meaning of the fundamental coordinates of thought. This notion was obviously tied to Innis' earlier discovery of the spatial and temporal bias of media, though, again, McLuhan's discovery was not situated in the domain of practical action but at the level of aesthetic experience. His important argument about printing was not merely that it changed the dominant conception of space, but that it altered what we took to be an aesthetically satisfying pattern of spatial arrangement, whether this was the arrangement of a page, a city, a house or a theory. Similarly, while printing altered our conception of time, it more importantly changed the dominantly pleasing patterns of rhythm. McLuhan was basically correct, then, in directing our consideration to the possibility that the new media of communication might be cultivating a taste for open rather than closed spaces, rimmed rather than axial patterns, historical and geologically modelled time rather than mechanical syncopation, or more generally a preference, in Mary Douglas' (1970) phrase, for "group over grid."

The importance of the questions McLuhan asked lay in his implicit attempt to apply hermeneutic insights to material objects, his stress on the new combinations and juxtapositions of experience created by modern technology, and his emphasis on the central place of aesthetic experience in all human action. I am opposed, as previously indicated, to McLuhan's notion that technology is autonomous, operating independently of human will and intention. Nonetheless, machines, once constructed, do operate over long periods of time entirely on the basis of their own internal realities.

McLuhan was a person of irresistible charm in intimate circles and I felt then, and feel now, that he was a critical figure in the evolution of our understanding of culture, media and communication. He did not spring from a platonic conception of himself, however. He wrote within a tradition and borrowed heavily from other scholars pursuing parallel lines of inquiry. But his contribution to that collective effort and achievement – ambiguous at best and on which no firm judgment is yet possible – has been decisive.

References

Albion, Robert. (1933, September). The communications revolution: 1760–1933. *Mechanical Engineering, 55*, 531–535, 573.

Douglas, Mary. (1970). *Natural symbols*. New York: Pantheon Books.

Innis, Harold. (1949). *Political economy and the modern state*. Toronto: Ryerson Press.

Innis, Harold. (1950). *Empire and communications*. Oxford: Oxford University Press.

Innis, Harold. (1951). *The bias of communication*. Toronto: University of Toronto Press.

Innis, Harold. (1952). *Changing concepts of time*. Toronto: University of Toronto Press.

McLuhan, Marshall. (1951). *The mechanical bride: Folklore of industrial man.* New York: Vanguard Press.

McLuhan, Marshall. (1960). *Report on project in understanding new media.* Urbana, Ill.: National Association of Educational Broadcasters.

McLuhan, Marshall. (1962). *The Gutenburg galaxy: The making of typographic man.* Toronto: University of Toronto Press.

McLuhan, Marshall. (1964). *Understanding media: The extensions of man.* New York: McGraw-Hill.

McLuhan, Marshall, with Fiore, Quentin, & Agel, Jerome. (1968). *War and peace in the global village.* New York: Bantam.

Mumford, Lewis. (1934). *Technics and civilization.* New York: Harcourt, Brace & Company.

Rosenberg, Harold. (1967). "He is a belated Whitman singing the body electric with Thomas Edison as accompanist." In Gerald E. Stearn (Ed.), *McLuhan: Hot and cool* (pp. 194–203). New York: Dial Press. (Originally published in the *New Yorker* as "Philosophy in a Pop Key.")

Shannon, Claude, & Weaver, Warren. (1949). *The mathematical theory of communication.* Urbana, Ill.: University of Illinois Press.

Weiner, Norbert. (1948). *Cybernetics; or, control and communication in the animal and the machine.* New York: John Wiley and Son.

Weizenbaum, Joseph. (1976). *Computer power and human reason.* San Francisco, Cal.: W. H. Freeman.

Wolfe, Tom. (1968). What if he is right? In *The pump house gang.* New York: Farrar, Straus and Giroux. (Originally published in *New York*, November 1965.)

RUTH KATZ AND ELIHU KATZ

4. McLuhan: Where Did He Come From, Where Did He Disappear?

Preaching from the threshold between the fall of "typographic man" and the rise of "electronic man," a Canadian professor of English named Herbert Marshall McLuhan became the guru of the media age following the publication of *The Gutenberg Galaxy* in 1962 and *Understanding Media* in 1964.[1] Brilliant, erudite and eccentric, the fame went to his head as he pontificated to industrial chiefs, advised publishers and prime ministers on the future of mankind, and appeared as himself in Woody Allen's *Annie Hall*. In books and articles, intellectuals, however disenchanted, continued to ask, "But what if he's right?" (Wolfe, 1968). And his biographer, Philip Marchand (1989), recalls a *New Yorker* cartoon in 1970 in which a young woman, emerging from a cocktail party, asks her escort, "Ashley, are you sure it's not too soon to go around saying 'Whatever happened to Marshall McLuhan?'" (p. 220).

This paper will try to answer these questions from a perspective of some 30 years. But it is not easy, first of all because it is difficult to read McLuhan. He refuses to hold still. He takes what Walter Benjamin calls "tiger leaps" inside the world of scholarship. He invents language of his own, well spiced with contemporary jargon. He contradicts himself, often intentionally. Every assertion is probably wrong. And he changes his stance – shifting attention from literature to the content of popular culture, and then to the forms in which the content resides; and shifting

1 This paper was prepared for a symposium in honor of Professor Yehoshua Arieli, held at the Van Leer Jerusalem Institute on June 25, 1996. It was revised for presentation at a session dedicated to Innis and McLuhan, organized by Dr. Marjorie Ferguson, at the annual meeting of the International Communication Association, Montreal, QC, May 1997. The present version is further expanded, thanks to the fellowship and hospitality of the Rockefeller Foundation's Bellagio Center; and prior to publication in this volume it appeared in the *Canadian Journal of Communication*, Vol. 23, No. 3, 1998 (reprinted with permission).

from the moral outrage of a critical theorist (in *The Mechanical Bride*, 1951) to the ostensibly value-neutral position of a cultural historian.

Some introductory guidelines

Let us begin by addressing some common assumptions about McLuhan, to each of which our answer is "yes, but." People ask, "If he's wrong on every detail, doesn't that disqualify him? Isn't he just a showman?" to which the answer is "yes, he's hardly a meticulous researcher, but no, his provocations popularized a long-brewing reorientation to the media of art and communication."

People ask, "Didn't he oversell technology?" to which the answer is "yes, but he, himself, disliked technology." "Wasn't he a technological determinist?" they ask, alluding to McLuhan's insensitivity to the harnessing of technology by the powers-that-be and societal definition of its uses and meanings. The answer is "yes, technology dictates to society but some of these very dictates are themselves liberating, freeing man to be more himself."

"Wasn't he in love with television?" The answer is "certainly more than with print." But he loved its form and feared its content, as we will show.

People think he was uninterested in testing his propositions. In fact, he tried but failed (Marchand, 1989). People think that McLuhan was the founder of the media studies that have sprouted everywhere. But the fact is that his name rarely appears among pioneer media theorists and he is held in rather low repute among social scientists who study mass communications. His fame spread, rather, among the humanists and leaders of literary establishments such as George Steiner, Jonathan Miller, Susan Sontag, Frank Kermode, and so forth (Stearn, 1967). But acknowledged or not, he stimulated, maybe revolutionized, our thinking about the social history and sociology of mass communication.

McLuhan's thesis

McLuhan is an historian of culture who posits that the prime movers of cultural change are communications technologies. He does not tell us how the media displaced each other – that is, how speech gave way to tom-toms, to alphabets, to scribal writing, to moveable type, to the printing press, cinema, telegraph, radio, television, and computer. But he does argue that each of these technologies successively changed the societies in which they predominated. In this sense, he is like other theorists of single causes, whether the technologies of energy (Wittfogel, 1957) or of production (Marx).

For McLuhan, technologies may be defined as extensions of man's senses and limbs, and thus almost all technologies are associated with communication and transportation, be they bicycles or eyeglasses or the radio.

The difference between McLuhan and other theorists of communications technology, including Harold Innis (1950), is that he is not satisfied to assert that media affect the organization of society, as, say, the automobile affected the urban environment. McLuhan's claim is that the technology (also) works indirectly on society by affecting the ways in which the brain processes information from each new medium, how the mode of processing affects the senses and thus personality, and how personality, in turn, affects social organization. One of his most provocative assertions is that the technologies of alphabetic writing, especially print, trained the brain to process visual information linearly, and such linear thinking – implying determination, causality, logic, detachment, delayed gratification – is then applied to the rest of life.[2] In a word, McLuhan is saying that the sequentiality of print socialized perception and thought to favor formal linear argumentation from a single (rather than multidimensional) point of view, thus to produce a personality that was inclined to invent perspectival thinking in art,

2   Earlier, Riesman, Denney and Glazer (1950) proposed a connection between types of personality (tradition-directed, inner-directed, other-directed) and the succession of media that characterize American epochs. Jonathan Miller praises McLuhan on this point: "He has done something which very few have done publicly before. That is: to focus attention on the devices through which we obtain knowledge. These aspects have largely been ignored in the past, or at least have been a province of philosophers or else of neuro-physiologists, and I think for the first time what McLuhan has done is to bring the nervous system right into the center of the discussion of ordinary communications and of human knowledge in general" (in Stearn, 1967, p. 235). We argue that McLuhan should have known more about the philosophers to whom Miller alludes.

assembly lines for industrial production, railroad lines for business, and the straight-thinking of science. The age of electronic media allegedly changed all that.

This is what McLuhan means by "the medium is the message." He tells us to pay less attention to the content of a medium than to its technology. The message, he implies, is what the medium tells us about *how* to think, not what to think. At other moments, McLuhan is satisfied that his most famous phrase calls our attention to the idea that the medium as "figure" changes the "ground" of the environment, as the computer, say, changes office routines, the writing of history, the decentralization of work, and so forth.

While he spells out the effects, in their time, of each of the predominant technologies, his main interest is in the contrast between media of "heart" and media of "mind." In the beginning was orality, the extension of the ear, the medium of heart. Unlike print that extends the eye individualistically, word-of-mouth is sociable, pluralistic, playful, favoring generalist and operational wisdom rather than specialist and classified information. Acoustic man experiences life simultaneously rather than sequentially, and sees the world more cubistically with competing aspects in the same single frame. Word-of-mouth favors communication in time across generations, and hence tradition and religion, whereas print pushes for communication in space, and hence towards the development of nations and empires (McLuhan, 1964).

It follows that the important difference among media, according to McLuhan, is in their openness, or ambiguity, and thus in the extent to which active participation is required from their audiences. This is what McLuhan means by "hot" and "cool." The more intense and unrelenting the stimulus, the less the involvement on the part of the audience, he says, classifying print and the disembodied voice of radio as "hot" because of their technological single-mindedness, and speech and television as "cool."[3] True to his technology, McLuhan argued that the television

---

3   The dichotomies eye /ear, heart /mind, oral / literate, hot /cool, and involved / uninvolved obviously overlap. For example, one cannot simply subdivide eye and ear into hot and cool, nor does McLuhan take the trouble to help us through these difficulties. In the case of hot /cool, however, he does imply that the terms are relative to any particular comparison of two media, suggesting that hot /cool is not a dichotomy but a scale of "hotter than."

viewer is required to subconsciously connect the dots on his television screen in order to complete the picture, and hence is more involved, more participatory. (This is what led to the joke that McLuhan owned a faulty television set.) The multiple senses addressed by television and its literalness – thought by most mainstream communications researchers to reduce involvement – makes television *more* involving for McLuhan, thus to resemble the participatory qualities of speech with its accompanying gestures, intonations, and so forth. Hence, for McLuhan, participatory television is the reintroduction of the culture of orality and a cooling down of the one-dimensional directedness of typographic culture. This is how McLuhan reads Kennedy's 1960 victory over Nixon: the cool Kennedy was compatible with the cool medium, whereas the overheated Nixon – we know from research – was thought to have bettered Kennedy among listeners to the hot medium of radio.

The electronic age has extended several of our senses simultaneously, and, through the awareness of ourselves and others that is said to be the product of such multidimensional involvement, we are better able to understand, and assume responsibility for, what is happening in our community, our nation, and our planet. Hence the concept of "global village." McLuhan contrasts the selfishness of typographic culture with the collectivism of electronic culture. It leads him to betray his moral bias, even if he claims to be a value-neutral observer. He wants us to understand that acoustic cultures – of sound, of heart, of simultaneity and multifaceted perception – take care of their own, better than the visual cultures which cultivate the self at the expense of the collectivity.

Apart from attention to form, there is also an acknowledgement of content. In his most original use of the term,[4] McLuhan proposes that the "content" of each new medium is its predecessor, that is, that the novel is the content of the cinema, phonograph records are the content of radio, and films are the content of television. By being framed anew in this way, each medium thereby undergoes "aestheticization." Thus, cosmopolitan television aestheticizes the Old West, for example, or a satellite view from the moon aestheticizes planet Earth.[5]

4   Other uses of "content" include the accepted reference to text, program, and genre, but also to personality and the aphorism that "the reader is the content of the poem" (Marchand, 1989, p. 34; see also p. 255).
5   Classically, the concept "aesthetization" implies distantiation of an object, which

But our purpose is not to demonstrate, yet again, that McLuhan contradicts himself, or that his likes and dislikes are based on prejudice and prior commitment, or that his jazzy dichotomies rest on dimensions that are not independent of each other. Rather, we wish to direct attention, however briefly, to certain academic roots that underlie his concerns, as well as to certain predecessors of whom he appears to be unaware.

Where did he come from?[6]

Where did McLuhan get these ideas? His critics and biographer agree on several sources, in addition to those he acknowledges himself. First, one should notice his personal history of marginality: He stems from northwest Canada; had an independent feminist mother and a weak father – both interested in words and in spirituality; converted to Catholicism in 1937; and brow-beat anybody who would venture to debate his wild insights and proclamations, even while wanting to be liked. He is thought to have benefited from the unusual insights that come from being a multiple outsider.

Intellectually, he was nurtured in two academic traditions, to which he was drawn after he became uneasy about his conventional studies of English literature and the classics. One of these is a complex array of disciplines that can be summed up by the label *aesthetics*; this dates to Cambridge in the late 1930s. Only later, after arriving in Toronto, did he become involved with technological theories, especially via Harold Innis who was a regular participant in McLuhan's weekly seminar (Carey, 1967). Innis was a Chicago-trained economist who had studied aspects of the political economy of Canada, such as the trade in furs

---

would introduce further confusion if, for example, a hotter medium became the content of a cooler one. This problem probably did not occupy McLuhan but it is perfectly reasonable to ask how the delivery of the content of one medium via the technology of another affects the "message" of one or the other, or both. The obvious experiment is to compare the experience of the "same" film screened on a movie projector and on television.

6   We rely heavily here on the fascinating biography of McLuhan by Marchand (1989). The Gordon (1997) biography was published after submission of this paper and we have not been able to consult it.

and fish (Creighton, 1981), and became interested in the role of "media of space" and "media of time" in shaping ancient and modern nations and empires. In his classic works on this subject (Innis, 1950; 1951), he relates the portability of media such as papyrus and writing to the extension of centralized spatial control by Rome and, later, Egypt, and the erection of monuments and writing-on-stone oriented cultures to religion and communication across generations.

But it was the experience of Cambridge that proved definitive for McLuhan (Marchand, 1989). His two main mentors, I. A. Richards and F. R. Leavis, were in the process of overthrowing the traditional study of literature, and infected McLuhan with their cognitive, aesthetic, and sociologically oriented programs. The New Criticism led by Richards sought to shift the focus of study away from the meaning and authorial intent of the text to its rhetorical powers, thus to shift attention away from "sight" and towards "sound," in the McLuhan sense. In Richards' view, the critic's job is to analyze how a poem is able to achieve its effects. He advised paying close attention to the working of actual words in context, not to their exact definitions and certainly not to vague adventures of the soul.

This thrust led to a renewed interest in perception and in the ways in which mental processing intersected with the powers of the text. The Cambridge group also turned to other arts, including music, moving away from the semantic in the direction of the syntactic – that is, away from content and towards structure and form. McLuhan became interested in Edgar Allen Poe for this reason, and in other modern poets, such as Eliot and Joyce, who were adding dimensionality – that is, more, more, more "sound" – to their poetry. At the same time, new emphasis was put on the role of the reader. Leavis – the other of McLuhan's primary teachers – said that to understand a poem, one had to reconstruct the poem in one's own mind. T. S. Eliot said that the chief use of meaning in a poem is to distract the reader so that the poem can work. In the same spirit, years later, McLuhan (1964) would say that content is the piece of meat the burglars give the watchdog so that the medium can do its work, forever aware of the manipulative powers of both media and messages.[7]

---

7   His classroom teaching and writings on popular culture (e.g., McLuhan, 1951) were innovative efforts to expose the working of popular culture.

Literature thus intersected with developments in aesthetics. For McLuhan, F. R. Leavis was more influential than Richards because he was interested not only in how a poem affects but in the functions of poetry as well (Miller, 1971). Meanwhile, Q. D. Leavis was conducting empirical research on the interaction of the writer and the reading public. The arts have a qualitative impact, a kind of immediacy, was the thrust of this argument. Differing from Richards, this approach emphasized the integrative "wholeness" of the artistic message, not its component parts. As a result, McLuhan – following Hopkins, Yeats and Eliot – oriented himself to the distinction between auditory and visual perceptual types. In his work on the trivium, McLuhan realized that dialectica (critical reason) could be applied to the visual, while rhetorica (persuasion) and especially grammatica (power of words) were associated with the media of sound; he also realized that the shifting balance among these three could be used to characterize different epochs (Marchand, 1989). His thesis on Thomas Nashe applied these tools of analysis and, upon his return to Canada, he defied convention by applying Leavis' approach to the study of how popular culture works (to teach students, he said, how to liberate themselves from its clutches). This was an early example of what is now called media literacy.[8]

McLuhan had a strong interest in art. He was fascinated by the idea of perspective and its links to linearity, as has already been noted. He was fascinated by medieval art that gave multiple views of a given object side by side, and noted the parallel to cubism, which did the same thing. He saw modern art as an important antagonist to the stringencies of visual culture.

These developments in literature and aesthetics coincided at Cambridge with work in neurology, as has been noted, in the psychology of perception, and in anthropology. Richards was explicitly interested in the ways in which the "nervous system processes and assimilates the information provided for it by the imaginative writers" (Miller, 1971, p. 29). This anticipates McLuhan's later interest in the division of labor between the hemispheres of the brain and his posthumous essay on the typographical European, subtitled "The 'Western' Hemisphere"

---

8   The discussion in the paragraphs that follow is documented in Katz and Hacohen (1998).

(McLuhan, 1978). Later, McLuhan would find special interest in the Sapir-Whorf hypothesis that languages – like the media – "shape the way we experience the world" (Marchand, 1989, p. 117). (Note that this falls short of the linguistic turn in philosophy which led beyond discussions of the age-old boundaries between logic and rhetoric, in an attempt to redraw the entire map of reason.)

Given his interest in aesthetics, it is surprising how little reference is made to the vast literature on the role of perception and mental processing of the arts that dates back to the eighteenth century. The "media literacy" of today came to the fore 200 years ago in a multitude of treatises that dealt with the differences among artistic media, as their dictates, boundaries, and uniquenesses interact with the senses which they engage and the types of mental processing which they trigger. Even more surprising than McLuhan's silence about these sources is the fact that they are apparently unremembered by the Cambridge community of the 1930s if one is to judge from literary critics and interlocutors of McLuhan. It is uncanny that these arguments and interdisciplinary explorations are almost a photocopy of arguments and explorations that enlisted a coterie of British men of letters, philosophizing about the arts almost two centuries earlier. In other words, the cognitive and aesthetic propositions to which McLuhan alludes, rightly or wrongly, can be traced back to eighteenth-century preoccupations with how the mind processes visual and auditory information. Like McLuhan and his Cambridge mentors, these writers – from Shaftesbury to Adam Smith – linked aesthetic concerns with moral philosophy and were deeply concerned, moreover, with related developments, especially in theories of language from Warburton and Condillac until Rousseau. That they are "unremembered" reminds us that science does not develop in a simple linear fashion; only when a paradigm takes center-stage do we look back to discover its precursors (Kuhn, 1970).

Briefly, the problem of perception came to the fore, together with other theories of man and society, as Europe became less self-centered and new worlds loomed on its horizon. Cultural variance gave rise to new universals concerning men while social universals gave rise to comparative studies of human organization, culture, language and ultimately to the embryonic social sciences. This was a moment in which empirical observation and inductive generalization displaced philosophical postulates, in which hypotheses about constructivist world-making vied with determinism, and in which Vico is the best-known name (see Vico, 1963).[9]

The interest in perception led to a search for evidence of how the mind works, just as it had done in Richards' Cambridge, and how the senses – especially seeing and hearing – are employed. The search led to the arts as a functional anticipation of the neuro-psychological laboratory, on the (brilliant) assumption that artistic problem-solving may reveal how the mind works. This was the point at which mimetic theories of artistic production were displaced by constructionist theories, and the arts were thought to be better perceived as different forms of world-making, given the different senses which they employ. In the process, the status of music, the art of the ear, changed from the art least able to imitate nature to the art that could, in effect, create coherent form without content, syntactic structures without semantic messages, effects without labels. That the structure of music "makes sense but not meaning" – that is, that "musical structure itself is the message" – became the envy of the other arts and paved the way towards abstract art.

In other words, the arts – seen as extensions of eye and ear – were no longer thought to be inferior to science but were conceived as different ways of knowing, and thus aesthetics became a branch of philosophy. Fascinating treatises were written about the differences among the arts and their different modes of symbolization. Mimesis was banished, along with the idea that each of the arts does the same thing, more or less, but by different means. Music, for example, was now seen as giving more direct access to experience than literature, anticipating Schopenhauer's view of music's primordiality (see Schopenhauer, 1950). Emphasis shifted to the ways in which the different arts selected

---

9   The mind, according to Vico (1963), operates symbolically, transforming all sensations into meanings, forever seeking coherence. The human mind does not change; what changes are the cultural artifacts which are the creation of human consciousness. The only basis for a science of culture and a metaphysics of mind are, therefore, historical investigations of the different encounters of human consciousness as they occurred at different times and situations. That there can be a "science of mind which is the history of its development ... that this process is traceable through the evolution of symbols – words, gestures, pictures, sounds, and their altering patterns and uses," is the boldest contribution of Vico's anthropological historicism, according to Isaiah Berlin (1979, p. 113).

content appropriate to their abilities and limits. Lessing (1957) is only the best known of a series of essayists who show how the media – whether painting, music, or poetry – set limits to the message.

It is a real surprise that McLuhan's far-reaching and self-serving literature search did not rediscover these fairly widespread deliberations on the differences among the arts, their modes of perception and representation, and their syntactic and semantic implications. He seems well versed in the debates over "making" versus "matching" in the Greeks and in Gombrich (1980) (in McLuhan, 1962, for example), but has missed out on a century of thinking which anticipates his own. Had he positioned himself on these shoulders, he would have been better situated to defend his thesis that cultures are based on choices, themselves cognitively constrained, whose consequences, however, are predetermined. It is fair to say that his emphasis on the *how* of thinking, rather than the *what*, rests on aesthetic theory concerning the limits of artistic media, on the one hand, and some theoretical assumptions concerning the nature of perception and cognition, on the other.

Why was he famous?

McLuhan was a vituperative provocateur, given to aphorisms and punning. For the 20 years or so since Cambridge, he was an *enfant terrible* in the several places he taught, and his publications attracted attention in respectable journals of literature and language. Portents of his fame came from his critical readings of popular culture – especially his tirades against the mechanization of man, henpecked by machines and women – and the analysis of the symbolic environment of advertising that culminated in *The Mechanical Bride* in 1951. He was discovered more widely through his contributions to the *Swannee Review* extolling the myth of the patrician South and its oral culture, set against the overheated industrialism of the typographic North. His agrarian romanticism led him to preach the virtues of community, to decry escapism, and to lean a little towards Franco fascism. He became even better known in the iconoclastic *Explorations in Communication*, a journal he edited with his creative seminar group, which was given a big boost by the Ford Foundation in 1952. McLuhan's groupies and converts, meanwhile, did a lot of public relations for their guru (Marchand, 1989).[10]

By the late 1950s, television was widely diffusing, and McLuhan began to take note of the dawning of a new age that would replace the era of the printed word and lead to a renaissance of cool acoustic space. Abandoning his critique of content, he switched to extolling the great potential of the new medium and its liberating and participatory qualities. This is the real beginning of his fame. He offered to all a hopeful future. He saw the evils of mechanization fading away, and with it the rise of globalism and the decline of the overheated nation-state. He believed that people would once again become aware of the world around them, thanks to the multiple perspectives that arise from shared and ubiquitous experience and simultaneous viewing by different kinds of people, and by the multiple senses that the medium requires for its decoding. In short, he proposed that we were on the verge of a world community connected by electric simultaneity, in which all stood to be empowered. He called it the Global Village.

This doctrine was comfortable to people on both sides of the set: It made viewers feel less guilty over the time spent watching television. Likewise, it deflected some of the criticism directed against the owners and producers of the mass media, who were relieved of responsibility for the possible effects of content. And, of course, there were his aphoristic pronouncements that attracted a lot of amused attention and the reaction, "What if he's right?"

For academics, he made communication the queen of the sciences, shifting attention away from whether this jingle is more effective than that jingle, to the role of media as technologies that affect cognition, personality, and social organization. It is a lot more satisfying to know that one's discipline has the best explanation for the Protestant Reformation or the rise of science, or of Hitler, than whether smart advertising campaigns really decide the elections.

---

10 In addition to the artists and writers who promoted him, there is a real, albeit small, "genius-scouting" public relations firm that adopted him and staged events in his behalf. One of the duo who ran the campaign is Howard Gossage whose essay on his find is reprinted as the lead article in Stearn (1967). For the role of promoters in securing the reputation of artists, see Lang and Lang (1990).

His message, in short, was a proposal not simply for understanding media, but for understanding cultural history and social change as a function of media predominance, and a lot of people were attracted to the all-but-unprovable thesis. And some still are (e.g., Meyrowitz, 1996). Moreover, now relinquishing concern over the manipulative potential of the media, his was a message of hope about a benign future, addressed to a world about to explode in the Cold War, Vietnam, the Kennedy assassination, the outbreak in the black ghettoes, and the retreat of the flower children.

Where has he gone?

Then he vanished. But did he?

First of all, he deserves credit for inspiring Eisenstein's (1979) rigorous study of the effect of the printing press and Ong's (1982) early work on the typographical teaching of Ramus. Both writers acknowledge their debt, even while distancing themselves – Eisenstein especially – from McLuhan's outrageous methodology.

Secondly, McLuhan's ghost can be found in cognitive studies. Nobody there takes notice, of course, but the fact is that McLuhan popularized the links among neurology, perception, the arts, and the media. In short, he did good public relations for the mind's new science, in spite of his failure to understand its subtlety and its rigor.

Then there is globalism. The satellite and the Internet have now virtually aestheticized television, as an outdated form, and the whole world is again talking about the Global Village. Indeed, applying technological determinism to the present moment, one cannot but conclude that the new media have outmoded the nation-state and that the world now consists of diasporas, on the one hand, and multinational corporations, on the other (Katz, 1996).

McLuhanism is evident in cultural studies as well. He was one of the first to make the study of popular culture academically legitimate (Schudson, 1987). On the other hand, he was naïve about power and, from this aspect, stands outside of cultural studies. But from the point of view of reception research, he stands well inside the tradition. When he was asked the perennial Canadian question, "What will happen to Canadian content on television if popular culture overwhelms us from across the border?" McLuhan replied, "If Canadians are viewing, that's Canadian content." His concern with involvement and participation are the essence of reception theory not only in communications research but in the study of literature as well (Radway, 1986).

McLuhan's footprints may also be traced to two further contemporary factions – except that these are mutually contradictory, just as he would have liked. One is the communitarian movement (Etzioni, 1995), which gives expression to McLuhan's yearning for home, hearth, sociability, and simplicity (Ferguson, 1970), in which oral communication and its technological mutations predominate. This is McLuhan's "ideal speech situation," without Habermasian rationality and, one should add, without McLuhan's pontifications.

The competing paradigm is postmodernism, which posits mutually alienated cultural communities, each with its own modes of thought and mutually exclusive aesthetic styles, living side by side in a world in which reality itself is called into question by the competing images which are said to represent it.

McLuhan would have liked being on both of these aircraft as they crash in virtual reality.

References

Berlin, Isaiah. (1979). Vico's concept of knowledge. In H. Hardy (Ed.), *Against the current: Essays in the history of ideas*. Harmondsworth: Penguin.

Carey, James. (1967). Harold Adams Innis and Marshall McLuhan. *Antioch Review, 27*(1), 5–39.

Creighton, D. (1981). Harold Adams Innis – An appraisal. In W. H. Melody, L. Salter & P. Heyer (Eds.), *Culture, communication and dependency: The tradition of H. A. Innis*. Norwood, NJ: Ablex.

Eisenstein, E. L. (1979). *The printing press as an agent of change*. Cambridge: Cambridge University Press.

Etzioni, Amitai. (1995). *New communitarian thinking: Persons, virtues, institutions and communities*. Charlottesville: University Press of Virginia.

Ferguson, M. (1970). Marshall McLuhan revisited: 1960s Zeitgeist victim or pioneer postmodernist. *Media, Culture and Society, 13*,

71–90.

Gombrich, E. H. (1980). *Art and illusion: A study in the psychology of pictorial representation*. Oxford: Phaidon Press.

Gordon, W. Terrence. (1997). *Marshall McLuhan: Escape into understanding*. New York: Basic Books.

Innis, Harold. (1950). *Empire and communication*. Toronto: University of Toronto Press.

Innis, Harold. (1951). *The bias of communication*. Toronto: University of Toronto Press.

Katz, E. (1996). And deliver us from segmentation. *Annals of the American Academy of Political and Social Science, 546*, 22–33.

Katz, R., & Hacohen, R. (1998). *Tuning the mind: How eighteenth-century deliberations on the arts prefigured the cognitive turn*. Manuscript submitted for publication.

Kuhn, T. S. (1970). *The structure of scientific revolutions*. Chicago: University of Chicago Press.

Lang, G. E., & Lang, K. (1990). *Etched in memory: The building and survival of artistic reputation*. Chapel Hill: University of North Carolina Press.

Lessing, G. (1957). *Laocoon: An essay upon the limits of painting and poetry*. New York: Noonday Press. (Originally published in 1766.)

Marchand, Philip. (1989). *Marshall McLuhan: The medium and the messenger*. New York: Ticknor & Fields.

McLuhan, Marshall. (1951). *The mechanical bride: Folklore of industrial man*. New York: Vanguard Press.

McLuhan, Marshall. (1962). *The Gutenberg galaxy*. New York: McGraw-Hill.

McLuhan, Marshall. (1964). *Understanding media: The extensions of man*. New York: McGraw-Hill.

McLuhan, Marshall. (1978). The brain and the media: The "Western" hemisphere. *Journal of Communication, 28*(4), 54–60.

Meyrowitz, J. (1996). Taking McLuhan and "medium theory" seriously. In S. T. Kerr (Ed.), *Technology and the future of schools*. Chicago: University of Chicago Press.

Miller, Jonathan. (1971). *McLuhan*. London: Fontana.

Ong, Walter J. (1982). *Orality and literacy*. London: Methuen.

Radway, Janice. (1986). *Reading the romance: Women, patriarchy and popular literature*. London: Verso.

Riesman, D., Denney, R., & Glazer, N. (1950). *The lonely crowd*. New Haven: Yale University Press.

Schopenhauer, A. (1950). *The world as will and idea*. London: Routledge. (Originally published in 1819.)

Schudson, M. (1987). The new validation of popular culture: Sense and sensibility in academia. *Critical Studies in Mass Communication*, *4*(1), 51–68.

Stearn, Gerald E. (Ed.). (1967). *McLuhan: Hot & cool*. New York: Dial Press.

Vico, G. (1963). *La scienza nova*. Milan: Rizzoti. (Originally published in 1744.)

Wittfogel, K. A. (1957). *Oriental despotism: A comparative study of total power*. New Haven: Yale University Press.

Wolfe, Tom. (1968). What if he is right? In *The pump house gang*. New York: Farrar, Straus, Giroux. (Originally published in *New York*, 1965.)

ARTHUR SIEGEL

5. Northrop Frye and the Toronto School of Communication Theory

Northrop Frye is one of the most important voices of the Toronto School of Communication Theory that had its genesis in the theories of Harold Innis and Marshall McLuhan. Innis was the starting point of Canadian communication theory. McLuhan described his own major books as a footnote to Innis' investigation. He took Innis toward a more inclusive cultural analysis, "though little remained of economics and politics that was recognizable."[1] A common denominator in Innis and McLuhan is their focus on the profound changes that occur in society – in culture, economics and political power structure – that may be associated with changes in communication technology. Their approach and subsequent work in this area by other Canadian scholars has become known as the Toronto School.

Frye acknowledged that the relation between his theories and those of Innis and McLuhan is rooted in the centrality of communications to the very existence of Canada. As Frye put it, "Canadians have been obsessed with communications."[2] This is reflected everywhere in our history: the building of bridges, canals, and the railway, and the construction of telegraph poles along the railway tracks in the 19th century. In the 20th century, Canadians pioneered some of the most important technological developments in broadcasting, including the invention of radio that could carry voice and music, the first radio station, long distance broadcasting and communication satellites for domestic radio and television. This communication obsession – tied to the struggle of nation building and

---

1   James Carey, "Canadian Communication Theory: Extension and Interpretations of Harold Innis," in Gertrude Joch Robinson & Donald F. Theal (eds.), *Studies In Canadian Communications* (Montreal: McGill University, 1975), p. 6.
2   David Cayley, *Northrop Frye in Conversation* (Concord, Ont.: Anansi Press, 1992), p. 123.

the viability of the state – led to what Frye called "very comprehensive theories of communication," like Innis' and McLuhan's. "I suppose," said Frye, "I belong to some extent in that category."[3]

One of Canada's legendary thinkers, Northrop Frye was internationally acclaimed for his work in literary criticism. He helped lay the foundations of Critical Theory. His concern with literature incorporated such concepts as identity, culture and community, which are central to communications. It was inevitable that his work would spill over into the development of communication theory.

Frye's career at the University of Toronto overlaps partly with Innis and McLuhan. They worked within a few blocks of each other, almost within shouting distance. The three renowned scholars did not interact directly and focused their principal attention in different directions. The Toronto School is not a formal institution. Rather, the name reflects the Canadian innovation in communications scholarship tied to the premise about the fundamental impact of the modes of communications on the shaping of society. The first stirring of a sense of continuity in the communication scholarships that was to evolve into this tradition came in the early 1960s – some ten years after Innis died – with the publication of Marshall McLuhan's *The Gutenberg Galaxy*. (There are other early important voices, including Eric Havelock.)[4] McLuhan had the loudest voice because it was amplified by the mass media that catapulted him to international fame and celebrity status. Two decades later, when Frye was asked about McLuhan's influence at its height, Frye allowed that he thought "McLuhan was being praised to the skies for the wrong reasons and then, after the vogue passed, being ignored for the wrong reasons. There is a great deal of permanent value in McLuhan's insights."[5]

Frye published more than 25 books. His principal communication concepts are embedded in his prolific writings in the field of literary criticism and the evolvement of literary theory. This may have distracted scholars for some years from fully realizing his contribution to the Toronto School. Today, he is perceived as a preeminent communication theorist. His proposal that "verbal structures (stories, myths, poetry,

3   Cayley, *Northrop Frye*, p. 124.
4   Eric A. Havelock, *The Muse Learns to Write* (New Haven: Yale University Press, 1962).
5   Cayley, *Northrop Frye*, p.162.

scientific discourse) mediate human relations" created fertile avenues of analysis.[6] The richness and originality of his broad ranging theoretical offerings are catalysts in providing new directions in communication studies. Frye's focus on concepts integral to the study of communication is not a post-Innis or post-McLuhan addition; it goes back to 1947 in the first book he ever published: *Fearful Symmetry*.[7] In this work, dealing with William Blake, he lays the groundwork for his theory of reality that is rooted in his seminal insights on cognition and perception. The theory of perception is central to Frye's work. He distinguishes between two ways of looking at the world. There is the objective view, seeing the real world as it is, and in this case the viewer is independent of the universe. The other *Weltanschaung* has humans at the center of things; it is grounded in subjectivity, imagination and myth. The analysis of the two views of the world leads Frye to the concept of double-vision (or dialectical vision).[8] Frye develops and elaborates on his communication insights in subsequent books, including *Modern Century* (1967) and *Critical Path* (1971). In the latter book, he puts forward the notion of "truth of correspondence," a scientific mantle for objectivity and expands on the dialectics of double-vision which enables us to perceive simultaneously the material as well as the imaginative dimensions.[9]

Frye also writes directly on media, exploring the different kinds of impact associated with differing modes of communications – oral, written and electronic. In *Modern Century*, he sends out warning signals about the roadblocks to communication that may be associated with electronic media: "erode privacy and increase introversion." In expressing concern about the implications of technology, he declares that the triumph of communication is the death of communication: where communication forms a total environment, there is nothing to be communicated."[10]

Robert Babe, in his study *Canadian Communication Thought: Ten*

6 Robert Babe, *Canadian Communication Thought* (Toronto: University of Toronto Press, 2000).
7 Northrop Frye, *Fearful Symmetry* (Princeton, N.J.: Princeton University Press, 1947).
8 Frye, *Fearful Symmetry*, p. 38.
9 Northrop Frye, *Critical Path* (Bloomington: Indiana University Press, 1971).
10 Northrop Frye, *Modern Century* (Toronto, Oxford University Press, 1967).

Foundational Writers, lays out in some detail the communication theories of Frye. He discusses the principal issues raised by Frye and notes this significance to contemporary scholarship.

> Frye's own mythopoeic world-view, as expressed in *Fearful Symmetry*, can be summarized by a number of axioms linking perception, imagination, the will, experience, knowledge, and truth. These propositions, in fact, are at the core of certain modern schools of communication thought – mentalism, social construction, symbolic interactionism, and post-modernism.[11]

Double vision has become an oversimplified shorthand label for Frye's communication theories as much as space-time and ear-eye are used to label Innis and McLuhan respectively. It is noteworthy that there is a consistency and continuity in Frye's work. In his first book, *Fearful Symmetry,* he introduces us to double vision; his last book appeared in 1991 a few months after his death, its title: *The Double Vision*. Our focus is largely on Frye's unpublished reflections – both in writing and in conversation – about communication in the Canadian environment, about Innis and, to a lesser extent, about McLuhan. Some of the material dates to the late 1960s and the early 1970s when Frye was formulating his vision of television. These early views remained a cornerstone of his thinking about mass media two decades later. Frye's involvement in communication is multi-dimensional. He was an active participant in shaping broadcasting in Canada through his position as a part-time Commissioner of Canada's regulatory body for broadcasting, the CRTC. This appointment virtually required him to think and write specifically about communication.

In the first instance, there will be an examination of Frye's posthumous interaction with the works of Innis. This will be followed by an examination of Frye's perceptions of the fundamentals of Canada and their implications for communications flow. The unpublished material provides distinctive footprints and elaborations of his theoretical insights.

---

11 Babe, *Canadian Communication Thought*, p. 236.

I Frye on Innis

Frye studied and edited Innis' writing – for, off and on, close to a dozen years (1968–1980). Innis died young in 1952 when he was deeply immersed in the writing of a history of communications.[12] He left behind, in handwriting, a great block of unfinished material. In 1968, Frye who had been newly appointed to the Canadian Radio and Television Commission along with CRTC research director Roderique Chiasson and André Martin, also of the CRTC, obtained permission from Mary Quayle Innis to edit the unfinished manuscript. Frye was editor of the manuscript, a task carried out with the support of many others. Frye became President of the Innis Communication Corporation, established to acquire copyright for *Dispersal and Concentration: Historical Aspects of Communications.*[13]

In his introduction to *Dispersal and Concentration,* written 30 years after Innis' death, Frye notes that by 1980 Innis' sources had become "questionable and obsolete." As an example he points out that Innis was quoting G.G. Coultin on bilingualism: "[it] implies a lack of clearness of speech and therefore of thought." More importantly, Innis did not have the benefit of critical and cultural theory, which in Innis' time was at best primitive. Consequently, "Innis must be read with a good deal of historical imagination with the realization that whatever issues do not seem central now must have been central once, and if they were once they are still potentially so."[14]

In the 22-page essay, Frye provides a sweeping analysis of Innis and lays out the principal pillars of Innis' theoretical framework as well as an interpretation of Innis' findings. He obviously likes Innis and sets him on the pedestal he deserves, referring to him as a landmark in the cultural history of Canada. Nevertheless, he never seeks to be

12 Harold A. Innis, *The Bias of Communications* (Toronto: University of Toronto Press, 1951). Harold A. Innis, *Empire and Communications* (Toronto: Oxford University Press, 1950).

13 Harold Innis, *Dispersal and Concentration: Historical Aspect of Communications,* edited by Northrop Frye (Chairman) in association with R.B. Chiasson, André Martin and Mary Wilson. Unpublished. Copyright: Innis Communications Corporation, 1982.

14 Northrop Frye, *Introduction to Dispersal and Concentration* (hereafter "Frye on Innis"), p. xii.

politically correct and is sometimes biting in his criticism, especially of the citations Innis relies on. Only a scholar of matching authority can offer criticisms, clarifications, and extensions that Frye provides in his unique reading of Innis.

Frye describes the Innis manuscript as an integral part of a social vision of scope and comprehensiveness unparalleled in Canadian culture. The broad-ranging approach from across a variety of disciplines reflects the notion that anything may be relevant to communications. There are great strengths in such an approach as it provides insights that are not bound by the jargon and borders of a discipline, but there are also weaknesses because it is not possible for any scholar to be equally strong in unlimited areas. The result, says Frye, is that "Innis is negatively as well as positively seminal. He will always be rewarding to study but he will also be in constant need for modification, revision and updating."[15]

Frye saw his essay as a contribution toward bringing Innis into the dialogue on major current issues, or, as he called it, our contemporary preoccupations. He had the benefit of 30 years of hindsight to carry out this task. But first, Frye moves backward in time, and focuses on what led Innis – a Canadian economic historian – to deal with communications. The early studies of the fur trade and the fishing industry and later his attention to the pulp and paper industry provided insight into the significance of exporting staples to foreign markets: "it leaves behind it a profoundly colonial mentality, proud of its natural resources but very different about its human ones, conditioned to accept somewhere else as the place where the main action is....Canadian history, Canadian immigration, and the way of Canadian life had all been profoundly affected."[16]

Innis' personal bridge to communication was that he examined not merely the economy of exported staples "but the larger question of the cultural use of the staple. He moved from economic history to a field where he was, in effect, taking all knowledge for his province."[17]

Basic to the thinking of both Frye and Innis is the Laurentian theory of Canadian expansion. As Frye points out, "Innis realized the importance

15 "Frye on Innis," p. xvi.
16 "Frye on Innis," p. xxvi.
17 "Frye on Innis," p. xiv.

of the east-west Laurentian axis, the thrust down the river to the Great
Lakes, fanning out from there into the far west and the north, that makes
sense of the map of Canada." This characteristic is critical for Canada
having a political development distinct from that of the United States.
This distinctiveness is a theme that Frye returns to in many of his
comments about communications. The east-west Laurentian axis is a
continuing factor in our communication environment: "The Laurentian
axis has vanished into the past, but its cultural consequences have
not."[18]

Frye did not come to the Laurentian Theory through Innis. He had
known of Innis as a university colleague who was chairman of the
Department of Political Economy at the University of Toronto, but did
not read his material until after Innis died. In fact, both Frye and Innis
published their complementary theoretical insights on this fundamental
characteristic of Canada at about the same time. Frye formulated this
theory when he wrote a review of Ned Pratt's *Towards the Last Spike* in
1952 for the *University of Toronto Quarterly*. [19]

Frye's awareness of the east-west axis had its genesis in 1939 when he
was returning by ship from two years of studies at Oxford. "I suddenly
realized that I was in the middle of the Gulf of St. Lawrence and I was
surrounded by five Canadian provinces, all of them invisible. You don't
get that kind of experience anywhere in the United States."[20] It was
for him the beginning of the understanding that the Canadian economy
developed from a big Laurentian thrust from the east to west. It took on
political shape with Sir John A. Macdonald, who thought in terms of
east to west movement, starting in Great Britain and federating Canada
as part of the British Empire on the way to India.

Frye introduces key dimensions of Innis' theory in simple and direct
language: "There is a general 'bias' (a word Innis uses frequently in
different contexts) predisposing the societies of the past either towards
time or towards space."[21] In time-biased societies, the emphasis was
on continuity and tradition and the media of communications had a
lasting quality about them (e.g., stone and clay tablets); the material

18 "Frye on Innis," p. xxvi.
19 Cayley, *Northrop Frye*, p.126.
20 Cayley, *Northrop Frye*, p.126.
21 "Frye on Innis," p. xvi.

used for writing was difficult to transport and expensive. Among the characteristics attributed to these societies are elitism, secrecy, the building of monuments (as a form of expression over time) and a vested interest by the powerful to keep knowledge in their own group.

The development of an alphabet, the production of paper and a duplicating process – all discussed in great detail in the Innis manuscript – brought about the conditions for making communication more accessible: there was a spread of literacy and communications could reach out over wider spaces. The spread, or spatial expansion, of communication became global after the industrial revolution. The technological achievements that led to space-biased societies resulted in challenges to the entrenched regime by new power groups in society.

Frye brings clarity to Innis' assertions about the implications of changes in communications: "It clearly seems to be Innis' view that changes in communications are involved in, or accompany, or in many cases are even the cause of, historical changes of attention."[22] The general principle involved is that "every ascendant class, in fact every pressure group within society, tries to establish a dominant or if possible a monopolized control over communication."[23]

The longevity of such monopolies is curtailed by the development of new technology of communication, something that happens in even the most stagnant societies. The new communication environment sets off new contexts, reflecting new forms of knowledge and thought. The struggle between power structures where every pressure group tries to establish dominance or monopolized control sets off a struggle within communication between classifying and disseminating information. The printing press, invented in the 15th century, in time resulted in a spectacular growth in the dissemination of communication to a situation where today "freedom of the press" is so established that it has developed a monopoly of its own.

Frye challenges the perception about the degree of permanence in the form of communications in time bound societies ranging from stone tablets to monumental structures like pyramids and cathedrals. "The monumental," says Frye, "turns out to be surprisingly fragile." He adds:

22 "Frye on Innis," p. xii.
23 "Frye on Innis," p. xvii.

It is the verbal that has the real power of survival in time, and this power is inseparable from the spatial power of cheap and expendable material and devices of multiplication. In other words, it is only the temporary that attains a real control of time.[24]

Frye suggests that Innis overemphasized the lasting power of time-biased communication.

The power struggle over communication is embedded in the theories of Frye, Innis and McLuhan. When this power struggle reaches a deadlock, Frye points out, opportunities open up for the individual. Such a power struggle in the 16th century within Christianity provided opportunities for the emergence of Renaissance humanism, Cinquecento painting and Elizabethan drama.[25] He extends this scenario to the struggle between Communism and Capitalism in our own times: "Twentieth-century science and literature have got what benefits they could from the absence of a final victory for either side."[26] (Frye was, of course, writing in 1980 before the implosion of Communism in what was then the Soviet Union.)

Frye uses Innis' own phrase, "the strategy of culture," to describe the process of imaginative wriggling out of a power struggle. Looking across the broad expanse of history, Innis provided three especially important opportunities when culture emerges from the struggle of opposites. They are:

- the creative and imaginative culture that emerges from a society in the middle of its power struggles;
- the law with its internal struggles;
- the objectivity of scholarship and scientific knowledge (institutionalized in the universities).

There are complexities and some contradictions in each of these categories in the struggle of opposites. Using knowledge from the fields of religion, music, science, painting, literature and drama, Frye illustrates the usefulness and difficulties associated with these three categories. Through example, he clarifies, elaborates, and brings

24 "Frye on Innis," p. xxviii.
25 "Frye on Innis," p. xix.
26 "Frye on Innis," p. xx.

contemporary relevance (that is, contemporary in the sense of 1980) to the issues explored in the Innis manuscript.

Frye points to Innis' concerns about the monopoly of print. "The technical achievements of the printed word today have made it an unchallenged medium of communications."[27] The result is a mass monopoly, or "the propaganda" that we criticize and associate with totalitarian countries, "without much noticing the effectiveness of a slightly different kind of propaganda in our own."[28] How do we deal with this problem? Innis turned his attention to broadcasting.

Innis, according to Frye, was interested in McLuhan's *The Mechanical Bride* (1951) that was a stepping stone to later books presenting a revolutionary theory where the electronic media were replacing print. McLuhan saw print as linear and time bound and the electronic media as having a simultaneous and many-sided impact. Frye notes that for McLuhan this was "primarily a psychological difference" although later he suggested it was also a physiological difference. Frye adds:

> What is disappointing about McLuhan's work, however, is the absence of any clear sense of the kind of social context in which electronic media function. Television in particular is geared to the rhythms of the social economy; however striking the psychological difference between its impact and that of print, the absence of any real social difference neutralizes nearly all of it. The usual television program, as the CRTC keeps rather irritably reminding Canadian broadcasters, is simply a talking journal, as the phrase "magazine format" indicates, a way of conveying the same words and images for the same social purposes. McLuhan felt, at least at first, that the electronic media would bring in a social revolution so pervasive that one could describe its social context only in terms of the future. But, as with other prophetic revolutionary theories, the existing power structures have refused to wither away on schedule.[29]

Innis thought that radio might provide the necessary challenge to the monopoly of the printed word. The revival of oral communication in

27 "Frye on Innis," p. xxvii.
28 "Frye on Innis," p. xxvii.
29 "Frye on Innis," p. xxix.

mass society makes mechanical or electronic reproduction essential. Radio was the principal electronic medium of Innis' time. (He died the year that Canadian television broadcasting was inaugurated, although Canadians could pick up U.S. border stations long before 1952.) There was optimism in the 1920s that radio would develop as an instrument for national and international dialogue and provide an opening for social and political interaction.[30] Radio was seen as a potential support structure for peace and international harmony. There was a search for a universal radio language – English, French, German and even Latin and Chinese were considered as possibilities – but most of the enthusiasm was for Esperanto, an artificial language created at the end of the 19th century.

Radio, however, did not evolve as a liberating force. Instead, the medium quickly became an instrument for propaganda with Nazi Germany and the Soviet Union providing especially powerful examples. Innis, as Frye points out, understood that Hitler was attempting to manipulate radio as a means of mass control and noted that this was not what he had in mind. Radio served as an instrument of war, political intimidation and propaganda long before it found a voice; news reports in Morse code were used in World War I (1914–1918) for propaganda. Broadcasting did not provide a ready answer.

Frye argued that Innis regarded "oral tradition" as a liberating agency to challenge the monopoly of the printed word. Innis refers to "oral tradition" at the beginning of *Empire and Communications* but is at once vague and imprecise in giving it meaning; he used the concept as a symbol for something he failed to identify. Frye's discussion of "oral tradition" begins with a clear statement of what it is not: it is not oral communication. "Oral communication, in its original form, belongs to an ancient world that can never come back."[31] Frye provides his own more contemporary interpretation of "oral tradition."

Some aspects of Innis' thoughts on oral tradition became clearer in the three decades between Innis' death and Frye's interpretation. Frye develops his argument through an example especially dear to him: literature. Canada witnessed an explosion of literary talent in the

30 For a history of radio as an instrument of propaganda see: Arthur Siegel, *Radio Canada International* (Oakville, Ont.: Mosaic Press, 1996).

31 "Frye on Innis," p. xxviii.

1960s and 1970s which precipitated important changes in the nature of Canadian writing. Frye refers to this as a qualitative change. Frye found that Canadian literature had developed a regional quality and argued that "the creative imagination needed a smaller and more cohesive unit than the vast sprawl of 'Canada' affords."[32] In essence the local and regional setting is an essential nucleus. This mirrors a pattern in the United States where literature has been strongly regional. American literature is the adding together of writers from Mississippi, New England, the Midwest and other parts of the American universe. The answer, thus, is the small unit and Frye argued in favor of the local.

> It looks as though the "counter-culture" we used to hear so much about is really the "strategy of culture itself, decentralizing where politics centralizes, differentiating where technology makes everything uniform, giving articulateness and human meaning to the small community where economy turns it into a mere distributing centre, constantly moving it in a direction opposite to that of the political and economic tendencies of history.[33]

This counter-movement of culture, that is, culture moving in the opposite direction to political and economic developments, applies to space, but, argues Frye, it is likely also to be true of time. In Innis' time-bound society there is an obsession with continuity without change in transferring the authority of institution to a new generation. Frye argues that there is a similar practice in the arts to follow established patterns. But over time new influences have to be accommodated. The expanded variety of traditions that become available to the artist – so visible today – opens up new thinking about culture.

> Culture tends to move backwards in time, away from the merely continuous, and towards the constant recapturing and rediscovery of the imaginative life in neglected tradition. It continues to do so even when "time bound" institutions are replaced or supplemented by "spatial" or marketplace monopolies.[34]

32 "Frye on Innis," p. xxx.
33 "Frye on Innis," p. xxx.
34 "Frye on Innis," p. xxxi.

Frye surveys the Innis manuscript he is introducing for evidence in support of his argument. He finds a good deal of data about the way in which the printing presses were used by Renaissance humanists to establish a market for scholarly editions of the Classics despite economic handicaps that appeared to make such an outcome impossible. They were fighting according to the directive of the strategy of culture: "in the opposite direction from the tendencies of the market." In the contemporary setting, artists, writers and the creative people in film and broadcasting are fighting similar battles.

For Frye, "oral tradition" makes sense as indicating the "headwaters of tradition. The end of the recreating backward movement in time that, in all forms of creation, brings the past to life as a new and enlarged form of present experience."[35] This elaboration on "oral tradition" is an extension of Innis' that provides new insights into Innis' as well as Frye's thoughts.

II Frye on Communications: In conversation

Frye died in 1991 and left behind unpublished material that provides his most direct pronouncements on the media of mass communications. His involvement in communication went far beyond the role of a theorist; he was also an active participant in shaping broadcasting policy in Canada through his position as a part-time Commissioner of the regulatory and supervisory agency for broadcasting. He also became a recognizable voice on Canadian radio and television.

The regulation of broadcasting dramatically changed in 1968 when Parliament in Ottawa passed the fourth Broadcasting Act, establishing the Canadian Radio and Television Commission as undisputed regulator of both public and private broadcasting. The regulatory body received extended power in 1976 when the Act was amended to include telecommunications under the jurisdiction of the CRTC (renamed the Canadian Radio-television and Telecommunications Commission).

Prime Minister Lester Pearson wanted a tame intellectual on the Commission and picked Frye. [36] The first chair of the CRTC, Pierre

35 "Frye on Innis," p. xxxii.
36 Cayley, *Northrop Frye*, p. 162.

Juneau, did not really care about Frye attending Commission hearings; he wanted him largely for discussions about theories of communication with the research department. Frye took this challenge seriously: "I worked reasonably hard at it."[37]

The head of the CRTC research was Roderique Chiasson, a Maritimer of remarkable breadth and much hands-on experience in film and television. Chiasson and his CRTC research colleague, André Martin, an important contributor to communications thought and research, developed a long-lasting relationship with Frye that continued through to the cooperative editing of the Innis manuscript discussed earlier.

While Frye was known for his shyness and his tendency to answer questions directly, often without elaboration, he felt comfortable talking freely with his two CRTC colleagues, communication thinkers in their own right. The Frye-Chiasson-Martin conversations ranged from the philosophy of communication to the technology and the regulatory dimensions of communication. Out of this dialogue, with penetrating questions and comments, evolved a meaningful record that helped Frye formulate his views in a more cohesive manner. This experience had a long-lasting effect on Frye's attitude to the media of mass communications, especially the broadcast sector. Many years later, in the 1980s, in such Canadian Broadcasting Corporation programs as IDEAS, and in published interviews,[38] Frye did not deviate much from his earlier views: the foundations of his outlook on mass media were shaped and refined in large part during his tenure as a CRTC commissioner.

Central to Frye's views are the fundamentals of Canada that form the communication environment. His interpretation of Innis' "oral tradition" concept where culture moves backward in time towards the headwaters of tradition appears to come out of the conversations. The search for fundamentals was itself a voyage backwards in time and a harvesting of the cultural heritage and traditions that have worked their way into the Canadian psyche from the earliest days of settlements to the present.

---

37 Cayley, *Northrop Frye*, p. 162.
38 For example: Cayley, *Northrop Frye*, and Robert D. Denham, ed. *Northrop Frye: A World in a Grain of Sand* (New York: Peter Lang, 1991).

The Canadian communications environment encompasses the geography and physical features, the climate, the defensive characteristics that secured the viability of the settlements, the negotiation tradition of national development in contrast to the revolutionary experience in the United States, the influence of immigration and the strong local and international feelings of Canadians in the absence of strong national feelings. Yet other concepts introduced by Frye into his communication thesis include the "latitude thing" (tied to his vision of the east-west axis) and the "longitude thing" which relates to the magnetic pull into American culture. He speaks to the colors of Canada – black and white – tied to the fierce winters. Canada's pastoral tradition, the presence of anarchism, its separatist tendencies, and the absence of class, all figure prominently in the Frye formula.

These concepts provide rich detail to Frye's big picture of the role of media of communications and their projected means to influence society. In essence, he looks at two sides of the communications equation relating to the interaction of media and society. To use his own language, they are: the *means* of media influence and the *response* to media influence. The dynamics of these two forces are shaped by the very essence of Canada, its people, languages, religions, and landscape.

The diagram below depicts Frye's views on media influence. The content of the media is a central component of this influence. The Canadian context determines in large part the meaning and relevance of the content. In the bottom half of the diagram (Means of Media Influence) the factors contributing to the shaping of the content are illustrated under the two broad classifications: Imaginative and Regulative. The upper half of the diagram (Response to Media Influence) depicts the likely outcome flowing from society's response to the content. Content that focuses on issues of true significance and concern promotes shared awareness of goals and objectives and thus contributes to identity formation. The content can also be a negative force in promoting hate and panic. (Principal features of the diagram are discussed below.)

For Frye, the important job, "the fundamental central job of communications is to create the community and dissolve the mob." In this thesis he skips a layer relating to the four critical functions of mass communication: information, interpretation, education, and entertainment. The sum total of these four essential tasks leads to the media having a role in holding society together, conveying the continuity

Diagram Illustrating Northrop Frye's Views on Media Influence

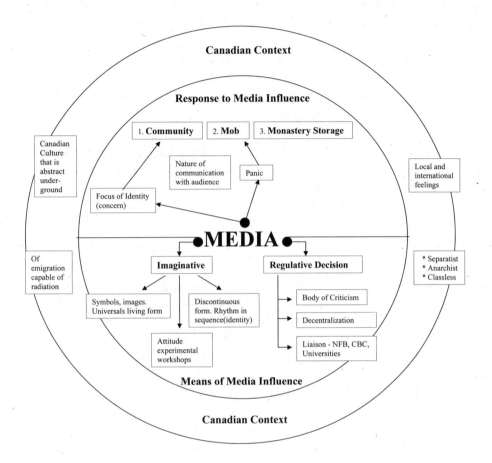

Source: Northrop Frye, Rod Chiasson and André Martin

of the culture and the values that define society.[39] In short, the media are the support structure for the community. For Frye, this is the primary goal which cannot be achieved unless the media carry out their essential tasks in a meaningful manner, free of censorship and other roadblocks.

39 For a more detailed discussion of the functions of mass communication, see Arthur Siegel, *Politics and the Media in Canada,* 2nd edition (Toronto: McGraw Hill-Ryerson Press, 1996), pp. 18–35.

The notion of community is at the heart of the Frye thesis: "community and communication are interdependent ideas." The community is locally and regionally based in the first instance. There has to be an awareness of the environment, "if you are not aware, you've really had it." The message from the communicator has to have relevance. As an example of relevance, Frye points out that all Canadians wanted to hear about the moon shot – the first landing on the moon – that was to take place the following week (July 21, 1969). "If one of those astronauts were a Canadian, the interest in this country would be a hundred times what it is." In summary, the challenge for the media is sensitivity to the environment, understanding the community it is reaching out to, and to reach out with relevance. These are key ingredients in creating ·identity.

If support structure of community is the primary goal, dissolving the mob is the complementary challenge. Those who constitute the mob need to be channeled into the community. The mob carries with it the danger of violence, violence without any teleological sense. The mob is activated by a response to a particular symbol, an arousal tied to the characteristic that a mob is only capable of simultaneous perception. Mob is of course inseparable from the notion of group.

Frye's comments about the mob came at a time of widespread street violence in the United States and many other countries. He had seen mob activity while visiting the University of California in Berkeley that had a People's Park, little more than a stretch of mud about the length of a city block. The mob saw it as a "Garden of Eden with a fence around it." The vision of the mob is often tied to protest marches. The mob, however, does not march: the mob drifts. "Somebody says, let's go and smash that shop," and so they go there and then they go somewhere else.

Using simple down-to-earth language, as he frequently did in conversation, Frye expanded on his visit to the University of California: "I'm still full of Berkeley – Telegraph Avenue [a landmark street in the University city] is a place which is full of what they call the 'street people.' In other words, it is a drifting mob without much sense of home."

The mob may have some internal groupings as in the case of Berkeley where there were small contemplative groups such as "people studying yoga and listening to some Tibetan Lama, this kind of thing."

Furthermore, there are other distinctions that can be made. There is a difference between a mob, surrounded by the police, shouting "get the pigs!" and a group listening to a folk singer such as La Bolduc (famous at the time, especially in Quebec) because she is speaking for the group that she is addressing, thus providing a focus of identity. Frye sees this latter example of community as a very opposite of the mob. The distinction is clear: the mob has a focus of hatred, the genuine community must have a "focus of identity."

Media have the means to help build community as well as create the mob. The nature of the communications experience is a key factor: in the positive sense it is focused on identity, concern with relevance to the community. Alternately, the response to media content can create panic, precipitate a focus on hatred and provide building blocks for the mob. There is a third dimension to the Frye thesis in response to media influence: Monastery Storage. It refers to the important function of the media as a storehouse for information and ideas, reflecting the culture of our times. It is the sum total of stored communication content that is a key aspect of the transmission of culture across the society and the transfer of the cultural legacy from one generation to the next.

Looking at the other side of the equation, Means of Media Influence, there are two major components: imaginative and regulative (see diagram). The imaginative relates to the process of shaping media content and incorporates changes that may be required over time and space to reflect changing patterns in learning and how messages are understood. Frye examines three dimensions of the imaginative: (1) symbols, images and universals, (2) attitude and (3) discontinuous form incorporating rhythm in sequence (i.e., the picture that emerges in our imagination over time from information coming from a variety of sources).

Frye speaks of the generation gap in society and the implications of this for communication. Over a 25 year period as a teacher at the University of Toronto, he noted a significant change in the learning process that in earlier days was almost entirely linear; communication was perceived as a step-by-step direction, turning the pages to get to the end. The younger generation, brought up on new styles of movies, television, folk and pop singers, can absorb simultaneously, in today's jargon, multi-tasking. There is then a distinction between two kinds of processes that succeeded each other in time: the linear participation and the simultaneous apprehension. The development of new media is a key factor in this process. It provides a new opening for learning. As Frye puts it:

> As you develop new media they tend to focus on the experimental side and older media then take over the teleological side. Television is very largely for presenting the world as it appears, radio and still more the newspapers become the teleological (side) of comment.[40]

Frye is enthusiastic about the modern audience with its acquired skills of simultaneous apprehension in communication. In the mid-20th century, education was teleological, a gradual unfolding, where students went from grade one to grade two, and so on. There were strict curricular parameters. Grade six materials could not encroach on grade seven materials. But as Frye put it, "all of this is junk now."

The regulative dimension of the Means of Media Influence (see diagram) is an issue that figures large in Frye's thinking. While media institutions are organized by individuals, there are constraints to the kind of tinkering that is possible in a democratic society. There are parameters created by language, geography and physical landscape, ideology, the nature of the political and economic systems, among other factors. Censorship is out of the question. But as the Canadian experience shows, regulation in broadcasting can be used in a positive sense, up to a point. Frye did not like regulation because he was worried about its potential use for censorship. He thought the CRTC was not always sure about its objectives, it needs to foster a climate of dynamic balance in broadcasting where creative people feel comfortable and receive recognition. The CRTC was overly concerned with economic issues – especially the profitability of broadcasting – and was not sufficiently focused on issues that troubled him: patterns of advertising and propaganda. At the same time he appreciated the merits of regulation, especially on such issues as panic and hate literature.

Frye has a broad view of the regulative dimension; it went far beyond the rulings of the CRTC. Communications policy, for example,

---

40 Excerpts of transcriptions of taped discussions between Northrop Frye, Roderique Chiasson, and André Martin, arranged under the title: "Communications About Canadian Fundamentals," p. 82, hereafter cited as *Excerpts*.

is sometimes carried out through tax rulings that, in practice, ensure Canadian ownership of the print media. Two areas of special interest that Frye views as regulative in nature are criticism and liaison.

A body of criticism from across the society, such as newspaper and magazine criticism, discussions in Parliament, audience complaints and other avenues of comment are important. So is the role of universities where communications was emerging as a discipline.

The people-to-people interaction, or as Frye calls it, the liaison aspect of regulative influence on the media has been largely overlooked. The CRTC has not served as a catalyst for liaison and neither did its predecessor, the Board of Broadcast Governors. The absence of a liaison structure is a disappointment because liaison could stimulate creativity and new ways of presentation. The National Film Board and the CBC could benefit from liaison especially in providing a connecting link between creative people.

Culture and Communication
Culture is indigenous and local; it cannot be planned. Communication is at the very heart of culture and serves as the building blocks of community, identity and unity. But Canada faces enormous challenges in the easy flow of communications that could make a meaningful contribution to evolvement of culture and identity. These challenges include the physical landscape, the uneven population distribution, the bilingualism of Canada in a multicultural environment and the American factor.[41]

Frye says the approach to Canadian culture should be to create conditions under which native energy can be released. But, as he noted, there is also a great wave breaking over the landscape which carries with it mostly the Americanization of Canada. He referred to the opening of the Canadian market, a passive and receptive market. At the same time, there were important happenings taking place in Canada: "It is just a matter of keeping doors opening so that they have a chance to emerge."[42]

He saw institutions like the CRTC, the National Film Board and the CBC as having been set up to help assure that there is a Canadian

41 Siegel, *Politics and the Media*, pp. 1–17.
42 *Excerpts*, p. 47.

dimension to our communications offering. Nationally subsidized forms of communications and cultural expression have been seen as essential for what has been called the marginal society of Canada.

On numerous occasions, Frye reminds us of the truth of John Grierson's powerful aphorism that identity is not something you analyze; it is something you create in actions. Identity, culture and communication are part of the same package. Frye inevitable returns to the dynamics of interaction, an interaction he sees everywhere, even in the rocks of Canada.

> It's got something to do with the rocks, too, there are so many damn rocks in this country, the pre-Cambrian shield is just lying all over the country, and the sense of the vegetation just pushing its way out of the rock, and the tremendous sort of mine culture in this part of the world. It's all part of the same cultural complex.[43]

Time and time again Frye emphasizes the local dimension of culture and the need for decentralization in broadcasting. The whole orthodox tendency, he pointed out, is in the wrong direction, a centralizing tendency. "It is founded on journalistic instinct which is deducted as part of headline news, and fans out from there ... this became a kind of habit."

Frye believes there has to be consensus for change because, in a sense, we all have a centralizing habit. "This habit is being formulated at the television station and the supermarket: we are all fed in the same processes."

"All culture," says Frye, "begins as a preventative against the inertia of habit." But change for the sake of change is not the answer because "you simply disturb one habit without fostering the other." He thought the CRTC could and should help to bring about decentralization in broadcasting. But it would require that everybody believed in the merits of decentralization, and would require a very strong decentralization apparatus to see the process through. "Otherwise it would be just a vacuum." He did not think the hour of decision for such CRTC activity had arrived; "it had better be postponed."

---

43 *Excerpts*, p. 4.

Regulation and the CRTC

Frye was not enthusiastic about the regulation of broadcasting but appreciated its necessity. He was one of the three CRTC commissioners on a Special Committee of Enquiry which concluded that "bias" is bound to occur in programs and we should not expect "perfect balance" or "total objectivity." While there is the "right to be wrong," at the same time to engage in "exaggeration" for dramatic effect may damage credibility.

He seems to be particularly influenced by the *Air of Death*, a CBC television documentary on the subject of pollution, broadcast in November, 1967, described at the time as perhaps the most controversial program in Canadian TV history.

In his conversations with Chiasson and Martin, Frye focused on his reaction to the program: "The reporting of the news is in the public interest, the creation of the news is against the public interest. Covering a student riot is in the public interest, but inciting the student riot in order to have a more interesting picture is against the public interest." There is an important difference between concern and panic. The arousal of concern over pollution is very much in the public's interest. At the same time the way the *Air of Death* program was handled led to a situation where the community of Dunnville, Ontario – featured in the documentary – found itself on one side, the mob on the other, "In this kind of thing, a mob always has a scapegoat. So to the tourist going to Dunnville, they say, everything is poisoned in Dunnville. And this is what I mean by panic. This is what is against the public interest."[44]

The thorny question of taste and morals was another difficult area in regulation. Expressions deemed obscene in the 1950s – the "famous four letter words" – were less than 20 years later in the 1970s no longer obscene. The obscene words in the 1970s were "nigger," "wop," "frog," words that create a mob, words that devalue a whole group of human beings. Defining "hate literature" that builds up a sense of hatred and contempt was a concern of legislatures across Canada. What had developed was a more realistic perspective of what is socially dangerous.

44 *Excerpts*, p. 62.

Separatism and Unity

Frye was sensitive to fragmentation pulls in Canada precipitated by language and regionalism that are, nevertheless, contained by the strong cohesive forces. He lays out both sides of the equation relating to national unity.

"Every part of Canada, he said at the end of 1968, "is separatist, it is not only Quebec." The Maritimes are separate from Canada which they think of as another country, the Acadians are separate from the Quebec French-Canadians, the English Maritimers are separate, and there are similar tendencies for separation in Newfoundland, the Prairies and British Columbia. To Frye's thinking, there was little difference between French Canadian separatism and the other kinds of separatism. The Quebec situation has a particular language factor, but he thought even that was not unique. It is the defense of language, however, "that has pushed it further in a political direction."

Elaborating on separatism, Frye speaks of Canada's conservative direction, which tries to hold the various regions within the union: "it's conservative and it's romantic and everything which is heroic in our history has to do with the drive to the west and the holding of our country together." At the same time there is the magnetic pull of the United States which resulted in half a million Maritimers living in New England. Ontarians moved to New York and the mid-western states. This pattern extends to the west. Because of language, the magnetic forces pulling to the south have not been as strong in Quebec.[45]

Immigration and Culture: The Anarchist Fact

Frye speaks of a strong anarchist fact in Canada. He said the radical movement of our time is anarchist and that means that it is local and separate and breaks down into small units. "That is our tradition and that is our genius." He speaks of the waves of immigration to Canada in the post-World War Two period and notes the large number of people who had been here for a short time. For example, in 1949, one out of every five Toronto residents had been there for less than a year. It has been a peaceful absorption.

45 *Excerpts*, p. 55.

We have not had race riots, we have not had ethnical riots, and we have not had the tremendous pressure collisions that they have had in the American cities because Canada is naturally anarchist. These people have settled down into their own communities, they work with other communities and the whole pattern of life fits in.[46]

Much energy can be harvested from this situation.

In contrast to the anarchist presence in Canadian culture, Frye sees no such link between Marxism and Canadian culture. International communism, the great radical movement of the 20th century, "took no hold in Canada at all, there were no Marxist poets or painters... there was no connecting point."

Canadian Content: Attitude
One of the basic problems for Canadian broadcasting is projecting Canadian Presence, that is, the mass media should focus on Canada, reflect the Canadian environment and interpret the world through Canadian eyes. The most cost effective approach for Canadian broadcasting, however, is to plug into the American stations and distribute American programming in Canada at a fraction of the cost of producing equivalent Canadian programs. (The practice goes back to the early days of radio.) This is a problem for the private broadcasters today but at the time Frye was discussing the issue (1968), the CBC was also heavy into American programming. Efforts to Canadianize broadcasting led to Canadian content regulations that helped to address the radio problem, but have not been particularly effective in commercial television. Canadian Presence on TV, for the most part, is regarded as a luxury and an obstacle to profitability and thus runs counter to the interests of the marketplace.

The CRTC's Canadian content requirements continue to generate great controversy. Frye was not enthusiastic about the approach to content regulation, which he referred to as the "55% and 60% thing." He wanted the criteria shifted from content to attitude.

There is a specific Canadian attitude toward world events. As soon as I cross the border and start teaching at American schools, I feel

like a Finn entering Russia or a Dane entering Germany. I have
moved from small observant country into a big power complex.
Now, that makes for a difference in attitude and as long as that
attitude is preserved, I wouldn't care too much about the content.
But the difficulty is of course that you can check up on content,
because it's quantity and you can't check up on attitude. What I
would like to see is 95% Canadian attitude.[47]

Frye frequently describes Canada as an observant country. He sees
"observant" as contemplative and not passive; it is not geared to
immediate action; it lacks a feeling of involvement. There is the danger
of collapsing into passivity, but he is not particularly concerned. "The
whole secret of wisdom is to be detached but not withdrawn."

Technology and Culture: New Media
One of the principal features of the Toronto School is the implication
of technological change in communication on the politics, culture and
social structure of society. Frye writes eloquently on this theme in his
introduction to the Innis manuscript (discussed earlier), but he is clearly
pragmatic about new media. Frye was sensitive to the fact that new
technologies have not always helped Canada to deal effectively with
the great challenges in communications flow. On the contrary new
technology has often provided new gateways for the influx of American
programs.

Frye sees the broadcast media as the technological development in
20th century communications that could cross the immense gaps in the
country's internal lines of communications and enable us to see the
larger Canadian picture. He had great concerns about how effectively
we were employing these new tools. An example came in 1968 when
he was briefed on the potentials of two-way communication that would
enable people to talk back to media; not only would they be receivers,
but also senders. He commented that communications is not just a
matter of finding walkie-talkie reporters interviewing people; it's not
just a matter of open-line programs. "When you are interviewing people
at random, you are still assuming that they are passive units. What you
will get is more or less reflex prejudices; and people fall in with this."

47 *Excerpts*, p. 38.

For him, meaningful communication is a dialogue.

Frye was distressed about the direction of broadcasting in Canada. He felt that the drive was on developing the technology to foster centralization at the expense of promoting culture, reminding us again of the local aspect of culture. As for globalization, or world diffusion, through the use of satellites, Canada was extending its energies on technology, on buildings and problems of programs.

Frye felt there should be an emphasis on thinking in terms of meaningful cultural content. "Things that hold society together reach out into the past." He was worried about a lack of appreciation of what Canada needs beyond hardware in communications: "We will set up the hardware with great speed and efficiency and there will be a long silence."

III   Frye in Theory and Practice

Frye was much more than an armchair theorist because his views were tested in the pragmatism as a regulator of broadcasting. One of his most important contributions to Canadian communication was his involvement with the Committee of Inquiry into National Broadcasting in 1977. He served reluctantly on this Committee which was organized by the CRTC shortly before Frye was slated to retire from the Commission. His presence, however, was required because of the prestige and sense of fairness he would add to a highly controversial situation.

The Parti Quebecois – which sought to take Quebec out of the federal union – was elected to power in the fall of 1976, and the country was in an uproar. Prime Minister Pierre Trudeau, Jean Chrétien, then serving as Justice Minister, and other cabinet ministers were highly critical of Radio Canada because they perceived the French language service of the Canadian Broadcasting Corporation as furthering the cause of separation and contributing to the electoral victory of the P.Q. Mr. Trudeau wanted a Royal Commission. For many people the attacks of Government on the media threaten freedom of the press.

The Committee of Inquiry worked diligently despite some roadblocks by the CBC in making relevant material available. The Committee's *Report* presents damning conclusions: "the electronic media in Canada, English as well as French, are biased to the point of subversiveness.

They are biased because, so far as they are able, they prevent Canadians from getting enough balanced information about Canada to make informed decisions regarding the country's future." But the most critical comment was: "As presented by the [broadcast] media, Canada is in a state of deep schizophrenia; if English and French Canadians were on different planets there could hardly be a greater contrast of views and information."[48]

The Committee of Inquiry asked Frye (along with CRTC Chairman Harry Boyle) to pen the *Report* on its behalf. In this *Report* he raises many of the concepts and ideas found in his conversations. He puts them together in a meaningful context, providing a blend of theory and practice. The *Report*, opposed the appointment of a Royal Commission. The *Report* is pure Frye. There is no trace of the tame intellectual in Frye's involvement.

The CRTC sometimes asked Frye to take on tasks that provided almost comic relief. An unpublished document called *The Frye Diet* displays his strengths and weaknesses as a television critic. He was fed (i.e., asked to watch) a dozen, or so, television programs and invited to comment on them. The programs dealt with music, politics, history, comedy, Olympic sports, beauty pageants, nakedness and the Sesame Street children's series. He uses the approach of literary criticism to provide an often humorous but also insightful analysis of the techniques of television and film.

Frye is always interesting, his chatter and his writing are clear, precise, and peppered with an underlying humour, as if he is chuckling to himself. His language can be salty and sexy, though invariably in good taste. When he refers to one particular quote that Innis uses, he describes it as being of imbecilic proportions but he quickly puts the comment in context and forgives the author.

This paper focuses on Frye's unpublished papers that provide insights into his theoretical vision of the media of communications. There is a summary of his major pronouncements and an attempt to elaborate where he took it for granted that his listeners (Chiasson and Martin) would be filling in the gaps on their own. When there is an attempt to expand the meaning of what he is saying, he is straightforward in

48 Committee of Inquiry into the National Broadcasting Service, *Report*. Ottawa: CRTC, July 1977, p. 62.

declaring that he does not agree. He summarizes his viewpoints in a dynamic manner.

Frye's concerns about Canadian unity were neutralized by his appreciation that there were strong ties that held the country together. The answer to Canadian unity is not to be found in bringing about uniformity, attempts at homogeneity would be counterproductive.

Canadian identity, Frye argued, has its roots in the diversity that is a product of the fundamentals of Canada: the physical characteristics, the climate, the regional variations, patterns of development along the east-west axis. The culture of Canada is local and needs to feed into a national information flow. Canadians everywhere have a local/regional stake that is tied (or needs to be tied) to the national communication network. The obvious repetition in this paper about the importance of the local aspect of culture is a reflection of the way Frye continuously repeats himself to emphasize the centrality of this point.

Frye died in 1991 at the age of 79. His views discussed here – except for the introduction to the Innis manuscript – were put forward two decades earlier. He was a thinker with firm opinions that remain vital today. He readily admitted changed outlooks without needing to explain away earlier views. It was only natural to him that scholarship would grow and evolve, not remain static. He was a teacher who changed his ways with the times. He welcomed change in society and saw his own generation as ironic in its outlook and adapted to the more utopian idealistic and revolutionary perception of the young.

His pronouncements about television were made nearly four decades ago. At the time, Frye was changing from black and white television to color. He did not take well to gadgets and for one reason or another was viewing black and white on his screen although he had made the conversion to color.

Television technology has come a long way since 1968 when Frye began his nine-year involvement in the regulation of broadcasting. He had an appreciation for the power of technology and was quick to admit that technological change had a momentum of its own that would overwhelm, or make redundant, regulation that stands in its way.

Frye, writing 20 years ago about Innis, said that the works of a scholar of 30 years earlier cannot be seen only in contemporary terms because the information and sources underlying that scholarship become questionable or obsolete. Can the same be said about Frye?

When he made the pronouncements discussed here, television was in its early stages, it was before the integration of communication satellites into the domestic broadcasting system in 1972. Computers were available but not a household item. There was no Internet and no e-mail. Digital television was only an emerging concept and experimental. The convergence of communication – in terms of technology and in the corporate boardrooms – was far off. The result of technological innovation has been greater centralization which Frye perceived as a real problem in relation to culture and communication. In the late 1980s, Frye's views had not changed significantly from those he held 20 years earlier. Technological change seemed to confirm his views rather than undermine them.

Frye was a theologian and ordained minister who did not believe in God as God is generally perceived. (Interestingly, McLuhan and Innis also had strong and distinctive religious influences in their thinking and lifestyle.) Frye was an important figure in the regulation of broadcasting who did not have much use for regulation. He watched television although he did not care for its programs. He emphasized organizational structure in society while recognizing the importance of anarchism. He championed protest at the same time that he sought to control the mob.

The apparent championing of opposites are not necessarily contradictions. Frye, like Innis, sees the progress of culture and society as a product of opposing forces; stalemate can open the path for creativity.

This paper examined in the first instance the linkage of Innis, McLuhan and Frye as the major Canadian theorists of what has become known as the Toronto School. One of the shared anchors was the study of the implications for society stemming from changing technology of communications. In the early 1950s, barely two years before his death, Innis explored the dominant modes of communications in ancient civilization and found that new technology brought with it power alignment, integration and change in society. In his unpublished manuscript, *Dispersal and Concentration*, Innis finds confirmation as he moves forward over the centuries. Each technology, Innis argued, carries with it a bias favoring time or space. The term technological determination is associated with such a theoretical framework. McLuhan, in his examination of the impact of print on western civilization, argued that print provided a fertile field for nationalism, industrialism, mass markets, universal literacy and mass education. McLuhan's principal focus, however, was on the implications for society stemming from electronic communication. His prophetic outlook generated great interest and at times significant criticism. There is a revived interest in McLuhan, attesting to the permanent value Frye attributed to McLuhan's work three decades earlier.

Northrop Frye, who includes himself in the theoretical company of Innis and McLuhan, gives particular attention to societal context and how this affects the influence of communication. Frye challenges some of the basic premises of both Innis and McLuhan. The three anchors of the Toronto School moved in different directions and thus provided a multidimensional and mosaic perceptive through their theoretical contributions.

Of the three, Frye was the most pragmatic; he had to be in that he was also a hands-on person in the regulation of broadcasting. One of Frye's most important contributions is Canadianism, the particular characteristics or fundamentals of Canada and their implications for communication needs, goals, and possibilities.

Frye's pragmatism extends to the problems and challenges of Canadian communications; he sees them as part of the reality condition of Canada and integrates the challenges into his schema. His very definitions of Canadian identity are rooted in the basic characteristics of the country. They are not handicaps. Anarchism, heterogeneity, weak nationalism, localism, regionalism, harsh winters, insecurities, these are forces – neither positive nor negative – that shape the Canadian context.

The Canadian contribution to communication technology and experimentations in the 20th century, ranging from the building of a Marconi receiving station at Glace Bay, Nova Scotia, to space technology – are at once outstanding and revealing. Outstanding because Canada is a relatively small county in terms of population, and revealing in that we perceived broadcasting technology as providing the best answer to building a communications network that could help bond the nation and provide a support structure for identity. It was typical of the 20th century, said Frye, "that you created the technology thing first."

Technology in itself is not the answer; technology needs to be used to carry content that fosters culture at its birthplace: the local community. A nationally imposed culture, if it were possible, would lead to uniformity that would threaten the fabric of Canada; Canada could lose its identity and its soul. As it is, Frye was troubled by the idea that Canada would remain an abstraction to Canadians. As Frye warns in his conversations, "we will set up the hardware with great speed and efficiency and there will be a long silence."

PART II

EXTENSIONS

PAUL FROSH

6. The Bias of Bias: Innis, Lessing and the Problem of Space

Intellectual trends are not always easy to predict. Yet it is fairly safe to assume that the writings of Harold Innis will figure very little in the emergence of new approaches in media theory or in the exploration of new areas of research. Like the image of Canada itself, Innis' work is treated very much as a "hinterland" within the main schools of Anglo-American communication studies: dauntingly large (in reference if not in volume), idiosyncratic, reassuringly "there" and yet relatively under-populated.

Regarding the latter – a poor analogy, perhaps, for the dearth of enthusiastic readers – it is Innis' writing style rather than his nationality that is usually felt to be at fault. Indeed, Innis' writing *is* notoriously difficult to bear for very long.[1] Unclear, repetitive, condensed and frequently contradictory, it comprises disjointed yet seemingly interminable descriptions of communications media and loosely connected details of political, economic, religious, technological and cultural developments, all staged across vast swathes of history and geography. There are very few interpreters and admirers of Innis who do not lament the result, or at least remark upon it with bemusement.[2] And once one does make it "through" the writing style, to use an unfashionable metaphor, Innis' thought – which in vulgar summary can appear so amenable to generalization and abstraction – turns out to be subtle, specific, prone to paradox. Above all, it suffers from what Judith Stamps has called "an almost aggressive tendency to undertheorize" (1995: 43). Compared to the invigorating prose, pithy quotability and

---

1 Though he's in fine company on that score: Adorno, Lacan, Derrida, to name only a few of the more fashionable thinkers.

2 See Blondheim (2003) for a fascinating discussion of the competing "explanations" of Innis' prose style.

compelling generalizing capabilities of someone like McLuhan, Innis just isn't sexy.[3]

McLuhan, of course, is the prime counter-example of Canadian success, alchemically transmuting some of Innis' qualities – referential sweep, idiosyncratic style of thought, a concern with technology – into a successfully exported brand. As a result, those working in new areas of research have found occasion to "return" eagerly to his work. To take only the most prominent example: quite a number of recently published books and papers have – with varying degrees of sophistication – proclaimed McLuhan's relevance to the era of computer-mediated communication, with some practically canonizing him as the tragic prophet of virtuality.[4] However insightful the more serious of these reappraisals may be as individual analyses, *en masse* they have been accompanied by a sonorous silence regarding Innis. Almost no published work has engaged with his thought in a way that implies that it might be remotely useful for understanding the advent and implications of new media.

Neglect on this scale is both a great shame and a missed opportunity

3   Stamps' book, an attempt to read Innis and McLuhan as critics of modernity and counterparts of Adorno and Benjamin, is one of the most sophisticated and impressive recent commentaries on Innis. This article is necessarily written in implicit dialogue with her ground-breaking work – and ultimately against her endorsement of one of Innis' basic premises: the ontological privileging of time over space, and of the oral tradition and sound over writing and "the visual."

4   A number of these claims appear in introductions to reissues of McLuhan's books (for instance, Lapham, 1994), or in contributions to anthologies of and on his writings (such as Moos [1997], Benedetti and DeHard [1997], [Eric] McLuhan and Zingrone [1997]), published in what are presumably more congenial times. Prominent reappraisals of McLuhan in the "digital age" include Marchand (1989), Levinson (1999) and – via Baudrillard – Genosko (1999). Among these, Horrocks' (2000) book is notable not only for its brevity but for its extremely acute and intelligent exploration of McLuhan's thought *and* its contemporary reassessment. The fashion for Baudrillard, and his own critical interest in McLuhan (see especially "Requeim for the Media" in Baudrillard, 1981), has also been a factor in the revival, with (a somewhat altered) McLuhan returning to English-speaking readers via French post-structuralism. Also reaching Anglophone readers in recent years is the German "media discourse analysis" of Freidrich Kittler, which has been traced to McLuhan, among others (notably Foucault, Lacan and Derrida) as an inspiration – including by Kittler himself (1999: the introduction by translators Winthrop-Young and Wutz is especially useful on these connections).

for the reinvigoration of communication theory. For Innis' thought, notwithstanding the notorious difficulty of his prose style, actually intersects powerfully with a number of central approaches within media and cultural studies, among them the political economy of communications and the sociology of culture. Additionally, Innis' central conceptual tool – the spatial or temporal "bias" of communications media – is strikingly relevant to many of the hottest topics on the media and cultural studies agenda (not to mention sociology): globalization and localization, the mediation of historical and collective memory, the distribution of power and knowledge, the social construction of space and time in modern and postmodern cultures, and of course – the impact of new technologies.[5]

It is impossible within the space of this short paper to do justice to the important congruities – as well as productive differences – between Innis' thought and some of these other approaches. Rather, I want to broaden the platform from which such comparisons might be launched in the future by revisiting, and rethinking, Innis' key distinction between spatial and temporal biases. I'll proceed at first by attempting to delineate the distinction more thoroughly as it appears in a small number of key texts (mainly the essays "The Bias of Communication" and "The Problem of Space," and certain sections of *Empire and Communications*).[6] Next I'll try to situate it in relation to another central space-time dichotomy in communications and cultural theory: the image/text distinction. This second section will hopefully bring out the structural affinities between Innis' "bias" over the orality/writing relationship – an anxiety usually reserved for a handful of highly literate scholars – and a far more widespread fear: that contemporary Western societies are dominated by visual images and pictorial media which threaten literate culture. Clearly, revisiting Innis' thought in this way will invoke different understandings of the space-time dialectic: as vectors affecting social and political structure through the distribution of knowledge; as the

5   Stamps also notes Innis' relevance to some of these concerns (1995: 4–6).

6   Admittedly this can seem a little narrowly focused. In my defence I would say, first, that Innis' writing on communication is sufficiently unified to allow one to recover his main themes from only a few texts without doing them too much violence; and second that such a focus facilitates an exploration of the texture of Innis' thought through relatively close textual analysis, something his writing style demands and rewards.

formal structures in which media produce representations; and as the key dimensions in which subjective and inter-subjective identities are created. Along the way I hope not only to explore Innis' continuing relevance, but to contribute to the debate about the significance of media to social organization and cultural experience.

Bias: Portability, Durability, Coding, Representation

To begin with, it is worth looking once again at the notion of "bias." What does Innis mean by the "bias" of a communication technology? The elliptical nature of Innis' writing makes answering this a difficult task. Perhaps the clearest and best known definition is given in the essay "The Bias of Communication," originally published in the book of the same name in 1951. On the first page bias is immediately connected to the question of knowledge *dissemination*: temporal bias results from the use of a heavy, durable medium generally not suited to transportation. Knowledge is thereby perpetuated across generations. Spatial bias results from the use of light, easily transportable but also highly perishable media, which disseminates knowledge across territory.

This is perhaps the best known definition of what Innis means by "bias." Connecting the physical properties of materials used in communication technologies – size, weight, longevity – to the distribution of knowledge, it is effectively a *political* notion. This is because such material properties allow for the distinctively different dominance of powerful social groups based on the unequal dissemination of information, or in Innis' terms: monopolies of knowledge (for time-binding media, religious hierarchies are the most popular example, while space-binding media favor the secular administrative elites of empires). Hence, what we can call "distribution bias" foregrounds the ways in which technologies allocate knowledge and power among groups by structuring spatial and temporal relations within a social organization. Innis' insight here seems to be that communication media are what Giddens (1990) calls "disembedding" mechanisms: systems that enable the "lifting out" of social relations from their particular context and their coordination across large stretches of space and time.[7]

---

7   Giddens' primary interest is, of course, the importance of disembedding mechanisms

And the key interest in space and time as fundamental parameters of communication technologies is also motivated by political concerns: the need for societies simultaneously to maintain their control over a given territory and to reproduce themselves temporally. This is why, for Innis, the bias of a technology is not merely a matter of potentiality, of enabling territorial expansion or cross-generational reproduction. It is also fundamentally a political *problem*: the bias of a dominant communication technology has to be counterbalanced somehow, by alternative media technologies or by other non-technological means, if a civilization is to protect itself from either the threat of spatial disintegration or of temporal exhaustion.[8]

Hence, in one of Innis' examples, the spatial expansion (after around 1580 B.C.E.) of ancient Egyptian political government over peoples of other cultures and religions – which followed the rise of (spatially biased) papyrus and the brush and the development of hieratic writing – "*compelled* [my emphasis] the king to attempt a solution to problems of continuity" (1999: 35). This solution was attempted mainly through the establishment of an imperial religion which did not distinguish between Egyptian and non-Egyptian subjects. Thus the spatial bias of a communication technology is counterbalanced by an *ideological* initiative. And this ideological initiative failed (as did this Egyptian empire, in Innis' account) because of the entrenched power and opposition of a social group – the priestly class – who enjoyed a monopoly of knowledge facilitated by a *prior*, time-binding, communication technology: hieroglyphic writing and stone. So different, competing monopolies of knowledge based upon what we might call (with apologies to Raymond Williams) "residual" and "emergent" time-binding and space-binding media may be *co-present* in social systems, producing historically specific tensions and struggles for dominance.

(particularly symbolic tokens and expert systems) for the emergence of specifically *modern* societies.

8   The need to "balance" the biases of different media is explicitly spelled out in *Empire and Communication*: "[Large scale political organizations] have tended to flourish under conditions in which the bias of one medium toward decentralization is offset by the bias of another medium towards centralization" (1972: 7. See also page 170).

It may not be clear from my description that the notion of bias, at least in Innis' hands, is very far from being a blunt instrument. Its use is always historically particular and highly sensitive to cultural and social context. And what is perhaps even less clear from this discussion, but no less important, is that the notion of bias cannot simply be a question of the *dissemination* of knowledge across territories and generations. On the second page of the same essay Innis writes:

> We can perhaps assume that the use of a medium of communication over a long period will to some extent determine the character of knowledge to be communicated (1999: 34).

We may grope our way to understanding what Innis means by the "character of knowledge" by returning to the example of ancient Egypt. The entrenched priestly class which opposed the move to an imperial religion was "supported by a difficult script." Hence a monopoly of knowledge, and the time-biased religious social hierarchy it established, was in part an effect of *coding complexity* – a complexity whose mastery required long initiation: i.e., coding complexity can be said to be time-biased in that it both favors and depends upon the selective transmission of communication skills across caste or class generations rather than their rapid extension across territories and populations. And such a "coding bias" is available as a political weapon: hence, according to Innis, pictorial writing was deliberately maintained despite the widespread availability of (space-biased) papyrus while the administratively more efficient use of consonantal signs was strictly limited. Thus there is nothing inevitable, in Innis' account, about the emergence or dominance of a communications medium. Technology is not an independent force, miraculously acting upon society and individuals from the "outside." The development and succession of media technologies is a political and social question connected to the power of the monopolies of knowledge that they themselves support.

Readers of Joshua Meyrowitz (1985) on electronic media and print will no doubt recognize Innis as an influence here. More intriguing, perhaps, are the connections we can discern between this notion of coding bias, particularly in its temporal form, and Pierre Bourdieu's analysis of "cultural capital" as a source for the reproduction of social hierarchies (1986, 1993). Bourdieu employs "cultural capital" to refer to those socially generated practical competences, transmitted across generations by the family and the educational system (and hence closely correlated to social class), by which individuals acquire the disposition and ability to decipher cultural products. In the case of "legitimate art," for example, such competence resides in the fundamental disposition, propagated through formal and informal education and institutionalized in museums and galleries, to decipher the object stylistically and aesthetically rather than functionally; that is, to perceive it *as an artwork*. Concomitantly, this competence is manifested in the ability to read certain stylistic features of the work as *pertinent*, their significance being determined by their location within a system, known to the viewer, of stylistic and generic classifications – a competence which is usually achieved, with varying degrees of completeness, in correlation to the familial, educational and occupational background of the individual viewer.

Reading Innis through Bourdieu in this way allows us to extend the notion of "coding" bias to the monopolistic diffusion of acquired cultural dispositions and competences, and to uncouple it from a purely technical framework. Coding bias is not simply about, say, the number or complexity of characters in a writing system. Rather, it is fundamentally a *social* phenomenon, concerned with the conditions of perception, readability and intelligibility and their different manifestation among social groups whose *inequality* they help to reproduce. Moreover, "coding bias" also refers to the perceived relative social *value* of the codified object and the code which supports it: as legitimate, desirable and enduring or as common, possibly repugnant and necessarily ephemeral. Obeying a historical logic that links scarcity and complexity to power, the harder it is to acquire a code, the more legitimate and desirable it becomes – along with the cultural products whose deciphering it governs. "Coding bias" then, in this reading, assumes one of its main modern Western guises in the specification, autonomy and exclusivity of "art" and "culture" themselves, where "coding complexity" – especially in the form of scholarly and "literary" literacy – has long been the rallying cry of those opposed to the purported "leveling" tendencies of mass culture. As bearers of a "common" heritage that is in reality restricted, and of an "aesthetic" non-monetary value that makes artworks extremely expensive, the codes of art and culture transcend time in the service of elite decipherment.

In addition to "coding bias" – broad as it is (or as I have made it) – Innis' phrase "the character of knowledge" also refers to the characteristics of a communicated message. An ideological initiative such as the Egyptian monarchy's attempted imperial religion requires transmission: here spatial communication technologies are employed to disseminate a potentially time-binding belief system that will provide the empire with temporal continuity. In another example, concerning the ancient Hebrews, "concentration on the abstract in writing opened a way for an advance from blood relationship to universal ethical standards" (1999: 39): space-binding phonetic writing facilitates a space-biased belief system (ethics become universal in that they extend spatially to everyone, as opposed to the temporal selectivity of biological descent). We can call this type of bias the "ideological bias" of media (a term that Innis of course never uses), and as the example shows such an ideological bias (temporal in the case of Egyptian imperial religion) can contradict the "distribution bias" supported by the physical properties of the dominant media technology (the spatial-bias of papyrus in the Egyptian empire). In fact, Sut Jhally (1993), in an effort to make Innis shake hands with Marx, effectively elides the need for societies temporally to reproduce themselves with the notion of ideology. For Jhally time-bias appears *necessarily* as a question of ideology – the survival of social relations over time based on legitimation and consensus – while spatial bias is principally about administration and the coordinated use of force. But this is unnecessarily reductive, an attempt to align Innis' thought with the main terms of the Gramscian model: coercion and hegemony. Startlingly and rather surprisingly, it does not take into account that ideological bias can be space-binding: the rise of imperialism as a modern ideology, working in tandem with globally space-binding communication technologies and administrative structures, is perhaps the classic case in point.

With this notion of ideological bias, and to a lesser extent coding bias, Innis' thought moves from questions of a medium's physical properties to those of its message and form, to its representational characteristics. This move is bulwarked by frequent and usually unelaborated comments that imply a perceptual predisposition, whereby, for example, a monopoly of communication "based on the eye" in modern print cultures is associated with a spatial bias.[9] It is these less developed assertions

9   See "A Plea for Time" in *The Bias of Communication*. Innis' description of

of perceptual monopoly and distinction that, according to James Carey (1992), constitute the limited zone of influence between Innis and McLuhan – and, in Stamps' analysis, link Innis, McLuhan, Adorno and Benjamin in a critique of the spatial-visual and an affirmation of the temporal-oral (more of which below). But the key point of this move from the material properties of technology to those of representation is that it signals an expansion of Innis' concerns from the realm of social organization to that of culture. Carey argues that while Innis does deal with both, the primary effect of the bias of media technologies is on social structure, and only secondarily on the characteristic culture which is thereby produced: it is this two-step influence on culture which presumably makes Innis' thought amenable to attempts, such as Jhally's, to integrate it with the base-superstructure model in Marxism. In other words, even the complex intertwining of different types of space-time bias – biases of distribution, coding, ideology, and perception – are borne out of a mainly *political* motivation, to account for the social organization of power in human history.

It is difficult and risky (as Carey acknowledges) to generalize in this way about Innis' notion of bias, since much of its lasting relevance is due not to its systematic coherence but to its dialectical sensitivity, the way it illuminates the historical complexities of the relationship between technology, social organization and culture (this is one of Stamps' main claims). Nevertheless, I think that it is fair to say that what remains *relatively* untheorized in Innis' thought is the way in which the space-time biases of media technologies do in fact work culturally. How, as *symbolic and expressive resources*, do they encourage particular forms of subjective experience, modes of feeling, thought and action among individuals, as well as types of social relationship between them and how might these be sufficiently patterned within a society and period so as to constitute a characteristically "biased" culture. How, as symbolic forms structured along a space-time axis, do communication media impact upon individuals' orientations of themselves and others in space and time? Such questions are of interest not only because their answer feeds back into ideology and hence into agency and social structure,

---

communication based on the ear in the form of electronic broadcasting appears to be even more spatially biased, as it erases national boundaries.

but also because they intersect in powerfully suggestive ways with another interlinked tradition of thought: that different media tend to produce types of representation that are definitively spatial *or* temporal, with consequences for the construction of subjectivity and social relationships.

Space / Time: Image / Text

Ruth and Elihu Katz (1998) have detailed the connection between McLuhan's thought and earlier generations of European writers on the differences among the arts. Given the central themes of McLuhan's oeuvre their primary interest was linked to philosophical and scientific thinking about perceptual distinctions, especially between visual and auditory processing. However, a long tradition of aesthetic and literary criticism has based itself on the claim that different media establish representational modes that are specifically organized around the dimensions of space and time. These distinctions are not perceptual per se – or at least not in Innis and McLuhan's sense. Rather, the central dichotomy running through this tradition is between pictorial and written media, image and text, both of which can of course be grasped as visual.

Most commentators on this tradition locate the birth of its modern theoretical elaboration in eighteenth-century debates on the relationship among the arts, especially the so-called "sister arts" of poetry and painting. The best known work in these debates is Lessing's *Laocoön: An Essay Upon the Limits of Poetry and Painting*, originally published in German in 1766. Lessing, in response to theories that maintained the fundamental similarity of the arts, promoted an antithetical principle which today we would call "medium specificity": that each medium is necessarily and naturally distinctive in both physical characteristics and signifying structure, and therefore also in its ideal representational object.[10] Crucially, the distinctiveness of media was anchored in the

---

10 The literature on Lessing is extensive. Aside from Mitchell's influential reassessment (1986), Schweizer (1972) gives a good account of the historical and philosophical context of Lessing's distinction between the arts, while Wellbery (1984) provides an interesting reading of Lessing through semiotic theory.

space-time dichotomy: painting, which uses forms and colors arranged side by side in space, can only represent objects existing side by side, while the consecutive signs of poetry can express only objects in time. The peculiar subjects of painting are therefore contiguous bodies, those of poetry – sequential actions.

Lessing's distinction requires a few comments. First, it is an ontological one: it seeks to anchor the specificity of a medium in a description of its essential qualities, its *being*. Painting is spatial by nature and by necessity (not contingently or ideally), poetry temporally so. Any indications of temporality in painting or spatiality in poetry are at best mere accidents, irrelevant to the true founding principle of the art, and at worst betrayals of self. Second, the distinction is based, as W.J.T. Mitchell (1986) notes, on a "homology" between the medium's physical structure, its representational content, and the mental processes of decoding: painting consists of forms displayed in space, the forms represent bodies in space, and their decoding by the viewer is assumed to be instantaneous – it has no duration. Now, this homology is very hard to maintain in the face of counter examples from the visual arts and from literature, as Mitchell's masterly deconstruction reveals: in fact its maintenance requires a return to my first point – that any such examples are treated as exceptional, as either extraneous accidents or dangerous acts of treachery.

Which leads to the third point: that the argument from necessity becomes an argument from desire. Paintings *should only be* spatial, poems temporal. As Mitchell points out, along with Noël Carroll (1988) in his discussion of the specificity thesis in cinema, such a move reveals the *ideological* function of the ontological distinction. For if media are naturally and necessarily (i.e., automatically) spatial or temporal, why do such essential characteristics have to be policed and protected by the strictures and recommendations of critics? Ultimately such distinctions usually serve an exclusionary purpose: not to describe a naturally occurring difference but to use nature as a cover for the enforcement of a cultural hierarchy. In Lessing's case (according to Mitchell) this hierarchy makes time superior to space and yet threatened by it; more precisely, it sets the spoken and written word above the visual image in a common iconoclastic move that attempts to preserve thought from infection by the illusionistic capacities of pictorial representation. Space here becomes the a priori of the *exterior* world, against which time, the a priori dimension of *inner* consciousness and thought, must be protected.

In other words the hierarchical distinction between verbal and pictorial representation parallels the distinction between time and space, which in turn parallels the distinction between mind and world. Obeying what Derrida calls "the logic of the supplement" (1976: 141–164), space, as the organizing framework of exteriority, appears as surplus to time ("a plenitude enriching another plenitude" [Derrida, 1976: 144]), and is also thereby a potential threat to its sovereignty, signifying its radical incompleteness ("It adds only to replace. It intervenes or insinuates itself in-the-place-of" [Derrida, 1976: 145]). What is interesting here, among other things, is that verbal (temporal) media and pictorial (spatial) media are understood to express the mind-world relationship in terms of *directionality*, and that directionality can be perceived as either benign or dangerous. In the case of verbal representation, with speech as the model and writing its (potentially subversive – Derrida, 1976) surrogate, mind travels outwards towards and into the world: the dynamic sequence of temporal signs reflects the succession of thought as it orders the flux of phenomena. Narrative, a temporal thought-form, shapes external reality. Pictorial representation, in contrast, through its illusionistic rendering of external space as a convincing replica of the world, threatens to travel inwards and enslave the mind (idolatry, fetishism), blurring the distinction between reality, sign and thought, petrifying mental processes and fixing them as a picture show.

Needless to say, this kind of space-time distinction, and its connection to the specificity thesis, has consciously and unconsciously underwritten many more recent claims about other pictorial and textual media. Popular and scholarly comparisons between cinema, television and the literary text are perhaps exemplary cases in this respect (see for example Arnheim's [1957] and Panofsky's [1992/1934] illuminating but problematic works on the cinema). Compounded on occasion by a dubious cross-fertilization with the distinction between high and low culture (see, for example, Booth, 1994, and Postman, 1985) it underpins some contemporary anxieties and assumptions about culture in a predominantly "visual" era (see Mitchell [2002] for an excellent discussion). It also enters debates about the future of the computer as either a site for hypertextual experimentation or for virtual reality, the former valorized as an extension of the textual potential of the codex, the latter stigmatized as the technological perfection of those (dangerous) "immersive" capacities of perceptual hallucination which originate in the pictorial model (Bolter, 1996).

How do Innis' writings engage with this representational distinction between spatial and temporal media? Innis' was certainly aware of this distinction, although his relationship to it is characteristically complex and opaque. Possibly its most striking appearance occurs in the essay "The Problem of Space," also from *The Bias of Communication*. It is initially worth noting that Innis quotes Lessing: "The oral tradition and its relation to poetry implied a concern with time and religion. 'The artist represents *coexistence in space*, the poet *succession in time*' (Lessing at the University of Berlin, 1810)" (102: italics in Innis).[11] What is intriguing about this quote is that Innis is not concerned with the image/text distinction per se, but with the way the quote supports his argument regarding the relationship of poetry to time and religion. As he states later on in the essay:

> Verbal poetry goes back to the fundamental reality of time. The poetic form requires a regular flexible sequence as plastic as thought, reproducing a transference of force from the agent to the object which occupies time and requires the same temporal order in imagination. (106)

Significantly, while the linkage between oral poetry and time is presented as a fundamental constant – an ontological correlation or homology between the "plasticity" of poetic form and the temporality of thought and imagination – the spatial nature of pictorial images seems to be historically contingent. Discussing pictorial art and vase decoration in Athens and Attica between 900 and 700 B.C.E., Innis claims that geometrical design:

> was finally replaced by pictorial representation which under the influence of literature reflected the fundamental principle of progressive narration especially in black figured vases. The ear and the concern with time began to have its influence on the arts

---

11 Innis gives his source as "Sir John Edwin Sandys, *A Short History of Classical Scholarship from the Sixth Century BC to the Present Day* (Cambridge, 1915), p. 294."

> concerned with the eye and space. The painter attempted to create
> an impression of a single scene in which time was not fixed but
> transitory and in which several actions took place at the same
> time. In the fifth century this method was rapidly displaced by
> a method emphasizing unity of time and space and in the fourth
> century a single action represented in a picture became dominant.
> (110)

There are two contradictory ways of reading this type of analysis and its
relation to the "medium specificity" thesis, both of which bring out the
tension between a "historical" or "materialist" Innis and an "ontological"
or "essentialist" one. The first is that Innis provides a refreshingly
de-ontologized and historically sensitive account of the spatial and
temporal biases of pictures and words within specific media ecologies.
While seeming to endorse as a given Lessing's claim that pictorial
representation is fundamentally an art "concerned with the eye and
space," Innis recognizes that it can nevertheless be heavily influenced
by "the ear and the concern with time," manifested in the development
of representational techniques that are narrational or temporally flexible.
Hence the image-text relationship is dynamic, subject to other, stronger
influences. Moreover, Innis' distinctions do not produce exactly the same
space-time "biases" as Lessing's. For example, Innis characterizes print
as spatially rather than temporally biased; partly because of its speed and
portability (distribution bias) but also partly because, in the West, it rests
on the abstraction of phonetic writing: writing, as Ong (1982) is at pains
to remind us, is a spatialization of speech. This kind of spatialization
establishes a different sort of homology. As in the example mentioned
above regarding the universalization of ethical standards among the
ancient Hebrews, the move to space-biased thought is a result of the
historically specific coincidence of portable technologies and semiotic
abstraction rather than pictorial form. In that sense Innis' analysis is
innocent of the charge of iconophobia that can be leveled at thinkers
who denigrate, with whatever degree of crudity or profundity, pictorial
representation in opposition to spoken and written texts. Additionally,
as I have pointed out, Innis allows for the co-presence of a distribution
bias that binds in one dimension, with coding and/or ideological biases
that bind in another. This reinforces the impression that Innis' thought
is not concerned with space and time as the fundamental terms of an

ontological distinction, but with their dialectical interaction in precise historical contexts.

Having said this, Innis' discussion of the transitions in ancient Athenian vase decoration can be read in a very different way. For Innis pictorial representation is in many ways a side-show, a useful cultural indicator but nonetheless a thoroughly dependent variable: it is *subject to* the dominant "biases" within a particular culture and media environment. These are determined by a different distinction to Lessing's: the fundamental opposition between speech and writing. What makes Athenian pictorial representation between 900 and 700 B.C.E. time-biased is the enduring dominance of the *oral* tradition. And what spatializes pictorial representation over the fifth and fourth centuries B.C.E., reducing temporal progression to a single action within one scene, is the transference from the spoken to the written word (109) in the same period.

This key distinction between time and space, oral and written, is not simply a dichotomy, of course, but also an ontological valorization of time and speech and their relation to thought, and a consequent denigration of space and writing.[12] Notwithstanding Innis' sensitivity to the interaction of media technologies, it is ultimately *writing* which bears the responsibility for spatial fixity and externalization. Here, in fact, we can see the main shift from Lessing to Innis: from an opposition between the verbal and the pictorial arts (with the former conflating speech and writing), to one between the spoken and the graphic (with the latter connecting writing and pictorial inscription). As painting is to Lessing, so writing is to Innis. And this valorization of speech ultimately serves to establish time as the sovereign of both individual and social being. Describing the oral tradition in Greece, Innis maintains that:

> It created standards and lasting moral and social institutions; it built up the soul of social organizations and maintained their continuity; and it developed ways of perpetuating itself. The oral tradition and religion served almost the same purpose. Language was the physiological basis of oral traditions, and religion was

---

12 The titles of Innis' essays allude to this preference. Time needs to be pleaded for ("A Plea for Time") – it is valuable and endangered: space, on the other hand, is a "problem."

the sociological mechanism through which traditions were established directed, and enforcing the co-operation of individuals in the interest of the community, maintaining group life, and creating a lasting organization of society independent of a living leader....In oral intercourse the eye, ear, and brain, the senses and the faculties acted together in busy co-operation and rivalry, each eliciting, stimulating, and supplementing the other. (105)[13]

I have quoted at length because this text, along with the passage already cited concerning the temporality of verbal poetry, starkly reveals the nature of Innis' romance with the "oral tradition" – spoken intercourse at the center of religious practice.[14] For in this tradition inner and outer, thought and its expression, utterances and their author, memory and history, individual and community, the brain and all the senses, are in harmony not simply politically but also in their being. Their interrelation is designated not by a manufactured border but by an ontological continuum. This foundation threatens to turn *any* external marking into a form of objectification, an abstraction on a discrete physical artifact of a characteristic previously available collectively because it was held in the minds and living speech of individuals. Thus while some communication technologies may be time-binding in terms of distribution bias (writing on stone, for instance), *all communication media bar speech* appear in these terms as objectifying spatial materializations of what had previously only occurred in time. Hence, it is important to recognize the trajectory within Innis' work which resonates with the fear of space that also subtends the image-text opposition in Lessing.

Two other brief examples will serve to flesh out this connection between the three media forms: oral speech, writing and pictures. The first is a detour via Plato, the second via McLuhan. In the chapter on "The Oral Tradition and Greece" in *Empire and Communications*, Innis approvingly quotes a famous passage from Plato's *Phaedrus* in which Socrates outlines one of his objections to writing:

13 The last sentence of this quote is of course an important thesis in McLuhan's thought.
14 Innis' "bias" in favor of the oral tradition is also explicit in other texts, notably "A Critical Review," also in *The Bias of Communication*.

> I cannot help feeling, Phaedrus, that writing is unfortunately like painting; for the creations of the painter have the attitude of life, and yet if you ask them a question, they preserve a solemn silence. You would imagine that they had intelligence, but if you want to know anything and put a question to one of them, the speaker always gives one unvarying answer. (1977: 56)[15]

Plato acts as the common source for both Innis' opposition to writing and Lessing's reservations about painting: both appear as non-dialogical and atemporal. What they have in common (graphic fixity) outweighs their superficial differences (the use of verbal/pictorial codes). Perhaps most problematic here is the threat of deception: writing, like painting, has "the attitude of life." Yet while painting produces the illusion of perceptual reality, writing produces the illusion of verbal dialogue and dialectical thought, even as it corrupts intelligence by making thought static, repetitive and ultimately dumb. Painting is the spatialization of the external world: writing, perhaps more worryingly, borrows the graphic powers of visual communication to spatialize speech-thought itself.[16] Hence Innis' work shares Plato's suspicion of fixity and externality, a suspicion that finds diverse expression not only in Lessing, but also in Marxist conceptions of "alienation" and "reification" (and their development in Debord's "spectacle"),[17] and in a host of assumptions regarding the deleterious effects of contemporary "visual" culture and media (especially television).

My second, more complicated detour is via a surprising analogy used by McLuhan throughout his Foreword to *Empire and Communications*. Discussing Innis' analysis of the balance between written and oral social structures, McLuhan claims that:

15 This is the translated text cited by Innis. The passage can be found, rendered slightly differently, in the translation of *Phaedrus* by Alexander Nehamas and Paul Woodruff. Indianapolis: Hackett. Section 275D–275E, p. 81.
16 My argument here is clearly informed by Derrida's (1981) famous analysis of Plato's critique of writing in *Phaedrus*.
17 This is one of Stamps' principal claims, and the basis of her comparison between Innis, McLuhan, Adorno and Benjamin. Lack of space prevents me from engaging in any detail with these claims, except to say that I think she fundamentally overestimates the role of the "oral tradition" in the work of Benjamin and Adorno, and totally ignores the problematic reductionism of Innis' conflation of space with vision and writing.

He saw that the figure-ground relation between written and oral is everywhere in a state of perpetual change. Material conditions can quickly reverse the relationship between written and oral so that, where literacy may be the ground of a culture in one phase, a sudden loss or access of written materials, for example, may cause the literate *ground* to dwindle to mere *figure*. (1972: ix, emphasis in original)

The word "idiosyncratic" hardly does justice to McLuhan's writing here. Not only does he describe Innis' thought on orality and writing by using the pictorial model of "figure" and "ground." He also reverses the conventional terms of that model, such that the "figure," that which stands out and commands attention in the foreground, is what one "dwindles" to when power is lost. "Ground" is thus the key term, as McLuhan makes clear right from opening lines of the Foreword:

If Hegel projected a historical pattern of *figures* minus an existential *ground*, Harold Innis, in the spirit of the new age of information, sought for patterns in the very ground of history and existence. (1972, v., emphasis in original)

This is an unusual way of saying that Innis searched for those effects of communication media that are most fundamental to social structure and experience but also (and as a result?) most overlooked by observers. It is unusual for two reasons. First, the metaphor of figure and ground establishes a way of thinking the dialectical relationship between the written and the oral: one medium may appear to be prominent, and is situated in the foreground of historical reality, while the other medium constitutes the "ground" – the existential substrate and necessary condition – of the historical reality itself. In other words, Innis' thought is conceived as a kind of world-picture. But that is not all: "figure" and "ground" are not simply pictorial elements somehow *given* in space. Rather, the terms describe the composition of a picture in relation to an observer: a world-*view*. This observer-relation is not merely one of proximity or distance (with the "figure" closer to the observer than the "ground"): it also involves and invokes the observer's powers of *attention*. "Figure" is what it is not only because of its position but also because of its conventional prominence within a representational order: it is the result of viewer habituation and expectation as much as of its placement within the frame. Innis' achievement – according to McLuhan – is to go against the grain of conventional viewing habits, to direct his own and his readers' attention at the ground rather than at the figure in a reverse gestalt-exercise.

So to think with Innis about the dialectics of orality and writing, time and space, is to think *pictorially* and *visually*. The third medium, which is subject, according to Innis' account of ancient Athenian vase decoration, to the prevailing influences of either oral or written communication and their temporal or spatial biases, becomes, in McLuhan's commentary, the defining form – the epistemological "ground" – of Innis' very thought and prose. Of course, one cannot see one's own ground. One thinks from within it, which is why Innis remains blind to the place of pictures and picturing in his own media theory. If we follow McLuhan's interpretation to its logical conclusion (and it is certainly intriguing if not necessarily convincing), this centrality of picturing to Innis' thought constitutes a "return of the repressed," the revenge of space and vision as the means by which to represent adequately the dynamic historical intersection of media technologies and forms – an intersection in which Innis officially sides with orality and time and in which pictures hardly figure at all.

Conclusion: Bias as a Critical-Descriptive "Hinge"

This centrality of picturing and vision can help to explain the tension between an "ontological Innis" who sees writing and space as fundamentally a "problem," and a "materialist" Innis who would affirm that societies, cultures and media are in essence *neither* temporal *nor* spatial, but dynamic spatial-temporal constructions. For Innis' project, as Stamps (1995) notes, is simultaneously descriptive and critical: it is not just a portrayal of the relationship between communication and political and social processes, but a consciously promoted view of that relationship which can be projected as a contemporary critique.[18] The pictorial model elides the analytical-depictive power of Innis' thought with its ethical and critical perspective: figure and ground are not just

18 Although Stamps certainly would not argue that Innis' thought is "pictorial."

there to be seen – not simply historical "patterns" to be disclosed, but are choices that the observer makes about how and where to look. Depiction gains critical force by being based on an "ontological" perspective about how things are (and hence should be) "fundamentally": critique gains legitimacy and purchase on the world through its deployment of depictive rigor.

The very use of the word "bias" itself makes manifest this duality of description and critique. Communication media have biases, as do civilizations. By this Innis means, as we have seen, that the dimensions of space or time are favored – either because of physical properties (distribution bias), formal and informational propensities (coding bias), or as a result of belief and policy (ideological bias). But scholars also have "bias":

> My bias is with the oral tradition, particularly as reflected in Greek civilization, and with the necessity of recapturing something of its spirit. "A Critical Review," Innis (1999: 190)

Innis' use of the word may be consciously playful, but his meaning in this passage is quite straightforward. Bias here is not primarily a spatial-temporal quality of things or societies under analysis, but an admission of the analyst's subjective inclination. "Bias" acts therefore as a kind of *hinge* between two types of discourse that in conventional "scientific" thought are often understood to be mutually exclusive: the one analytical, descriptive, detached, scholarly and registered dispassionately in the third person; the other personal, critical, self-reflexive, engaged and registered in the first person.

This conflation has the effect of giving critical and ethical force to Innis' historical argument. But it can also lead to an impoverishment of that argument, whereby the necessity for a fundamental split between space and time produces a kind of analytical inertia, with media and societies categorized all too neatly according to the space/time, oral/written dichotomies. Furthermore, it can encourage the reductive simplification of "time" and "space" themselves, whereby the ontologizing of their relationship and effects makes it impossible to explore the details of their *construction* in specific historical contexts. This is a particular problem when one sets Innis' notions of time and space alongside the works of theorists engaged in the analysis of modernity. For when applied locally, as it were, Innis' space-time dialectic is highly suggestive but, of itself, an insufficient critical tool. It becomes most fruitful to thought when set against other terms, employed by a variety of social and cultural historians and theorists (Foucault, Lefebvre, Giddens, Virillio, Bauman and Castells spring to mind), that specify *modes* of temporal and spatial relationship: place and flow, stability and mobility, stasis and speed, continuity and discontinuity, liquid and solid, disembedding and abstraction.

Nevertheless, Innis' work does provide a broadly productive framework for comprehending our epoch's communication ecology, and its relationship to space and time, *historically* – as part of the longue durée in which media systems and social formations emerge, expand and decline. The "materialist" Innis provides us with a benchmark "grand narrative" of human communication, one relatively free of the evolutionary or teleological determinism that underpins other grand narratives, and against which we can situate more local studies. It is worth repeating the central thesis of that narrative: Throughout human history communication media have been fundamental to the determination of the spatial and temporal dynamics that structure social organization, the characteristics of human knowledge, and the representational modes at the core of cultural experience. And such "determination" is not essential or absolute, but a historically contingent and dialectical affair, inviting and necessitating political, social and cultural counter-biases. The determination of historical dynamics by communication media is thus, according to Innis, necessarily open to alteration and remedy – no less in the age of information than in any other.

References

Arnheim, R. (1957). *Film as Art*. Berkeley: University of California Press.

Baudrillard, J. (1981). *For a Critique of the Political Economy of the Sign*. St. Louis: Telos Press.

Benedetti, P., & DeHard, N. (Eds.). (1997). *Forward Through the Rearview Mirror: Reflections on and by Marshall McLuhan*. Ontario: Prentice Hall Canada.

Blondheim, M. (2003). Harold Adams Innis and his Bias of Communication. In Katz et al. (eds). *Canonic Texts in Media*

Research. Cambridge: Polity.

Bolter, J. D. (1996). Ekphrasis, Virtual Reality and the Future of Writing. In Geoffrey Nunberg (Ed.) *The Future of the Book* (pp. 253–272). Berkeley: University of California Press.

Booth, W. (1994). The Company We Keep: Self-Making in Imaginative Art, Old and New. in H. Newcomb (Ed.) *Television: The Critical View* (pp. 503–515). Oxford: Oxford University Press.

Bourdieu, P. (1986). *Distinction: A Social Critique of the Judgement of Taste*. London: Routledge.

Bourdieu, P. (1993). *The Field of Cultural Production*. trans. Randal Johnson. Cambridge: Polity Press.

Carey, J. (1992). *Communication as Culture: Essays on Media and Society*. New York: Routledge.

Carroll, N. (1988). *Philosophical Problems of Classical Film Theory*. Princeton: Princeton University Press.

Derrida, J. (1976). *Of Grammatology*. Baltimore: The Johns Hopkins University Press.

Derrida, J. (1981). Plato's Pharmacy. *Dissemination.* Chicago: University of Chicago Press.

Genosko, G. (1999). *McLuhan and Baudrillard: The Masters of Implosion*. London: Routledge.

Giddens, A. (1990). *The Consequences of Modernity*. Cambridge: Polity Press.

Horrocks, C. (2000). *Marshall McLuhan and Virtuality*. Cambridge: Icon/Totem Books.

Innis, H. (1972). *Empire and Communications*. Toronto: University of Toronto Press. Originally published in 1950.

Innis, H. (1999). *The Bias of Communication*. Toronto: University of Toronto Press. Originally published in 1951.

Jhally, S. (1993). Communications and the Materialist Conception of History: Marx, Innis and Technology. *Continuum 7.*

Katz, R., & Katz, E. (1998). McLuhan: Where Did He Come From, Where Did He Disappear? *Canadian Journal of Communication, 23,* 307–319.

Kittler, F. (1999) *Gramophone, Film, Typewriter.* Stanford University Press, Stanford.

Lapham, L. (1994). Introduction to M. McLuhan, *Understanding Media: The Extensions of Man* (pp. ix–xxiii). Cambridge, Mass.:

MIT Press.

Lessing, G. E. (1969). *Laocoön: An Essay Upon the Limits of Poetry and Painting*. New York: Noonday Press. Originally published in 1766.

Levinson, P. (1999). *Digital McLuhan: A Guide to the Information Millennium*. London: Routledge.

Marchand, P. (1989) *Marshall McLuhan: The Medium and the Messenger*. New York: Ticknor and Fields.

McLuhan, M. (1972) Foreword to H. Innis, *Empire and Communications*. Toronto: University of Toronto Press.

McLuhan, E., & Zingrone, F. (Eds.). (1997). *Essential McLuhan*. London: Routledge.

Meyrowitz, J. (1985). *No Sense of Place: The Impact of Electronic on Social Behaviour*. Oxford: Oxford University Press.

Mitchell, W.J.T. (1986). *Iconology: Image, Text, Ideology*. Chicago: University of Chicago Press.

Mitchell, W.J.T. (2002). Showing Seeing: A Critique of Visual Culture. *Journal of Visual Culture*, *1*, 165–181.

Moos, M. A. (Ed.). (1997). *Media Research: Technology, Art, Communication: Essays by Marshall McLuhan*. Amsterdam: G+B Arts International.

Ong, W. J. (1982). *Orality and Literacy: The Technologizing of the Word*. London: Routledge.

Panofsky, E. (1992). Style and Medium in the Motion Pictures. In G. Mast, M. Cohen & L. Baudry (Eds.) *Film Theory and Criticism* (pp. 233–248). Oxford: Oxford University Press. Originally published in 1934.

Postman, N. (1985). *Amusing Ourselves to Death: Public Discourse in the Age of Show Business*. New York: Elisabeth Sifton Books – Viking.

Schweizer, N. (1972). *The Ut Pictura Poesis Controversy in Eighteenth Century England and Germany*. Frankfurt: Herbert Lang.

Stamps, J. (1995). *Unthinking Modernity: Innis, McLuhan and the Frankfurt School*. Montreal: McGill-Queens University Press.

Wellbery, D. (1984). *Lessing's Laocoon: Semiotics and the Age of Reason*. Cambridge: Cambridge University Press.

GENE ALLEN

7. Monopolies of News: Harold Innis, the Telegraph and Wire Services

The sending of a telegraphic message from Baltimore to Washington in May 1844 is widely recognized as a milestone in the history of communication. It introduced to the world a technology that exponentially increased the speed of communication; more radically, as James Carey has observed, the telegraph separated communication and transportation for the first time, with far-reaching consequences for the treatment of information as a separate and valuable commodity.[1] It transformed the way business was transacted, setting the stage for an era in which the "visible hand" of large business corporations increasingly dominated the economy of North America and Europe; and it led directly to the emergence of perhaps the most powerful journalistic institution of the 19th and early 20th centuries, the news agency or wire service.[2]

The telegraph profoundly changed the way communication took place in the dimensions of time and space, two categories that are central to the seminal studies of communications and history which Harold Adams Innis carried out in the 1940s and early 1950s. In Innis' analysis, practices of communication organized around different technologies led societies to focus either on space or time as central organizing principles, and thereby conditioned their growth and decline.[3]

---

1   James Carey, "Technology and Ideology: The Case of the Telegraph," in Carey, James, *Communication as Culture: Essays on Media and Society* (New York: Routledge, 1992; first published 1988), p. 203.

2   Alfred D. Chandler, *The Visible Hand: the Managerial Revolution in American Business* (Cambridge, Mass.: Harvard University Press, 1977), pp. 77, 209–10, 245.

3   The inelegant phrase "communication practices organized around different technologies" is intended to signal that Innis should not be seen as a technological determinist, but as one who understood technologies as operating in specific contexts of economic and political power.

Surprisingly, though, in his wide-ranging catalogue of communication innovations, Innis paid relatively little attention to the telegraph and its offspring, the telegraphic news agency; a recent compilation of his work, for example, includes in its index 15 references to parchment, six to papyrus, one to news services and none to the telegraph.[4]

Scattered throughout Innis' work, however, numerous brief references to the telegraph can be found. The goal of the present paper is to draw these together and identify the concerns and analytical issues that underlie them – not, I hope, as a taxonomic exercise in i-dotting and t-crossing, but in an effort to imagine what a more concerted Innisian account of the telegraph and news agency might look like, in the spirit of Carey's invitation to approach Innis' writings as "not merely things to read but things to think with."[5] Then, by considering Innis' ideas in relation to the early history of the Canadian Press news agency, I hope to point out some of their strengths and limitations and offer some suggestions about how Innis' legacy can most fruitfully be used.

The telegraph: an agent of decentralization?

Innis, as has been noted above, never provided a systematic or extended account of the telegraph. Rather than examining it on its own, he invariably approached the telegraph as one element in a larger account of the newspaper industry in the 19th and 20th centuries. The following quotation, in which the telegraph is chiefly of interest as one among

---

4   I am indebted to Menahem Blondheim for pointing out the absence of the telegraph in Innis' work, and for suggesting that I look into the question more closely. Blondheim previously raised this issue in "Wiring the Maritimes: Technology, Economy, and Communication Policy in the Development of Canada's Eastern Lines of Telegraph," a paper presented at the Jerusalem Conference on Canadian Studies, Jerusalem, June, 1998.

    For the index entries, see Harold Innis, *Staples, Markets and Cultural Change*, ed. Daniel Drache (Montreal and Kingston: McGill-Queen's University Press, 1995), pp. 499, 500, 504. (In fact, the essays collected in this book do include several references to the telegraph, but they are not listed in the index.)

5   Carey, "Space, Time and Communications: A Tribute to Harold Innis," in Carey (1992), p. 142.

several innovations that affected the development of newspapers, is typical of his approach:

> The newspaper, with the technological advances evident in the telegraph, the press associations, the manufacture of paper from wood, the rotary press, and the linotype, became independent of party support and became concerned with an increase in circulation and with all the devices calculated to bring about such an increase to meet the demands of advertising.[6]

Why, one might ask, did Innis not study the telegraph by itself, but only as it affected the development of another communications medium? The answer, I believe, reflects the way Innis' account of the newspaper industry fits into his overall project of seeking to understand the influence of communication on history.

At the risk of oversimplification, Innis' approach to communication can be summed up as follows. Media of communication powerfully shape the societies that give rise to them. Every medium has a bias, or tendency, either to emphasize duration and continuity (that is, the messages it conveys last for a long time) or to be suitable for quick and widespread dissemination of messages through space. These biases become entrenched, leading to imbalances, monopolies of knowledge held by particular groups, and, at the extreme, violent disruption. Every entrenched medium is eventually challenged and supplanted by media that emphasize the bias it rejects – a medium focusing too narrowly on time and continuity, for example, will eventually fall to one with a corrective emphasis on space, expansion and novelty, and vice versa. "Monopolies of knowledge ... developed and declined partly in relation to the medium of communication on which they were built and tended to alternate as they emphasized religion, decentralization, and time, and force, centralization, and space."[7] This is a way of describing history that focuses on dynamism and change at a broad structural level; it is an attempt to explain how power is distributed and exercised and how

---

6   Harold Innis, "On the Economic Significance of Cultural Factors," in Innis (1995), p. 306.
7   Harold Innis, *Empire & Communications*, rev. by Mary Q. Innis (Toronto: University of Toronto Press, 1972; first published 1950), p. 166.

different kinds of power and different kinds of societies succeed one another.

In practice, the tracing of these developments in relation to particular communications media in Innis' work can seem confusing and even contradictory. It is helpful to remember that he was usually attempting to describe a process of change: one form may just be starting to emerge out of another (so that both coexist in a shifting balance); a development which initially seems to strengthen a particular bias may eventually have the opposite effect by virtue of the rigidities it creates. Such a pattern of shifting and overlapping explanation is evident in Innis' account of the newspaper industry.

At the broadest level, Innis was interested in the openness and adaptability of societies, and this concern is central to his analysis of the newspaper industry.[8] He was particularly interested in how the mass-circulation newspaper (which first appeared in the 1830s, and became dominant after 1890) differed from earlier forms of print media, and how it differed from radio as it emerged in the 1920s and 1930s.[9] Innis argued that the newspaper promotes an obsession with the immediate, which is to say, a neglect of time and continuity. It is fundamentally an institution that emphasizes space.[10] The actual effect on space is

---

8 William Christian, preface to *The Idea File of Harold Adams Innis*, ed. William Christian (Toronto: University of Toronto Press, 1980), pp. xi–xiii. For a valuable overview that draws together the different strands of Innis' work throughout his career, see Drache, "Introduction: Celebrating Innis: The Man, the Legacy and our Future," in Innis (1995), pp. xiii–lix.

9 For the dominance of mass-audience newspapers later in the 19th century, see Richard L. Kaplan, *Politics and the American Press: The Rise of Objectivity, 1865–1920* (Cambridge: Cambridge University Press, 2002), p. 120.

10 Innis (1972), 170: "In the United States the dominance of the newspaper led to large-scale development of monopolies of communication in terms of space and implied a neglect of problems of time." See also "On the Economic Significance of Cultural Factors," where he approvingly quotes the 19th-century French politician François Guizot: "'It [democracy] readily sacrifices the past and the future to the interest of the present,' and that evil was accentuated by the reign of the newspaper and its obsession with the immediate." In Innis (1995), p. 308.
At another point, though, Innis observes that the capital-intensive and monopolistic character of the modern newspaper tends to emphasize the dimension of time: "significance of monopoly of position of newspaper – influence over long period rather than short run – monopoly and heavy capital investment – mobilizes opinion

complicated, though. At one level, newspapers and their constituent technologies allow the spread of information over ever larger areas, but they do not necessarily strengthen the nation as a geographical unit. For Innis, the newspaper of the later 19th and 20th centuries was primarily a force for decentralization – especially as contrasted with the nationalism engendered by earlier forms of print and the centralizing influence of radio.[11]

---

as in case of parties – stabilizing influence. Competition with small sheets – parties follow imperfect competition in newspaper. ..." Innis (1980), p. 38.

11 Innis argued that radio, which appealed to the ear rather than eye, replaced the newspaper's emphasis on decentralization and space with an orientation toward centralization and time: "The disastrous culmination of a monopoly over space ending in the First World War and the depression was followed by a monopoly over time." This allowed political leaders like Al Smith and F. D. Roosevelt to appeal directly to voters, over the heads of critical editors: "The traditions of decentralization of the press were replaced by new traditions of centralization and continuity reflected in a fourth term for the President." Innis, "Technology and Public Opinion in the United States," *Canadian Journal of Economics and Political Science* 17 (Feb., 1951), p. 23. (This important article is also reprinted in Innis, *The Bias of Communication* [Toronto: University of Toronto Press, 1951, reprinted 1991], pp. 156–189.) See also n. 107 on the same page: "Schumpeter in his Business Cycles has emphasized the importance of the Kondratieff cycle but has neglected the problem of organization of communication by which innovations are transmitted. As monopoly of communication with relation to the printing press was built up over a long period under the protection of freedom of the press and accentuated discontinuity and the destruction of time, it eventually destroyed itself and compelled a recognition of a medium [i.e., radio] emphasizing time and continuity."

In some respects, Innis saw newspapers as similar to print media in general, which particularly emphasized the geographical space of the nation; like earlier forms of print, one of the ways in which mass-audience newspapers organize people is according to their written languages and national subdivisions. In some cases, this could have centralizing tendencies, as when a written language was standardized over larger areas by means of print. However, here again Innis emphasized the decentralizing possibilities of print: "The modern state with political boundaries influenced by the paper and printing industries has been profoundly affected by the industrial revolution and the application of steam power to the paper and printing industries ... . The divisive influence of these industries has been evident in the division of regions speaking the same language, as in the separation of the United States from the British Empire, in the emergence of the British Commonwealth of Nations, and in the growth of regionalism centring around large metropolitan areas." Innis, "The Concept of Monopoly and Civilization" in Innis (1995), p. 388.

What interested Innis most about the telegraph was how it influenced the extent of the space which newspapers could effectively dominate – in Innis' terms, the space in which they could exercise a monopoly. One of the most important consequences of the telegraph (and the wire service) in Innis' view was that it altered the balance between nation, region, and locality, and between large and smaller cities. Before the advent of the telegraph, newspapers in North America took most of their out-of-town news from other publications, which arrived through the mail in an arrangement known as the exchange system.[12] Smaller centers relied mainly on the out-of-town news they received from the nearest metropolitan newspaper, giving the large city substantial influence over its hinterland. "Low rates of postage on newspapers favoured the larger centres," Innis wrote, "and newspapers in the smaller centres became servile imitators in 'tone, temper and opinion.'"[13]

Both in Britain and the United States, the arrival of the telegraph and the news agency (which made telegraphic news widely available and affordable) changed this state of affairs.[14] Smaller cities could now receive up-to-date international and national news directly, at the same time their big-city counterparts did. This tended to break up the monopolies of space which papers in London or New York had exercised. Beginning in the 1850s, Innis wrote, provincial newspapers in Britain "were quick to seize the advantages of the telegraph, and were able to compete. on a basis of equality with *The Times*. ... *The Manchester*

12 Richard A. Schwarzlose, *The Nation's Newsbrokers*, Vol. 1, *The Formative Years: From Pretelegraph to 1865* (Evanston, Ill.: Northwestern University Press, 1989) pp. 4–6; Paul Rutherford, *The Making of the Canadian Media* (Toronto: McGraw-Hill Ryerson, 1978), p. 13. See also Richard B. Kielbowicz, *News in the Mails: The Press, Post Office, and Public Information, 1700–1860s* (New York: Greenwood Press, 1989).

13 Innis (1951), p. 8, quoting S.N.D. North, *History and Present Condition of the Newspaper and Periodical Press of the United States* (Washington, D.C., 1884), p. 112.

14 Innis, "The Newspaper in Economic Development," *Journal of Economic History*, Vol. II, Supplement (Dec. 1942, reprint), pp. 10–11: "The Associated Press was formed to provide news to a large number of papers at low cost." Menahem Blondheim has strongly argued that the unprecedented organizational requirements of a wire service were the crucial factor rather than cost alone: Blondheim, *News over the Wires: The Telegraph and the Flow of Public Information in America, 1844–1897* (Cambridge, Mass.: Harvard University Press, 1994), p. 59.

Guardian and other provincial papers gained access to the debates in the House of Commons and were able to exert sufficient pressure to bring about government ownership of the telegraph system."[15] Thus, "[t]he monopoly of London strengthened by the railway was destroyed by the invention of the telegraph which encouraged provincial competition after 1868."[16]

Intriguingly, this analysis leads in more than one direction. On one hand, metropolitan centers like New York lost some influence over their hinterlands in an economic or geographical sense and had less influence nationally as well.[17] But at a political level, the centrifugal forces which Innis described also gave U.S. metropolitan newspapers more independence from party control based in Washington and the state capitals. Over all, the telegraph had important political consequences by strengthening local and regional orientations and weakening a national focus.

> The telegraph and the fast press in the metropolitan areas destroyed the power of party … . Instability weakened the position of a central authority after 1840. Power shifted from Washington and issues were no longer settled in Congress. The metropolitan press destroyed a centrally directed government. Buchanan was the last president to have an administration organ in Washington.[18]

The observation that the same developments weakened metropolitan newspapers in one respect and strengthened them in another is typically Innisian.

15 Innis (1942), p. 14.
16 Innis, "The Bias of Communication," in Innis (1995), p. 347.
17 Innis (1951), p. 11: "The limitations of the metropolitan press became evident in the essentially local character of its circulation, the decline in influence of weekly newspapers, and the increasing importance of newspapers in small centres. The telegraph emphasized the importance of news with the result that the newspaper was unable to meet the demands of a national medium."
18 Innis (1951), p. 11. See also p. 10: "The telegraph weakened the system of political control through the post office and the newspaper exchange. The monopoly over news was destroyed and the regional daily press escaped from the dominance of the political and the metropolitan press." In his notebooks, Innis took this argument even further: "Break up of local party domination in Richmond, Washington and Albany with newspapers with rise of fast press in metropolitan centres destroyed single governing authority and brought civil war. Innis (1980), p. 19.

Innis clearly attached great importance to the telegraph's, and the news service's, effect on patterns of regional dominance. One event in newspaper history to which he paid considerable attention was the struggle between New York and midwestern U.S. newspapers for control of Associated Press from the 1860s to the 1890s. As early as the 1860s, Joseph Medill of the *Chicago Tribune* denounced the New York-based AP – at the time, a consortium of powerful metropolitan publishers rather than the cooperative organization it later became – as "a most pernicious and crushing monopoly."[19] In Innis' view, following the analysis outlined above, the telegraph had contributed to the growing independence of midwestern newspapers, but tensions between Chicago and New York did not disappear. "Western newspapers were at a disadvantage in time since news tended to spread from east to west, and complaints arose regarding the dominance of New York papers over business information. New York interests had an advantage in market reports and western papers held that this advantage was particularly serious since they were compelled to pay high prices for the service."[20] Innis described the eventual takeover of the agency by Associated Press of Illinois in the 1890s (a successor of the earlier Western Associated Press) as "the destruction of a parochial monopoly of New York newspapers by newspapers which had emerged in relation to the demand for news in the West and the growth of a monopoly in response to the demands of the telegraph."[21] In both Britain and the United States, the telegraph and news services profoundly changed the regional distribution of economic and political power and of influence over public opinion.[22]

19 Innis (1951), p. 15.
20 Ibid., p. 14.
21 Ibid., p. 16. The monopoly Innis refers to is presumably the news agency.
22 A further aspect of the development of mass-circulation newspapers was the stratification of audiences along class lines. Innis argued that the telegraph contributed to the growth of evening papers, which were usually aimed at a working-class audience; in the 1880s, "[e]vening papers flourished with the increasing interest in sport facilitated by reliance on the telegraph throughout Great Britain." Innis (1942), p. 13.
    See also Innis (1951), p. 18; Innis, *The Press: A Neglected Factor in the Economic History of the Twentieth Century* (London: Oxford University Press, 1949), p. 27.

News and the monopoly of knowledge

In the foregoing discussion, Innis' use of the term "monopoly" is fairly straightforward. In measuring the ebb and flow of metropolitan influence over hinterlands, it recalls his earlier work as an economic geographer. In another aspect of his analysis of the telegraph and news agency the term is used more broadly, based on the classic economist's sense, but going beyond it.

The cooperative news agency (such as Associated Press or its Canadian counterpart, Canadian Press) is a remarkable institution. Unlike private agencies such as Reuters or United Press, the news cooperative is owned by its member newspapers. It requires a high degree of cooperation in sharing news – the exclusive possession of which is highly valued – among businesses which are, at least theoretically, competitors. Only the necessity of creating a sophisticated organization to manage the gathering and distribution of telegraphic news, the advantages of spreading the relatively heavy cost of transmission among scores and even hundreds of subscribers on shared circuits, and the related advantage of having sufficient weight to bargain effectively with telegraph companies were sufficient to mitigate the usual competitive instinct.

One crucial feature of news cooperatives' structure kept the balance between competition and cooperation relatively stable. Newspaper competition operates almost exclusively within a local circulation area; thus, a paper in Chicago could readily share news reports with a paper in Los Angeles without fear of losing readers or advertisers to it, but would not be willing to do the same for another Chicago publication. Cooperative news agencies reflected this reality by enshrining in their by-laws the so-called "right of protest," by which a member newspaper could prevent a direct competitor in its city from being admitted to the cooperative (or make membership punitively expensive).[23] This strict limit on new memberships created a monopoly even stronger than the economist's definition describes. Not only did AP, as the single seller

---

23 AP was forced to abolish this system in response to a Supreme Court anti-trust ruling in 1945; Schwarzlose vol. 2, 22. The issue had come before the courts as early as 1900; see William F. Swindler, "The AP Anti-Trust Case in Historical Perspective," *Journalism Quarterly* 23 (1946): pp. 40–57.

of a desirable commodity (in this case, news), have the power to set its own price without regard to competition; by imposing administrative limits on access, it consistently refused to supply many would-be buyers at any price. (AP also imposed other limits on its members, refusing to allow them to buy news from or supply news to any competing agency.) While the news agency may have reduced the size of a metropolitan newspaper's hinterland, within that zone the dominance of a paper with access to AP copy was strengthened. This clearly is what Innis had in mind when he observed that "(r)egional monopolies of metropolitan newspapers have been strengthened by monopolies of press associations."[24]

This recognition of the news agency's tendency to create stronger (though physically less extensive) monopolies provides a counterweight to Innis' emphasis on decentralization. In "A Plea for Time," for example, he argued that with the development of mass-circulation newspapers, small cities "were gradually dwarfed by the rise of large cities. ... Large centres became centres of news for distribution through press associations and in turn press associations became competitive with an emphasis on types of news which were mutually exclusive."[25] One might take this argument a step further. An obvious characteristic of the news-agency system is that large numbers of subscribing newspapers print identical stories, and the places where these stories are written, edited and distributed have a powerful position in the whole network. When one considers the journalism business as a whole, rather than focusing on individual newspapers, the widespread use of news-agency copy could also have centralizing tendencies. Innis did not develop this argument, however; while the telegraphic news agency did contribute to stronger monopolies in his view, they remained at the regional level.

The concept of the monopoly of knowledge is central to Innis' thinking. In effect, this refers to a specific group's ability to control important information, notably by controlling the technologies and

---

24 Innis (1972), p. 170. Blondheim, p. 161, states that by 1879 an AP franchise in New York was worth $500,000 and one in Chicago was worth $100,000.

25 Innis (1995), p. 370. Even here, though, Innis tends to gravitate to the decentralizing side of the argument: "The increasing efficiency of press associations brought a decline in the number of scoops claimed by individual papers and led to increasing dependence on local news and features." Innis (1949), p. 20.

skills by which information is gathered, processed and disseminated. For Innis, a monopoly of knowledge is typically associated with a society's over-reliance on a medium that emphasizes either time or space, and is the cause of instability which eventually sets the stage for a reaction in the other direction. But in the field of communication, such monopolies are particularly difficult to eradicate. "Mankind constantly being caught in his own traps," Innis wrote in the sketchy, allusive notes subsequently published as his Idea File, "language and systems developed and most difficult to break down – significant that reforms come latest in control of communications, i.e., paper duty last to be removed – interest in monopoly of A.P. the last to be recognized. Control of methods of expression makes improvement more difficult."[26]

For Innis, one of the imbalances fostered by AP's monopoly of knowledge was political: a bias in favor of the Republican Party. "The power of the Associated Press in facilitating mobilization of the resources of Republican newspapers in a united front was evident in the election of McKinley in 1896. ... With the exception of the Wilson period the monopoly of the Republican press persisted until the election of F.D. Roosevelt in 1932."[27] Eventually, rival newspapers which were excluded from AP supported competing news agencies such as E. W. Scripps's United Press agency and Hearst's International News Service; these also offered a political alternative to AP, which "was regarded as conservative, capitalistic, and guilty of holding back news for the morning papers."[28] A crucial development in this competition was a

26 Innis (1980), p. 74. See also p. 75: "Slow development of attacks on trusts in fields of communications an indication of difficulty of securing competition in fields of knowledge."

27 Innis (1951), p. 17. Innis describes Hearst's attempts to gain political office as a Democrat as "in part a result of the necessity of combatting the monopoly of the Associated Press."
    The question of political bias in news-agency copy is disputed. For many years the prevailing view has been that news agencies eschewed or at least reduced bias; this is largely based on Donald L. Shaw's influential article, "News bias and the telegraph: a study of historical change," *Journalism Quarterly* (Spring 1967), 3–12, 31. This view has recently been sharply questioned by Blondheim, pp. 174–188, who documents AP's strong Republican bias in the 1870s and 1880s. It is interesting to note that Innis' version is more in keeping with Blondheim's view.

28 In order to compete effectively, though, Scripps and Hearst had to establish extensive chains of their own to reap the same economies of scale that underlay

U.S. Supreme Court ruling in 1918 forbidding non-AP members from reprinting published AP reports. "Property right in news was established and the monopoly of the Associated Press strengthened."[29]

It should be noted, though, that the most restrictive aspects of AP's monopoly were limited to it and similarly organized cooperatives. Private news agencies like Reuters might enjoy a near-monopoly over the provision of foreign news in some areas of Britain, but the service was available to anyone who could pay for it; indeed, one of the cornerstones of Julius Reuter's business strategy was that the service be offered to all comers on a basis of absolute equality.[30] All news agencies share certain monopolistic tendencies by virtue of the control they exercise over what news is reported and how it is distributed, thus directly affecting the view of the world that millions of widely dispersed readers receive.[31] However, the highly restrictive monopoly of knowledge that Innis cites in relation to Associated Press is not an essential characteristic either of the telegraph or the news agency *per se*. The institutional forms that grow up around a particular technology can vary in significant ways.

Innis also argued that the telegraph and news agencies played an important part in the development of a new economic and business model for the newspaper industry generally. In his account, newspapers grew during the late 19th and 20th centuries mainly because advertisers wanted a way of reaching consumers. Newspapers became larger to accommodate increased volumes of advertising (a process that required

---

AP's success, which had "disastrous results to independent newspapers." Innis (1951), pp. 18–19.

29 Innis (1951), p. 18. For the 1918 ruling see Schwarzlose, vol. 2, p. 242.

30 Donald Read, *The Power of News: The History of Reuters* (London: Oxford University Press, 1992), p. 45.

31 Schwarzlose, vol. 1, p. 121: "[C]reation and operation of a newsbrokerage [news agency] increasingly deprived an editor of the ability to make daily decisions on selecting and editing stories from beyond his community. Newsbroking centralized the gathering, assembling and distributing of news stories in the hands of the broker, who might be many miles away and was functioning with motivations or perspectives differing from those of the local editor. Such tendencies toward centralization and monopolization of news movement are a continuous theme of newbroking's history, and find parallel expression in each of a succession of national communications systems, of which telegraphy was only the first."

cheap and regular supplies of newsprint), and developed sensationalistic methods to promote larger circulations, especially among less-educated readers – again, a goal of advertisers. Sheltered behind the unquestioned doctrine of freedom of the press (especially in the United States), the mass-circulation newspaper with its focus on crime, gossip, sex and scandal established a monopoly beyond the merely political, diminishing the possibilities of genuine understanding among its readers:

> Technological advance in communication implies a narrowing of the range from which material is distributed and a widening of the range of reception in which large numbers receive, but are unable to make any direct response. Those on the receiving end of material from a mechanized central system are precluded from participation in healthy, vigourous and vital discussion. ... The lumpy character of new developments in communication and the appeal to lower levels of intelligence by unstable people accentuates instability if not insanity.[32]

The telegraph and news service contributed to these developments, in Innis' view, by increasing the supply of news – one of several resources (a supply of cheap paper, better presses, a more efficient distribution system) that the new approach to the newspaper business required.[33] In one sense, the supply of news is a straightforward notion – subscribing newspapers would have received a much greater volume of timely, publishable daily copy via AP than they had through the postal exchange. But quantity is not the only issue; Innis was also drawing attention to a new kind of information, one that adds a further dimension to the idea of the monopoly of knowledge. Compared to news made available through the exchange system, telegraphic news is more timely, reports events and facts rather than discussing ideas, and arrives in a predictable way.

32 Innis (1949), p. 37. See also his comment on p. 27 that the growing importance of afternoon papers suggests "(t)he implications of the press in the twentieth century" – "Evening papers catered to individuals who had exhausted the possibilities of concentrated mental power and demanded relaxation and entertainment rather than information and instruction."
33 Sometimes the formulation is reversed and a growing demand for news is said to have brought the telegraph into wider use. "The demand for news to increase circulation hastened the development of the telegraph and the organization of news services." Innis (1972), p. 161.

It is, in short, information that is more like a commodity, suitable for use in the industrial process that newspaper publishing had become.[34] Without this regular supply of *daily* news, the large daily newspaper publishing many pages of advertising would not have enough content to attract a large readership.

The telegraphic news agency thus brought a new way of conceiving the world to newspaper readers. It is the wire service which made it possible for millions of readers, widely separated in space, to see reports of the same events, expressed in the same words, each day. One might argue that this, rather than the newspaper *per se*, is the crucial institution in creating the "imagined communities" which Benedict Anderson describes as the core of modern nationalism.[35] Various influential accounts of the emergence of a new kind of news in the 19th century have emphasized the importance of objectivity, factuality, or a broader range of content.[36] Just as important, though, are the ideas of regularity and consistency: news as a regular succession of daily events from around the nation and the world, described in an increasingly consistent way. In this conception, today's news will be different from yesterday's, to be sure, but "the news" as an overall category is more predictable, its arrival in sufficient quantity more reliable, its form less variable. This is a creation of the telegraphic news agency, and this idea of what news is has persisted relatively unchanged to the present day. Although Innis did not use the phrase, one of the telegraph's major legacies might be described as the monopoly of news.

---

34 The spread of literacy and the public school system, Innis argued, had created "new types of readers concerned with events rather than ideas," and early attempts at cooperative newsgathering in the pre-telegraphic era suggest "the significance of emphasizing facts in spread of communication." Innis (1980), p. 122. On news as industrial commodity, see Carey, "Technology and Ideology," in Carey (1992), p. 211.

35 Benedict Anderson, *Imagined Communities* (New York and London: Verso; rev. ed., 1991), p. 33.

36 See, for example, David Z.T. Mindich, *Just the Facts: How "Objectivity" Came to Define American Journalism* (New York and London: New York University Press, 1998); Michael Schudson, *Discovering the News: A Social History of American Newspapers* (New York: Basic Books, 1978). For a recent history that focuses on the development of consistency in the physical appearance and organization of newspapers, see Kevin Barnhurst and John Nerone, *The Form of News: A History* (New York: The Guilford Press, 2001).

The telegraph's centralizing tendencies

Beyond the newspaper industry, the growing supply of news had broader economic effects. Innis noted that rudimentary news services had operated as early as the mid-16th century, mainly to provide up-to-date price information for commercial clients.[37] Around that time, the stock exchange at Antwerp "required a permanent news service to provide information on the rating of business houses of different nationalities."[38] In one of his Idea File notes, Innis draws together different threads in a highly suggestive way:

> Growth of market opinion – rise of price structure – Lyons, Antwerp, Amsterdam organization of news services as basis of opinion. Shift from political and ecclesiastical hierarchies – rise of state as instrument of credit. Role of Netherlands as republic in contrast with monarchies. Impersonal method of appointments of price system compared with competitive examinations, nepotism, etc.[39]

Here Innis is describing the role of information in what he elsewhere calls the penetration of the price system, a historical development of great significance.[40] The growth of newspapers in the 19th century accelerated this process, and in doing so broke up monopolies of knowledge: "development of newspapers means destruction of monopolies of price information – equilibrium theory, i.e., Marshall, paralleling increasing influence of press in spread of information."[41] In addition, "(t)he railroad and the telegraph steadily increased the efficiency of advertising media – chiefly weeklies, monthlies and quarterlies – which created a national market."[42]

---

37 "News-letters were used by the Fuggers after 1554 and printed sheets developed with improvements in postal services organized by monarchies." Innis (1972), p. 146.

38 Ibid., p. 147.

39 Innis (1980), p. 30.

40 See Innis, "The Penetrative Powers of the Price System on New World States," in Innis (1995), pp. 66–87.

41 Innis (1980), p. 122. Alfred Marshall (1842–1924) was one of the founders of neoclassical economics.

42 Innis, "On the Economic Significance of Cultural Factors," in Innis (1995),

Innis' discussion of advertising parallels to some extent his treatment of the telegraph. On one hand, he emphasizes the underlying technology's decentralizing tendencies: thus he stresses that daily newspapers were more closely restricted to their local circulation areas, leaving weeklies and monthlies to develop the national advertising market (especially for such consumer products as patent medicines). At the same time, though, local newspapers became steadily more dependent on advertising, which led in the aggregate to an intensification of market involvement on the part of readers everywhere and therefore a deepening of advertising's overall influence. The telegraph and wire services contributed indirectly, but crucially, to this development, mainly by providing a sufficient quantity of up-to-date news to attract large audiences and to allow the publication of a daily news vehicle of sufficient size to support the growing volume of display advertising. In any case, the telegraph was not the only technology, nor was the news service the only institution, that contributed to the spread of advertising or the price system, but they were important elements in the combination of forces that underlay it.

Clearly, although Innis never focused explicitly on the telegraph in any substantial way, his analysis of it is both subtle and far-reaching. By emphasizing its decentralizing aspects, though, Innis paid less attention to how the telegraph extended control over space and extended the reach of institutions and political authority.

---

p. 306. "Correspondence between individuals and firms with slow navigation ... was inadequate to meet the demands of large-scale industry and large-scale consumption. The rapid and effective dissemination of information was essential to the effective placing of labour, capital, raw materials, and finished products. Oscar Wilde wrote that 'private information is practically the source of every large modern fortune,' and the demand for private information hastened the development of communications. The application of steam power to the production of paper, and, in turn, of the newspapers, followed by the telegraph, and the exploitation of human curiosity and its interest in news by advertisers anxious to dispose of their products created efficient channels for the spread of information. The state, acting through subsidies, the post office, libraries, and compulsory education, widened the areas to which information could be disseminated. Democratic forms of government provided news and subsidies for the transmission of news." Innis, "On the Economic Significance of Cultural Factors," p. 303. Innis also argued that the decentralization of the daily press brought about by the telegraph and news services meant that only weeklies or monthlies could develop national circulation and influence: *ibid.*, p. 303.

At one level, this was simply a matter of physical expansion. In Canada, for example, the telegraph reached Fort Garry in the Red River colony (present-day Winnipeg) in 1871, more than a decade before the transcontinental railway did; similarly in the United States, the telegraph reached San Francisco in 1861, eight years before the railway.[43] There was a natural symbiosis between railways and telegraphs, but since the telegraph was much cheaper to build and operate, it was well ahead of the railway in exercising control over space. Once built, the telegraph allowed politicians and bureaucrats to exercise much closer control over diplomats or military officers in the field (prompting Britain's ambassador in Vienna to complain about "the telegraphic demoralization of those who formerly had to act for themselves"[44]). In the United States, the federal government's control of the telegraph system during the Civil War was an important, and consciously exploited, military advantage; a by-product of this was that Associated Press became, in effect, a government news agency for the duration of the war.[45] In economic terms, the telegraph gave corporations much greater control at a distance over their operations, and (as Innis noted indirectly) tied a growing number of commodities and their producers around the world into an integrated market.

The telegraph was typically a single channel and thus ideally suited to monopoly control, a fact reflected in government ownership in Britain, France and most other countries and the dominance of Western Union in the United States.[46] Internationally, the dominant news agencies of Britain, France and Germany were sufficiently powerful that in 1870 they divided the world into exclusive territories, in which each had a monopoly in supplying news from abroad and gathering it for foreign distribution

---

43 Harold Innis and A R. M. Lower, *Select Documents in Canadian Economic History* (Toronto: University of Toronto Press, 1933), p. 734; Blondheim, p. 145.

44 Tom Standage, *The Victorian Internet: The Remarkable Story of the Telegraph and the Nineteenth Century's On-line Pioneers* (Walker and Company: New York, 1998), pp. 156–159.

45 Menahem Blondheim, "'Public Sentiment is Everything': The Union's Public Communications Strategy and the Bogus Proclamation of 1864," *Journal of American History* 89:3 (December 2002): 869–899.

46 Innis' understanding of the monopolistic characteristics of the St. Lawrence trade and communication corridor in Canada might readily apply to the telegraph as well.

– a further indication of what Innis might call the "space-binding" qualities of the telegraphic news agency. With some modifications this system remained in place for 60 years. If not an outright monopoly, it was a closely controlled and long-lasting oligopoly of global space.[47] One might readily extend to all news agencies Menaham Blondheim's conclusion that AP was "one of the most powerful centripetal forces shaping American society in the modern era."[48]

Nor did Innis pay much attention directly to the telegraph's significance in terms of time. This reflects a peculiarity of his overall approach: when Innis spoke of a bias toward time, he really meant a bias toward duration – he was not speaking of a continuum between media that send messages slowly and media that send them quickly. For Innis, media that transmit information relatively quickly – paper, for example, or the telegraph – were said to have a bias toward space rather than time. He did acknowledge their speed, but considered this primarily in terms of its effect on space rather than time *per se*. Rich and productive though it is, the space-time dichotomy does not favor systematic consideration of speedy media such as the telegraph in relation to time.

When Innis acknowledged that the telegraph contributed to a great increase in the speed of transmitting information, he followed the pattern noted earlier of considering it among other innovations that affected the development of the newspaper industry.

> The newspaper has been a pioneer in the development of speed in communication and transportation. Extension of railroads and telegraphs brought more rapid transmission of news and wider and faster circulation of newspapers; and newspapers, in turn, demanded further extension of railroads and telegraph lines. ... Speed in the collection, production and dissemination of information has been the essence of newspaper development.[49]

47 Read, pp. 53–58.

48 Blondheim (1994), p. 7. As noted on p. 175 above, Innis recognized that news agencies exercised great influence through their central position in the distribution of news, which tended to counteract the decentralizing forces identified elsewhere. But the balance of his interpretation remains overwhelmingly in favor of decentralization.

49 Innis (1942), p. 31. Elsewhere Innis put great emphasis on the introduction of fast presses; see, for example, "The Bias of Communication," in Innis (1995), p. 347.

The telegraph played a crucial part in this speeding up. The key point is that it reduced or eliminated time differentials in access to important information among different localities, and in this sense it broke down monopolies of knowledge.[50] But as Blondheim has observed, it has its own monopolistic tendencies in relation to time.[51] The telegraph is a "pipeline" technology. Messages move through it sequentially, so that whichever message enters the pipeline first is delivered first; it has an important temporal advantage over the second message in the queue, as does the second over the third, and so on. Furthermore, though an individual telegraphic signal is instantaneous, a message of even a few words (with each letter representing one or more separate signals) takes much longer to encode, transmit and decode; this, combined with other delays in transmission (by the routing of messages through different circuits, for example) magnifies the first-comer's advantages.[52] Conditions of access are therefore crucially important, and when a user has sufficient bargaining power to guarantee preferential access (as was the case between AP and Western Union), monopolistic advantages ensue.[53]

How much help, then, is Innis in seeking to understand the telegraph and the institutions that grew up around it? As we have seen, he never sought to explain the telegraph as a separate technology, but considered it as one of several media of communication that contributed to the development of the newspaper industry. Despite his emphasis on decentralization, Innis' discussions of the telegraph and the news agency point toward an underlying tension: they broke down monopolies in some respects, but strengthened them in other ways. In particular, the telegraph and the news agency broke down monopolies of knowledge by disseminating information widely and quickly (making it possible

50 As Carey has pointed out, the telegraph moved speculation into the dimension of time rather than space and led to the creation of futures markets. "Technology and Ideology," in Carey (1992), pp. 217–218.
51 Blondheim (1994), pp. 60–63.
52 The encoding and decoding of messages (as in Morse code) was time-consuming; on average, a skilled operator could transmit or receive 30 words a minute, or around 1,800 words an hour. One key to Julius Reuter's success was his ability to knit together poorly connected telegraphic circuits efficiently, thus transmitting messages more quickly than competitors could; Read, p. 18.
53 Blondheim (1994), p. 43.

for small-town newspapers to provide their own, timely, versions of national and international events, or allowing small-town merchants to know the price of wheat in Chicago or Liverpool at the same time their big-city competitors did). At the same time, the institutions that controlled the telegraphic and news networks (such as Associated Press and Western Union) were highly monopolistic in structure. The two tendencies coexisted, the balance varying at different times. For a present-day researcher, the attempt to understand this balance offers a powerful analytical approach to questions of wire-service and telegraphic history.

News agencies and regional competition: the founding of Canadian Press

The development of Canadian Press illustrates the value of an Innisian approach to wire-service history. CP was not established until 1917, very late in comparison to Associated Press and Reuters. From 1894 until 1910, the AP franchise in Canada was held by the Canadian Pacific Railway and AP copy was distributed to Canadian newspapers exclusively via the CPR telegraph. After the CPR stopped offering the service in 1910, it took seven years for Canadian publishers to establish their own functioning news cooperative – the chief asset of which was the AP service – and this only came about under the highly charged circumstances of wartime and with the aid of a substantial government subsidy.[54] Although individual Canadian newspapers were often innovative and successful, one is struck by the overall weakness of the Canadian industry in this respect, and by its willingness simply to tag along with American developments.[55] Innis' ideas help to explain why this was so; indeed, this situation illustrates one of his chief concerns, the

---

54 M.E. Nichols, *(CP) The Story of The Canadian Press* (Toronto: Ryerson Press, 1948), pp. 5–130.

55 See Paul Rutherford, *A Victorian Authority: The Daily Press in Late Nineteenth-Century Canada* (Toronto: University of Toronto Press, 1982); and Minko Sotiron, *From Politics to Profit : The Commercialization of Canadian Daily Newspapers, 1890–1920* (Montreal: McGill-Queen's University Press, 1997)

difficulty of maintaining particularity in an increasingly homogeneous (i.e., American-dominated) world.[56]

The idea of the monopoly of space applies to various aspects of CP's history. It is of crucial importance that the American telegraph network had reached Canada and the maritime provinces of British North America by the late 1840s.[57] This meant that once AP was in operation, channels were already in place that would allow its distribution north of the border. Although the border imposed significant organizational and institutional conditions on the use of AP material in Canada, the telegraph as a connected system increasingly drew all of North America together into a single, continental space – a clear indication of its expansionist spatial bias.[58] Furthermore, since AP had an effective monopoly in the provision of international and American news for most of the later 19th century, there was little reason for Canadian newspapers to establish their own service as long as AP news could be acquired at a reasonable cost. Once established, the AP monopoly tended to be self-perpetuating.

The regional dimension of spatial monopolies was especially apparent in Canada. The first steps toward the creation of a Canadian news agency were taken in Winnipeg. In 1907, three competing dailies in the city joined forces to oppose a decision by the CPR's telegraph department to increase substantially the rates it charged for the AP service; at the same time, the volume of AP material would be cut.[59] Despite the CPR's dominant position, other telegraph companies served Winnipeg, and other news agencies such as United Press and Hearst's

56 Drache, "Introduction," in Innis (1995), pp. xvi, xxii.
57 The extension of the telegraph system into New Brunswick and Nova Scotia took place under the direct influence of Associated Press. AP wanted the fastest and most secure possible connection with Halifax, where the Cunard mail steamers, carrying the latest European news, made their first North American landfall. The through line from Halifax to New York went into operation in 1849; see Blondheim (1994), pp. 81–83, 87. The telegraph from New York reached Toronto via Buffalo in 1846; Schwarzlose vol. 1, p. 82.
58 Chandler (1977), p. 200, notes that as an essentially long-distance medium, the telegraph was powerfully pushed toward systematization and consolidation.
59 Nichols, p. 20. Canadian Associated Press, a more limited service to provide cable news from Britain, had been set up in Toronto in 1903, aided by a government subsidy of $15,000. Rutherford (1982), p. 113.

International News Service were eager to compete with AP. Taking advantage of these circumstances, the Winnipeg publishers formed an organization called Western Associated Press, putting together a service of international and Canadian news for newspapers throughout western Canada from non-AP sources and distributing it as far as possible over telegraph lines of the CPR's competitors. As M.E. Nichols, one of WAP's founders, recalled, the fact that competing newspapers did not circulate in the Canadian west made doing without AP conceivable: "As a last resort [the Winnipeg publishers] could rest on the principle that news is news until it is read (no radio in those days), and the only intruding competition to consider was from a city in the United States 500 miles distant from Winnipeg and a Canadian city 1,200 miles away."[60]

Newspapers in Toronto and Montreal had no interest in the western experiment, mainly because the threatened CPR price increase did not apply to them. But more fundamentally, the status quo was quite acceptable because of their favorable position in the continental system of telegraphic news distribution. Being reasonably close to New York, they received the AP report with minimal transmission charges. Equally important, Ontario and Quebec were relatively densely populated with newspapers, which could be served by fairly compact telegraphic circuits. The costs of distance were thus quite low, and lowered further in being divided among many subscribers. For Winnipeg and points west, a contrasting set of locational circumstances led to a much less favorable result. The 1,200 miles that separated the city from eastern competitors and the relative scarcity of other newspapers to share the cost of transmission over a long circuit led to much heavier telegraphic charges. Thus, even before the 1907 price increase, Toronto morning papers paid 40 per cent of what their (much smaller) counterparts in Calgary or Saskatoon paid for the same AP service.[61]

Winnipeg's location involved issues of power and editorial control as well. An important aspect of the telegraphic news agency's monopolistic structure is that "downstream" locations are greatly affected by decisions made at "upstream" transmission points about how much and what kind of material to send. Winnipeg's reasons for dissatisfaction with

60 Nichols, p. 21.
61 Toronto morning papers were paying $20 a week for AP service circa 1910, as against $50 a week for Calgary and Saskatoon; Nichols, pp. 55, 64.

the CPR's proposal to deliver the AP report from Minneapolis instead of Montreal are revealing: while the AP report received in Montreal was an acceptably complete version of the AP international-news file, the version that arrived from Minneapolis had been previously edited down at Detroit and again at Chicago in order to meet the interests of "newspaper readers in the middle western states." In the process, Nichols wrote, "(n)ews of general public interest, and especially cable [i.e., international] news, went out of the report as state news went in."[62] Since the western Canadian papers were not members of AP, but simply purchasers of a commodity that was made available as is, they had little ability to influence what they received – except if they succeeded in organizing a Canadian cooperative in which they might hope to have some influence.

In 1910, the CPR decided after an unfavorable regulatory decision to sell its AP franchise to a holding company of Canadian publishers. At the same time, the Great North Western Telegraph Co., which was mainly active in eastern Canada, gave up its service of providing domestic news. Nichols saw these events as the termination of 50 years in which telegraph companies had been the main providers of telegraphic news to Canadian publishers. In the United States, as Richard Schwarzlose has noted, the struggle between news agencies and telegraphers for control of news-agency business continued for 30 years after the Civil War, but the publishers represented in AP succeeded in maintaining their independence.[63] In Canada it appears that the telegraph companies were relatively stronger – exercised, in Innis' terms, a more effective monopoly – and the publishers (collectively at least) were relatively weaker than in the United States. Had it not been for the decision of the Board of Railway Commissioners that led the CPR to give up the AP franchise, the CPR might have maintained its control for many years beyond 1910.

Why did the technology of the telegraph have a stronger position than publishers – the producers and main consumers of news content – in Canada? The reason may have been that in no individual, strategically located city were publishers able to establish the dominance over telegraphic news that New York publishers exercised (initially at least)

---

62 Ibid., pp. 27, 28.
63 Schwarzlose, vol. 2, p. x.

in the United States. The early history of Associated Press is a tale of high-handedness and arrogance towards its subscribers, especially by the organization's autocratic general manager, Daniel Craig.[64] In Canada, by contrast, publishers in Montreal and Toronto were more or less evenly matched in strength; in the holding company that was established in 1911, for example, the Ontario and Quebec section had two separate divisions, one controlled in Toronto and one in Montreal. Neither city exercised the crucial "gateway" functions in relation to the rest of the Canadian newspaper market that New York AP exercised in the United States, reaping the monopolistic advantages that went along with its location at the originating end of the telegraphic news pipeline.

But the main obstacle to the establishment of a functioning Canadian news agency was the division of costs for leased-wire service over what were called the "unproductive gaps" in the Canadian telegraph system. Between Toronto and Winnipeg, Calgary and Vancouver, and Montreal and Saint John, New Brunswick, there were long distances (1,200 miles, 640 miles, and 480 miles, respectively) with no daily newspapers on the main telegraphic circuit to bear a share of the cost. As Blondheim has noted, the economics of news-agency operation tend strongly to reinforce monopoly: in terms of breadth, volume, quality and cost of coverage, it is virtually impossible for any competitor to overcome an established news agency's advantages in distributing the same news report to numerous subscribers on one reasonably compact telegraphic circuit.[65] Where there are only a few subscribers over long distances, an equally powerful economic logic works in the opposite direction, creating instability – or, as in the Canadian case, preventing the very establishment of a news agency without extraordinary outside intervention. Thus the years between 1911 and 1917 were largely spent in fruitless arguments over whether newspapers in Ontario and Quebec should subsidize the leased wire to Winnipeg that was the crucial connecting link in a national system. The western viewpoint, as Nichols expressed it, was that Ontario and Quebec publishers should "pass on some of the benefits of their preferred position to territorial divisions whose geographical position penalized them," while the central Canadian

---

64 Schwarzlose, vol. 1, pp. 186–191; Blondheim (1994), pp. 109, 125
65 Blondheim (1994), p. 100.

publishers just as adamantly insisted it was not their responsibility to pay for transmission beyond their provincial boundaries.[66] The impasse was not resolved until the federal government agreed in 1917 to contribute an annual subsidy of $50,000, which covered the cost of leased wires over all three unproductive gaps.[67]

The early history of Canadian Press recalls strongly a concept that shaped Innis' earlier work on the economic history of Canada – the notion of excess capacity. Innis' work on the cod fishery, the fur trade, the Canadian Pacific Railway and the history of transportation in Canada generally emphasized what might be called the costs of distance.[68] The operation of costly trade networks or systems of transportation at much less than full capacity had wide-ranging consequences, shaping patterns of immigration and settlement at different periods and emphasizing cycles of expansion or retrenchment in the fur trade or the wheat economy.[69] Excess capacity tended to create both rigidity (a lack of

66 Nichols, p. 85.
67 Nichols, p. 129. The subsidy was withdrawn in 1924.
68 Harold Innis, *A History of the Canadian Pacific Railway*, reprinted with a foreword by Peter George (Toronto: University of Toronto Press, 1971; first published 1923).

———; *The Cod Fisheries: The History of an International Economy* (Toronto: University of Toronto Press, 1940, reprinted 1978).

———; *The Fur Trade in Canada: An Introduction to Canadian Economic History* (Toronto: University of Toronto Press, 1956, reprinted 1970).

———; "Unused Capacity as a Factor in Canadian Economic History," in Innis (1995), pp. 139–154

Innis and Lower (1933).

In his introductory notes to the section on the telegraph in *Select Documents in Canadian Economic History*, Innis notes the similarity of its history to those of the railway, roads, air mail, and the telephone: "[A]ll tend in their first stages to get their east-west connections through the already completed American systems. All-Canadian (and in the case of overseas shipping, cables, etc., all-British) routes come later and often from sentimental or political motives. Local development and extension is the next stage" (p. 213).

69 "Problems of unused capacity have had the effect of quickening and accentuating the long-run general trends of economic development and have necessitated governmental intervention as a steadying or remedial factor. ... Governmental intervention as a means of solving problems during a period of expansion creates problems to be solved by new types of government intervention during a depression." Innis, "Unused capacity," in Innis (1995), p. 152.

adaptability) and instability and eventually to require government intervention. The unproductive gaps that stood in the way of establishing Canadian Press parallel almost exactly the problems of distance that complicated the financing and building of the Canadian Pacific Railway, a subject which Innis had studied closely in the early 1920s. One of the attractions of an Innisian account of CP is that it underscores the links between Innis' earlier work as an economic historian (based on primary sources and focused on Canada) and his later research as a communications theorist (focused on secondary sources, synthesis, and the world outside Canada).

Innis' explanation of how the telegraph affected relations between large and smaller cities also applies to Canada. Nichols, the Winnipeg newspaperman who has written the only published history of CP, commented on the competition between newspapers in Toronto and those elsewhere in the province in a passage that strongly echoes Innis' account of the relations between newspapers in London and New York and their respective hinterlands:

> Obviously there was a competitive situation in the smaller cities, the local papers struggling to hold the circulation available in their limited areas and the metropolitan papers eager to push in. The weaker the smaller paper in national and external news, the more vulnerable it was to invasion by the big fellow.[70]

But the availability of the Canadian Press service changed the competitive balance. It allowed the smaller papers to receive:

> a standardized news service differing only in volume from the complete service which is the backbone of the news content of metropolitan papers. Nothing of major interest to the Canadian reader can happen, at home or abroad, that is known to the big city paper in advance of its communication to its provincial contemporary.[71]

The tendency toward decentralization that Innis noted in his overall account of the telegraph and news agencies was clearly at work in Canada as well.

70 Nichols, p. 87.
71 Ibid.

Innis' interest in the relations between large and smaller entities applies more broadly to CP's history. It is clear that AP as an institution exercised a powerful influence in the establishment of Canadian Press. In 1914, Melville Stone, AP's general manager, presented the Winnipeg-based Western Associated Press with an "ultimatum – it is not too strong an expression – demand[ing] that the Canadian Press, Limited [the publishers' holding company for AP rights] be nationalized with a supreme central executive and headquarters. The Western Associated Press must go out of business."[72]

Why would Stone have taken such a position? He probably had two concerns: first, that a relatively weak organization like WAP might be less able to discipline its members, leaving open the possibility that news which AP considered its exclusive property would end up in the hands of non-AP members; and second, that WAP had a record of dealing with AP's competitors. Stone must have been aware that WAP had begun its career by using non-AP services, and he may have known that WAP was negotiating with another U.S. news agency (presumably United Press or Hearst's International News Service) as late as 1914. In July 1917, British Columbia newspapers were told of Stone's complaints that "a rival American news service" was receiving Canadian news that should go only to AP.[73] At CP's first annual meeting the previous month, Stone repeated in person his insistence that there should be "a strong central governing body" for the Canadian news service – no doubt because only such a strong organization could enforce the monopoly over how its members used the service that AP had worked so hard to achieve.[74]

Just as AP's major asset in its early years was possession of the latest European news off the Cunard steamers, so the AP service of American and international news was the most valuable thing that Canadian Press had to offer its members. This gave AP a great deal of leverage over the fledgling organization. There are several ironies in this situation. Stone, who had been a Chicago publisher and representative of the midwestern

---

72 Canadian Press Archives (Toronto), Western Associated Press files, printed statement of Sept. 24, 1914.

73 Canadian Press Archives, File 9–0, "Meetings general 1917–1918," minutes of annual meeting, June 13, 1917; minutes of meeting, British Columbia section, July 1917.

74 Canadian Press Archives, minutes of annual meeting, June 13, 1917.

insurgents in their battle against control by New York-based AP, had no sympathy for the similar regional aspirations of Winnipeg-based Western Associated Press 20 years later. By 1910, the tendency toward decentralization which so impressed Innis had given way to a renewed movement toward centralization and monopoly.

It is important to remember that Innis studied media of communication not simply for their own sake, but because they helped explain why societies rose and fell, and why the relations of dominance and subordination between societies were as they were. In considering CP's origins, it is noteworthy that a powerful American-based organization demanded the establishment of a strong Canadian junior partner that could overcome centrifugal tendencies. While the Canadian government's interest in a better supply of Canadian war news cannot be minimized, it is nonetheless true that a major national institution in Canada came into being in substantial part because of American pressure. As a stable, though subordinate, partner, a strong Canadian news agency effectively enhanced the influence of an American monopoly. At the same time, though, the institution that thereby came into existence can only have strengthened a sense of shared nationality among Canadian newspaper readers. As in the United States, the tension between monopoly and particularity persisted.

Centralization and decentralization: a shifting balance

My purpose in the foregoing is not to relate the entire history of Canadian Press, but simply to suggest how Innis' ideas might assist in such a project. Clearly, his notions of the monopoly of space and decentralization are highly applicable. (While more recent scholars have gone further in elaborating the monopolistic characteristics of the telegraphic news agency – characteristics which affected the course of developments in Canada – at least one of them was inspired by Innis, so that here we have Innis at one remove.[75]) The notion of excess capacity, which arose in Innis' earlier studies of Canadian economic history, is

75 Both Schwarzlose and Blondheim emphasize the monopolistic aspects of AP's history, Blondheim doing so in an explicitly Innisian framework (1994), pp. 2–4.

also helpful in understanding the evolution of telegraphic news services; it might apply to other countries that, like Canada, are not as central in the international information economy as the United States or Britain. Innis' awareness of Canada's paradoxical nature applies here as well: not only a nation whose role in some measure has been to manage more efficiently its successive subordinate relationships with Britain and the United States, it is also one whose very existence (along with the institutional supports, like Canadian Press, which it established) raises at least the possibility of a more independent direction.

In all, the implicit analysis of telegraphic news that underlies Innis' account of the newspaper industry provides many useful tools for thinking with. It must be acknowledged, though, that his emphasis on decentralization – understandable though it may be in the context of Innis' interest in newspapers as a way-station between the nationalism of print and the centralization of radio – seems overstated when one looks at the telegraph specifically. Yet it would be equally problematic to describe the story as one of centralization only. It is more enlightening to consider telegraphic news in relation to a shifting balance between centralization and decentralization, a balance which changes over time and may display elements of both tendencies at any given moment. Hinterlands of metropolitan newspapers can shrink while their local dominance grows stronger; the increasing autonomy of individual newspapers may be undermined when one considers the telegraphic news agency as an institution that serves and shapes the whole industry; one type of national political culture may be weakened even as the national (and international) economy takes deeper root. Innis' powerful structures of explanation yield a version of history that is coherent but not one-dimensional, never losing its capacity to account for change in new and surprising ways.

XIAOQUAN ZHAO

8. Revitalizing Time:
An Innisian Perspective on the Internet

Introduction

Harold Innis died at a time when television was making its entry into ordinary households. Fifty years later, television is already an "old" medium. A variety of new media based on digital technology have come about and started to be widely used. The Internet is an outstanding representative of these new media. It carries a colossal amount of information and disseminates it with an unprecedented level of efficiency. Such enormous capacity residing in a single medium would be simply unimaginable to Innis' contemporaries (with the exception, perhaps, of Marshall McLuhan). Living in this Internet age, we cannot help but wondering: What would Innis have to say were he to live today? How would his notions of space and time be applied to the Internet? Would he consider the Internet as yet another spatially biased medium, or a revolutionary technology that could serve to salvage the time element in our collective cultural experience? This paper will seek to answer these questions.

Many believe that Innis was essentially a pessimist (Carey, 1989; Blondheim, 2003). This claim is apparently based on the gloomy commentaries Innis made of the media environment in the modern history of the Western civilization. This history, according to Innis, was marked by media technologies that exhibit a strong bias toward space. Printing, and the various media forms based on this technology, enabled the dissemination of information over vast territories. The dominance of these media consequently cultivated a social-cultural favoritism toward expansion, military force, nationalism, commercialism, specialization, and mechanization. On the other hand, religion, tradition, community, and other manifestations of a concern for time were marginalized at best, and destroyed at worst. With these observations, Innis warned his readers of a dangerous and ever-growing obsession with space in the Western civilization, and pleaded for a resurrection of time (Innis, 1951).

I would argue, however, that Innis would not be as pessimistic today. The Internet, unlike the traditional print and electronic media, may be able to diminish society's bias toward space. Before embarking on explanation, there are two issues that have to be dealt with first. One concerns whether it is at all worth the effort to apply Innis' theory to the contemporary media environment. The other, also the more important one, concerns what analytical framework should be derived from Innis' theory and applied to the Internet, if such application is indeed meaningful.

Current relevance of Innis

In his critique of Innis, Blondheim (2003) writes:

> The relevance of canon has two dimensions: the text's continuing power to engage, and its continuing power to explain. Innis's work has proved mostly successful on the first account, less so on the second…Innis's work has failed, on the whole, to serve as a foundation for understanding later-day real-world developments, as media and their institutional environments changed and the broader social, political, and cultural landscape changed with them. (p. 178)

Blondheim's evaluation of Innis' theory is not unfair. As he noticed, over the last half century, "[F]ew if any observers resort to [Innis'] ideas or make reference to his texts in attempting to interpret the rapid and radical changes in the communication environment" (p. 28). While this is true, it should also be noted that, at the turn of the century, a series of endeavors have emerged trying to analyze the cultural significance of various new media specifically using Innis' communication theory (e.g., Comor, 2001; Menzies, 1999; 2000). These endeavors, in fact, represent only part of the recent resurgence of technological theories, which is apparently sparked by the recognition of the enormous impact of new media technologies on contemporary society. A representative work in this resurgence is *Digital McLuhan* (Levinson, 1999), in which

the many prophecies McLuhan made decades ago are reassessed in
the world of digital media. Innis, however, is not in the center of the
limelight; like years ago, he is still shadowed by the more dramatic
and magnetic image of Marshall McLuhan. But his theory is also
gaining attention and is being regarded as a useful analytical tool in the
examination of the newest development in the media (Menzies, 2000).

Another possible reason that, in Blondheim's eyes, might have caused
the lack of application of Innis' theory to the contemporary world is
Innis' "bias" as an "involved public man, academia leader, and policy
maker" (p. 29). This bias is centrally reflected in his concern with the
future of the Western civilization. His roles as "public man, academia
leader, and policy maker" urged him to sound an alarm for the Western
civilization's "suicidal" obsession with space, while the dynamic in his
theory leads readers to expect a revival of the time bias as a corrective.
This, according to Blondheim, is an inconsistency and it compromises
the current relevance of Innis' ideas. Blondheim's observation of the
discrepancy between the theoretical implications of Innis' work and his
realistic concerns is accurate. But this discrepancy does not necessarily
impair the meaningfulness of Innis' theory in the new media environment.
In fact, both Innis' theory and his alarm were meant to urge us to put the
contemporary world under close and constant scrutiny. His alarm warns
us of the magnitude of the problem, while his dynamic theory gives us
hope and method to find a solution. This duality of Innis' ideas is thus a
reason for, rather than a reason against, the application of his theory to
the current and future media environment.

Thirdly, a fair case can be made that Innis' theory has not generated
much interest in contemporary application because it was not well
formulated in the first place. Blondheim and many others have
acknowledged the impenetrability of Innis' writing. He never really
elaborated his concepts in great detail; even concepts as central as
bias, time, and space could only receive a short condensed introduction
before they were thrown into overwhelming and meticulous historical
analysis. This certainly deterred many potential followers. But again,
this lack of explicit formulation is also a reason why Innis' theory can be
very engaging – it invites interpretation and elaboration, and it provides
multiple footings on which various levels of theorization and analysis
can be done. In view of this, the next part of this paper will seek to
extract an appropriate analytical framework for our investigation by

explicating Innis' theoretical approach and central concepts.

Innis' dialectical approach

Dialectics is a prominent characteristic of Canadian communication scholarship; it is also the approach Innis employs in his study of communication (Babe, 2000). A dialectical approach views all entities as the result of the dynamic interaction between opposites. The opposites are often different properties of the entity. They range from simple physical properties to large-scale social economic forces, all depending on the entity in question and its development stage. The interaction between opposites may result in tension and clash. It could also result in equilibrium, but such equilibrium in all likelihood will not last forever. In other words, struggle and contradiction between opposites are absolute; balance and reconciliation are only relative. From a dialectical point of view, everything can be defined as a relation. The atom is a relation between the positive and negative electrons. The society, in classic Marxist terms, is a relation between the production forces and the production relations. Dialectics sees history as composed of ongoing confrontations and resolutions between opposites. Both internal and external forces can kindle the confrontation within a relation. Consequently, dialectics emphasizes not only the internal strengths of the two opposites, but also the specific context in which the given relation exists.

Innis' perception of world history is a perfect exemplification of a dialectical relationship. He conceives of history as the trajectory of human society's movement along the continuum between time and space. Between these two opposites, a certain society at a given point of history can always be located. The relative proximity of the society toward either of the two poles indicates a certain kind of bias. The bias will constantly face resistance from the other end. When the bias becomes excessively strong, the reaction from the other side will also become powerful. As a result, the tension within society will build up and in time will lead to a correction, often violent correction, of the current bias. Balance between time and space, of course, is also possible. When a society reaches about the midpoint of the time-space continuum, bias will be minimized and a relative harmony will be achieved.

This dialectical nature of world history, according to Innis, derives primarily from the dialectical characteristics of the media technologies that have fueled the evolution of human society. Innis believed that every medium of communication, because of its particular properties, possesses a bias toward either time or space. He writes:

> According to [a medium's] characteristics it may be better suited to the dissemination of knowledge over time than over space, particularly if the medium is heavy and durable and not suited to transportation, or to the dissemination of knowledge over space than over time, particularly if the medium is light and easily transported. The relative emphasis on time or space will imply a bias of significance to the culture in which it is embedded. (1951, p. 33)

This short passage, in a crude way, defines a medium's bias in terms of its physical properties. But this definition, to Innis, is more a heuristic than a rigid categorization. It is a point of departure to think about the multiplicity of dialectical interactions that underpin the determination of the initial bias of the media and the transformation of such bias into defining cultural characteristics. Innis' historical analysis has demonstrated abundantly that the dialectic mechanism not only operates within each medium, but also functions between coexisting and/or competing media. More important, it has also demonstrated that the relationship between media technologies and cultural environment is not unidirectional. While shaping culture, media themselves are also shaped by external cultural forces.

These three kinds of dialectical interactions, I think, constitute the central thesis of Innis' communication theory. Obviously, these interactions are not parallel to one another. They are necessarily intertwined and constantly shedding influence on each other's development. In the following section, these dynamic interactions will be explained in terms of three levels of biases: medium bias, media bias, and cultural bias. These three levels of bias will then serve as an analytical framework for our investigation.

The analytical framework

Medium bias

According to Innis, any medium is defined by the relation between its time and space elements. The relative power of the two opposites is the internal determinant of its bias status. Viewing from another angle, however, it is also apparent that each medium has the potential to serve either as a time medium or a space medium or both. The stone can certainly be transported over space; the papyrus can also be used to store information over time. However, such use of these media does not take advantage of their relative strengths, and therefore does not represent the typical ways in which they have been used in history.

This is part of the reason why, as mentioned earlier, Innis' attribution of the time/space bias to media's physical properties should not be taken too rigidly. Nor should the physical properties be regarded as the only yardstick that can be used to measure bias. In fact, sometimes the external environment may play a bigger role in deciding a medium's bias. Angus (1998), for example, points out that in Innis' analysis, the same medium, water, exhibited different biases in different societies. In ancient Egypt, considerable importance was attached to the accurate prediction of the annual flooding of the Nile. As a result, a concern over time was fostered and tremendous efforts were directed toward designing and improving calendars in order to keep track of time. In Babylon, on the other hand, people were concerned with irrigation of their land. This problem led them to opening canals and eventually resulted in spatial expansion. Thus, the same medium, water, while possessing the same material properties, was biased toward time in one society and space in the other.

As is evident in his analysis, Innis certainly was not unaware of this dynamic between bias primarily shaped by internal characteristics and bias influenced by external conditions. However, he did not make a clear point on this issue. This negligence may have led many people to believe that physical characteristics are the only decisive element in his concept of media bias and consequently to criticize him for being overly simplistic.

Finally, it is also important to realize that time and space are essentially shorthand for a variety of media functions and effects. While the basic function of any medium is disseminating information, either over time or over space, this function almost immediately develops into many other functions once the medium comes into contact with society. Indeed, what motivated Innis' plea for time was not a disinterested observation that the dominant media of his day were most suited for the dissemination of information over space, but a sharp and poignant awareness that these space-biased media performed significant social, political, and cultural functions that were driving Western civilization farther away from the state of equilibrium (Innis, 1951). These higher order functions are not discernible when the medium is observed in isolation. Therefore, when trying to determine the bias of a medium, we should always put it in context. We should take into account not only its bias in the physical sense, but also the bias' higher-level manifestations. This inductive method is especially relevant in the new media environment, where the physical properties of the media are becoming increasingly harder to define. But this should not impair the relevance of the concept of bias, because we can still identify the bias in such media by examining the patterns of information flow they produce and the many social-cultural functions they fulfill.

Media bias

The relationship between coexisting media is frequently alluded to in Innis' texts. While an individual medium may display a particular bias, such bias may or may not represent the general bias in the entire media environment, and thus may or may not become the defining factor in the cultural environment. Innis' historical analysis seems to have identified three mechanisms that may decide the relationship between individual medium bias and general media bias. One mechanism is dominance, i.e., a certain medium serves as the predominant communication vehicle in a given society and overrides the biases of other coexisting media. One is balance, i.e., biases of different media cancel each other out and reach a relative balance. The third is coordination, i.e., multiple media share the same bias and together shape the characteristics of the social-cultural environment.

The mechanism of dominance is evident in most of Innis' analysis. Through domination, a medium may suppress the biases of other coexisting media and exert disproportionate influence on society. Pyramids in ancient Egypt, papyrus in the Roman Empire, and parchment in the Middle Ages, they were all the dominant media in their respective social-historical settings. The dominant and subordinate positions of coexisting media, again, are dually decided both by their technological advantages and external influences. For example, the dominance of parchment in the Middle Ages was not only a result of its durable quality, it was also contingent on many natural and cultural factors, such as the rise of Islam in the seventh century, which cut off the supplies of papyrus to the West from Egypt (Innis, 1972, p.16).

Societies containing a balanced media environment are infrequent in history. In such cases, the biases of two or more coexisting media manage to cancel each other out and the overall bias of the communication system therefore is minimized. This situation, according to Innis, is most conducive to stability and prosperity. "Large-scale political organizations such as empires...have tended to flourish under conditions in which civilization reflects the influence of more than one medium and in which the bias of one medium toward decentralization is offset by the bias of another medium towards centralization" (Innis, 1972, p.7). An example of such societies is ancient Greece, where the time bias of speech successfully resisted the space bias of writing, which resulted in the flowering of Greek culture in the fifth century (Innis, 1951, p. 68).

The mechanism of coordination, on the other hand, recognizes the possibility of shared bias between different media. This mechanism was particularly evident in Innis' analysis of his contemporary media environment, where various print media appeared to be jointly pushing the Western civilization toward an extreme bias toward space. This mechanism also seems to be at work with radio and television. Innis did not examine television, but he did consider radio as representing a counter force to traditional print media, particularly newspapers (1951, pp. 81–82, 188; 1972, p. 164). However, Innis' reading of radio was hasty and proved inaccurate in the long run. While Innis believed that radio, via its (early) emphasis on participation, could lead to dialogical communication, enhanced democracy, and enlightened public opinion, later development of this medium, and television as well, has attested to the prevalence of a one-way communication model, which, driven by an interest in profit, emphasizes only penetration, market segmentation, and specialized programming (Comer, 2001). Radio and television, therefore, have served to continue the space bias in the Western civilization, most notably in the United States.

Cultural bias

As mentioned earlier, the dialectical interaction between media and culture is not independent of the time-space interactions both within an individual medium and between coexisting media. In the previous two sections, we have repeatedly referred to the mutual influences between medium or media bias and social cultural conditions. The influence of culture on media, as we have observed, is centrally reflected in a variety of social and historical contingencies, which may facilitate the emergence of certain media technologies and cultivate particular kinds of bias within those technologies.

The influence of media on culture, as our analytical framework shows, may take place in a series of steps. Starting from medium bias, a single medium may be able to foster certain kind of social and cultural practices, but such practices will remain limited and/or local until this medium becomes the representative of the general media environment. Once a medium bias has evolved into the dominant media bias in a given society, changes and modifications will then occur on a large scale, and eventually the cultural character of that society will be redefined. But, how does this happen? Through what mechanism does the bias of communication transform into the overall bias of culture?

A central mechanism Innis discovered that explains the impact of communication on culture is monopoly of knowledge. He argued that the technological capacities of the media fundamentally influence the way knowledge is disseminated in society. When a medium, or a mix of media, becomes the predominant vehicle of information storage and/or circulation, its bias will tend to define the nature of knowledge, decide in whose hands the knowledge will be controlled, and dictate who will get access to this knowledge, hence creating a monopoly of knowledge. This monopoly, in turn, will decide what kind of institutions will emerge, what kind of politics will be practiced, and what kind of value system will be adopted by society at large. The resulting institutions, political practices, and value system, added together, represent an overall bias in society, which, in accordance with its source in communication, can be summarized as either a bias toward time or a bias toward space.

This rather lengthy interpretation of Innis' communication theory has identified three levels on which new media such as the Internet can be examined. Firstly, we should look at the medium from both within and without, and gain insight into its potential bias. Secondly, we should put the new medium into the context of other existing media and find out whether its bias is dominant in or representative of the entire media environment. Thirdly, we should investigate the particular pattern of knowledge dissemination that will be enabled by the technological capacities of this medium and then consider the kind of modifications or changes it may bring to the contemporary society once it is able to define the media environment.

Internet the medium

The physical senses of both time and space are "radicalized" by the Internet (van Dijk, 1999). The huge web of coaxial cables, fiber optics, phone lines, and computers has linked together the remotest corners of this world. In this sense, the Internet does appear to have a strong potential to serve as a space medium. However, the time element in the Internet is equally significant, not only because it promises instant transmission of information at any time of the day, but also because tons of information is stored and being stored on the Internet, and will remain accessible not only for later use, but also for later generations. Considering this, isn't the Internet also a strongly time-binding medium?

This contrast is only a superficial reflection of the complex relation between time and space when it comes to the Internet. But it already presents a dilemma to an Innisan perspective. The problem of time and space, in the context of electronic media in general, has attracted the attention of many theorists (Giddens, 1990; Harvey, 1989; Meyrowitz, 1985). Giddens (1991), for example, considers time-space distantiation as the most important characteristic of modernity, and observes that modern societies are stretching further and further across both time and space thanks to the rapid development of communication and transportation technologies. Harvey (1989), on the other hand, observes a trend of time-space compression. To him, the growth of electronic communication networks has made distance and time increasingly irrelevant – synchronized stock exchange not only wipes out the difference of locations, it also diminishes the role of time by generating great profit or loss within the immediacy of a few seconds.

Neither of the above two viewpoints derives directly from the examination of the Internet. But they both seem to be valid depictions of this new communication medium. Indeed, the Internet cannot only push distance to the extreme; it can also completely erase the difference between here and there. Similarly, we can not only immerse ourselves in the past online (a virtual tour of a medieval monastery, for example), we can at the same time enjoy the instant access to whatever information we desire. Such elastic and radical senses of time and space, however, do not necessarily lead to a conclusion that the Internet is not biased. As a matter of fact, when we reach beyond the physical senses of time and space and look at the higher-level manifestations of the Internet's bias, it will become obvious that the Internet is indeed biased toward time.

Firstly, the flexibility in time management promised by the Internet seems to suggest that it is biased toward time. In "A Plea for Time" (1951), Innis contended that in modern Western civilization, time is not only trivialized, it is also spacialized, i.e., linearized and mechanized. The Internet, relying on no rigid schedule, seems to be freeing time from the tyranny of space – time no longer has to be linear; it no longer has to be divided into chunks and succumb to the monitoring of the clock. People with access to the Internet no longer have to worry about missing the primetime – they can do whatever they want at whatever time they please. In this way, time "flows" again within the human experience.

A second characteristic of the Internet that strongly points to its time bias is the numerous online communities that have appeared. A tragic consequence of Western civilization's obsession with space, according to Innis, is the marginalization of religion, tradition, and community. Today, more and more people are turning to the Internet to recover a sense of belonging, to search for common interests and spiritual guidance. The flourishing of virtual communities thus not only suggests a reawakening of the concern for time, it also provides a realistic venue for a highly segmented society to regain its cohesiveness.

Yet another time-related characteristic of the Internet is its facilitating role in civic engagement (Wellman, Haase, Witte & Hampton, 2001). Using this dialogic medium, civilians cannot only exchange political views among themselves; they can also directly communicate with policy makers who used to be largely unreachable television icons. The level of political participation promised by the Internet, however much it has been appreciated so far, gives us reason to hope that a truer or fuller sense of democracy may be realized in the Internet age.

Having pointed out these exemplifications of the time bias in the Internet, a word of caution is in order. It should be reemphasized that any medium bias is a relative bias. For the Internet, this relativity is especially important not only because the medium itself has a very strong space element, but also because it has arrived in a strongly space-biased media environment. With this in mind, we now turn to the relations between the Internet and other coexisting media.

Internet and other media

As discussed earlier, the bias of an individual medium may not necessarily represent the general media bias in a given society. This is exactly the case with the Internet. Although we are calling the current times the Internet age, the Internet only accounts for a small portion of the general media fodder consumed by our society. Traditional media are still exerting great influence, and the overall media bias in the contemporary Western world is still toward space (Deibert, 1999).

However, we should not lose sight of the speediness of the Internet's development. Although the Internet has existed for more than three decades, its core component, the World Wide Web, did not take off until 1993. Since then, this new communication medium has developed at a lightening speed. By September 2000, there were 377.65 million people online around the world (Nua, 2000). By July 2005, this number skyrocketed to 938.71 million (Internet World Stats, 2005). Of course, compared with the penetration rate of television, these figures are still too small. But the growth of Internet is definitely impressive, and we have reason to believe that it will become more and more prominent in the future media environment.

Given such momentum of the Internet, how should we understand its relations to the other media? What kind of mechanism, i.e., dominance, balance, or coordination, is and will be at work in the general media environment? The answer based on the status quo is obvious: The Internet is still dominated by television. Television remains the biggest medium today. Its preoccupation with spacial expansion is still defining the primary characteristics of the Western civilization. However, when looking into the future, there seems to be a great possibility that either dominance by the Internet or coordination between the Internet and other media will eventually come about. I say so not only because of the rapid growth rate of the Internet, but also because the Internet appears to be a marvelous substantiation of McLuhan's provocative idea that the content of every medium is just another medium (1964). Indeed, the content of the Internet includes almost every other media. Once online, one can watch television and movies, make phone calls, read newspapers and literature, and check personal mail. With such enormous technological capacity, the Internet has a serious prospect of becoming the medium of all media one day. When this comes true, the dominance mechanism and coordination mechanism will become one, because the Internet, by itself, will constitute the entire media environment.

If the Internet indeed becomes the dominant medium or the generic medium in the future, we would expect its time bias, i.e., the bias toward free flow of time, community, civic engagement, etc., to become the general bias in communication. Only by then will the Internet truly start its challenge to the Western culture's obsession with space. Only by then will its corrective force be fully exercised and fundamental changes on a massive scale begin to happen.

Internet and society

Finally, we should recognize the multiple ways in which the bias of the Internet interacts with the contemporary social and cultural environment. The Internet has always been under the influence of a variety of external forces, ranging from the demands of the state to the interests of business corporations. The concern over national security in the US has played a crucial role in the creation of the Internet, and to a great extent shaped its decentralized character. Capitalist interests, however, are also using the Internet to expand their reach. Not only is the Internet used as an efficient way of transmitting business information, various forms of E-commerce have also mushroomed to turn the World Wide Web into yet another mass market. The profit-making drive behind these practices is in large measure responsible for the incessant pursuit of greater bandwidth, faster connections and more powerful processors (Deibert, 1999).

However, such external influences, working in different directions, have not altered, and probably will not alter, the Internet's bias toward time. The reason is that they have not been able to, or wanted to, change the particular pattern of information flow on the Internet. This information flow pattern, as discussed earlier, is the central mechanism through which the Internet's time bias may eventually transform into an overall cultural bias. Unlike traditional broadcasting media, the information flow on the Internet is not unidirectional. Instead, it is marked by an ever-growing degree of interactivity. Everybody on the Internet can choose to be either the information sender or receiver or both. There is no central source of knowledge. Everybody can contribute to the growth of knowledge online. At the same time they can also easily access the knowledge contributed by other Internet users. This particular mode of knowledge accumulation and knowledge sharing is indeed very similar to the oral tradition that Innis so admired (1951, pp. 6–12). In the oral culture, speech was the dominant medium. Knowledge was chanted and recited and stored in the collective memory. In such societies, knowledge was not monopolized; it was "multipolized" in the brains of every society member who shared the responsibility in maintaining and enriching the collective memory. Bound together by this shared memory, the oral people achieved a strong sense of time, tradition, community, and spirit.

The Internet is indeed functioning as the collective memory for the Netizens. While it is too early to tell if it will successfully dissolve the traditional monopoly of knowledge created by the print and earlier electronic media, its particular pattern of information flow nevertheless gives us the strongest reason to believe that the Internet may be able to revive the sense of time in the Western civilization. The premise, of course, is that it grows strong enough to overcome the other media and their deep-rooted obsession with space.

Conclusion

The alarm Innis sounded is still ringing. The contemporary Western civilization is still celebrating its bias toward space. The advent of the Internet, however, is presenting a realistic opportunity for the resurrection of time. My preliminary analysis has shown that the Internet, although defying the physical sense of time and space, is essentially a time-biased medium. Its short history has already provided evidence for its capacity to emancipate time from mechanization, to create communities for the lonely and the isolated, and to enhance civic engagement. Besides, the Internet's particular mode of information flow also seems to be conducive to a collective control over knowledge, which may then lead to fundamental changes in the social, political and cultural structures of the Western civilization. Of course, for all these to come true, the Internet needs to first assume a defining role in the general media environment. This may not be happening soon. But it is important that we appreciate the great potential of the Internet and cherish the hope it brings to us.

References

Angus, I. (1998). The materiality of expression: Harold Innis' communication theory and the discursive turn in the human sciences. *Canadian Journal of Communication, 23*, 9–29.

Babe, R. (2000). Foundations of Canadian communication thought. *Canadian Journal of Communication, 25*, 19–37.

Blondheim, M. (2003). Harold Adams Innis and his "Bias of Communication." In E. Katz, J. D. Peters, T. Liebes, & A. Orloff (Eds.). *Canonic texts in media research: Are there any? Should there be? How about these?* (pp. 156–190). Cambridge: Polity.

Carey, J. (1989). *Communication as culture: Essays on media and society*. Boston: Unwin Hyman.

Comer, E. (2001). Harold Innis and "The Bias of Communication." *Information Communication & Society, 4*, 274–294.

Deibert, R. (1999). Harold Inns and the empire of speed. *Review of International Studies, 25*, 273–289.

Giddens, A. (1990). *The consequences of modernity*. Stanford, Cal.: Stanford University Press.

Harvey, D. (1989). *The condition of postmodernity: An enquiry into the origins of cultural change*. Oxford: Polity.

Innis, H. (1951). *The bias of communication*. Toronto: University of Toronto Press.

Innis, H. (1972). *Empire and communications*. Toronto: University of Toronto Press.

Levinson, P. (1999). *Digital McLuhan: A guide to the information millennium.* New York: Routledge.

McLuhan, M. (1964). *Understanding media.* New York: McGraw-Hill.

Menzies, H. (1999). Digital networks: The medium of globalization, and the message. *Canadian Journal of Communication, 24,* 539–555.

Menzies, H. (2000). The bias of space revisited: The Internet and the information highway through women's eye. In Acland, C. & Buxton, W. (Eds.) *Harold Innis in the new century,* (pp. 322–228). McGill Quenn's University Press.

Meyrowitz, J. (1985). *No sense of place: The impact of electronic media on social behavior.* New York: Oxford University Press.

Nua (2000). *How many online?* Retrieved Dec. 10, 2000, from http://www.nua.ie/surveys/how_many_online/index.html

Van Dijk, J. (1999). *The network society: Social aspects of new media.* London: Sage Publications.

Wellman, B., Hasse, A. Q., Witte, J., & Hampton, K. (2001). Does the Internet increase, decrease, or supplement social capital? *American Behavioral Scientist, 45,* 436–455.

Internet World Stats. (2005). *Internet usage statistics – The big picture.* Retrieved Aug. 16, 2005, from http://www.internetworldstats.com/stats.htm

RITA WATSON

9. Articulating McLuhan:
A Cognitive-Pragmatic Perspective on the Consequences of Communication Media

A revival of interest in McLuhan has been occasioned by a new resonance his ideas have found as the media environments of the twenty-first century unfold. The immediacy, intimacy and simultaneity of communication enabled by electronic media, the erosion of political and national boundaries and the flattening of cultural and social hierarchies are only a few recent developments that reflect his early predictions (Carey, 1998; Meyrowitz, 2002). While former critics are revisiting his theories, the impression persists that McLuhan may have come up with the right ideas for the wrong reasons. He flouted not only the rules of rational argumentation, but also its very premises. While this does not invalidate McLuhan's ideas, it may begin to explain the vehemence with which many academics reacted against him after his work and reputation had risen to popular acclaim in the 1960s (Miller, 1971).

The cornerstone of McLuhan's argument is that technologies of communication have a pervasive and transparent influence on mind and society. We are all affected, but we are not aware of it. The linear, phonetic-alphabetic texts used in Western culture, for example, were argued to engender in their users a propensity for linear, rational, detached thinking, for forming chains of inference and inferring the relation of sequence to causality (McLuhan, 1962, 1964) The modern advent of electronic media, as it supplanted alphabetic literacy, would create a return to a pre-literate society, a "re-tribalized," globally-realized, village-like orality.

This paper examines McLuhan's argument about the cognitive consequences of the media of communication by examining the oral-literate transition.[1] What influence can a change in the medium of

---

1 The transition from manuscript literacy to print, highly significant in any discussion

communication be expected to have on cognition, and, through the minds of the individuals who constitute it, on collective life?

The Nature of Consequences: Writing Systems and Cognitive Bias

In articulating what the consequences of the oral-literate transition might be, we can now avail ourselves of theory and empirical results that were unavailable to McLuhan. It is easier to rule out what the consequences of written media are highly unlikely to be, on both evolutionary and developmental counts.

On a literal reading of McLuhan, his claims are quite radical: alphabetic literacy is causally linked to the emergence of higher cognitive functioning, rationality and causal inference. But the appearance of writing is clearly too recent a phenomenon to account for the emergence of these abilities. Environmental effects on evolution are slow. The human brain has probably not changed appreciably since the Pleistocene era, roughly around the time that language appeared (cf. Cosmides & Tooby, 1994; Premack & Premack; 1995). Consequently, the basic ability to monitor our own thoughts, that is, to plan, reflect, analyze, infer causality and so on, is unlikely to have emerged much later than this.

Developmental evidence also suggests that children acquire metacognitive abilities sometime during the period of language acquisition, before schooling and the acquisition of writing. They can make predictions based on an understanding of mental states sometime around the age of four years (Astington, 1993) and understand some aspects of intentionality even earlier (Leslie, 1994). Even more compelling, there is empirical evidence that infants in the first year of life have expectations about sequence and causality in the physical world (Leslie, 1987; Spelke & Newport, 1998: Spelke, in press). There does not, then, seem to be a basis in either human evolution or development for arguing that writing plays a causal role in the emergence of higher

---

of consequences of literacy, is not addressed in this paper; discussion and additional sources can be found in Olson, Harris, and other references cited below.

cognitive functioning, which is now generally held to be grounded in the basic, universal endowment of humankind.

This does not, however, rule out the possibility that writing creates a bias in the cognitive preferences of its users, a more articulate and defensible claim that is more consonant with recent views about the consequences of writing for cognition: written language provides us with the conceptual categories for thinking about language (Olson, 1994); texts influence forms of consciousness (Chafe, 1994; Ong, 1976; 1982); writing produces evidence which is not memory-dependent (Harris, 1986; Havelock, 1963; 1976); writing lifts speech out of its context and turns it into an object of thought (Ong, 1976; 1982); and so on.

The Uniqueness of the Phonetic Alphabet

Substantial evidence exists that acquiring phonetic alphabetic orthographies alters the perceptual judgements of it users. Research on the development of phonemic segmentation skills shows that when young children learn to read, typically in the early years of schooling, their judgements about the units of spoken language change. They begin to segment the stream of speech into units that correspond to the alphabetic categories they are learning. Prior to learning how to read, they will say that the word "bat" is composed of two sounds, "b" and "at"; and make similar judgements about other three letter words, such as "cat" or "pit" or "ball." After they learn the alphabet, they will change their judgements, and say that the word "bat" consists of three sounds, corresponding to the three letters of which the word consists (Goswami, 1991; Goswami & Bryant, 1990; Trieman, 1985; 1992). Crucially, this change occurs when the word is orally presented, not read. Thus, learning a phonetic alphabetic script changes the perceptual/ cognitive categories that underlie children's thinking about language. These results have been extensively replicated, and the evidence seems incontrovertible.

It is an error, however, to assume that this effect is unique to alphabetic scripts. While we cannot travel back in time to test the learners of cuneiform scripts in the scribal schools of ancient Mesopotamia, their school texts are readily available for examination. These texts clearly show a similar awareness of orthographically-determined categories. An Akkadian school text from Girsu dated from 2250 B.C., in the British Museum Western Asiatic collection (BM #87217[2]), shows a list of names sorted not by any property of their reference, or content, but rather by their orthography: they are arranged according to the initial syllable, or orthographic sign, of the names. This is the equivalent of organizing a dictionary alphabetically, all words beginning with the letter "a" coming first. The text is organized by a category derived from the use of a system of writing, and thus shows a clear influence of the technology of communication – cuneiform writing – on the conceptual organization of its users.

McLuhan erroneously claims that pictographic and hieroglyphic writing were used in Babylonian cultures to give a "pictorial expression" to oral meanings. Babylonian cuneiform was pictographically derived, but developed into an abstract syllabic writing system. It was indeed unwieldy, but this was not solely attributable to the representational properties of the script or the large number of signs that had to be memorized. It was at least partly a function of the available technologies: stylus on heavy clay tablets or chisel on equally-inconvenient stone (Horowitz, personal communication[3]). Nor is it tenable to view the alphabet as the endpoint of a progression toward better orthographies:

> Describing a syllabary in alphabetic terms makes it seem defective, when in fact alphabets do not represent a perfect or unambiguous correspondence of symbols to linguisitic units. Neither alphabets nor syllabaries succeed in perfectly representing speech. The bias towards the alphabet may derive from the conceptual categories of alphabetic literate scholars.
> (Harris, 1986, p. 38)

Like the scholars referred to by Harris, McLuhan may thus have been influenced by his own literate bias. Claiming that the cognitive consequences of writing are the result of the representational superiority of the phonetic alphabet *with respect to the content that it conveys* also

---

2   An Akkadian school text from Girsu, dated 2250 B.C.E. British Museum Western Asiatic Collection reference # 86271. A list of names beginning with the same cuneiform sign.

3   Wayne Horowitz, Dept. of Assyriology, The Hebrew University of Jerusalem.

glaringly contradicts his primary dictum: that the effects of media are independent of content.

The Greek adaptation of the then-widely-used Phoenician alphabet may have been too small an order of change to be a primary influence underlying the major changes in mental and cultural life that McLuhan and other members of the Toronto School attributed to it (Lloyd, 1990). The phonetic alphabet was not as unique as formerly thought in the ancient world. Other early writing systems were adapted to represent diverse languages, and even the cuneiform script, initially syllabic, was used to create an alphabet (Robinson, 1995).

Maintaining an orthography-specific view of the consequences of writing also has the effect of marginalizing other writing systems. Logographic and other scripts have persisted into the modern era, notably in the great civilizations of Asia, and it is improbable that non-alphabetic literates are somehow cognitively or culturally challenged. Claims that Chinese speakers lacked the ability to think counterfactually because counterfactual statements were not grammaticalized in their language were challenged and disproved (Au, 1983). Interestingly, some new evidence suggests that Asians do show a less-pronounced categorical bias than Westerners on cognitive sort tasks, and a greater tendency to remember background detail as well as foregrounded figures in visually-presented scenes, although a generation in the alternate culture will weaken or eliminate these observed differences (Nisbett, 2003).

The cognitive consequences of the use of phonetic alphabets, then, are most likely to be in the nature of a use-based extension of existing cognitive abilities in "alphabetically-enabled" directions (cf. Olson, 1994). It also seems probable that any orthography, including cuneiform or logographic scripts, would have an impact on its users' conceptions of language. Acquiring an orthography requires the creation of the conceptual categories needed for mapping the signs of an orthography onto the stream of spoken language: orthographically-derived concepts are necessary to read or write a given language using an acquired script. In any domain of knowledge, even playing tennis or driving a car, learning a skill generates new categories and concepts specific to its application. There is no reasonable argument against this, and at this level, there is no doubt that the "technology" of writing has cognitive consequences.

It is possible that some consequences or biases may ultimately be found to vary in concert with specific writing systems, but there are far broader, more general changes involved in the oral-literate transition: from aural to visual representation, from impermanence to permanence, from undifferentiated "streams" of spoken language to the discrete, inscribed segments of written language, from the largely unconcious and effortless acquisition of spoken language to the largely conscious and effortful acquisition of writing systems. It seems far more likely that these factors would account for more far-reaching cognitive consequences than the relatively narrow, specific differences between individual scripts. Broader principles are in play, and theories may be better formulated in orthography-general rather than orthography-specific terms.

In addition, there is reason to expect that the cognitive consequences of communication technologies, such as the medium of writing, would have at least some universal properties, even if specific consequences were found to vary with specific technologies. Writing and other technologies of communication are ultimately extensions of spoken language, and most theories of language and its acquisition, while allowing for linguistic variation, claim a significant degree of universality. Ordinary spoken language, the original medium or "technology" of communication, may thus be the optimal starting point for determining what the general cognitive consequences of communicative technologies might be.

The Standard Model of Communication

Unexamined assumptions about spoken language underlie most theories of communication. The standard, or code, model has long dominated thinking about linguistic communication (Kempson, 2001; Sperber & Wilson, 1986; 1995). The standard model assumes that *encoded meaning* – the text or spoken words – governs the interpretation of messages.

Sophie says, for example: "It's cold in here." The standard model assumes that her listener understands her by *decoding,* or unpacking the meaning in the *code,* or language: the four words that she utters. In the ordinary use of language, decoding occurs in a largely effortless manner below the level of consciousness. Alternate interpretations of Sophie's words can be derived as necessary to understand what she is trying to say. *Unencoded meaning,* or *context,* is used for this purpose. *Context* consists of all non-linguistic aspects of the communication event: the space-time coordinates and physical environment shared by the speaker and hearer; the face-to-face relation between them and the social conventions and conversational principles (cf. Grice, 1989) to which they both may adhere, to greater or lesser extents.

Context could alter the interpretation of Sophie's utterance in the following way: her listener, who is also her host, loves fresh air, even in the middle of winter. Because of this the window is wide open. Sophie is reluctant to rudely demand that he close the window, so instead she shivers and says indirectly, "It's cold in here." If her listener is both attentive and conversationally competent, he will understand that she would prefer the window closed. Whether or not he acts on this information is, of course, dependent upon non-communicative factors. The point is that on the standard model, *context* serves to enrich an interpretation that has already been derived from the *code.*

McLuhan's theory of the cognitive consequences of phonetic-alphabetic literacy is conceptualized on this standard model. This is evident in the nature of the claim: the source of the influence of the phonetic alphabet is argued to be its representational superiority with respect to the messages it conveys. This only makes sense on the standard model, a view of communication that situates meaning in the code. Similarly, the characterization of text understanding as "decontextualized" (cf. Ong, 1976; 1982) demonstrably derives from the way context is construed on the standard model: the shared, physical, face-to-face environment of speakers and hearers that serves as an optional source of enrichment of already-decoded messages.

The limitations of theories based on the standard model become evident when they are applied to existing empirical results. An example is the large study of literacy and cognition carried out by Scribner and Cole (1981). This study attempted to replicate Luria's (1976) results: a greater preference for hierarchical category organization and a more developed ability to reason from linguistic premises in literate individuals when compared with their non-literate counterparts. Scribner and Cole compared different kinds of literacy found in the Vai population of Liberia: non-literates, mono-literates who use writing primarily for day-to-day purposes like list-making or letter-writing; literates schooled in traditional oral-recitation methods and literates schooled on the

Western, text-analytic model. They found no cognitive consequences for literacy *qua* literacy. The significant difference was between those schooled on the Western model and everyone else. Schooling, then, and not literacy, was presumed by Scribner and Cole to underlie the cognitive consequences that Luria had attributed to literacy.

Theories of literacy based on the standard model are defeated by results that seem to imply no cognitive impact of acquiring a script, of simply learning how to read and write. Attributing the difference to "schooling," as Scribner and Cole do, may appear to be justified, but does not help us to articulate the source of the effect, since schooling is such a multifaceted, complex process that defies simple definition. Even more problematic, explaining these results as a consequence of schooling rather than literacy opens an improbable divide between some conceptions of language and others. Conceptions of phonemic units, as we have already seen, are clearly and demonstrably influenced by literacy. How is it, then, that conceptions of the larger morphological units of which they are a part – words – appear to remain unaffected, as is suggested by Scribner and Cole's (1981) findings?

If we abandon, for the moment, the standard, code model of communication and instead explore a cognitive-pragmatic (Carston, 2002; Kempson, 2001; Sperber & Wilson, 1995) model, could a more coherent account of these apparently inconclusive and contradictory results be formulated?

A Cognitive Pragmatic Model

On a cognitive-pragmatic model of spoken language, *encoded meaning* is never sufficient to derive a message interpretation, or proposition (Kempson, 2001; Sperber & Wilson, 1995). Only an incomplete meaning, or an *incomplete logical form*, can be derived from a text or spoken language. *Unencoded meaning, or context,* is used simultaneously with the code, as an integral aspect of the interpretation process, rather than as an optional, post-decoding enrichment process as in the standard model of communication (above).

Context on a cognitive-pragmatic account is *selected* rather than given, and *cognitive* rather than physical. *Context* here is not defined by the shared space-time coordinates of face-to-face interlocutors as it is on the standard model. It is rather *a set of assumptions* that the hearer/ reader/receiver brings to the process of interpretation: beliefs, prior knowledge, and selective representations of the shared situation. *Context* here is not an enrichment device operating on a meaning specified by the linguistic code. It is essential – interpretations cannot be derived without it. Interpretation is a property of minds, not of sounds, marks on a page, displays on monitors or screens; meaning is a property of neither pictographs nor pixels, neither phonemes nor letters. The meaning of messages is an attribution made by the interpreters and users of these devices, and is always derived in a cognitive environment.

Context, on this account, can thus never be absent if interpretation is taking place. The absence of a shared physical environment that occurs when written language replaces oral discourse is thus not equivalent to an absence of context. It is rather a change in the sources and kind of information that is available to a listener/receiver/reader in the process of interpretation, a change in the kinds of assumptions that can be made.

If we return to Sophie's utterance with this account in mind, it becomes clear that the words "It's cold in here" are not adequate to specify her meaning. The indexical expressions "it" and "here" are insufficient to determine an interpretation outside the listener/receiver/reader's cognitive environment (see Bar Hillel, 1954, for an extended discussion of the prevalence of indexicals in ordinary language). Even "cold" is a relative term: compared to what? Sophie's host apparently does not share her interpretation of the meaning of "cold." A shared physical environment alone cannot resolve these interpretive problems.

On a cognitive-pragmatic model, if the listener/receiver/reader does not succeed at first in deriving a relevant interpretation, another cognitive environment – that is, a different set of assumptions – will be selected in which to re-interpret the utterance or text. An infinite regress – the generation of an unlimited number of contexts – is prevented by the principle of relevance (cf. Sperber & Wilson, 1995): a listener/ receiver/reader of a message wants to derive *maximum cognitive effects* (meaning) by investing the *minimum effort*. The listener evaluates a message in a cognitive environment which consists of the knowledge and assumptions that are active at the time a given message is received – an activation determined by the immediately preceding utterance or event. The *minimum effort* half of the relevance equation restricts the number of assumptions activated – only assumptions necessary to derive a relevant meaning will be activated. In most natural language communication situations – an utterance in conversation, a radio or television broadcast, a sentence in a newspaper or novel or on a computer or television screen – understanding is an effortless and largely transparent process (see Carston, 2002; Kempson, 2001; Sperber & Wilson, 1995, for full accounts of current cognitive pragmatic theory).

In this model, then, meaning is not conveyed by the code alone, nor by a sequential interpretation based first on code interpretation and then subsequently on an enrichment process that draws on the shared physical context of interlocutors. Meaning is rather derived in a cognitive context selected by the listener/receiver/reader in which all relevant sources of information are simultaneously considered. The code is only one source, albeit an important one, of information.

This altered conception of communication helps to articulate theorizing about cognitive conseqences of the oral-literate transition in the following ways. First, the characterization of the oral-to-literate transition as one of a dichotomous and discontinuous shift from contextualized to decontextualized interpretation of encoded meaning is not sustained. Second, the way in which texts might work to effect cognitive consequences is different on the standard and cognitive pragmatic models.

The interpretation of texts differs from the interpretation of spoken language on both the standard and the cognitive-pragmatic models: the temporal, impermanent representation of a spoken message makes it less available for reflection, while the spatial, fixed representation of a written message makes it more available. On the standard model, cognitive consequences are due to the simple presence of the text and the absence of shared face-to-face situation. On a cognitive pragmatic model, however, the consequences of a written medium are not absolute, but rather contingent on the role played by the medium in the process of deriving meaning.

If interpretations are easily recovered, the role of the text may not be that different from the role of spoken language, at least as far as higher cognitive processes go. That is, if no reflection or analysis is required in order to arrive at an interpretation, then a fixed, permanent representation presents no obvious advantage and, in this sense, could simply stand in place of a spoken message. However, in cases of ambiguity or complexity, extended inferential processing are required. The listener/receiver/reader needs to generate more than one cognitive context in which to repeatedly evaluate the information contained in the code. Such extended inferential processing could be significantly *advantaged* by fixed, permanent representations of the code without being *determined* by specific properties of the representation itself.

On a cognitive-pragmatic account, then, the cognitive implications of a written medium are neither a straightforward consequence of its fixed, spatial, permanent qualities, nor of its representational adequacy with respect to the message that it conveys. It is rather a consequence of the role that the code plays in the inferential process of interpretation in the cognitive environments of the listener/receiver/reader, a role that can be expected to vary with the interpretive requirements of the message that it conveys.

On a cognitive-pragmatic model, Scribner and Cole's (1981) results are more comprehensible. The absence of any measurable cognitive consequences for simple uses of reading and writing by Vai mono-literates is because no extended inferential processing is required in either the writing or interpretation of lists and personal letters. The fixed, permanent qualities of writing provide a simple extension of memory span of the writer (lists of single items) or an extension of the presence of the writer in time and space (personal letters). These are both real-world advantages, but do not necessarily confer an advantage in the process of inferential understanding, and, not surprisingly, yielded no measurable cognitive conseqences in this study.

Similarly, a cognitive-pragmatic model would not predict that traditional schooling that focuses on memorization alone would necessarily have consequences. Texts in this case clearly provide memory and time-space advantages over oral transmission, but while they are certainly available for reflection and analysis, if none is carried out there would be no necessary consequences for the development of higher level cognition. In contrast, schooling on the Western model requires the analytic uses of written texts, the repeated and extended processing of abstract, philosophical and scientific discourse, and text-based problem-solving. Under these uses of texts, Luria's (1976) findings were replicated: an increased preference for hierarchical categorical organization in both object sort and word definition tasks, an increased ability to reason from verbal premises, and so on.

When complex, interpretive processes have to be performed, then, the fixed, permanent representations provided by a written text confer an advantage in the process of inferential understanding: the text can be repeatedly returned to and used as a source of information in successive attempts at inferential understanding involving any number of changes in the set of assumptions invoked in the cognitive environments of the reader/receiver.

It must be said that in advancing the cognitive-pragmatic model over the standard model it does not necessarily follow that theories based on the latter are wrong. The theories advanced by McLuhan and other members of the Toronto School about the consequences of literacy defined the field of literacy studies, the early postulates of which do stand. They would, for instance, correctly predict the phonemic segmentation results discussed above, the most incontrovertible evidence for consequences of literacy. In this case, the simple presence and use of writing does appear to have cognitive consequences. The phonemic segmentation results irrefutably show that simply acquiring a script, with no higher level processing, leads to the development of new conceptual categories.

It is also significant, with respect to theories on the standard model, that when writing first appeared in ancient Mesopotamia, among the very first kinds of texts to appear were "categorical": lexicons, or lists of words (e.g., BM Reference # 93005[4]), and lists of place names such as were found in the school text described above. Again, the simple presence of the written form seems to influence conceptual organization. It is difficult to state conclusively that oral cultures had no formal lexicons, but surviving oral forms – narratives, poems, omens, myths and the like – show no evidence that they did. The closest thing to a list structure in oral traditions might be the kind of geneologies familiar from the Old Testament, in which progenitors and descendents are enumerated. But the items here are not strictly members of a list, like "objects" or "words." Geneologies are accounts of kinship structures,

---

4   Stone vocabulary showing the Akkadian equivalents of 48 Kassite (middle Babylonian) words. 1200–800 B.C.E., British Museum Western Asiatic collection, reference # 93005; while this artifact is relatively late with respect to the appearance of writing, it illustrates the general form of lexicons and list structures that characterize very early Mesopotamian texts, cf. Horowitz.

of individuals embedded in a network of biological relations, rather than a list of equivalent entries a category labelled "kin."

While list structures do appear to be linked to the simple presence and use of a writing system, the claims of McLuhan, Havelock, and others that the phonetic alphabet played a unique role in this development are not supported. The very earliest of written documents contain list structures and suggest that any form of writing would lead to the development of an explicit conceptualization of "category." The Rhind mathematical papyrus of ancient Egypt and early Mesopotamian scientific texts attest that writing in any orthography would lead to a "categorical insight" and the use of lists and explicit taxonomic structures in the exposition of ideas.

Finally, the possibility also exists that the failure to find measurable cognitive consequences as a consequence of the simple presence of writing and non-complex uses of text in the Scribner and Cole study could be due to the measures and tasks that were used: they may not have been sensitive enough to discriminate a change.

The disadvantage of the standard model, then, is simply that it is restricted to code-based hypotheses. The advantage of the cognitive-pragmatic model is that any source of information, and diverse ways in which those sources of information figure in the interpretation process, can be brought to bear in a coherent manner when trying to identify the consequences of changes in communication media.

Re-evaluating Cognitive Consequences

a) Hierarchies

McLuhan's claim about hierarchical bias was not just cognitive, it was social: it manifested itself in the organization of literate societies and would break down, he claimed, as electronic media became dominant. Social hierarchies do appear to be flattening, as the privileged sinecures of literary elites are eroded by the affordances of electronic media (Carey, 1998; Meyrowitz, 2002). Hierarchical category organization, however, is a universal characteristic of mind (Atran, 1990), and while evidence suggests that it is amplified by literacy, it is unlikely to be entirely flattened by a return to orality, even a partial one, engendered by electronic media.

Would a bias toward increased hierarchical organization in cognition, amplified by the uses of literacy, be related to the amplification of a similar bias in the organization of society? A conclusive answer is a beyond the scope of this paper, but a speculative remark may be in order. Luria (1976), in the first large empirical study of the cognitive consequences of literacy in post-revolutionary Russia, documented an increase in hierarchical cognitive organization among literate townsfolk when compared with their pre-literate, rural counterparts when measured by object sort and word definition tasks. These findings were replicated by Scribner and Cole (1981) in a literate population educated on the Western model, as already discussed.

A cognitive-pragmatic model suggests why the analytic uses of text would lead to a hierarchical bias in cognitive organization: the repeated processing of a single word or expression in successive instances of inferential interpretion requires a paratactic extension of that word or expression in a vertical axis of substitution within a linear text. As each possible meaning or interpretation of a single item is considered and reinterpreted, categorical or semantic relations within individual conceptual domains would necessarily be attended to, in contrast to the syntactic or thematic relations that dominate the continuous, uninterrupted processing of connected discourse. This could quite conceivably lead to an emphasis on and strengthening of hierarchical categorical organization in semantic knowledge. This paratactic or hierarchical dimension has been argued to be the dominant mode of interpretation in analytic or scientific uses of language (see Olson & Torrance, 1996).

Whether or not a cognitive bias of this kind would have a spill-over effect, manifesting itself in the organization of a literate society is not only a difficult question to answer, it is a difficult question to pose: what would constitute evidence? It is, however, a plausible speculation, since hierarchical bias in cognitive organization is one domain of the consequences of literacy that has evidentiary support.

b) Transparency and Pervasiveness
As noted at the beginning of this chapter, McLuhan claimed that the consequences of communication media were both transparent and pervasive: we are all affected to a significant degree but are aware neither of the influence itself nor of its extent.

Dennet (1994; 1998) attributes the development of higher cognitive processes to spoken language: language functions to identify our thoughts, enabling us to keep track of them in the "grand central station of the mind" and allowing greater awareness and control over our mental processes. The price to be paid for these linguistically-enhanced cognitive abilities is that the use of our labelled thoughts entails the transparent effect of the terms we use to label them. Thought is inescapably colored by the properties of language: we have "language-infected" cognitive states.

For Dennet, then, the effects of *language* on thought are transparent, in that we are unaware of their effects, and pervasive, in that the use of any language will necessarily invade thought. It seems a relatively small inferential leap to McLuhan's notion that the "technologies" of communication other than natural language would have consequences for mind, and that these effects might be similarly transparent and pervasive.

McLuhan seems to be surprisingly right-headed on this larger issue, if somewhat scant on its articulation.

c) Determinism, Constructivism or Bias?

Much of the initial burst of criticism leveled at McLuhan labeled him a technological determinist (cf. Carey, 1998; see Blondheim, this volume, for an account of similar criticism of Innis). Recent reinterpretations of McLuhan emphasize, rather, his claims about bias. McLuhan, it hardly bears repeating, was influenced by his mentor Innis' work on the bias of communication. But while Innis emphasized the time or space biases of different communication technologies, McLuhan was more concerned with the perceptual-cognitive biases inherent in the listener/reader/receiver: the "ear" of traditional oral cultures versus the "eye" of the literate world. The subject of this paper has been cognitive bias more generally construed – the enhancement or extension of existing cognitive capacities in ways supported by the technologies of communication, such as writing – and it has been argued that this interpretation of McLuhan is more defensible on grounds of cognitive theory than his more radical claims.

Beyond Innis' and his own notions of bias, McLuhan's thought was also influenced by ideas in earlier, unacknowledged traditions of inquiry. Katz and Katz (this volume) identify the influence of Vico, and also of the Sapir-Whorf hypothesis, which it is interesting to note is currently enjoying a revival of sorts (Bowerman & Levinson, 2001). Carey (1998) identifies an influence of Mumford among others, and situates McLuhan in a tradition of technology/mind theorizing and social constructivist thought. McLuhan's place in the cognitive sciences, if one were to be had, would be in the constructivist camp, to the extent that his views are reminiscent of Vygotsky's (1962), Bruner's (1986) and more recently of Tomasello's (Tomasello, Kruger & Ratner, 1993) constructivist claims that social and cultural interactions play a constitutive role in cognitive development. On this view, the "tools" of communication are constitutive of the development of mind.

McLuhan viewed any tool or technology, communicative or otherwise, as having pedagogic "value": tools and instruments are "vehicle(s) for instructing men and women… in culturally acquired modes of thought and action" (Carey, 1998). It may be more than coincidence that McLuhan's work first appeared in print within a few years of the translation into English and publication in the West of Vygotsky's (1962) work, and concurrently with significant changes in prevailing views about the mind (Bruner, 1986; Gardner, 1987). As Katz and Katz (1998) point out, McLuhan may have influenced and/or been influenced by the birth of the new cognitive science.

Conclusions

Writing was the first technology that significantly extended communication beyond the limitations of spoken language. It has been used for over five thousand years, and its influence has not waned. The era of electronic communication, far from replacing it, appears to have led to an explosion of writing: since the arrival of television, the publication of books has risen by 2.8 percent a year (cited in Jefferson, 2003). In spite of electronic publishing, the proliferation of printed, academic journals is the bane of university librarians with limited shelf space. The Internet, and computer technology in general, makes such extensive use of the printed word that it is fair to say computer literacy both entails and extends the use of the written word, rather than supplanting it.

Are electronic media likely to cause a wholesale resurgence of a pre-literate, oral, tribal mentality? Not if they require basic literacy to take advantage of them. You can't surf the Internet if you can't read the commands and other information on the screen. Pre-literates or illiterates are excluded from the world of electronic communications as much as from the world of books, journals and newspapers. Literate humankind, embodying as it does generations of literate cultural practices and conventions, cannot become pre-literate, at least not in a single generation.

The new media, however, clearly make demands beyond those of either simple oral communication or literacy as it has been known until now. They demand simultaneous processing of multi-modal representations in diverse spatio-temporal configurations, with varying degrees of fixity and temporality. Some version of a cognitive-pragmatic model may have the potential for conceptualizing the cognitive consequences of new, multi-modal representational media. Diverse constellations of coded and unencoded, verbal and visual, print and electronic information can be conceptualized as shifting sources of inference within the cognitive-interpretive environments of listeners/receivers/readers.

The framework sketched in this paper is a suggestion of how questions about the consequences of new media for cognition could be formulated by focusing on the shifting role different codes and representational media play in the interpretive process. Claims expressed in fixed, ungeneralizable, code-specific terms may have less potential in successfully addressing questions of cognitive consequences of the new media. A coherent set of principles is more likely to be developed if it can be generalized across diverse codes and representational media.

The framework presented here also suggests that the cognitive consequences of communication media are not wholly independent of the messages conveyed, as McLuhan argued, but appear to be at least partially independent due to the role that media play in message interpretation.

References

Astington, J. W. (1993). *The child's discovery of the mind*. Cambridge, Mass.: Harvard University Press.

Atran, S. (1990). *Cognitive foundations of natural history: Towards an anthropology of science*. New York and Cambridge, UK: Cambridge University Press.

Au, T. K.-F. (1983).Chinese and English Counterfactuals: The Sapir-Whorf Hypothesis revisited. *Cognition*, 15.

Bar Hillel, Y. (1954). Indexical expressions. *Mind*, 63, 359–379.

Bowerman, M., & Levinson, S. C. (2001). *Language Acquisition and Conceptual Development*. Cambridge, UK: Cambridge University Press.

Bruner, J. S. (1986). *Actual minds, possible worlds*. Cambridge, Mass., and London, UK: Harvard University Press.

Carey, J. W. (1998). Marshall McLuhan: Geneology and legacy. *Canadian Journal of Communication,* Vol. 23, No. 3.

Carston, R. (2002). Linguistic meaning, Communicated meaning and cognitive pragmatics. *Mind & Language,* Vol. 17, pp.127–148.

Chafe, W. (1994). *Discourse, consciousness and time*. Chicago: University of Chicago Press.

Cosmides, L., & Tooby, J. (1994). Origins of domain specificity: The evolution of functional organization. In Hirschfeld, L., & Gelman, S. (Eds.). *Mapping the mind: Domain specificity in cognition and culture*. Cambridge, UK: Cambridge University Press.

Dennett, D. (1994). Language and intelligence. In Khalfa, J. (Ed.). *What is intelligence?* Cambridge: CUP.

Dennett, D. (1998). Reflections on language and mind. In P. Carruthers, J. Boucher (Eds.). *Language and Thought,* pp. 284–294, Cambridge: Cambridge University Press.

Gardner, H. (1987). *The mind's new science*. NY: Basic Books.

Goswami, U. (1991). Learning about spelling sequences: The role of onsets and rimes in analogies in reading. *Child Development*, 62, pp. 1110–1123.

Goswami, U., & Bryant, P. (1990). Rhyme, analogy, and children's reading. In Gough, P.B., Ehri, L.C., & Treiman, R. (Eds.). *Reading Acquisition*. (pp. 49–64). Hillsdale, NJ: Erlbaum.

Grice, P. (1989). *Studies in the way of words*. Cambridge, Mass.: Harvard University Press.

Harris, R. (1986). *The Origin of Writing*. Illinois: Open Court.

Havelock, E. (1963). *Preface to Plato*. Cambridge: CUP

Havelock, E. (1976). *Origins of Western literacy*. Toronto: OISE Press.

Jefferson, M. (2003). On writers and writing: Overcoming graphomania. *New York Times Book Review,* Nov. 23, pp. 31.

Katz, R., & Katz, E. (1998). McLuhan: Where did he come from, where did he disappear? *Canadian Journal of Communication,* Vol. 23, No. 3.

Kempson, R. (2001). Pragmatics: Language and communication. In Aronoff, M., & Rees-Miller, J. (Eds.). *Handbook of Linguistics.* London: Blackwell

Leslie, A. (1994). Pretending and Believing: Issues in the theory of ToMM. *Cognition,* 50, 211–238.

Leslie, A. (1987). Do six-month-old infants perceive causality? *Cognition,* 25, 265–288.

Lloyd, G. (1990). *Demystifying mentalities.* Cambridge: CUP.

Luria, A. (1976). *Cognitive development: Its cultural and social foundations.* Cambridge, UK: Cambridge University Press.

McLuhan, M. (1962). *The Gutenberg galaxy.* Toronto: The University of Toronto Press.

McLuhan, M. (1964). *Understanding media: The extensions of man.* New York: McGraw-Hill.

Meyrowitz, J. (2002). Canonic Anti-Text: Marshall McLuhan's Understanding Media. In Katz, E., Liebes, T., & Orloff, A. (Eds.). *Canonic Texts in Media Research.* Cambridge: Polity Press.

Miller, J. (1971). *Marshall McLuhan.* New York: Viking.

Nisbett, R. (2003). *The geography of thought: How Asians and Westerners think differently... and why.* NY: Simon & Shuster, the Free Press.

Olson, D. R. (1994). *The world on paper.* Cambridge: Cambridge University Press.

Olson, D. R., & Torrance, N. (1996). *Modes of thought: Explorations in culture & cognition.* Cambridge: CUP.

Ong, W. (1976). *The presence of the word.* New Haven, Conn.: Yale University Press.

Ong, W. (1982). *Orality and literacy: The technologizing of the word.* London: Methuen.

Premack, D., & Premack, A. J. (1995). Origins of human social competence. In Gazzaniga, M. (Ed.). *The Cognitive Neurosciences.* Cambridge, Mass.: The MIT Press.

Robinson, A. (1995). *The Story of Writing.* London: Thames &

Hudson.

Scribner, S., & Cole, M. (1981). *The psychology of literacy*. Cambridge, UK: Cambridge University Press.

Spelke, E. S., & Newport, E. (1998). Nativism, empiricism, and the development of knowledge. In Lerner, R. (Ed.), *Handbook of child psychology, 5th ed., Vol. 1: Theoretical models of human development*. NY: Wiley.

Spelke, E.S. (in press). Developing knowledge of space: Core systems and new combinations. In Kosslyn S.M., & Galaburda, A. (Eds.). *Languages of the Brain*. Cambridge, Mass.: Harvard Univ. Press.

Sperber, D., & Wilson, D. (1995). *Relevance: Communication and cognition*. (2nd Edition; first published 1986). Oxford, UK and Cambridge, Mass.: Blackwell.

Tomasello, M., Kruger, A. C., & Ratner, H. H. (1993). Cultural Learning. *Behavioral and Brain Sciences,* 16, 495–552.

Treiman, R. (1985). Onsets & rimes as units of spoken syllables: Evidence from children. *Journal of Experimental Child Psychology*, 39, 161–181.

Treiman, R. (1992). The role of intrasyllabic units in learning to read and spell. In Gough, P.B., Ehri, L.C., & Treiman, R. (Eds.). *Reading acquisition* (pp.65–106) Hillsdale, NJ: Erlbaum.

Vygotsky, L. (1962). *Thought and language*. Cambridge, Mass.: The MIT Press.

PART III

APPLICATIONS

HILLEL NOSSEK AND HANNA ADONI

10. The Global Village, the Nation State and the Ethnic Community: Audiences of Communication and Boundaries of Identity

Introduction

The nation state, with its recognized borders, political and civil bodies, and national culture, is a complex political entity, whose very existence, some would say, is presently under threat. This may be the consequence of two seemingly contradictory social trends, which emerged during the end of the last century and continued into the beginning of this one. These trends are globalization, on the one hand, which promotes social relations with the wider, global community, often by transcending the boundaries of the nation state, and multiculturalism, which reinforces the consciousness of ethnic communities living within the nation state, allowing them to stay in touch with their communities of origin outside the nation state.

The concepts "nation state" and "ethnic community" are problematic and, to some extent, overlap. The bases for many liberal democracies are built on a dominant ethnic community which is politically expressed in a common territory, sovereignty, language and culture, and occasionally, if not invariably, in a common religion too. Historically speaking, one could say that nation states often developed from ethnic communities which amassed political and cultural power that became the source for the boundaries of their political entity and for the rule of a cultural hegemony (Anderson, 1983). Other ethnic communities continued to exist within these entities as minority communities whose members enjoyed full citizenship rights, although lacking independent political definition as a group.

To some degree, the definition of an ethnic community is the result of social construction following social negotiation over political, social and cultural interests. The term "ethnic community" embraces different classes of groups. Some communities are founded on common ethnic roots, others on shared language and culture, still others on a common religion.

Whenever a single social group possesses all of these variables, it becomes a distinct ethnic community, as for example the Arab minority in Israel. However, many groups, for example, Israel's community of immigrants from the former Soviet Union (FSU), and communities from different parts of the Diaspora, which have settled in Israel, see themselves as ethno-cultural communities with a common language and culture. Sometimes communities accept their minority identity, and just seek recognition for their unique identity and the chance to nurture their culture side by side with that of the hegemonic majority. Other times, communities may wish to remain distinct from the majority and form an autonomous framework, even a separate nation state. The dismantlement of the eastern bloc of countries and the liberalization processes in existing nation states have caused old and new demands to surface. Some of these have been fully met, with states breaking up into new states, e.g., the FSU and Yugoslavia, in other cases, there may be intensification of existing claims, as in Spain, Italy and elsewhere. From the mid-twentieth century onwards, as a result of decolonization processes and the globalization of the employment market, new ethnic communities have sprung up alongside the older ethnic communities, e.g., the Hispanic community in the USA, the Indians and Pakistanis in Britain, the Turkish community in Germany, and many others.

Globalization leads to crossing or even disregard for the boundaries of nation states and is manifested in terms of economics, tourism and communication. International trade promotes brand names like Adidas, Nike, McDonalds, Coca Cola, etc., which are sold and marketed to consumers worldwide, while international tourism allows a growing number of people to visit foreign countries. On the other hand, post-materialist ideas provide a new ethos, focusing on environmental conservation and encouraging anti-globalization activism (Downing, 2001; Levitt, 1983; Morley & Robins, 1995; Schlesinger, 1993; Sreberny-Mohammadi, 1996). The new communication technologies put us in touch with people with similar interests all over the world, encouraging the sense of being part of a wider, global community, which while essentially virtual, nevertheless exerts an influence on the individual's life.

Both globalization and multiculturalism will probably be affected by multi-channel communication systems, which, on the one hand, address a supra-national audience, while on the other hand, liberate ethnic minorities from dependence on the establishment, allowing them relative autonomy in communication terms. Multi-channel communication systems have helped to strengthen pan-global solidarity and domestic, minority-group solidarity on the community level, and helped people to keep in regular, daily contact with their countries of origin. It is so in the case of Israel's immigrants from the FSU and its Arab minority. This can set the stage for inter-ethnic group conflict, to the degree of undermining the stability of the nation state, and, as noted before, in extreme cases, such as Yugoslavia and the FSU, can result in total dismemberment (Geertz, 2000; Morley & Robins, 1995; Schudson, 1994; Tamir, 1998).

However, we would like to suggest that another possible scenario exists. The novel social reality and new communication environment created by new technologies can help people choose between different social identities or else use the available media to support multiple social identities. The question is then whether these media further the construction of one identity at the expense of others, or whether it is possible to construct complex identities, which, as Stuart Hall (1991; 1993) claimed, form the essence of the modern immigrant's social existence. The article discusses the role of old and new media consumption, reading books and newspapers, watching TV, and using the Internet, in the construction of social identities whose reference frameworks are relevant to Israelis: Israeli society, the Jewish People, the global community and the ethnic and ethno-cultural communities in Israel.

Two important theoretical approaches – the technological approach and the functional approach – in communication research will assist in this investigation, which tries to understand what the new communication technologies imply in terms of nurturing different social identities.

Communication Technologies as Agents of Social Change
The origins of the technological approach, also referred to as the Toronto school, are commonly traced to Canadian researcher Harold Innis

(1951), who theorized that civilizations are shaped by the dominant medium of communication at any given point in time. Innis suggested that the principal medium of communication in every historical period addresses the need to transfer information through time and space with optimal efficiency, and causes the "displacement" of an earlier medium, which then becomes obsolete (Blondheim, 2003).

Innis' celebrated disciple, Marshal McLuhan (1962), adopted this idea and analyzed the social impact of the advent of the printing press and television. His underlying premise was that the protracted use of a dominant medium would influence the dominant culture, the social structure and the cognitive processes of individuals. He also contended that the linear nature of print provided fertile ground for the development of rational thinking as well as for modern nationality, economy and science (Katz & Katz, 1988).

One of McLuhan's most pertinent arguments concerns the relationship between the technology of the printing press and the development of national consciousness, which provided a springboard for the political creation of the European nation states. McLuhan argued that the printing press helped to formalize and spread the lingua franca, thus laying the social foundation for the emergence of new political systems, i.e., nation states. Benedict Anderson's highly influential book, *Imagined Communities* (Anderson, 1983), also examined the impact of printed books on modern capitalism and nationalism.

McLuhan argued that the twentieth century spelled the end of *The Guttenberg Galaxy* (McLuhan, 1962), when print was the dominant medium, and that television will not only displace and replace print in the end, but also influence the nature of information, human cognitive structure and the structure of social systems. McLuhan has further argued that television is a message in its own right, and exposure to it encourages a structural, Gestalt form of perception. He also suggested that television messages should be viewed as a whole, which one cannot understand if the individual elements are regarded in isolation. This contrasts with the linear nature of print where the message is conveyed by one element following another in sequence. Based on this idea, he predicted that a new cognitive structure would emerge that would be more appropriate to the complexity of modern experience, and would ultimately replace the printed, linear type of thinking.

McLuhan predicted that the preeminence of television would also affect worldwide social and political structures. Television, he said, would blur national boundaries, creating a kind of global village and produce a reversion to the tribalism that marked social and political systems before the advent of printing. In his later work, McLuhan refined his original displacement thesis, suggesting four categories of interaction between different media: amplification, displacement, retrieval and reversal (Levinson, 1999). The four categories of interaction among media can be translated into four basic questions: (1) Which aspect of communication does each type of medium amplify? (2) Does the new medium conserve any element of the existing dominant medium? (3) Has the new medium displaced its predecessor? and (4) When the new medium achieves its full potential, into which medium will it either revert or evolve?

Although McLuhan proposed four states of interaction, the dynamic among them follows the classical, dialectic thesis-antithesis-synthesis model. The first two initial phases of the process are amplification (thesis) and displacement (antithesis), while the third and fourth phases, viz., retrieval and reversal, represent the synthesis phase, which gives rise to the new thesis. In light of the "recent" additions to the realm of technology, of the computer and the Internet, one could argue that the synthesis stage will probably involve the convergence of two or more media (Adoni & Nossek, 2001).

In addition, from an entirely different direction, historical research supports McLuhan's ideas, while questioning his methods of substantiating them. For hundreds of years, books and literature written in national languages were the basis for the construction of national identity. Reading was a fundamental social activity for both socializing the nation's youth and newcomers wish to join the nation state. As noted earlier, Anderson (1983) put forward a similar argument concerning the relationship between the printing press and books, and the emergence of the European nation states through the formalization, dispersion and transformation of national languages into "languages of power." Thus, texts in national languages became national cultural assets of lasting value, providing the foundation for social integration and the national identity.

Post-modern theories that stress the power of images and the role of the media in their creation and dispersal have revived ideas highlighting the technological aspect of the media (Meyrowitz, 1985; Postman, 1982). Forsaking the Marxist worldview, French philosopher Jean Baudrillard adopted a technological approach, which he took to new heights when he argued that the electronic media, by which he meant mostly television, have the effect of totally transforming the social construction of reality (Baudrillard, 1983). Baudrillard claimed that in post-modern societies, there has been a change in relations between signifier and signified. Previously, it was clear that reality was "over there," and that signifiers were abstract symbols intended to convey that reality (De Saussure, 1915). Nowadays, however, suggested Baudrillard, signifiers have taken control of reality and consciousness, and we find ourselves living in an "ecstasy of communication," i.e., a riot of constantly multiplying signifiers, forever signifying other signifiers.

Functional Theory and the Neo-Functional Approach to Communication

An important assumption advanced by functional theory was that the media answer a range of social needs, both on the micro level of the individual, and on the macro level of the social system. In macro terms, communication media are agents of control and social cohesion, since they transmit information and support the social consensus, besides promoting social change (Lazarsfeld & Merton, 1948; Merton, 1968).

On the micro level, the "uses and gratifications" approach, based on functional theory, which focuses on media functions, posits that an audience of active consumers exists, which seeks to meet psycho-social needs through selective exposure to particular media and contents (Blumler & Katz, 1974; Katz & Adoni, 1973; Katz et al., 2000; McQuail & Windhal, 1993; Rosengren, Palmgreen & Wenner, 1985; Rosengren & Windhal, 1972). According to empirical studies based on this theory, each medium specializes in satisfying different types of needs, and there is a functional division of labor between them (Adoni, 1985; 1995; Neuman, 1986; 1991). Thus, for example, books appear mainly to serve the cognitive needs associated with learning, the accumulation of knowledge, and with the aesthetic experience. Newspapers, the second print medium, are regarded as providing general information and updating readers on political matters. Television is seen as meeting the need for information, providing a form of escapism and for socializing with friends. Escapist and aesthetic needs can also be met through books and film, and the need for current information is mainly supplied by radio. These studies also demonstrated the interchangeability of different media. Low functional interchangeability is apparent between books and television since they do not meet the same needs (Himmelweit & Swift, 1976; Katz, Gurevitch & Hass, 1973). Neuman (1986; 1991) came to similar conclusions, suggesting the need to examine media functions with reference to synergy theory, which argues that media consumers develop an ability to choose between different media, and take optimal advantage of what they offer to meet specific needs.

After several years of great popularity with media researchers in the 1970s, the "uses and gratifications" approach drew heavy fire and was then sidelined as a theoretical framework. Students of communication, who took a qualitative approach to media studies, criticized the "uses and gratifications" theory for relying exclusively on positivist theories and quantitative methodology. Some rejected "uses and gratifications" for being overly "psychological" and only concerned with individuals' needs, and for making it difficult to explain matters of a general social nature. Moreover, whereas almost all studies based on this approach have focused on how consumers evaluate the various media (television, books, newspapers, etc.), they largely tended to neglect the contents of the message conveyed. Another criticism is that the main methodological assumption, namely, that people have the ability to evaluate their own uses of the various media, is not convincing enough.

Notwithstanding the criticism, the "uses and gratifications" approach is currently undergoing a process of reassessment. In a comprehensive survey, McQuail (2001) rejected some of the criticism, contending that numerous studies have used this approach and contributed to our understanding of how media consumers use the media when faced with a large selection of media from which to choose. Lately, due to the rapid adoption of new communication technologies, there has been a resurgence of interest in this approach, which appears especially appropriate for studying the multi-channel media environment.

A trend, which emerged during the last decade, stressed the fact that the media are integral part of social reality and that all types of media consumption should be considered social activities. Similar to "uses and gratifications" research, this approach also focused on media consumers, and their uses of media were perceived as activities taking place within a certain social context. This approach was formulated by a group of European researchers, who labeled it "media use as social action" (MASA) (Renckstorf & McQuail, 1996; Renckstorf, McQuail & Jankowski, 1996; Renckstorf & Wester, 2001). While this novel approach was based largely on the functional approach to communication research, we can follow Alexander's example and refer to it as neo-functional, i.e., that it is concerned with the connection between the individual's social action on the micro level, and the socio-cultural system on the macro level (Alexander, 1990). Media influence is not measured by the success of targeted, short-term effects on consumer audiences (as, for example, in advertising or election campaigns), but in terms of long-term processes involving social reality construction and identity formation. When exposed to a symbolic reality, a person's unique social and cultural traits produce a subjective reality, in which they both act and help in its formation (Adoni & Mane, 1984). Based on these ideas, it may be proposed that media usage is essential in constructing people's collective identities. These identities are developed in childhood and reinforced in adulthood, and are vital for the continued survival of the nation state (Adoni, 1979; Adoni & Adoni, 1994; First, 1997).

This blend of the "uses and gratification" approach together with approaches emphasizing personal interpretation in a defined socio-cultural framework, as elaborated by Press (1994) in her discussion of "reception theory," has led to methodological innovations. These innovations involved combining studies based on audience surveys and statistical data processing with studies of the meaning of the social activity of media consumption, and employed qualitative methods, such as focus groups and in-depth interviews (Vettehen, Renckstorf & Wester, 1996).

The theoretical framework of this present study brings the Toronto School approach together with neo-functional ideas, where the emphasis is on the social significance of media consumption and its contribution to the construction and reinforcement of social identities. The technological approach, which ascribed tremendous power to media technology as an agent of change, led to speculations regarding the weakening of national identity, alongside a growing affinity to the global community on the one hand, and the ethnic community on the other. The rival hypothesis, which is founded on the basic functional assumptions, maintains that the new patterns of media consumption may enable the simultaneous development of multiple, national, global and ethnic identities.

Israel: A Case Study

In Israel, in the early 1990s, a multi-channel media system emerged very rapidly and replaced a monopolistic system that had existed for decades. Today, Israel's new media map contains three national television channels (one public and two commercial) and cable TV offering a very wide range of channels, national channels, global satellite channels, channels broadcasting from other countries – Europe, neighboring Arab countries, the United States. The national cable channels also offer a domestically produced Russian channel, a channel serving the religious community, and a music channel. An Arabic channel and a news channel are also in the pipeline. A direct broadcast satellite (DBS) is also available, offering subscribers a similar choice of channels.

As a result of this large supply, over 80% of Israeli households have multi-channel television systems. Both the cable companies and the satellite company provide home Internet connection; over 50% of households own a PC, and over 30% are already Internet-linked. Many people also use the Internet at work (Adoni & Nossek, 2001). The new media map also contains 14 commercial regional radio stations as well as dedicated radio stations for the Arab minority and religious community, two national, public radio stations, and some 150 local pirate radio stations. Print media include several national dailies and hundreds of local weekly newspapers, books in Hebrew and publications translated into Hebrew (mostly from English), on a variety of literature and reference subjects.

For many years, Israel's media played a vital and calculated role in the acculturation of new immigrants and the development of their Israeli identity, as part of the Zionist "melting pot" strategy for Israeli society. Nowadays, new media policies and usages combine with globalization and multicultural trends to promote the new multicultural "salad bowl" conception of Israeli society, which has replaced the old "melting pot" idea (Nossek, 2002). The arrival of one million immigrants from the former Soviet Union, who chose to retain their original language and culture rather than rapidly and unequivocally reject their original culture, offers an outstanding example of this trend. This immigration wave coincided with the intensification of Israeli Arab minority aspirations for cultural autonomy, which was nourished by the fact that the skies had opened to neighboring Arab countries media and global Arabic channels.

Israel's socio-cultural development in conjunction with this cocktail of traditional and new media technology serves as a unique timeframe for exploring the way media consumption reinforces or undermines trends toward multiculturalism and globalization. Thus, Israeli society can serve as a case study of a multi-ethnic and multi-channel media environment. As always in a research based on a case study, there is a tension between the findings concerning the idiosyncratic developments in one society and the possibility of their generalization to other societies. As elaborated above the Israeli society shares with other Western societies several important attributes, and therefore the findings relating to the media functions in the social construction of identities might be relevant to other multi-ethnic Western societies characterized by multi-channel media environment.

Our research questions focused on the contribution of media usage to nurturing four social identities pertinent to Israeli media consumers. The four identities are (1) Israeli identity (identification with Israeli society), (2) Jewish identity (identification with the Jewish people), (3) global identity (identification with the global community) and (4) ethno-cultural identity (identification with one's ethno-cultural community).

Research Populations and Research Methods
In September 2001, we conducted a telephone survey among a representative sample of the urban adult Jewish population, which consisted of 520 interviewees (aged 21+). We also conducted sessions with nine focus groups of 10–12 members each. The groups consisted of men and women age 20–60 from different ethno-cultural groups and geographic regions, who had varying levels of education and religious observance.

The findings relate to the responses to 16 questions regarding the use of each medium (reading books, reading newspapers, watching television, and Internet usage). For each activity, interviewees were asked to indicate the degree to which the usage of each medium reinforced a particular social identity (Israeli, Jewish, global, ethno-cultural). The study examined three factors relating to the four identities: (1) the affective factor, i.e., the emotional sense of belonging to these groups; (2) the cognitive factor, i.e., the acquisition of knowledge and information with regard to each of these groups, and (3) the instrumental factor, which pertains to behavioral practices relevant to these groups. An index was constructed showing how the various types of media contribute to reinforcing the four identities. Pearson's correlations were computed for the degree of interchangeability between the media activities for constructing identities.

Findings

Media use and Israeli identity
The highest number of survey interviewees (72%) believed that reading newspapers contributed to the construction of their Israeli identity. Watching television and reading books were second and third respectively, and the Internet was not far behind (see Table 1).

Table 1:
Mean Percentage of Respondents Who Reported that Media Use Contribute to the Social Construction of Identities (%)

Media Consumption Activity / Social Identity	Reading Books (N=430)	Reading Newspapers (N=276)	Watching Television (N=376)	Surfing Internet (N=156)
Israeli[35]	49	72	60	43
Jewish[36]	61	47	54	24
Global[37]	43	48	52	52
Ethnic[38]	32	28	32	24
Average	46	49	50	36

Analysis of focus groups discussions provided interesting insights into why people engage in these activities and their significance in terms of identity enhancement. Language emerged as the most salient characteristic regarding the relationship between reading and Israeli identity. Focus group participants reported that the fact that they read in Hebrew is what makes them feel that reading connects them to society. As one group member put it (Iris, age 30, post-secondary education) – "Hebrew is our style. It lets you get into the character. With any other language, I can't flow with the text. When I read Hebrew I feel Israeli."

According to focus group members, reading newspapers keeps them up to date about Israeli current situation and, rather surprisingly, serves as a source of information about normative Israeli behavior. Newspapers also supply information that helps people decide how to vote in elections. Iris – "I read Yediot Ahronot ("Latest News" – leading, popular newspaper). I skim the headlines in the morning, and then read it from cover to cover in the afternoon. The same on weekends. *I read the paper to belong.*"

Many of the survey respondents said that watching television helped strengthen their Israeli identity, besides developing their global identity, and a large majority of them said that television helped them keep up to date with what was happening in Israeli society. About two-thirds said that television made them feel part of Israeli society, provided them with information on the government's performance, and helped them follow current events. Almost half the survey respondents indicated that television helped them in deciding how to vote in the elections. As one focus group member put it explicitly (Rachel, age 54, university education) "Television strengthens your feelings of patriotism and national pride; so do the newspapers."

Focus group members mentioned three television genres that made them feel that television connected them with Israeli society: (1) Israeli-produced television series and Israeli films – regardless of their artistic quality, these helped to strengthen the sense of Israeli identity by connecting individuals to past or present experiences that are uniquely Israeli and not necessarily universal. Included in this genre were series such as *"Tironut"* (*"Basic Training"*)[1] or *"Shabatot Ve'Hagim"*

---

1   *"Tironut"* followed the experiences of a group of soldiers during basic training. The individuals portrayed represented different sectors of Israeli society.

("*Sabbaths and Holidays*")[2]; (2) the second genre consists of sports programs showing Israel competing against foreign teams; also, sports subjects specifically related to Israel; (3) the third television genre comprised Israeli news broadcasts, and broadcasts by foreign TV news networks. It seems that people watch foreign news broadcasts at times of security related tension or during a crisis, in order to understand how the world sees Israel, or learn more about events on the domestic front. Whatever the case, people watch and use these outside resources to connect with Israel, not to connect with the world.

Focus group participants referred specifically to the role of these genres in bolstering people's sense of connection to Israel society. Tsvia (B.Ed.) – "I never miss "*Rak BeIsrael*" ("*Only in Israel*").[3] I laugh the whole time – we laugh at ourselves. I loved "*Florentine*"[4] (another series). I could relate to the setting and the characters. I really enjoyed "*Laga'at Ba'shamaim*" (series) ("*Reaching for Heaven*")[5] with Orly Zilbershatz."[6] Aliza (MA degree) – "I loved some of the Israeli soaps. Take the series "*Shabatot Ve'Hagim.*" It was so true to life, and authentic. It showed what life is like in Israel. I also enjoyed the less popular series, like "*Zinzana,*"[7] which was very realistic and showed Israel's conflicts and problems. I also enjoyed "*Ha'Machon*" ("*The Institute*"),[8] even if it didn't reflect my own profession very positively. Ella (high school + courses): "I also like the Israeli soap operas. I really

2   A drama series showing relationships between friends, couples, and families. Depicts life in contemporary Tel Aviv.

3   A weekly television satire.

4   Florentine is a Tel Aviv neighborhood, which recently became "gentrified," changing from an area occupied by light industrial businesses in the south of the city, to one which attracts twenty-somethings. The series follow a group of young people in the neighborhood, addressing subjects like being gay, marital infidelity, etc.

5   This series portrays a family coping with the father's decision to become religiously observant.

6   Popular Israeli actress

7   The word "*zinzana*" comes from the Israeli underworld. The series is set in a prison, and follows the lives of prisoners and their families. The main character, the prison governor, is based on a real person, and he is seen confronting crime both professionally and within his family.

8   "The Institution" is a psychiatric clinic and the series describes the personal and professional lives of the staff people who work there.

identified with the stories shown in "*Ha'Masait*" ("*The Truck*").[9] It showed different social groups within Israeli society. It was about us. I really enjoyed those series."

As for sports programs and documentaries, Kfir (23, completed high school) – "When you watch Hapoel Tel Aviv (football team) play, you feel part of the country," David (student, 39, immigrated to Israel 20 years ago) – "The film "*Kippur*,"[10] which was screened on *Yom Hazikaron* (Israel's Remembrance Day for Fallen Soldiers) showed us what it was really like." Ilana (high school + courses) – "Some series, like "*Passport*,"[11] make you want to travel and see foreign countries. Eyal Peled[12] and Moshonov[13] are very interesting because they deal with your own country. For example, Moshonov did a program about Latrun.[14] You know about such places, but there's also a lot you don't know about them. It makes you want to go there on the weekend. Find out more about them – not just superficially. The program "*Arabesque*"[15] taught us about our neighbors. It was excellent. It explained what life is like across the border, and you say to yourself, 'They're people just like us.' You learn to understand them. If you understand them, you can live with them."

Those who watched *both Israeli and foreign news* described their reasons for doing this regularly, and passed indirect criticism on Israeli broadcasting services and official and unofficial censorship. Rachel (54, university education) – "I watch television to stay up to date. I watch the foreign news to see what the world thinks about us. How foreign journalists see us." Bosmat (32, university education) – "I also

9 Drama series about life in a poor town in southern Israel. It centers on a truck driver struggling to make a living.
10 Film by Amos Gitai about the Yom Kippur War, which tells about a unit of combat soldiers, who fought in a bloody battle on the Golan Heights.
11 A program combining tourism with celebrity guests. Each week, another Israeli celebrity travels and reports on a different travel destination.
12 Eyal Peled is an Israeli television journalist specializing in world travel. The program discusses different travel destinations each week.
13 Moni Moshonov is a popular Israeli actor and comic. The program presents places of interest in Israel.
14 Latrun is an historical site quite near Jerusalem where an important battle was fought in 1948, during Israel's War of Independence.
15 "Arabesque" is an Israel television program in Arabic.

watch the foreign news because of the war with the Palestinians. I want to know what they're saying. They present interviews we don't see on television here. You find out more about what the other side is saying." Yardena (B.Ed.) – "Since the Intifada began, I watch CNN and Sky news more than Israeli news. Not just the news. I watch interviews relating to Israel. I want to know what they think of us. It's very important to me. The Israeli news gets on my nerves because the commentators keep stressing the same things and keep stirring up conflict. CNN's coverage irritates me in a different way." Rami (47, systems engineer) – "I watch CNN out of habit, I hope to hear things we aren't told in Israel." Ilana (university education) – "When a terrorist attack strikes, I watch foreign channels. I want to compare, to see the perspective from outside Israel. I want something more objective, with less panic. Sometimes, the footage of the attack site is more explicit. When I need to distance myself a bit emotionally, I switch to Sky."

Although reading books came third in terms of helping people connect with Israeli society, the focus groups provided us with interesting insights into the way in which reading bolsters people's sense of Israeli identity. It is not just reading per se that has this effect, but reading books in Hebrew and reading books about the history, personalities and physical and human landscapes of Israeli society. These kinds of books contain associations for their readers that serve to unite people who were born and raised in Israel and are connected to the Israeli experience. As one focus group participant explained:

Orna (MA degree) – "I prefer Israeli literature, written in Hebrew by Israeli writers (*sifrut ivrit mekorit*), books about life here, like Meir Shalev's books[16]; I can relate to them better than translations of foreign books. I relate on an emotional level, I know what they are talking about. There are shared associations. For example, books by Gavriella Rotem.[17] I was amazed at how I could relate to her associations."

16 Popular Israeli author who often deals with his own childhood on the small cooperative settlement of Nahalal. His books blend descriptions of Israel's landscapes, personal stories interwoven with the history of the Jewish settlement in Israel.

17 Author whose her book "*Hamsin ve'tziporim meshugaot*" ("Heat Wave and Crazy Birds") about Israel in the 1950s became a bestseller.

Concerning the Israeli identity, focus group participants referred to Israeli authors such as Amos Oz[18] and A.B. Yehoshua.[19] As Orna (see above) said, "I usually prefer Israeli writers, like A.B. Yehoshua…they speak our language, they can touch us."

The things people avoid reading also tells us something about Israeli identity. According to the focus group members, they do not read, or read very little literature written by Palestinians or authors from neighboring Arab states. One woman, Aliza (MA degree), put this very succinctly "…I don't read their work, though I think one should. I have a big problem with translations of Arab and Palestinian literature. The work is emotionally loaded. It's important, but I'm not interested." On the other hand, people read books about the Israeli-Arab conflict. We can conclude from this that not only reading constructs the boundaries of national identity, but also that it is strongly tied to the dominant ideology and current politics.

The focus group findings corroborated those of the survey, showing that a large proportion of respondents who used the Internet also do it in relation to their Israeli identity. The main reason is use of the Hebrew language and the type of information available from Israeli sites. As one participant, Bezalel (aged 34, university education), said: "It is easier to read in Hebrew. I mainly use Israeli websites." Another participant, Gidon (45, university education), said: "Most of the websites I use are Israeli. Israeli sites are adequate for my needs."

In sum, for all types of media under discussion, the Hebrew language and Israeli subject matter appear to be key factors in structuring an Israeli identity. However, there also seem to be differences among various media. Survey respondents and focus group participants think that reading newspapers and watching television contribute more

18 Respected novelist and thinker. Works include "*Michael Sheli*" ("My Michael"), describing the life of a young Jerusalem couple in the 1960s against a background of the Jewish-Arab conflict. Beside his many published books, Oz also writes for the daily newspapers and voices his opinion on topical issues, mainly the Israeli-Palestinian conflict.

19 Respected veteran author and journalist. His many works deal with different aspects of Israeli society: these include "*Ha'meahev*" ("The Lover") dealing with a young girl's entry into adulthood during Yom Kippur War. "*Ha'shiva me'Hodu*" ("Back from India"), about a romance between a young doctor and a mother searching for her sick daughter in India, and others.

to their Israeli identity in terms of everyday connection with what
is happening in Israeli society as well as the opportunity to receive
information "about ourselves" from foreign point of view. Survey
respondents ranked reading books and the Internet in third and fourth
place respectively, while focus group participants revealed a completely
different contribution to the Israeli identity. Much like newspapers and
television, the role of the Internet was associated with keeping abreast
of Israel's current events and politics by focus group participants. We
believe it was ranked lower than newspapers and television because it
is a relatively new medium although it is quite safe to say that its use
will increase in the near future. In contrast to the other three media,
they claimed that books affect Israeli national identity most profoundly.
Israeli readers share the experience of being Israeli with Israeli writers,
they feel they have common linguistic and cultural heritage as well as a
common Israeli identity, which is constructed and reinforced by reading
Israeli literature in Hebrew.

Media Use and Jewish Identity
Reading books, more than any other media consumption activity, helps
in constructing Jewish identity and strengthening the bond with the
Jewish people and its heritage. Over two-thirds of interviewees shared
this point of view, both with respect to the cognitive aspects of this
identity (learning about the Jewish history and the Holocaust), and
regarding their sense of belonging and active participation in the Jewish
holidays. Over half the respondents reported that watching television
and reading newspapers contributed to their Jewish identity, while only
a quarter of respondents thought the Internet did this (see Table 1).

From the focus group discussions, we learned that for religious and
non-religious people alike, regardless of their ethnic origin, reading
about Holocaust is one of the most important factors in constructing
their Jewish identity. Yardena (B.Ed.): "When I was 20 (my family is
originally from Iraq) I couldn't relate to the Holocaust. Then I married
a man from a kibbutz whose background was European, and his parents
were Holocaust survivors. This brought me face to face with people
who had been through it – my mother-in-law, saved bread during the
war. I read Katchetnik[20] obsessively. Also, my brother-in-law wrote his

20 Author and Holocaust survivor, he wrote many books on the Holocaust. His real

doctorate thesis on the Holocaust and I became obsessed with reading and learning about it. I'm calmer about it now. My first encounter with it was within the family. Then it spread to other levels. The subject makes you want to learn more. Perhaps it connects me to their pain." Aliza (MA) – "I read in order to identify. There were a lot of Holocaust survivors where I grew up. My parents lost their families in the Holocaust. Today too, I think it is extremely important to read so as not to forget. The environment where I grew up had no connection to the Holocaust and I really wanted to understand it – how it could have happened. I thought a lot about what I would have done had I been there. I would devour books by Katchetnik, Zilberman, and Kichel.[21] One reason is that we must never forget. I think that they didn't teach us enough about the other 13 million non-Jewish people who were murdered. My curiosity led me to visit a concentration camp. I still find it unfathomable. I've got a 14-year-old daughter and she has a lot of difficulty with the Holocaust. She won't read anything about it. She's always asking me whether it could happen again. Not because of the Intifada, she started asking me long before. I don't like history or biographies; I like stories with a mixture of both." Tsila (55, university education) – "When did I started reading about the Holocaust? When I became a teacher. It was hard for me to read factual material on the subject, so I forced myself to start reading fiction. I don't like Holocaust movies. Give me a book; I can cope with books."

To sum up, one can say that reading books contributes to the Jewish identity more than any other media consumption activity. Holocaust literature is considered the most important genre in this respect. In fact, some readers see Holocaust fiction as more accessible than historical works, which are harder to digest. Television and newspapers also contribute to strengthening Jewish identity, while television contributes mainly through fictional series, and through Holocaust movies and documentaries such as Landsman's "Shoah."[22] Both survey respondents

---

name was Yehiel Dinur, but he wrote under the name Katchetnik, which was the nickname of a concentration camp prisoner. His real name emerged for the first time at the Eichmann trial in Jerusalem (1961) where he gave evidence.

21 Authors who wrote books about the Holocaust.

22 Director Claude Landsman's famous documentary for which he interviewed dozens of Holocaust survivors.

and focus groups participants felt that the Internet made least contribution to reinforcing their Jewish identity.

Media Use and Global Identity

Our findings clearly substantiate the hypothesis that the Internet is particularly helpful in the construction of a global identity. Over half the respondents reported that the Internet helped them most in this aspect. Note, however, that multi-channel television helps connect people to the global community at least to the same extent. Using the Internet to stay in touch with people all over the world was the only element of the global community mentioned by a very high percentage of respondents. This is how one focus group participant described the connection between the Internet and global identity: Orna (MA) – "My home page on the computer at work is the "New York Times." I remember reading an article on the first page on September 11, and then passing it around for others to read. I read English fluently. Now I am learning Spanish, so I visit Spanish newspaper sites. I rarely watch television."

The focus groups gave interesting insights into the role of multi-channel television in constructing a global identity. Focus group members had the following to say about the news: Itzik (29, student) – "I like to know what's going on. I watch the foreign channels because they broadcast things we don't get in Israel, like the NBA." Shimon (60, technician) – "I also watch French broadcasts on channel TV5. The news is different to what you get here. It's important for me to know what they are telling them over there." Ido (27, university education) – "There is news on the foreign news channels that isn't shown here, like what's happening in the world … I also watch MTV, music."

Virtual "globe trotters" are individuals who enjoy the feeling that they have been everywhere, though without leaving their room; cable television helps them achieve this blissful state. This was expressed in many different ways:

Nissim (36, university education) – "I like hearing English spoken. I travel the world using my remote control." Hedva (52, university education). "I watch CNN. It's in English so you learn the language. Sometimes they screen things that the local censor hasn't passed yet. The current events in English enrich your knowledge of the rest of the world." Alex (student, settled in Israel 12 years ago) – "You have the best of several worlds. You can see things that aren't available in Israel, like talk shows." Gershon (41, university education) – "I'm always hopping from one foreign channel to another. I love the Moroccan version of 'Millionaire.'[23] I like quiz shows. I learn about the subjects people know about in other countries." Ilana (high school education + courses) – "I really like television. For example, I like 'Oz'[24] ... I also like 'Law and Order.'[25] *I enjoy seeing what America is like.*" And finally, Ruti's (university education) pithy statement: *"It brings the world home to us."*

Even at a time of multi-channel television and widespread Internet use, books and newspapers still help readers to strengthen their connection with the global community and construct a global identity. As one focus group participant, Aliza (52, MA), aptly said: "Reading is very complex, it takes me to other places and the same time it takes me to inner places. When I read translated literature, it takes me to other places, though I do enjoy reading about familiar places, like America and England." Other people put it differently: Alex (student, immigrated to Israel 12 years ago) "A book hasn't got a country. It doesn't matter where the writer comes from. A book gets translated and people from different countries can enjoy it." Someone else emphasized the escapist function of reading: Udi (university graduate) – "I enjoy diving into a different kind of world, so I'm drawn to books which describe different atmospheres, different places."

The most salient finding regarding the use of media to construct a global identity is the equivalence between Internet and television. Despite the predominance of these activities, reading newspapers and books also contributes to the formation of a global identity by allowing people to learn about distant countries, different cultures and different ways of life all over the world. As shown in earlier studies (Adoni & Nossek, 1997; Nossek & Adoni, 1996), the present era of globalization is marked by a desire and need to connect with the global community and construct a new global identity.

23 Versions of the "Millionaire" quiz show exist throughout the world. Contestants, answer general knowledge questions, and stand to win a lot of money.
24 American series about a prison high security wing.
25 American series.

Media Use and Ethno-Cultural Identity

As with constructing an Israeli identity, in the case of an ethno-cultural group, it seems that reading books, and to a lesser extent watching television broadcasts in the language of the ethno-cultural group, plays an important role in structuring ethno-cultural identity.

Statements by focus group members clearly indicate a relatively new phenomenon, namely that middle-aged people born in Israel, or people who arrived to Israel at a very young age, read books written by members of their parents' ethno-cultural group, and use these books to help them identify or reconnect with their ethnic origins. Several focus group participants described this succinctly: Ora (university education) – "A recently published book I found I could really relate to was *Boei Doda Nirkod* ("Let's Dance Auntie").[26] I could relate personally to the subject matter, and it made me feel extremely nostalgic. The language used reminded me of my childhood with my parents." Leora (B.Ed.) – corroborating what Ora said – "It is about growing up in the Bulgarian community in Jaffa."

Ilana (high school + courses) made the same point about another ethno-cultural group: "I like reading books written by my uncle. He wrote a lot of books about Yemenite Jews, His name is Rabbi Shlomo Gamliel. I enjoy books about life in Yemen and the early years in Israel. His books all describe the suffering in Yemen. His stories are the stories of my parents' lives. That is why I sometimes sit down and read them." Gershon (41, university education) – "I read books by writers who came from Iraq, Sami Michael, Eli Amir.[27] They write about things I can relate to. My father is Polish, but my mother is Iraqi. I can really relate to stories about life in Iraq and the early days of Israel."

Ruti (university education), another focus group member, said: "I mainly read Israeli authors... though I also read Spanish works. I joined a group of women that got together to share books. Most of the women only read Spanish books. Now the group meets once a month in somebody's house. We buy books and exchange them, and

---

26 A book relating to the Jewish community of immigrants from Bulgaria in the fifties that lived together in Jaffa.

27 Known Israeli novelists writing about the Jewish life in Iraq and the Jewish immigrants from Iraq in Israel.

chat about them and eat. The books are usually works translated into Spanish, mainly novellas, which isn't a genre I like. I read them because I like being part of the group. I don't watch telenovellas on television. With books you can see, your imagination works. Telenovellas are so superficial I can't stand them. The women in the group watch them. They don't read Hebrew so they watch Spanish shows. They aren't newcomers to Israel. I came to Israel when I was quite young, and I was a teacher, so I can read in Hebrew. They came later and got jobs which didn't require much reading in Hebrew."

Some people read Yiddish works with the same thing in mind. For example, Ilana (university education) – "I enjoy Itzik Menger's[28] ballads very much. I read them in the Yiddish original. It's my way of connecting with the bygone world. My parents spoke Yiddish, that's how I know it."

It is important for people to feel connected to the past of their ethno-cultural community. This applies to both individuals from European and North African / Middle Eastern backgrounds. For example, Miriam (59) – "I watch television shows and movies in Arabic from Egypt and Jordan." Nurit (38) – "I watch some programs simply because I understand Arabic. I watch the Channel 1 (Israel TV) news in Arabic."

Israel has two large ethno-cultural groups: the Israeli-Arab community and the community of immigrants from the former USSR. Members of both communities communicate with family and friends in their own language and almost always read books in their mother tongue (Adoni, Cohen & Caspi, 2002).[29]

Most Arab members of the focus groups reported that they read Israeli newspapers to keep up with Israeli politics. In fact, they do not really have a choice, as there are practically no daily papers in Arabic, though they all read local, weekly Arabic newspapers. Educated individuals read some literature and often buy books in Hebrew to read to their children, because there are no books in Arabic. Several participants stressed this point, e.g.: Latifa (MA student, teaches Arabic) "Jaffa has not got a library where you can borrow Arabic books. There is no

28 Renowned Yiddish poet.
29 In each community, a small percentage of people (10%) do not use the media in any language.

pedagogic library either. I have to go to Tel Aviv. I get books from the *'HaMeshulash'* ('The Triangle')[30] and the north. I mostly read books on education. I don't read politics; I am interested in Arabic poetry and literature, by writers like Mahmoud Darwish[31] and Fadua Tukan.[32] I enjoy fiction – short stories – because of lack of time to read. I read classics like Jubran Jubran, Najib Mahfouz[33] and Elia Abu Madi and Taufiq el Hakim. If you want to read something enjoyable, read Jubran. I read it for the eloquence of the language. I read Hebrew more for pleasure; I take books that the librarian recommends."

One participant commented that an interest in Muslim mysticism and religion could also contribute to the construction of the ethno-cultural community. Mahmoud (44, high school education) – "...I read books in Arabic on mysticism and religion. Most of them are Jordanian, and some from Egypt. They discuss Islam and mysticism, with religious commentaries. They open the channel of love towards other people and for the religion itself. The books are written by religious sages. This is what I am interested in at the moment – religion and the Quran. My father used to read the Quran all the time. I follow his tradition. I have a friend who is a writer, his name is Mahmoud Abbasi; he writes all kinds of booklets, which I read."

From statements by Arab respondents we can learn that the most important media for staying in touch with the Arabic language and Arab culture are television and radio. People showed a preference for foreign stations, particularly Al Jazeera, and for news programs and movies from neighboring Arab countries.

One focus group member summed up the contribution of the media to constructing his ethno-cultural identity: Raid (35, university education, psychologist) – "When I want news, I turn to Al Jazeera or to newspapers sites on the Internet that you can't get in Israel and which are not influenced by the Israeli government. For example, London newspapers that you can't get here. European newspapers make you

---

30 Area in central Israel with a large concentration of Arab towns and villages.
31 Admired, veteran Palestinian poet and thinker.
32 Well known Palestinian poetess from the city of Shechem (Nablus).
33 Nobel Prize winner, leading Egyptian author.

feel more connected to the Arab communities there. You also need to know what is happening in Dubai and Kuwait. ...The Syrians represent Arab culture at its best ... Their standard is very high. As an Arab, I can be proud of them."

Immigrants from the former USSR who have been living in Israel for more than a decade still read material in Russian because it is easier and they can relate better to the contents. However, some people said they are no longer interested in what happens in the former USSR. This is what they said: Natalie (25, student, 12 years in Israel) – "You can get books, Russian books, but they represent a different mentality. A book that's been translated into another language is understood completely differently... it is more of a connection with the language. Translated works lose something in the translation. The plot is the same, but it has a slightly different nuance." Neli (university education, 12 years in Israel) – "I also feel that I don't understand what is happening there. It isn't as relevant anymore. I'm closer to what is happening here. My relationship with Russia is over." Alex (student, 12 years in Israel) disagreed – "Even if an adult knows Hebrew, it is hard to divorce yourself from your birth culture."

Focus group participants thought that Russian newspapers, radio REKA,[34] and books in Russian, encourage intra-community and inter-generational ties as opposed to helping immigrants construct an Israeli identity. The immigrants also use the Internet to stay in touch with relatives back in the former USSR. In Neli's words: "It helps me stay in touch with my family. It's very useful for my mother because it's quick and cheap."

Functional Interchangeability among Media in their Contribution to Identity Construction

The findings show that social identities are, to an extent, constructed by the consumption of all four media – reading books and newspapers, watching television and using the Internet. The functional differentiation among the media, i.e., the fact that a different one is emphasized each time in the construction of different identities, leads to our next question,

---

34 Public radio broadcasts intended for new immigrants in different languages, especially in Russian and Ethiopian.

namely which consumption activities are functionally interchangeable, and which are functionally specific in terms of their contribution to the construction of a specific social identity.

Where two media meet the same needs, studies based on the functional approaches demonstrate varying degrees of interchangeability between patterns of consumption for different types of media (Adoni & Nossek, 2001; Himmelweit & Swift, 1976; Katz, Gurevitch & Hass, 1973). McLuhan suggested that where there is a high level of functional interchangeability, in other words, when one medium meets a given need more effectively than another, a fall in consumption of the least effective medium might result. An intermediate state is also possible, in which both media will be used for the same purpose, although the emphasis in each case will be different. An example of this is television news broadcasts, which are visual, and radio news broadcasts, which outstrip television in terms of speed of delivering the news to the public. Similarly, both television and Internet meet people's need for information and keeping abreast of current events, albeit in different ways. In these cases, we would expect both media in question to be used to meet the need for information and for both to persist. An alternative would be for a number of media to merge to form a new medium, which would meet the combined needs represented by the constituents. Internet is an example of a converged medium. Another hypothesis suggests that in cases of low functional interchangeability, people would continue to use different media side by side since they provide mutually exclusive functions. For example, reading books has a low level of interchangeability with the Internet since the needs they meet are non-interchangeable: in the Internet case, email serves the need to nurture interpersonal connections, while reading books answers both intrapersonal needs and social need such as constructing a national identity.

We can examine media interchangeability by comparing the correlation between the consumption of two different media and their contribution to shaping social identity based on respondent evaluations. For example, we can examine the correlation between the contribution of reading newspapers and of watching television to the construction of Israeli identity. Based on respondent evaluations, 24 correlations were calculated for the contribution of all possible pairs of the use of four media (books, newspapers, television and Internet) to the construction of the four social identities examined (Israeli society, the Jewish People, the global community and the ethno-cultural community).

Table 2:
Functional Interchangeability between Pairs of Media Usage for the
Construction of the Same Social Identity (Pearson's correlations)

Media/ Social Identity	Books/ Television	Books/ Internet	Books/ News-papers	Newspapers/ Television	Newspapers/ Internet	Internet/ Television
Overall inter-changeability	.42	.32	.48	.58	.43	.50
Israeli	.44	.25	.31	.47	.15	.32
Jewish	.58	.26	.57	.58	.47	.56
Global	.44	.30	.50	.54	.35	.51
Ethno-cultural	.60	.49	.53	.70	.70	.62

According to the correlations between respondent evaluations of the contribution of the examined media use to constructing social identities (Table 2), the highest level of interchangeability was between reading newspapers and watching television. The second highest level of interchangeability was between the Internet and television, and the third highest level of interchangeability was between reading books and reading newspapers. The lowest level of interchangeability was between the Internet and books. On the other hand, television was found to be the most versatile medium since it was interchangeable with both the printed media and the Internet.

The picture becomes more complicated when we examine the degree of interchangeability of media use for the construction of specific social identities. Regarding Israeli identity, the highest degree of interchangeability was found between watching television and reading books and newspapers. This interchangeability appears to be influenced by the importance of Hebrew when choosing books and television programs and the informative content of newspapers and television. The fact that television and books and newspapers are entirely different technologically does not appear to affect users' evaluation of the function that they fulfill. The level of interchangeability between the two printed media was also much lower. The lowest degree of interchangeability for Israeli identity was found between using the Internet and reading books and newspapers.

Regarding construction of Jewish identity, as in the case of the Israeli identity, the highest level of interchangeability was between reading books and newspapers and watching television. Here too, the lowest correlation was between reading books and using the Internet.

Regarding construction of a global identity, the highest level of interchangeability was between watching television and reading newspapers, apparently because the aim of both these media is to provide information about the global community. A high level of interchangeability was also found between reading books and reading newspapers, while, once again, the lowest level of interchangeability was between reading books and using the Internet.

We found a different pattern of interchangeability for media contribution to constructing an ethno-cultural identity. There was a high level of interchangeability for all possible pairs of media. The highest level of interchangeability was between reading newspapers and watching television and between reading newspapers and using the Internet. Analysis of the findings showed that the highest overall level of media interchangeability was for constructing ethno-cultural identity.

A different pattern of media interchangeability was found for constructing an ethno-cultural identity as compared with the pattern of media interchangeability in constructing the three other social identities. Whereas, with the three remaining identities, there is apparently little interchangeability between the Internet and the printed media, in the case of ethnic-cultural identity, the Internet and the printed media show greatest interchangeability. From this, we can infer that the printed media play an exclusive role in shaping the other three identities. In terms of shaping ethno-cultural identity, however, no single media seems to make any outstanding contribution.

Discussion and Conclusions

The role of communication technologies in fostering social identity can only be explained in terms of an integrated theoretical framework incorporating both the technological and functional conceptualizations of media study. Based on this integrated conception, the present study explored the contribution of four media (books, newspapers, television, and Internet) to constructing four social identities in Israeli society: Israeli identity, Jewish identity, global identity, and ethno-cultural identity. It also examined whether certain media function interchangeably and if some "specialize" in constructing certain identities.

As the theoretical discussion revealed, new communication technologies are integral to two significant social trends of the early twenty-first century: multiculturalism and globalization. Although these trends seem contradictory in terms of social identity construction – multiculturalism implying ethno-cultural segmentation and globalization a unified global culture – despite their obvious differences they are perceived by scholars of media and society as a threat to national identity: the core of the nation-state and its culture. Proponents of the technological view maintain that new media technologies, i.e., television and Internet, threaten national identity since they obscure nation state boundaries and encourage identification with the global community on the one hand and to ethnic community on the other. This conception essentially applies media displacement theory to identity construction, assuming that strengthening one identity will cause the displacement of others. Conversely, functional theory argues that new media consumption patterns foster the development of multiple – national, global, and ethnic – identities.

Research based on combination of the two theoretical perspectives yielded a broader insight, namely, that media technology is indeed a powerful agent of social change, whereas the differential functional uses of the various media can indeed determine the direction of the social change concerning the social construction of identities. The findings of the present study did not corroborate McLuhan's media displacement hypothesis. Rather, they show that the use of both printed media and television serve in the construction of social identities and that there is a high degree of interchangeability between them. One possible explanation for this is that in a multi-channel environment, people tend to use several media to meet the same social needs. Indeed, this was substantiated by focus group participants, who stressed the complementary functional relationship between reading and watching TV.

The findings also demonstrated that media consumption is indeed an important social activity that influences the social construction of identity, thus affecting trends in both globalization and multiculturalism. In general, our findings support McLuhan's early insights that reading printed media, i.e., books and newspapers, in the reader's national language, helped to sustain national identity, which was the essence of the nation state. Regarding television, the present findings are somewhat unclear. On the one hand, agreeing with the media technology approach, we found that television, especially cable and satellite TV, helped to construct people's ties with the global community. New technology users are also more connected to the global community than the national, terrestrial television viewers of the 1960s, when Toronto School researchers first conceived their vision of the "global village." However, our findings also demonstrated that television served in constructing national and ethno-cultural identities as well as the global identity.

Watching television, reading newspapers, and reading books contributed significantly to constructing an Israeli identity. Compared to the results reported in studies of Israeli leisure patterns (Katz & Gurevitch, 1976; Katz et al., 2000), television still seemed more useful than any other media in constructing various social identities, though there is only a small gap between television and the other media. It was found in this study that the role of television in constructing social identity has changed since 1990, when multi-channel television and subsequently the Internet appeared on the media scene in Israel. One apparent consequence of this multiplicity of channels and dispersal of viewing is that television is no longer the dominant media in constructing Israeli national identity. For similar reasons, we argue, television currently has a greater impact on the construction of global and ethno-cultural identities, which in turn amplifies multicultural trends.

As was the case back in 1970, newspapers emerged here as the most important media for constructing Israeli identity. Interestingly, in both the Arab and Russian communities, which are recognized for their strong ties to their own culture, reading Hebrew newspapers appears to be the first choice for constructing an Israeli identity, while reading books fostered the construction of these populations' ethno-cultural identity. One could still argue, similar to Katz et al. (2000), that books and newspapers have not lost their special role in people's lives, despite Israel's multi-channel media environment.

As one would expect, both Internet and television were found to foster global identity. Interestingly, the Internet, which was extremely effective in this sense, also helped in constructing an Israeli national identity. However, the Internet was found to have less impact than other media on constructing Jewish and ethno-cultural identities. Moreover, we found a low functional interchangeability between the Internet and other media, chiefly the printed media, in terms of constructing social identities.

However, it is worth noting that as the Internet has yet to achieve its full potential in the multi-channel environment, its impact on the construction of social idetities may increase in the future due to the many options for new ways of communication that it offers, and the growing number of its users.

Contrary to apprehensions regarding the fragmentation of identities or global uniformity, the findings support the claims of researchers such as Hall (1993) and Gillespie (1995), that the media indeed play a role in constructing multiple identities. As our earlier studies showed (Adoni, Caspi & Cohen, 2002; Adoni & Nossek, 1997; Nossek & Adoni, 1996), one can be both a citizen of the world and an active member of an ethno-cultural community without conceding one's national identity. The ability to develop multiple identities and negotiate between them both on the personal level and in terms of the social system offers at least a partial solution to the threat from both multiculturalism and globalization to the political framework of the nation state.

Acknowledgements

Our thanks to the Burda Center for Research on Innovative Communication at Ben-Gurion University for providing the research grant to fund the qualitative data collection. Thanks also to the Smart Institute at the Hebrew University, and the School of Communication, College of Management, for the research grants which allowed us to conduct the survey. Thanks to the Dialog Company and its CEO Dr. Yitzhak Dayan for undertaking the quantitative fieldwork, and to Ms. Smadar Shtraks for the statistical processing. Thank are due also to the Granitim Company for organizing the focus groups meetings.

Special thanks also to research assistant Ms. Ronie Kolker for processing the focus group transcripts and accurately editing the bibliography. Thanks are also due to Ms. Sharon Ashkenazi for helping to process some of the focus groups transcripts and Ms. Ruth Freedman for her excellent editing.

References

Adoni, H. (1979). The functions of mass media in the political socialization of adolescents. *Communication Research, 6*(1), 84–106.

Adoni, H. (1985). Media interchangeability and co-existence: Trends and changes in production distribution and consumption patterns of the print media in the television era. *Libri*, 3, 202–217.

Adoni, H. (1995). Literacy and reading in a multimedia environment. *Journal of Communication*, 45, 152–174.

Adoni, H., & Adoni, U. (1994). Jews, Israelis and citizens: National identity and patterns of political involvement among Israeli adolescents. *Jewish Political Studies Review*, 3–4, 175–209.

Adoni, H., Cohen, A. A., & Caspi, D. (2002). The consumer's choice: Language, consumption and hybrid identities of minorities. *Communications. The European Journal of Communication Research*, 27, 411–436.

Adoni, H., & Mane, S. (1984). Media and the social construction of reality: Towards an integration of theory and research. *Communication Research*, 11, 323–340.

Adoni H., & Nossek, H. (1997). "Ani," "Israeli" ve"ezrach ha'olam": Ha'televizia be'chvalim ve'hashlachoteia al ksharim chevrateim ["Me," "Israeli" and "citizen of the world": Cable television and its implication on social connection]. In: Caspi D. (Ed.). *Tikshoret ve'demokratya be'Israel [Media and democracy in Israel]* (pp. 97–115). Tel Aviv: Van Leer Institute and HaKibbutz HaMeuchad Ltd. (in Hebrew).

Adoni H., & Nossek, H. (2001). The new media consumers: Media convergence and the displacement effect. *Communications. The European Journal of Communication Research*, 26 (1), 59–83.

Alexander, J. C. (Ed.) (1990). *Action and its environments: Toward a new synthesis*. New York: Columbia University Press.

Anderson, B. (1983). *Imagined communities: Reflections on the origin and spread of nationalism*. London: Verso.

Baudrillard, J. (1983). *Simulations*. New York: Semiotext(e).

Blondheim, M. (2003). Harold Adams Innis and his Bias of Communication. In: Katz, E., Peters, J.D., Liebes, T., & Orloff, A. (Eds.). *Canonic Texts in Communication Research* (pp. 156–190). London: Polity Press.

Blumler, J., & Katz, E. (Eds.) (1974). *The uses of mass communications*. London: Sage.

De Saussure, F. (1915). *Course in general linguistics*. London: Peter Owen.

Downing, J. (2001). *The Seattle IMC and the Socialist Anarchist Tradition*. Washington, D.C.: ICA pre-conference "Our Media, Not Theirs." May, 2001.

First, A. (1997). Television and the construction of social reality: An Israeli case study. In: McCombs, M., Shaw, D.L., & Weaver, D. (Eds.). *Communication and democracy*. New Jersey: Lawrence Erlbaum.

Geertz, C. (2000). *Available light: Anthropological reflections on philosophical topics*. Princeton, New Jersey: Princeton University Press.

Gillespie, M. (1995). *Television, ethnicity and cultural change*. London: Routledge.

Hall, S. (1991). Ethnicity, identity and difference. *Radical America*, 24, 4.

Hall, S. (1993). Culture, community, nation. *Cultural Studies, 7* (3), 349–363.

Himmelweit, H. T., & Swift, B. (1976). Continuities and discontinuities in media usage and taste: A longitudinal study. *Journal of Social Issues*, 32, 133–156.

Innis, H. (1951). *The bias of communication*. Toronto: University of Toronto Press.

Katz, E., & Adoni, H. (1973). Functions of the book for society and self. *Diogenes*, 81, 106–118.

Katz, A., Hass, H., Weitz, S, Adoni, H., Gurevitz, M., & Schiff, M. (2000). *Leisure pursuits in Israel: Changes in patterns of cultural activities 1970–1990*. Tel Aviv: Open University.

Katz, E., Gurevitch, M., & Haas, H. (1973). On the use of the mass media for important things. *American Sociological Review*, 36, 164–181.

Katz, E., & Gurevitch, M. (1976). *The secularization of leisure*. London: Faber & Faber.

Katz, R., & Katz, E. (1988). McLuhan: Where did he come from, where did he disappear? *Canadian Journal of Communication*, 23, 307–319.

Lazarsfeld, P. F., & Merton, R. K. (1948). Mass communication, popular taste and organized social action. *The Communication of Ideas* (pp. 492–512). New York: The Institute for Religious and Social Studies.

Levinson, P. (1999). *Digital McLuhan*. New York: Routledge.

Levitt, T. (1983). The globalization of markets. *Harvard Business Review*, May/June,

McLuhan, M. (1962). *The Gutenberg galaxy*. Toronto: University of Toronto Press.

McQuail, D. (2001). *With more hindsight: Conceptual problems and some ways forward for media use research.* Paper presented at the 2nd International EJCR Colloquium, October 18–20, 2001, University of Nijmegen, The Netherlands.

McQuail, D., & Windhal, S. (1993). *Communication models* (2nd Ed.). London: Longman.

Merton, R. (1968). *Social theory and social structure*. New York: The Free Press.

Meyrowitz, J. (1985). *No sense of place*. New York: Oxford University Press.

Morley, D. & Robins, K. (1995). *Spaces of identity*. London: Routledge.

Neuman, S. B. (1986). Television, reading and the home environment. *Reading Research and Instruction*, 25, 173–183.

Neuman, S. B. (1991). *Literacy in the television age: The myth of TV effect*. Norwood, NJ: Ablex.

Nossek, H. (2002). Israeli society: Democracy and liberalization. In: Nossek, H. (Ed.). *Israel in the early 21st century: Society, law, economy and communication*. Tel Aviv: Gome-Tcherikover Publishers.

Nossek, H., & Adoni, H. (1996). The social implications of cable television: Restructuring connections with self and social groups. *International Journal of Public Opinion Research*, 8 (1), 51–69.

Postman, N. (1982). *The Disappearance of Childhood.* New York: Delacorte Press.

Press, A. L. (1994). The sociology of cultural reception: Notes toward an emerging paradigm. In: Crane, D. (Ed.). *The sociology of culture* (pp. 221–247). Oxford, UK: Blackwell.

Renckstorf, K., & McQuail, D. (1996). Social action perspectives in mass communication research: An introduction. In: Renckstorf, K., McQuail, D., & Jankowski, N. (Eds.). *Media use as social action* (pp. 1–18). London: John Libbey.

Renckstorf, K., McQuail, D., & Janowski, N. (Eds.). (1996). *Media use as social action*. London: John Libbey.

Renckstorf, K., & Wester, F. (2001). An action theoretical frame of reference for the study of television news use. In: Renckstorf, K., McQuail, D., & Jankowski, N. (Eds.). *Television news research: Recent European approaches and findings*. Berlin: Quintessenz Books.

Rosengren, K. E., Palmgreen, P., & Wenner, L. (Eds.). (1985). *Media gratification research: Current perspectives*. Beverly Hills, Cal.: Sage.

Rosengren, K. E., & Windahl, S. (1972). Mass media consumption as a functional alternative. In: McQuail, D. (Ed.). *Sociology of Mass Communications* (pp. 166–194). Harmondsworth, Middlesex: Penguin.

Schlesinger, P. (1993). Wishful thinking: Cultural politics, media and collective identities in Europe. *Journal of Communication, 43*(2), 6–17.

Schudson, M. (1994). Culture and integration of national societies. In: Crane, D.C. (Ed.). *The sociology of culture* (pp. 21–45). Oxford, UK: Blackwell.

Sreberny-Mohammadi, A. (1996). The global and the local in international communication. In: Curran, J., & Gurevitch, M. (Eds.). *Mass media and society* (2nd ed., pp. 177–203). London: Edward Arnold.

Tamir, Y. (1998). Two concepts of multiculturalism. In M. Mautner, A. Sagi & R. Shamir (Eds.). *Multiculturalism in a democratic and Jewish state* (pp.79–92). Tel Aviv: Ramot.

Vettehen, P. H., Renckstorf, K., & Wester, F. (1996). Media use as social action: Methodological issues. In: Renckstorf, K., McQuail, D., & Jankowski, N. (Eds.). *Media use as social action* (pp. 32–42). London: John Libbey.

NAVA COHEN-AVIGDOR AND SAM LEHMAN-WILZIG

11. Rare to Medium: A Full Taxonomy of Elements for Assessing How Well (Done) the Internet's Unique Capabilities are Currently Exploited by e-Magazines

The fast pace of the Internet's technological evolution and its somewhat unique character as a *multimedium* constitute a challenge for both practitioners and scholars alike. One such challenge is to understand its sundry capabilities and exploit them to the fullest[1]: to what extent, at this relatively early stage of the Internet's development, are its practitioners maximally using its (full) potentialities? The comprehensive list provided in this article offers a solid basis for analyzing[2] and comparing the extent to which the technical capabilities of the Internet are impacting the substantive contents as well as the communicative mode of transmission. While our case study focuses on e-magazines, the question addressed is universal: how different are they from their print counterparts at this relatively early stage of the Internet's development?

The current research surrounding the Internet has dealt mainly with its social and cultural impact through the communication connections that it engenders. Various studies have looked at the Internet from a variety of perspectives: content, policy, community and society, commerce, gender, CMC and interaction between users, plus some others. However, as Andrew J. Flanagin et al.[3] noted a few years ago,

---

1   This is the central focus of the doctoral study from which the subject of this chapter is taken: Nava Cohen-Avigdor, "Utilizing the Special Abilities of the Internet in Women's Journalism: An Analysis of the Penetration/Growth Stages of e-Magazines and the Self-Defense Stage of Print Magazines" (Ramat Gan: Dept. of Political Studies, Public Communications Program, Bar-Ilan University, 2005).

2   For each, we analyzed the *entire* e-magazine (or print-based site) and not just certain parts (e.g., homepage).

3   Andrew J. Flanagin, Wendy Jo Maynard Farinola, and Miriam J. Metzger, "The

there exists a lacuna regarding the Internet's technological structure and how it influences Internet use. As we shall see below, several researchers ask whether this medium's new technological capabilities ("elements") are fully incorporated by content producers – or whether, alternatively, the Internet producers are making mistakes similar to their predecessors when earlier new media came into being: "application conservatism" – the rear-view mirror syndrome, as McLuhan and Fiore[4] put it – based on repeating the production patterns found in older media. Just as it took time for television producers to turn the "medium" into something "well done" (from early radiophonic TV to more visually-based programming), an important question today is how "well done" is the current Internet use of this new medium's "language," in the specific area of e-magazine content. Academic scholarship can go far in showing the way to fuller exploitation of this new medium's capabilities, as Newhagen and Rafaeli suggest.[5]

However, before such an undertaking can be accomplished, a prior task awaits us: producing a comprehensive taxonomy of the possibilities inherent in Internet journalism sites. As will be shown below, there have been several preliminary attempts at listing important elements along a host of categories, but all are partial at best. Thus, we have set out not only to bring together all such (relevant) previously mentioned elements, but to add still others not discussed in the literature. Such a comprehensive list can then serve as a baseline for assessing the relative success or failure of sites to utilize the vast panoply of capabilities that the Internet/Web theoretically offers surfers/readers.

It must be noted at the start that the term "Internet" is problematic, as Adams and Clark note.[6] Discussing the various factors offered by previous researchers that influence its character, they conclude that the Internet is both a *macromedium* (comprehensive in scope and global in

Technical Code of the Internet / World Wide Web," *Critical Studies in Media Communication* 17(4) (2000): 413.

4   Marshall McLuhan and Quentin Fiore, *The Medium is the Massage: An Inventory of Effects* (New York: Bantam, 1967): n.p.

5   John. E. Newhagen and Sheizaf Rafaeli, "Why Communication Researchers Should Study the Internet," *Journal of Communication* 46 (1) (1996): 4–13.

6   Tyrone Adams and Norman Clark, *The Internet – Effective Online Communication* (New York: Harcourt College, 2001): 29.

size; also enabling the dissemination of even the shortest messages for the smallest audience), and also a *metamedium* (a platform for older media, e.g., telephone, print, broadcasting). Our preference is to call the Internet a *multimedium*,[7] i.e., a combination of the two categories: *macromedium* and *metamedium*. It should be noted that the Internet is inherently different from the other main mass media (newspapers, radio, TV) in that while it retains some mass elements, it also has a distinct "demassified, individual and interactive nature."[8]

Obviously, our approach is based on the theoretical approach of technological influence on communication patterns developed by Harold Adams Innis and Marshall McLuhan.[9] While these two pioneers did not agree on all points, the central idea of *technological* centrality in the process of media evolution is the common thread running throughout their works. We do not directly attempt to prove or disprove their theory, but rather accept it as the starting point for our analysis of the connection between the Internet's technological capabilities and the content producers' use of them. Indeed, it was so at the very start: studies of the history of the Graphical User Interface show that its initial

7   See: Nicholas W. Jankowski and Lucien Hanssen, eds., *The Contours of Multimedia: Recent Technological, Theoretical and Empirical Developments* (U.K.: University of Luton Press – Academia Research Monograph 19, 1996); Roger Fidler, *Mediamorphosis: Understanding New Media* (Thousand Oaks, Cal.: Pine Forge, 1997): 25.

8   Nicholas W. Jankowski and Lucien Hanssen, "Introduction: Multimedia Come of Age," in *The Contours of Multimedia, ibid.*: 8.

9   Eric McLuhan and Frank Zingrone, eds. *Essential McLuhan* (London: Routledge, 1995); Michel A. Moss, *Marshall McLuhan Essays: Media Research, Technology, Art, Communication* (London: Overseas Publishers Association, 1997); Gary Genosko, *McLuhan and Baudrillard: The Masters of Implosion* (London: Routledge, 1999).

For the original works of this school's founders, see: Harold Adams Innis, *The Bias of Communication,* Introduction by Marshall McLuhan (Toronto: University of Toronto Press, 1951), reprinted (U.S.A.: 1964); Marshall McLuhan, *The Gutenberg Galaxy – The Making of Typographic Man* (New York: Mentor, 1962); Marshall McLuhan, *Understanding Media – The Extensions of Man* (New York: Mentor, 1964) and the Reprint Edition, with an Introduction by Lewis H. Lapham (Cambridge, Mass.: MIT Press, 1994); Marshall McLuhan and Quentin Fiore, *The Medium is the Massage, op. cit.*

phases were very much influenced by communication theoreticians who emphasized technological influence.[10]

The choice of technological influence as a starting point is not merely ours: in his book *Digital McLuhan*, Paul Levinson argues that McLuhan's theories are more relevant than ever in explaining the nature and influence of new media technologies, e.g., the Internet. As he put it: "How is selecting the news we want to read, hear about, and watch on the Internet different from its presentation via newspapers, radio, and television?"[11] Indeed, there has been a recent upsurge in scholarship from the perspective of communication technology influence.[12]

The most obvious change emanates from the process of media convergence (accelerated by the Internet) in which, according to Herbert,[13] present contents – especially information – undergo recoding or reformatting into a new type of product, transmitted through a wide array of telecommunications media, satisfying different needs of sundry audiences. The Internet, especially, enables information to be produced and consumed textually, orally and/or visually in ways different from previous broadcast media; this is both an opportunity and a challenge for the content providers, now faced with learning a new professional "language" of almost unlimited potential – and in McLuhanesque terms, dealing with a "colder" medium than before. Taylor,[14] emphasizing the pressures of convergence, says much the same thing: new, hybrid forms of media demand creative, interactive approaches in order to *fully* realize the almost unlimited potential of the Internet.

10 Susan B. Barnes, "Bridging the Differences Between Social Theory and Technological Invention in Human-Computer Interface Design," *New Media & Society* 2(3) (2000): 353.

11 Paul Levinson, *Digital McLuhan – A guide to the information millennium* (London: Routledge, 1999): 2.

12 Barnes, "Bridging the Differences Between Social Theory and Technological Invention," op. cit.: 354.

13 John Herbert, *Journalism in the Digital Age: Theory and Practice – Broadcast, Print and On-Line Media* (Oxford: Focal Press, 2001): 16–17.

14 Paul A. Taylor, "McLuhan's Millennium Message," *New Media & Society* 2 (3) (2000): 373–381.

Theoretical Background

As noted above, in this chapter we will offer a comprehensive list of the many elements that a text-based site could usefully apply on-site. There are books[15] that have dedicated a few chapters to the elements of the medium in general (from different points of view), and there have been a few studies[16] that have focused on several such elements (see below). Others have compared print and e-newspapers, among them Alloro et al.[17] who compared the contents of 54 biomedical print and e-magazines, asking whether the former is slated to disappear.[18] Li[19] analyzed the graphics and design changes in three major American

15 For example: Jakob Nielsen, *Multimedia and Hypertext: The Internet and Beyond* (San Francisco: Morgan Kaufman, 1995; Originally published in Boston, Mass.: AP Professional); Adams and Clark, *The Internet – Effective Online Communication*, *op. cit.;* Chris Mann and Fiona Stewart, *Internet Communication and Qualitative Research: A Handbook for Researching Online* (London: Sage Publications, 2000); and more.

16 Herre van Oostendorp and Christof van Nimwegen, "Locating Information in an Online Newspaper," *Journal of Computer-Mediated Communication* 4(1) (1998); downloaded from http://www.ascusc.org/jcmc/vol14/issue1/oostendorp.html (Oct. 22, 2002). Tanjev Schultz, "Interactive Options in Online Journalism: A Content Analysis of 100 U.S. Newspapers," *Journal of Computer Mediated Communication* 5(1) (1999); downloaded from http://www.ascusc.org/jcmc/vol5/issue1/schultz. html (June 4, 2001). Nicholas W. Jankowski and Martine van Selm, "Traditional News Media Online: An Examination of Added Values," *Communications* 25 (1) (2000): 85–101. Sylvia M. Chan-Olmsted and Jung Suk Park, "From On-Air to Online World: Examining the Content and Structures of Broadcast TV Stations' Web Sites," *Journalism & Mass Communication Quarterly* 77(2) (2000): 321–329. Jakob Nielsen and Marie Tahir, *Homepage Usability: 50 Websites Deconstructed* (U.S.A.: New Riders Publishing, 2002). Molly E. Holzschlag and Bruce Lawson, eds., *Insite Usability: The Site Speaks For Itself* (U.S.A.: Glasshaus, 2002); and others.

17 Giovanna Alloro, Cristina Casilli, Maurizio Taningher and Donatella Ugolini, "Electronic Biomedical Journals: How they Appear and what they Offer," *European Journal of Cancer* 34(3) (1998): 290–295.

18 Their conclusion: print papers will not disappear in the near future because of technological problems that will not be resolved quickly, e.g., low resolution of print type on the screen.

19 Xigen Li, "Web Page Design and Graphic Use of Three U.S. Newspapers," *Journalism & Mass Communication Quarterly* 75(2) (1998): 353–365.

papers that decided to put out an e-version as well; Nielsen[20] did much the same (mostly design) on a theoretical level. Peng et al.[21] studied the latest trends of U.S. e-paper sites, focusing on classified ads, readers, contents and services offered. In short, all these studies touch on some unique Internet elements – but either limited in the number of such elements or in the site sections studied. To our knowledge there has been no attempt to *comprehensively and systematically* list them *all* through a study *in situ.*[22]

To be sure, "new" is not necessarily "improved." The ultimate purpose of changing the design of, and adding elements to, a new-old medium is to improve the consumer's experience, i.e., to render it more usable. This means that each element must offer some *real* (and really *useful*) "added value" to the user. Therefore, we take as our lead the term "usability" that constitutes a common thread in Internet studies of the technology and the medium's "form"; we list only those elements that offer such extra value for the end user as others have done. For example, van Oostendorp and van Nimwegen[23] explored several elements of e-papers' usability, especially their influence on different reading techniques (e.g., scrolling and hyper-linking) for finding information dispersed throughout the site. We too study reading/searching techniques through an expanded list of traits regarding Links (horizontal, vertical, sub-linking to other sites) and also Accessibility to sections/services (e.g., Purchases, Archives). Too often, only seasoned, veteran surfers are capable of discovering these, rendering the site only partly usable for the average reader.

20 Jakob Nielsen, "Differences Between Print Design and Web Design" (Jan. 24, 1999); downloaded from http://www.useit.com/alertbox/990124.html (Jan. 25, 2001).

21 Yeuh Foo Peng, Tham Irene Naphtali and Xiaoming Hao, "Trends in Online Newspapers: A Look at the US Web," *Newspaper Research Journal* 20 (2) (1999): 52–63.

22 The specific case study of the doctoral dissertation from which the present article is taken involves 30 women's magazines – electronic and print. The women's magazine is the largest selling type of magazine in the Western world. This offers two possibly conflicting elements: 1. leading print magazines tread warily in the new medium so as not to kill the golden goose; 2. they have a strong economic incentive (and wherewithal) to put some eggs in the new media basket.

23 Oostendorp and Nimwegen, *Locating Information in an Online Newspaper*, *op. cit.*

Two relatively recent books do deal comprehensively with the extent
of usability: *Homepage Usability*[24] that analyzed only the Home Page;
and *Usability: The Site Speaks For Itself,*[25] covering the entire site.
However, the former dealt with all types of sites (commercial, e-stores,
computer firms, TV channels, as well as CNET and USA Today, among
others). The latter is closer to what we hope to accomplish; *Usability:
The Site Speaks For Itself* dealt in-depth with six complete sites, among
them BBC News and Economist.com, basing its recommendations on
the practical experience of Webmasters (Website developers, designers
and strategists). In the book's introduction, Molly E. Holzschlag[26] notes
that "usability" predates the Web[27] and certainly is a non-absolute,
i.e., subjective, matter – with Webmasters still involved in a learning
process. The Economist.com Webmasters decided on eight parameters
(what we call "elements"): Identity; Navigation; Page length; Clean
content; Strong header; Consistency; Frequency; and Balance.

Our list goes well beyond these parameters. On the other hand,
because of the huge taxonomic complexity of what we have set out to
do, this chapter will not attempt to also test the relative "added value" of
each of our elements regarding usability. We leave such an investigation
to a future time – perhaps when e-magazine sites will include most of
our elements.

Returning for a moment to the Nielsen and Tahir book,[28] it is generally
accepted that the homepage is far and away the most important part of
any content site because of its high visibility (only infrequently will
a surfer arrive first at an interior page through some horizontal "deep
link" from another site). The authors offer 113 homepage usability
guidelines, some relevant to other pages and some not. However,
many of their guidelines are not reader-oriented but rather *provider*-
oriented – from a pronounced commercial marketing perspective, not
altogether relevant for our purposes. Our list, on the other hand, is
reader-oriented. Nevertheless, several of their points are well taken.

24 Nielsen and Tahir, *Homepage Usability, op. cit.*
25 Holzschlag and Lawson, eds., *Usability, op. cit.*
26 Holzschlag and Lawson, eds., *Usability, ibid.., 2.*
27 The disciplines that have formed the foundation of Web "usability" are: User Interface
    Design; Human Computer Interaction (HCI); Graphical User Interface(GUI).
28 Nielsen and Tahir, *Homepage Usability, op. cit.*

For example, whereas the main purpose of a print magazine's cover page is to encourage the consumer to purchase that magazine instead of its many competitors at the newsstand, the homepage is arrived at consciously by the reader so that here it needs to "pull" the surfer into internal pages, given the great ease of jumping ship to other online magazines. Other differences relate to "content turnover": unlike print vehicles, e-magazines (or e-papers) must change at least part of their contents more than the official publication frequency would indicate (e.g., hourly within a "daily" newspaper; weekly or even daily within a "monthly" magazine). Finally, given the ease of hypertext jumping within a site, the e-magazine's homepage necessarily must offer far more information than its print counterpart regarding the contents. Thus, our list opens with the critical homepage, based on five central elements related to surfing quality, information accessibility and site orientation (some of these elements are also examined over the entire site).

The need for a comprehensive taxonomy is evident from the universal conclusion that Web content sites do not come close to utilizing the technical capabilities at their disposal. For instance, in a content analysis study of 100 American e-papers Schultz[29] found very little interactivity opportunities (e.g., e-mail; Discussion Forums; Chat-Rooms; Letters to the Editor; Poll/Surveys) for the readers. Jankowski and van Selm[30] looked at seven daily e-papers and six TV news e-sites from the U.S., Canada and Holland, and found that they included in varying measure multimedia, discussion and feedback. Their study offers six elements for studying (un)successful sites in the future: Hyperlinks, Discussion groups, Feedback, Archives, Multimedia, and Updating news. We include these as well.

Finally, Chan-Olmsted and Park[31] – in their large-scale study of 300 TV news sites – looked at three major categories: homepage contents (3 variables); overall site contents (8 variables); and overall site structure (18 variables). They also found that there was not a lot of interactivity and personalization. Rather, these stations chose to stick to their traditional fare of news presented in rather straightforward fashion: "The emphasis on news-oriented content presents a less risky

29 Tanjev Schultz, "Interactive Options in Online Journalism," *op. cit.*
30 Jankowski and van Selm, "Traditional News Media Online," *op. cit.*
31 Chan-Olmsted and Suk Park, "From On-Air to Online World," *op. cit.*

business approach because a station will be able to minimize costs by re-formatting the content it already owns and provide the utility currently sought by most audience Web users. As the Web grows and the delivery technology improves, the TV broadcasters will eventually enter a stage of Web development that requires more product differentiation."[32]

This also seems to be print journalism's approach. Their entrance into e-journalism was accompanied by two economic fears: 1) heavy outlays undercutting the organization's profitability, especially as almost all Web content is free; 2) losing paying readers of the print paper who will find the same material online. These considerations go a long way in explaining the conservative technical and graphic decisions regarding content and design, i.e., not fully utilizing the medium's capabilities. In any case, we too list several of these comparative contents elements.

The Internet (and the Web within it) is not merely a top-down medium but also holds many peer-to-peer possibilities. Derrick de Kerckhove's[33] analysis of the Web stresses its "tribal" character (McLuhan's terminology[34]) and as such involves "shared" language, not "imposed." Levinson[35] goes so far as to claim that the Internet has truly transformed our world into McLuhan's "global village" as every online villager can create a dialogue with any other surfer.[36] Thus, as de Kerckhove notes, the Web is both collective and personal. Finally, the language is "oral" (textual immediacy) but also copied and stored – in Innis' terms, overcoming the limitations of both space and time.

Of necessity, all these characteristics are represented in our list of elements. For instance, chat rooms are the purest expression of orality on the Web, whereas the huge archives and data banks store information in amounts not heretofore possible. Many e-papers understand the

---

32 *Ibid.*: 337.

33 Interview with de Kerckhove in: Kevin Kelly, "What Would McLuhan Say?" *Wired* (Archive Oct. 4, 1996); downloaded from http://www.wired.com/wired/archive/4.10/dekerckhove.html (Jan. 3, 2001).

34 See: Marshall McLuhan and Bruce R. Powers, *The Global Village* (New York: Oxford University Press, 1989).

35 Levinson, *Digital McLuhan, op. cit.*, 7.

36 This point leads directly to the issue of gatekeeping on the Net, of major importance regarding the communication process. However, because of the complexity involved we shall not deal with this question despite its indirect connection to the medium's traits.

value of chat rooms and give them prominent place (along with topic-specific forums). Archives can also be found on such e-papers in various guises[37] – from entire issues preserved in original form, to internal search engines, to select articles connected to central links according to subject or section within the site.[38]

Innis also investigated many of the printed page's influences on the reader, among them the severance of communicator/audience connection.[39] To a large extent, both Internet synchronous and asynchronous interactivity neutralizes this problem, enabling new types of connection between the two parties – and thus we include interactivity in our list as well.[40] Newhagen and Rafaeli see interactivity as one of the five major elements of the Internet (the others being multimedia, hypertext, packet switching and synchronicity).[41]

Levinson goes even farther, claiming that interactivity is the prime factor underlying many surfers' "addiction" to the Internet.[42] Rafaeli and Sudweeks agree to some extent: "Interactivity plays a role in creating the attraction of networks and in generating their growth patterns."[43] Al and Laura Ries view interactivity as the defining element differentiating the Internet from all other mass media – in the long run determining what will be an appropriate part of the Net and what not.[44] Indeed, Nielsen views the Internet in the future as being completely interactive![45] Nevertheless, as Rafaeli and Sudweeks conclude, we still have a while

37 Some now charge money – a growing phenomenon on the Web.
38 The Internet has become the source for more information retrieval than any other – books, magazines, television and telephone. Andrew J. Flanagin et al., "The Technical Code of the Internet," *op. cit.*, 417.
39 McLuhan and Zingrone, eds. *Essential McLuhan, op. cit.*, 307.
40 Chan-Olmsted and Suk Park, "From On-Air to Online World," *op. cit.* We list below seven elements related to interactivity.
41 Newhagen and Rafaeli, "Why Communication Researchers Should Study the Internet," *op. cit.*
42 Levinson, *Digital McLuhan, op. cit.,* 11.
43 Sheizaf Rafaeli and Fay Sudweeks, "Networked Interactivity," *Journal of Computer Mediated Communication* 2 (4) (1997). Downloaded from http://jcmc.huji.ac.il/vol2/issue4/rafaeli.sudweeks.html (June 6, 2001).
44 Al Ries and Laura Ries, *The 11 Immutable Laws of Internet Branding* (New York: HarperCollinsPublishers, 2000).
45 Jakob Nielsen, "Differences Between Print Design and Web Design," *op. cit.*

to go before formulating a complete theory of interactivity[46] – in part because of the multi-varied nature of the phenomenon. As Kiousis points out, interactivity is both a media function and a "psychological factor that varies across communication technologies, communication contexts, and people's perceptions."[47]

If Innis was interested in how the audience becomes disconnected from the mass communicators, McLuhan took a different tack, regarding media as "extensions of our human selves,"[48] i.e., enabling a reaching-out of our senses. Radio, for example, extended our ears. From this perspective, the Internet can be said to "extend the extensions" through its ability to combine within it the specific and discrete extensions of each previous medium. He would most probably have viewed digital technologies (e.g., the Internet) as extending our central nervous system beyond our natural analog capabilities through the dissemination of our thoughts and ideas around the globe via e-mail, chat, forums and the Web as a whole.

As McLuhan thought it incumbent upon us to understand the function of each of our senses (through whatever medium: skin, eyes, tongue) in order to fully comprehend our physical and social environment, so too is it important to list and categorize the various unique capabilities of the Internet based on the sundry media within it. In other words, the Web contains capabilities derived from textual media (e.g., diverse ways of presenting texts; emphases on key words; still photos), from electronic media (e.g., film; the possibility of "zooming" in and out of pictures; moving items; flash; audio), and even new capabilities not found in classical media (e.g., synchronous and asynchronous interactivity, such as chat, forums, or instant polls, as well as self-publishing). Only by delving into each element and accompanying capability can we completely comprehend the full potential of this communication complex along its physical (Net technology) and social (influence) dimensions.

To this one must add, in light of McLuhan's dichotomy, the convergence of hot and cool media within one technological infrastructure

---

46 Rafaeli and Sudweeks, "Networked Interactivity," *op. cit.*

47 Spiro Kiousis, "Interactivity: A Concept Explication," *New Media & Society* 4 (3) (2002): 355.

48 Marshall McLuhan, *Understanding Media, op. cit.*

– obviously rendering the (multi)medium an even more complex affair. The interactive characteristics render the Internet a cool medium, and as the technology improves this facility the medium becomes ever "colder." Nevertheless, given the presence of other elements the hot character of the Internet is not about to disappear soon.

Related to this is the paradox noted by Innis and McLuhan that as electronic media abolish time and space, they can also bring people closer together, i.e., strengthen social relationships, by using the social capabilities of each medium converged within it. Here the sum is indeed greater than its parts, leading to a capability not found (at least not to the same extent) in other mass media: the development of "community." From the perspective of our subject here – e-journalism – as incorporation of more Internet elements (especially the interactive ones) continues apace within a magazine or portal, so too does it become a useful vehicle for developing a community ethos.

To be sure, such a community might be somewhat different than what has come before, given that "the medium is the message." There are two aspects to consider here, as Carey points out in his introduction to Innis' book *Changing Concepts of Time*:

The spatial bias of modern media, the attempt to extend lines of communication further and further, from center to margin, from the capital to the hinterland, in order to exercise definitive control over the environment, including the humans that inhabit that environment inevitably shrinks time down to the present, to a one-day world of the immediate and the transitory.[49]

Thus, the Internet enables its users to cast their social net wider than ever before, in a fashion that is almost global (were it not for the language barrier). Virtual communities need no longer be local or national; they transcend geographical (and even cultural) borders. *The New York Times* Internet edition, for example, already today has more non-New York readers than its print edition has local readers. However, as the above quote makes clear, such "community" might come at a price of an overly transitory perspective.

Just as Innis provides a cautionary tale to what McLuhan calls the extensions of man on a macro-social level, so too in the micro e-journalism context one has to be wary of overextension. Much

---

49 Harold Innis, *Changing Concepts of Time* (U.S.A.: 1952): xv.

like Narcissus, we can become overly taken with our expanding self. First-time designers are especially prone to this problem. As Rieder notes,[50] this phenomenon was common among those who designed the overall Web and the Webmasters of particular sites. They were so taken by their mastery of Web code that in effect their creativity was shut down. As a result, the early designers narrowed the possibilities of the servomechanisms of the medium, turning into quasi-robots, exaggeratedly mimicking each other without any measure of sophistication. Publishers and editors, with even less understanding of the underlying architectonic difference between the Web and previous media, tended to throw text into the Web without much thought and called it an "e-newspaper."[51]

The result: Web pages clinging to older design models overloaded by "gadgets," without much real utility to the surfer. Rieder advises designers to think about the design of Web pages less from a technical perspective and more from one emphasizing the ideal surfing (reading, etc.) experience, i.e., to distance themselves somewhat from pure technological determinism – or at least from technical overload (on Web pages, sometimes "less is more"). As Staci Kramer argues: "There should be a limit on the number of moving elements on any page at any given time... . [I]t's hard to focus on the usually fine work offered by msnbc.com when msn butterflies are fluttering, program notes are rotating and banner ads are taking turns. Ditto for CBSnews.com and its no fewer than five moving front-page elements. The part of me that desperately wants news Web sites to make money is in direct conflict with the part that gets distracted by the way the retail space is being used."[52] For this reason, our list also includes "design overload" (amount of info and available services; graphics complexity) as well as ease of orientation on the homepage and the site as a whole.

---

50 David Rieder, "Bad Web Design: The Internet's Real Addiction Problem," in *Web. studies: Rewiring Media Studies for the Digital Age*, ed. David Gauntlett (London: Oxford University Press, 2000): 97.

51 Newhagen and Rafaeli, "Why Communication Researchers Should Study the Internet," *op. cit.*

52 Staci D. Kramer, "DIY News: News Web Sites Offer Tools for Assembling Free-Ranging Newscasts," *Online Journalism Review;* downloaded from http://ojr.usc. edu/content/story.cfm?request=660 (Nov. 7, 2001).

This brings us to the question of the place of the surfer in the Web news/information experience. Overall, Websites are comprised of short texts with the readers "surfing," "scanning," and/or "linking" (jumping) from one text to the next. According to Nielsen,[53] surfers overwhelmingly prefer short, objective, straight-to-the-point writing, with 79% scanning text compared to a mere 16% who read every word of the item/document. As a result, he suggests that in order to enable such text to be readily scanned, editors should bold key words, present substantive sub-headlines, list major points in bullet form, place each idea in its own paragraph, and build the article in pyramid fashion.[54]

According to some pundits, this sort of media "consumption" requires very little intellectual effort on the part of the user. Indeed, the amount of material on the Web is vast and yet there is no "standard" for determining what is worthwhile and what not (for example, other than the homepage, e-papers don't have "pagination," so that one lacks the ability to discern the relative importance of an item on page 2 compared to one on page 34). In such a situation, information retrieval becomes almost accidental (or driven by other considerations, e.g., search engines that place "paid-for" sites higher in their results list). Moreover, despite the "unlimited" potentialities of the Internet, the underlying operating program structure is relatively circumscribed. This results – if we were to use a McLuhanesque approach – in passivity, laziness, superficiality, and the inability to evaluate the informational value of data and facts.[55]

On the other side of the fence are those, like Levinson, who forcefully argue that surfing the Web is nothing like the passive experience of TV viewing. Rather, it holds the promise of personal creativity – "we create it and remake it by using it" – just as we did in the acoustic space before the advent of print and the age of literacy.[56]

How to account for such different assessments of Internet use? The answer lies in the multifarious nature of this multimedium, full of

---

53 Jakob Nielsen, "How Users Read on the Web" (1997a); downloaded from http://www.useit.com/alertbox/9710a.html (Jan. 9, 2001).

54 Jakob Nielsen, "Measuring the Usability of Reading on the Web" (1997b); downloaded from http://www.useit.com/alertbox/readingmetrics.html (Jan. 9, 2001).

55 Pasovsky, Uri, "DominatingTakeover" [Hebrew], *Haaretz*, Nov. 28, 2000: 14–17.

56 Levinson, *Digital McLuhan, op. cit.*, 6.

contradictions or at least paradoxes: it is collective but also personal; it has huge amounts of information but no hierarchical structure; the Web page is physically two-dimensional but also multi-dimensional (what with time elements and the ability for action to take place on the screen);[57] the whole technology is quite complex but also very user-friendly.

Given the debate and the medium's many facets, it would be hard to overestimate the critical importance of understanding the design of the underlying technology, as Flanagin et al. emphasize.[58] This includes the physical form of each Web device (PC, cell phone, PDA, TV), social procedures involving its use (where? when?), and of course the medium's functional capabilities/limitations. All of these render the medium a "cool" one in McLuhan's terms[59] – soft, shadowy, blurred, changeable, demanding greater participation from the user. The Web, full of hyper-links, is a clear case of "a verdant breeze wending its way through every leaf in the hothouse of knowledge, not only cooling but pollinating as it moves along," as Levinson poetically puts it.[60]

In sum, while the Web (and its meta-infrastructure, the Internet) has been a catalyst for new forms of journalism[61] (including women's

---

57 A Website design is essentially different from a printed page design, among other things because of the scrolling element characterizing the latter as well as the layering ("Windows") technique. Jakob Nielsen, "Differences Between Print Design and Web Design," op. cit.

58 The emphasis on technical code is based on: Andrew Feenberg, Alternative Modernity: The Technical Turn in Philosophy and Social Theory (Berkeley, Cal.: University of California Press, 1995a). Andrew Feenberg, "Subversive Rationalization: Technology, Power, and Democracy," in Technology and Politics of Knowledge, eds. Andrew Feenberg and Alastair Hannay (Bloomington, Ind.: Indiana University Press, 1995b): 3–22.

59 Marshall McLuhan, Understanding Media, op. cit.

60 Levinson, Digital McLuhan, op. cit., 117.

61 Maggie O'Brien, "Newspapers on the Internet – With a case study of the Nando Time," Research Paper, Junior MagZINE Journalism at the University of Texas Austin (1999); downloaded from http://uts.cc.utexas.edu/~maggs/paper.html (Jan. 9, 2001). Keith Kenney, Alexander Gorelik and Sam Mwangi, "Interactive Features of Online Newspapers," First Monday 5(1) (2000): 217–235;downloaded from http://www.firstmonday.org/issues/issue5_1/kenney/index.html (June 21, 2003).

62 Lisa Hamm-Greenawalt, "Women's sites understand community," Internet World

magazines[62]), it is still far from realizing its full potential. Few are the site producers that fully utilize the interactive potential of this medium that could lead in principle to an entirely new form of communication.[63] Because the e-paper grew out of the print paper milieu, and despite it being a rather different product in its very essence, it mostly continues to preserve the structural model of its forebear.[64]

Towards a Taxonomy of Elements: Problems and Rationale

Internet communication is not limited to text alone. Mann and Stewart note[65] that as the Internet's capabilities and bandwidth increase, enabling wider use of voice and pictures/video, the limitations inherent in the keyboard disappear. This places Web surfing on a plane markedly different from print and other classic media, with its own cultural and psychological (not just technological) codes.

We intend here to delineate the full panoply of Web/Internet capabilities from the perspective of the e-magazine (and by extension, news journalism) user – a sort of Internet Codex. These will be presented on three levels of organization in descending order: first, broad *categories* that relate to the two types of journals (Internet and/or print); second and within each category, the sundry *elements* or "traits" that are found in each type of journal (e.g., homepage, design, advertising, etc.); and third, the specific *variables* within each element (e.g., whether the ads are interactive or not; method of payment for content, if at all, etc.). As suggested by the first level, this list will include not only those aspects unique to the Web/Internet (the main part of the list), but also elements

5 (29) (1999): 56–9. Downloaded from http://www.findarticles.com/m0DXS/29_5/55818628/p1/article.jhtml (Feb. 1, 2001).

63 Kevin Crowston and Marie Williams, "Reproduced and Emergent Genres of Communication on the World Wide Web," *The Information Society* 16 (3) (2000): 201–216.

64 Melinda McAdams, "Inventing an Online Newspaper," *Interpersonal Computing and Technology Journal* 3(3) (1995): 64–90; downloaded from http://www.sentex.net/~mmcadams/invent.html (June 5, 2001).

65 Mann and Stewart, *Internet Communication and Qualitative Research, op. cit.*, 217.

that are found in both print and electronic versions of magazine (and news) sites, albeit in different measure. Before doing so, however, it must be noted that such an enterprise is fraught with difficulties and inherent vagueness.

Two examples will suffice at this stage to indicate the problems involved: scope of the site and number of ads. The volume of a magazine can easily be measured through the number of pages of equal size found therein. But how is one to count the number of e-pages if we cannot easily follow the pagination due to links, pop-up pages, constantly changing ads and the like – not to mention the fact that the length of scrolled pages is not standardized! Similar difficulties attend anyone trying to follow the number of ads and their size: how does one count a banner with internally changing ads in rotation? Does one include a pop-up that appears only after a certain amount of reading time or only for specific surfers (based on their cookie information)? Worst of all, it is difficult to follow a site's evolution (unless one is willing to survey its entirety each day), precisely because of its dynamism and especially the fact that many sites do not save (or permit unlimited access to) previous editions.[66] If one wishes to analyze the Web edition of *The New York Times*, is that the 6:00AM, 12:20PM or 8:40PM edition? (*The NYT* updates every 20 minutes.) Ditto for a monthly magazine, in which certain sections or columns can change every week or even more often!

There is little doubt, therefore, that in researching the dynamic and ever-changing Web environment a great deal of intellectual flexibility is called for, demanding creative solutions (within accepted academic rules of the game). Blind acceptance and continuation of prior research methods used with traditional, static media will render future research increasingly difficult and even irrelevant regarding the Internet, for this novel medium demands the use of fresh approaches and categorization.

To be sure, not all sites necessitate the same level of innovative thinking. It is comparatively easier to define (e.g., frequency of

---

66 Overcoming these hurdles, in this doctoral research we have managed to find several e-magazines with previous editions still existent – which enable us to compare "then" and "now," offering a truly historical picture of the producers' learning process from the start.

publication) an e-magazine site that has a parallel print magazine. Here there already exists a recognized, clearly delineated and defined media product that can be compared with the newer e-artifact. However, when we approach an entirely new e-magazine that has emerged from the Web, sans print edition, the situation and concomitant definitions tend to be murkier. There are sites that clearly describe themselves as magazines/newspapers and there are others self-defined more as "virtual communities," with everything that this implies as noted earlier. In both cases, the contents and services offered are still loosely based on the print magazine archetype, but with very wide leeway to add a broad array of activities not found in classic print media.

This leads to the next point. As Rivett correctly argues,[67] it is important to keep in mind that Web texts cannot be understood divorced from their production and consumption patterns – that also may vary greatly, not only from surfer to surfer but also over time. Thus, any analysis must be carried out in the context of its being a fast-growing medium. We would thus expect that in future studies based on our taxonomy a fairly large gap will emerge between what the producers functionally offer on their magazine/newspaper Websites and what they *could* be offering.

Even the use of the term "Website" (or "Web") is somewhat problematic. As mentioned earlier, the Internet is both a medium of communication and also a *metamedium,* i.e., the underlying infrastructure for several specific media: e-mail, telephony, group discussion, Web surfing, etc. While this distinction is a useful one, it is not always very practical. E.g. – an e-magazine might at first be taken for a replacement of the print medium (a *Web* site), but given that it may also carry discussion forums, e-mail, and other types of "non-magazine" (i.e., *Internet*) use, we cannot clearly distinguish between the e-magazine in its "medium" and its "metamedium" guises – that is, between its "Web" and "Internet" modalities. Thus, up to this point we have tried to be precise in using "Internet" and "Web" in their proper place. For the sake of simplicity, however, we shall henceforth use only the term "Web" in the context of the e-magazine, with the understanding that it relates to the Web *plus* other Internet functions such as e-mail, forums and the like.

---

67 Miriam Rivett, "Approaches to Analysing the Web Text: A Consideration of the Web Site as an Emergent Cultural Form," *Convergence* 6 (3) (2000): 34.

How did we go about deriving the list below? First, we drew from the extensive literature as surveyed above. Then, as part of a larger, doctoral dissertation study, 30 different women's magazines (a few Israeli; most American) were analyzed: 10 of the most popular print magazines (e.g., *Good Housekeeping, Ladies Home Journal, Elle, Self,* etc.), 10 e-magazines put online by these ongoing print magazine, and 10 new e-magazines found exclusively online (e.g., *Girl Zone, All That Women Want, Women's e News, iwomen,* etc.). It should be noted that selecting Websites is a precarious affair because of the institutional instability inherent in this still early development stage of the Web – new sites are being added each day, many sites disappear just as quickly,[68] and for those which do survive, internal design/format/content change is almost de rigueur.[69] Thus, the Web researcher should try to analyze the subject under scrutiny in "real time"[70] and not after the fact, for the specific site may not be around soon thereafter!

In order to account for the above considerations and prevent some of these pitfalls, we decided on the following approach: 1) 10 print magazines and 20 sites were analyzed over a six-month period. 2) We carried out one full investigation each month as the magazines and the sites appeared/were updated. In short, 180 entire magazine "issues" were studied, from July – December 2002. 3) The e-magazines were also followed periodically *between* each new issue, to understand the possibilities regarding sectional changes and ongoing interactive communication with the readers.

It should be noted that the list displayed below is completely *non-content dependent*, and thus can be applied to other news/content sites on the Web[71] – perhaps even to the other new, content-oriented media

68 See, for example, Sally J. McMillan, "The Microscope and the Moving Target: The Challenge of Applying Content Analysis to the World Wide Web," *Journalism & Mass Communication Quarterly* 77 (1) (2000): 80–98. She found that around a sixth of all health Websites disappear within a year.
69 Giovanna Alloro et al., "Electronic Biomedical Journals," *op. cit.* Marcia J. Bates, and Shaojun Lu, "An Exploratory Profile of Personal Home Pages: Content, Design, Metaphors," *Online and CDROM Review* 21(6) (1997): 331–340.
70 McMillan, "The Microscope and the Moving Target," *op. cit.*
71 There exists the possibility that for "daily" *e-newspaper* sites some minor revisions/additions might have to be made to our list – most probably in the internal indicators within some of the variables.

in the future. Having said that, however, we cannot make a claim for completeness (despite our "Codex" comment above) – for the simple reason that technological improvements and future inventions will almost undoubtedly add more elements to the Web arsenal. To take but one offbeat example, a company called "Digiscents" (now defunct) successfully developed a way to add the sense of *smell* to the surfing experience![72] Certainly massive broadband, wireless surfing, and even ultimately the full development of Virtual Reality will augment the Web with further characteristics and potentialities.

Our list is divided into four broad media categories, each of which has several elements: 77 are unique to the Web; 14 are common to print and e-magazines; 5 are unique to print magazines[73]; 15 are relevant to a comparison between the same magazine's print and Web editions. Altogether, our taxonomy includes 110 elements and their respective variables.

By adding up the coding results of these elements and also combining them into larger categories (as will be detailed below), researchers will be able in the end to do four things: a. assess how well the full panoply of potentialities is currently being utilized; b. analyze the extent to which the cumulative learning process of media adaptation has taken place over time; c. compare the similarities and differences between print and Web magazines in general; d. understand the differences between "sister" magazines – print and Web – and how each is used to complement the other.

Elements and Variables[74]

Elements (and respective variables) Unique to e-Magazines
*A. **Homepage**[75]: 1. Orientation Around the Page* (hard – easy); *2.*

---

72 Anna Salleh, "Now you can smell it – online," *Science News* (April 18, 2001); downloaded from www.abc.net.ac/science/news/stories/s278744 (Jan. 13, 2003).

73 A few of these five are relevant to the larger doctoral study from which this chapter is drawn.

74 One technical note: in order to shorten the long list, the following elements do not present the full range of all the internal variables but rather list only the extremes (placed within parentheses).

75 Because the homepage is the most important and widely read section – from which

Amount of Info and Available Services (none – large number); 3. *Site Index Enabling Easy Access* (no – yes); 4. *Start of Articles or Full Articles* (no – yes); 5. *Ability to Make the Page Your Homepage* (no – yes).

All subsequent categories and variables refer to the entire Website.

B. **Contents** *(readability)*[76]: 6. Structure/Concision of Writing (over 1000 words – up to 200 words); 7. Ease of Eye Scanning With Key Words *Highlighted* (none – in every article); 8. Ease of Eye Scanning With Key Words *Bulleted* (none – in every article).

C. **Design** *(graphics complexity)*[77]: 9. *Graphics Maneuverability – Surfer Can "Zoom" Pictures* (none – every page); 10. *Graphics Movement – Items Move* (none – every page); 11. *Graphics Movement – Animation Clip* (none – every page); 12. *Graphics Movement – "Flash" Technology* (none – every page).

D. **Synchronous Interactivity:** 13. *Online Chats*[78] + *Topic Variety* (none – 10+; low – high); 14. *Polling Surveys*[79] + *Topic Variety* (none – 10+; low – high).

---

in most cases the surfer begins to investigate the site – we chose to commence the list with this element and devote several variables to it, some of which are relevant only to the homepage (e.g., variable 5) and others that can be studied on other pages as well (e.g., variable 1).

76 Variables 6–8 could also be listed under the category "Design." We chose to leave them together here under "Contents" because these are important aspects of textual change and style of writing unique to the Web. See Jakob Nielsen, "How Users Read on the Web," *op. cit.;* Jakob Nielsen, "Measuring the Usability of Reading on the Web," *op. cit.* This is also the reason that variable 6 has not been placed among the elements common to both print and e-magazines.

77 In continuation of the previous note, in this "Design" element we decided to place only variables that relate to graphic design. Everything on a dynamic HTML page is an object that can move with the proper programming. Variable 9 relates to the ability of the surfer to enlarge all or some of the pictures (or parts of a picture). Variable 10 refers to short and permanent movement of a section, e.g., the site's logo flashing, while variable 11 relates to animation clips (permanent or changing). "Flash" (variable 12) uses sophisticated movement not found in the other variables.

78 Many magazines/newspapers have synchronous (real-time) chats that enable somewhat moderated but mostly free discussion with other readers. This service is built into the site and does not demand any special program or knowledge on the part of the participants.

79 Many sites run polls on sundry subjects, thereby reinforcing reader involvement. The results are ongoing so that the surfers can see the immediate effect of their

*E .Asynchronous Interactivity:*15. *Online Forums*[80] + *Topic Variety* (none – 10+; low – high); 16. *E-Mail*[81] *Between Writers and Readers* (none – every article).

F. Hyper-Text (linking within and outside the site): 17. *Horizontal Linking* (none – all articles); 18. *Vertical Linking* (none – all articles); 19. *Sub-Heading Links Within the Article* (none – all articles); 20. *Links to Other Sites* (none – all articles).

G. Search Engines (internal and external): 21. *External to Other Sites* (no – yes);

22. *Internal within the Site* (no – yes).

H. Frequency/Extent of Contents Updating/Changing Within the Same Issue:

23. *Frequency of Change Within the Same Issue* (none – four+); 24. *Extent of Change in Previous Variable* (none – most of the site); 25. *Difference in Frequency of Change Between Parts of Site* (no – yes).

I. Frequency/Extent of Graphics Updating/Changing from Issue to Issue[82]:

26. *Frequency* (none – every new issue); 27. *Extent* (none – the whole site);

---

vote – quite different from print media polling that has significant time delays in reporting the results.

80 The forum is an asynchronous discussion group and/or bulletin board, occasionally moderated, so that the responses do not always immediately appear on the site. On rare occasions, the site will have an invited guest appear for an hour or two, announced ahead of time, in which case the forum becomes more synchronous.

81 To be sure, readers can send letters to a print magazine as well. However, e-mail changes the entire dynamics of such an exchange quantitatively and even qualitatively (quick editorial response), so that such bottom-to-top-to-bottom communication becomes an inherent part of the reading/surfing experience, an ongoing relationship between readers and writers.

82 Variables 26–28 were not placed in the overall category of "Joint Elements" (print and e-magazines) because the design changes are substantively different here, a result of each medium's different nature. Whereas print magazines very rarely change their overall design, overall Website design change is far more frequent, and specific design changes are constant – seen as part and parcel of contents change. All this because of the technical ease in which Web design changes can be undertaken as well as surfers' greater openness (even expectation) regarding such change.

28. *Difference in Frequency of Change Between Parts of Site* (no – yes).

J. **_Advertising & Classifieds_**[83] *(existence and surfing disruption):* 29. *Banners* (none – every page); 30. *Pop-Ups* (none – every page); 31. *Flash Ads* (none – every page); 32. *Miscellaneous Ads* (none – every page); 33. *Surfing Disruption as a Result of Ads* (high disruption – none).

K. **_Archive (accessibility and scope):_** 34. *Exists* (no – yes); 35. *Ease of Access to the Archive* (complicated – easy); 36. *Scope of Contents* (much less than the original site – the whole site); 37. *Archived from the Start of the Site* (no – yes).

L. **_Video/Audio:_** 38. *Video Clips/Interviews, etc.* (none – large amount); 39. *Slide Presentations* (none – large amount); 40. *Audio* (none – large amount).

M. **_Quasi-Portal (widening the magazine's framework)_**[84]: 41. *Quasi-Portal* – e.g., index of sites, other magazines, etc. (no – yes).

N. **_Sending and Downloading Material:_** 42. *Icon for Printing* (none – all articles);

43. *Icon for Sending Article by e-mail* (none – all articles); 44. *Ability to Save Page to Hard Disk* [85] (none – every page); 45. *Download Audio File to Hard Disk* (no – yes); 46. *Download Video File to Hard Disk* (no – yes); 47. *Personalizing e-Newsletter – Choosing Topics to be Notified About* (no – yes); 48. (If "Yes") *Variety of "Editing" Possibilities* (very few – very many); 49. (If "Yes") *Ease of this Service* (not easy [over

---

83 The Internet enables ads using techniques not possible in print. Flash and pop-ups are clearly different than static print ads, but even banners are different as they usually have an internal rotation of several ads, each appearing in turn every few seconds. The banner too can use Flash or other technologies, not to mention some sites that match the banner to the specific surfer based on cookie identification. Variable 29 measures the number of banners and not the overall number of content messages found within them.

84 This means structurally and permanently widening the purview of the magazine, as a different content and commercial concept – not through temporary links (in articles) to other sites but rather within a framework that is structured from the start with other sites in mind, while retaining a focus on a specific topic area. For example, the magazines *Cosmopolitan* and *Good Housekeeping* are part of a women's portal entitled iVillage – despite each having its own e-address, staff, contents, etc.

85 In certain cases one cannot save an e-page or one can save only part of it (e.g., without picture, ads, etc.).

7 steps] – very easy [2 steps]); 50. *Receiving Uniform Newsletter from the Site* (no – yes).

O. **Following (Spying On) the Site's Surfers**: 51. *Required Registration During Initial Entrance* (no – yes); 52. *Password to Enter* (no – yes); 53. *Automatic Identification and Surveillance* (no – yes, i.e., existence of "cookie" or other means of spying).

P. **Shopping**: 54. *Shopping Ability* (no – yes); 55. (If "Yes") *Ease of Shopping* (difficult [over 7 steps] – easy [up to 2 steps]).

Q. **Payment for Site Access/Services**: 56. *Payment for Access to Whole Site* (no – yes); 57. *Payment for Access to Certain Parts of Site* (no – yes); 58. *Added Services for Payment* (no – yes); 59. *Added Services for Free* (no – yes).

R. **Technical Quality & Support**: 60. *Surfing Speed*[86] (over 20 seconds from one page to another – up to 5 seconds); 61. *Technical Problems* (none – many);

62. *Technical Support* (none – very extensive).

S. **Ease of Surfing and Orientation**: 63. *Orientation Around the Site* (complicated – very easy); 64. *Automatic Jump from Bottom to Top of Page through Link* (no – every page); 65. *Automatic Jump to Homepage from any Page via Link* (no – every page). 66. *Site Index Linking to Other Pages* (no – every page); 67. *Site Map* (no – yes);

68. (If "Yes") *Map Orientation* (complicated – easy to use).

T. **Community Communication**: 69. *Reader Production of Contents* [e.g., blogs, talkback, camera-phone & text items from the field] (none – all possibilities).

70. *Signing Site Guest Book* (no – yes); 71. (If "Yes") *Incentive* (no – yes); 72. *Direct Connection to Editor* (no – yes); 73. *"About Us" – Site Information*[87] (no – yes); 74. *"What's New on the Site"*[88] (no – yes); 75.

---

86 Based on regular speed (56K modem) and not broadband. Of course, this can also depend on time of day, day of the week and other technical aspects. In the future, when broadband becomes more common, this variable's indicators will have to be amended.

87 This is an important variable for e-magazines. It does not refer to basic information such as editorial names and titles, but rather to a wide-ranging "column" encompassing lots of information about the magazine, including its history, purposes and at times even what other media have written about it.

88 Many surfers enter the *same issue* several times (the same day or over the course of the month) so that the site must enable them to easily identify what has been

Automatic Translation of Contents to other Languages (no – yes); 76. *Privacy Policy Listed* (no – yes); 77. *"Write to Us"* (no – yes).

Joint Elements of Print & e-Magazines
U. **Contents (Scope, Variety, Credits) & Advertisements**: 78. *Scope – # of pages* (up to 50 – over 800); 79. *Regular Sections* (none – 16 and up); 80. *Variety of General Topic Areas* (none – 16 and up); 81. *Writers' Credits* (none – in all articles); 82. *Advertisements* (none – every page).

V. **Design Complexity**: 83. *Number of Pictures* (none – every page); 84. *Tables and Graphs* (none – every page); 85. *Design Variety – Different Graphic Elements on Page* (none – large variety); 86. *Design Density* (overly dense – clean and spacious).

W. **Feedback/Communication**: 87. *Address for Correspondence* (no – yes);

88. *Fax/Phone Number* (no – yes); 89. *E-mail address* (no – yes).

X. **Target Audience**: 90. *Target Audience Defined* (no – yes).

Y. **Gifts and Discounts**: 91. *Incentives For Readers/Surfers* (no – yes).

Elements Unique to Print Magazines
Z. **Supplements**: 92. *Separate Supplements* (no – yes); 93. *Print Catalogues Distributed* (no – yes); 94. *Distributing a Product Sample* (no – yes).

AA. **Design Change**: 95. *Paper's Overall Format Change* (none – yes).

BB. **Article Length**: 96. *Length of Articles* (over 1000 words – below 200 words).

Element Comparison of Same Brand: e-Mag and Print
CC. **Identical Product**: 97. *Same Cover Photo* (identical – totally different);

98. *Same Headlines* (all identical – none the same); 99. *Same Logo* (no – yes);

---

recently added: variable 74 (flashing "new"; prominently placing the date of the latest update, etc.).

100. *Same Contents* (all identical – none the same); 101. *Graphic Design Similarity* (totally identical – no similarity); 102. *Similar Advertisements* (all identical – none the same).

⟨ *DD. __Editorial Cooperation__:* 103. *Print Mag Points Readers to e-Mag* (no – yes/frequency); 104. *E-Mag Points Readers to Print Mag* (no – yes/frequency);

105. *E-Mag Enables Subscription to Print Mag* (no – yes); 106. *Cooperative Sections Between the Two Mags* (no – yes/how much); 107. *Subscription to Print Mag Enables Access to E-Mag* (don't need it – yes, for any e-material).

EE. __Editorial Personnel__: 108. *Both Mags have Same Editor* (no – yes); 109. (If yes) *Is the Editor's Column Identical?* (no – yes); 110. (If no) *Does a Different Editor's Column Appear in e-Mag?* (no – yes); 111. *Same Editorial and Writing Staff in Both* (mostly the same – mostly different).[89]

Conclusion

When a new medium enters the scene, there tends to be a lot of oohing and aahing about its amazing capabilities.[90] However, this does not in any way guarantee its quick success or even "correct" use in the early stages of development and diffusion. Indeed, the very wondrousness of the technology may tend to hide the more serious question of what society should be doing with it – and how best to utilize it.

The Internet and Web have not been immune to this. Indeed, it took over 20 years for the Internet (e-mail, forums, etc.) to begin to look like a true mass medium. The Web, commencing in the early 1990s, grew much more rapidly in the number of users (in part because of the earlier experience of the Internet), but this was not *because* of full use of its capabilities but rather *despite* those capabilities remaining mostly

---

89 We chose "mostly" and not "all" because the list of staff names is not always complete.

· 90 For an excellent illustration of the wide-eyed wonder in which most of our modern communication technologies were greeted, including telegraph, telephone, typewriter fax machine, home computer, and others, see: Merritt Ierley, *Wondrous Contrivances: Technology at the Threshold* (New York: Clarkson Potter, 2002).

dormant in most of the mainstream Websites, especially those involved in e-journalism.

Innis and McLuhan would not have been surprised at this "slow" pace, for they were well aware that full new-media utilization is a long-term process. However, in at least one sense, we are witness here to McLuhan being stood on his head. He emphasized how new media can revolutionize new ways of thinking; we suggest that no less valid is the dictum that *new ways of thinking can revolutionize new media*. In other words and in the final analysis, until producers *and/or users* learn how to make the most of the true capabilities of a new medium, it will remain "new" only in the technical – and not functional – sense.

In the more specific case of e-journals, we can expect to find that at this relatively early stage of the Web's young life, most magazines will display only a relatively small number of the elements that are unique to the medium. There are several reasons for this.

First, economic resources are limited, not only for new sites, but also for sites being set up by print magazines. Second, most of the users will be print magazine readers, generally conservative in their media consumption patterns. Third, early stages of a new medium are marked by much trial and error – the Webmasters as well as the editors are learning the ropes, not only regarding what can be technically done, but also what the readers want. Finally, print magazines "anchor" their daughter e-magazine within their own conceptual framework, so that such "dual magazines" suffer *naturally* from built-in editorial and design conservatism.

This last point leads to a second expectation: new e-magazines without print affiliation will utilize a wider array of Web traits than those with print magazine affiliation. This does *not* necessarily mean that they will be more commercially successful, because the affiliated magazines have a huge audience base from which to draw on as compared to new e-magazines that have to start from scratch. But if we ignore for a moment audience share and revenue, it stands to reason that the new e-magazines – unencumbered by historical (print) tradition – will be more likely to experiment with the new possibilities inherent in this multi-faceted, new medium. In any event, as our larger study found,[91]

91 Nava Cohen-Avigdor, "Utilizing the Special Abilities of the Internet...," *op. cit.*

this is not the case (at least regarding women's e-magazines). The major reason is quite banal: money. The print-based e-magazines have a much more solid financial base, and thus are able to invest far money in the technological infrastructure.

Whatever the nature of the financial backer, a promising possibility for both types is the use of the e-magazine to create and constitute the central axis for a virtual community around the main subject of the magazine. In this sense, the task of Website editors is different from their print counterparts. Whereas the latter use the magazine as a medium for *top-to-bottom* communication, the former use such content as a lever for *peer-to-peer* (forums, chats, instant messaging, etc.) as well as for *bottom-to-top* (i.e., reader to writer/editor) communication. The technical possibilities of interactivity on the Web change the *essence* of the magazine experience as well as its development.

Why development? Almost all mass media until now – and certainly those familiar to Innis and McLuhan – were basically uni-directional, i.e., messages were transmitted from content producers to audience consumers. This meant that the learning process of fuller new medium exploitation was a matter for the producers almost exclusively. There was little the TV viewer could do in the 1950s to change programming content other than switch between the few channels offered.

The Web, on the other hand, not only offers millions of programming possibilities so that audience choice is vastly greater and thus "readership ratings" more effective in influencing the production of content, but even more important is the highly interactive nature of the medium. This, in effect, turns surfers into "prosumers" (to use Toffler's famous term[92]), who can directly influence content production through ongoing interaction with the editorial staff as well as by independently setting up their own sites and actually producing content (e.g., blogging). To once again quote Levinson above: "we create it and remake it by using it."[93]

Given that their numbers are far greater than the sum total of professional e-content producers, and that many of them are inclined to be more adventurous and open to new possibilities than the "professional" producers (usually trained in some previous medium), one can expect

---

92 Alvin Toffler, *The Third Wave* (New York: Bantam Books, 1981): 11.
93 Levinson, *Digital McLuhan, op. cit.*, 6.

the learning curve to rise sharply in the years ahead. To that end, we trust that our taxonomy of e-magazine Website elements and variables constitutes a significant step towards such fuller exploitation of this truly revolutionary new medium – for producers and users alike.

References

Adams, Tyrone and Clark, Norman, *The Internet – Effective Online Communication* (New York: Harcourt College, 2001).

Alloro, Giovanna, Casilli, Cristina, Taningher, Maurizio, and Ugolini, Donatella, "Electronic Biomedical Journals: How They Appear and What They Offer," *European Journal of Cancer* 34(3) (1998): 290–295. Downloaded from http://www.elsevier.nl/gej-ng/10/17/42/37/34/30/abstract.html (6 Feb. 2001).

Barnes, Susan B., "Bridging the Differences Between Social Theory and Technological Invention in Human-Computer Interface Design," *New Media & Society* 2(3) (2000): 353–372.

Bates, Marcia J. and Lu, Shaojun, "An Exploratory Profile of Personal Home Pages: Content, Design, Metaphors," *Online and CDROM Review* 21(6) (1997): 331–340.

Carey, James W., "Harold Adams Innis and Marshall McLuhan," in *Mass Media and Mass Man,* ed. Alan Casty (New York: Holt, Reinhart and Winston, 1973), 75–82.

Chan-Olmsted, Sylvia M. and Park, Suk Jung, "From On-Air to Online World: Examining the Content and Structures of Broadcast TV Stations' Web Sites," *Journalism & Mass Communication Quarterly* 77(2) (2000): 321–329.

Crowston, Kevin and Williams, Marie, "Reproduced and Emergent Genres of Communication on the World Wide Web," *The Information Society* 16 (3) (2000): 201–216.

Feenberg, Andrew, *Alternative Modernity: The Technical Turn in Philosophy and Social Theory* (Berkeley, Cal.: University of California Press, 1995a).

Feenberg, Andrew, "Subversive Rationalization: Technology, Power, and Democracy," in *Technology and Politics of Knowledge,* eds. Andrew Feenberg and Alastair Hannay (Bloomington, Ind.: Indiana University Press, 1995b), 3–22.

Fidler, Roger, *Mediamorphosis: Understanding New Media* (Thousand Oaks, Cal.: Pine Forge, 1997).

Flanagin, Andrew J., Farinola, Wendy J. Maynard, and Metzger, Miriam J., "The Technical Code of the Internet / World Wide Web," *Critical Studies in Media Communication* 17(4) (2000): 409–428.

Genosko, Gary, *McLuhan and Baudrillard: The Masters of Implosion* (London: Routledge, 1999).

Hamm-Greenawalt, Lisa, "Women's sites understand community," *Internet World* 5 (29) (1999): 56–59. Downloaded from http://www.findarticles.com/m0DXS/29_5/55818628/p1/article.jhtml (1 Feb. 2001).

Herbert, John, *Journalism in the Digital Age: Theory and Practice – Broadcast, Print and On-Line Media* (Oxford: Focal Press, 2001). First Published 2000.

Holzschlag, Molly E. and Lawson, Bruce, eds., *Usability: The Site Speaks For Itself* (USA: Glasshaus, 2002).

Ierley, Merritt, *Wondrous Contrivances: Technology at the Threshold* (New York: Clarkson Potter, 2002).

Innis, Harold Adams, *The Bias of Communication,* Introduction by Marshall McLuhan (Toronto: University of Toronto Press, 1951). Reprinted (USA: 1964).

Innis, Harold Adams, *Changing Concepts of Time,* (USA, 1952). Introduction by James W. Carey, Reprinted (USA: Rowman & Littlefield Publishers, 2004).

Jankowski, Nicholas W. and Hanssen, Lucien, eds., *The Contours of Multimedia: Recent Technological, Theoretical and Empirical Developments* (UK: University of Luton Press – Academia Research Monograph 19, 1996).

Jankowski, Nicholas W. and Hanssen, Lucien, "Introduction: Multimedia Come of Age," in *The Contours of Multimedia: Recent Technological, Theoretical and Empirical Developments,* eds. Nicholas W. Jankowski and Lucien Hanssen (UK: University of Luton Press – Academia Research Monograph 19,1996), 1–21.

Jankowski, Nicholas W. and van Selm, Martine, "Traditional News Media Online: An Examination of Added Values," *Communications* 25 (1) (2000): 85–101.

Kelly, Kevin, "What Would McLuhan Say?" *Wired* (Archive 4 Oct. 1996). Downloaded from http://www.wired.com/wired/archive/

4.10/dekerckhove.htmL (3 Jan. 2001).

Kenney, Keith, Gorelik, Alexander, and Mwangi, Sam, "Interactive Features of Online Newspapers," *First Monday* 5(1) (2000): 217–235. Downloaded from http://www.firstmonday.org/issues/issue5_1/kenney/index.html (21 Jan. 2003).

Kiousis, Spiro, "Interactivity: A Concept Explication," *New Media & Society* 4 (3) (2002): 355–383.

Kramer, Staci D., "DIY News: News Web Sites Offer Tools for Assembling Free-Ranging Newscasts," *Online Journalism Review* (7 Nov. 2001). Downloaded from http://ojr.usc.edu/content/story.cfm?request=660 (11 Nov. 2001).

Levinson, Paul, *Digital McLuhan – A guide to the information millennium* (London: Routledge, 1999).

Li, Xigen, "Web Page Design and Graphic Use of Three U.S. Newspapers," *Journalism & Mass Communication Quarterly* 75(2) (1998): 353–365.

Mann, Chris and Stewart, Fiona, *Internet Communication and Qualitative Research: A Handbook for Researching Online* (London: Sage Publications, 2000).

McAdams, Melinda, "Inventing an Online Newspaper," *Interpersonal Computing and Technology Journal* 3(3) (1995): 64–90. Downloaded from http://www.sentex.net/~mmcadams/invent.html (5 Jun. 2001).

McLuhan, Eric and Zingrone, Frank, eds., *Essential McLuhan* (London: Routledge, 1999).

McLuhan, Marshall, *The Gutenberg Galaxy – The Making of Typographic Man* (New York: Mentor, 1962).

McLuhan, Marshall, *Understanding Media – The Extensions of Man* (New York: Mentor, 1964). Reprint edition, with an Introduction by Lewis H. Lapham (Cambridge, Mass.: MIT Press, 1994).

McLuhan, Marshall and Fiore, Quentin, *The Medium is the Massage – An Inventory of Effects* (New York: Bantam, 1967).

McLuhan, Marshall and Powers, Bruce R., *The Global Village* (New York: Oxford University Press, 1989).

McMillan, Sally J., "The Microscope and the Moving Target: The Challenge of Applying Content Analysis to the World Wide Web," *Journalism & Mass Communication Quarterly* 77 (1) (2000): 80–98.

Moss, Michel A., *Marshall McLuhan Essays: Media research,*

technology, art, communication (London: Overseas Publishers Association, 1997).

Newhagen, John E. and Rafaeli, Sheizaf, "Why Communication Researchers Should Study the Internet," *Journal of Communication* 46 (1) (1996): 4–13.

Nielsen, Jakob, *Multimedia and Hypertext: The Internet and Beyond* (San Francisco: Morgan Kaufman, 1995). Originally published by Boston, Mass.: AP Professional.

Nielsen, Jakob, "How Users Read on the Web" (1997a). Downloaded from http://www.useit.com/alertbox/9710a.html (9 Jan. 2001).

Nielsen, Jakob, "Measuring the Usability of Reading on the Web" (1997b). Downloaded from http://www.useit.com/alertbox/readingmetrics.html (9 Jan. 2001).

Nielsen, Jakob, "Differences Between Print Design and Web Design" (24 Jan. 1999). Downloaded from http://www.useit.com/alertbox/990124.html (25 Jan. 2001).

Nielsen, Jakob and Tahir, Marie, *Homepage Usability: 50 Websites Deconstructed* (USA: New Riders Publishing, 2002).

O'Brien, Maggie, "Newspapers on the Internet – With a case study of the Nando Time," Research Paper, *Junior MagZINE Journalism* at the University of Texas Austin (1999). Downloaded from http://uts.cc.utexas.edu/~maggs/paper.html (9 Jan. 2001).

Pasovsky, Uri, "DominatingTakeover" [Hebrew], *Haaretz* 28/11/2000: 14–17.

Peng, Foo Yeuh, Naphtali, Irene Tham, and Hao, Xiaoming, "Trends in Online Newspapers: A Look at the US Web," *Newspaper Research Journal* 20 (2) (1999): 52–63.

Rafaeli, Sheizaf and Sudweeks, Fay, "Networked Interactivity," *Journal of Computer Mediated Communication* 2 (4) (1997). Downloaded from http://jcmc.huji.ac.il/vol2/issue4/rafaeli.sudweeks.html (6 June 2001).

Rieder, David, "Bad Web Design: The Internet's Real Addiction Problem," in *Web.studies: Rewiring Media Studies for the Digital Age,* ed. David Gauntlett (London: Oxford University Press, 2000), 96–102.

Ries, Al and Ries, Laura, *The 11 Immutable Laws of Internet Branding* (New York: HarperCollinsPublishers, 2000).

Rivett, Miriam, "Approaches to Analysing the Web Text: A Consideration of the Web Site as an Emergent Cultural Form," *Convergence* 6 (3) (2000): 34–56.

Salleh, Anna, "Now you can smell it – online," *Science News* (April 18, 2001). Downloaded from www.abc.net.ac/science/news/stories/ s278744 (13 Jan. 2003).

Schultz, Tanjev, "Interactive Options in Online Journalism: A Content Analysis of 10 U.S. Newspapers," *Journal of Computer Mediated Communication* 5 (1) (1999). Downloaded from http://www.ascusc. org/jcmc/vol5/issue1/schultz.html (4 June 2001).

Taylor, Paul A., "McLuhan's Millennium Message," *New Media & Society* 2 (3) (2000): 373–81.

Toffler, Alvin. *The Third Wave* (New York: Bantam Books, 1981).

van Oostendorp, Herre and van Nimwegen, Christof, "Locating Information in an Online Newspaper," *Journal of Computer-Mediated Communication* 4 (1) Sept. (1998). Downloaded from http://www.ascusc.org/jcmc/vol14/issue1/oostendorp.html (22 Oct. 2002).

RAPHAEL COHEN-ALMAGOR

12. Conceptualizing the Right to Privacy: Ethical and Legal Considerations

> *Publication is a self-invasion of privacy.*
> *The more the data banks record about each one*
> *of us, the less we exist.*
>
> Marshall McLuhan

Preliminaries

We all care about our privacy. We all would like to keep some part of it outside the public domain. However, this is becoming increasingly difficult as technology advances and the media are struggling to fill time slots and empty pages. When news is becoming entertainment (infotainment) and private stories become public spectacle, individual lives can be mercilessly exposed to the glaring spotlight of unwanted publicity. In delineating the boundaries of intrusion, distinctions are made between children and adults; between public figures and ordinary citizens; between people who choose to live in the spotlights, and ordinary citizens who stumble into the public forum, and between ordinary citizens doing something of public significance and those who do not. I discuss the tragic death of Princess Diana and then examine the Quebec *Charter of Human Rights and Freedoms* and Chapter III of the *Civil Code of Quebec [1994]* that were invoked in a recent Supreme Court case, *Les Editions Vice-Versa Inc. v. Aubry* concerning the use of a person's photo without asking for her permission. Siding with the Court's majority in this case it is asserted that the public's right to know does not allow scope to magazines to take photos of people to decorate their covers without the people's consent.

I should explain the rationale for addressing these two case studies. Diana's complicated relationships with the British media and the *Aubry* case in Canada have attracted attention in the respective countries. In a way, the two stories exemplify the two different cultures: the British and the French-Quebec culture. The British media give less credit to privacy than their French counterparts.[1] The two stories also supplement one another and exemplify the public-private distinction when the media intrudes on people's privacy. The Diana story is different from the Canadian *Aubry* case in several aspects. Diana was a celebrity whereas Aubry a private person; Diana was constantly reported in the newspapers whereas Aubry's photo was used only once for artistic and commercial purposes; Diana's case evoked public moral outrage whereas Aubry's case was minor by comparison involving violation of the law; Diana tried to avoid going to courts whereas the *Aubry* case was resolved by the courts; Diana's case is far more complicated involving many intricate issues: the use of the media to blunt Royal power; the ability, or inability, to sustain privacy when one party encourages media coverage and utilizes the media for private purposes. In addition, there is the further issue of children as a protected class of people.

However, there are also similarities between the two cases: both raise a host of legal and ethical considerations; both were **not** cases of photojournalism; instead, the attractive images of both Diana and Aubry were splashed on journals' covers with the purpose to increase sales of newspapers; the privacy of both women was intruded upon without their consent; both felt that they were exploited by the media to advance their own partisan interests. Both cases illustrate the need to outline boundaries to free expression and free press.

With due appreciation for the liberal inclination to provide wide latitude to freedom of expression, we must also acknowledge the "democratic catch" and the need for prescribing the scope of tolerance. The right to free expression and free media, supplemented and strengthened by the concept of the public's right to know, does not entail

---

1   In the United States, freedom of expression and public information prevail over the right to privacy except where the information's sole purpose is commercial. In the United States, the mere idea of establishing a body like the British Press Complaints Commission, discussed *infra,* would set a firestorm of debate. The absolute language of the First Amendment, "Congress shall make no law respecting an establishment of religion, or prohibiting the free exercise thereof; or abridging the freedom of speech, or of the press," is taken almost literally. Cf. Philip Meyer, *Ethical Journalism* (Lanham, Maryland: University Press of America, 1987), pp. 3–16; http://caselaw.lp.findlaw.com/data/constitution/amendment01/

the freedom to invade individual privacy without ample justification.[2] The media should adopt some social responsibility standards to retain some credibility in the eyes of the public.[3]

In the liberal framework, the concept of "rights" is understood in terms of a need that is perceived by those who demand it as legitimate and, therefore, the state has the responsibility to provide it for each and every citizen. Rights are primary moral entitlements for every human being. In this context one could differentiate between rights that guarantee certain goods and services, like the right to welfare and to healthcare, and rights that protect against certain harm or guarantee certain liberties, like the right to freedom of expression and to exercise choice.[4]

Another pertinent distinction is between an individual's rights with regard to the state or government and an individual's rights with regard to his or her fellow citizens. Rights, conceived to be legitimate, that must be met by the state (e.g., the right to life, to shelter, and to associate), justify taking political actions to fulfill them. Rights regarding other individuals who act illegitimately justify the use of coercive measures against those individuals either by concerned citizens (right to self-defence, to privacy, or to protect one's property) or by the state.[5]

---

2 See Section 8 of the *Canadian Charter of Rights and Freedoms*, and Article 17 of the *International Covenant on Civil and Political Rights:* "No one shall be subjected to arbitrary or unlawful interference with his privacy, family, home or correspondence, nor to unlawful attacks on his honour and reputation." U.N.T.S. No. 14668, Vol. 999 (1976).

3 Cf. Commission on Freedom of the Press (Hutchins Commission), *A Free and Responsible Press* (Chicago: University of Chicago Press, 1947); Robert W. McChesney and John C. Nerone (eds.), *Last Rights: Revisiting Four Theories of the Press* (Urbana and Chicago: University of Illinois Press, 1995), esp. pp. 77–124. See also Dan Caspi, "On Media and Politics: Between Enlightened Authoritarianism and Social Responsibility," in R. Cohen-Almagor (ed.), *Israeli Democracy at the Crossroads* (London: Routledge, 2005).

4 Cf. R. Cohen-Almagor, *Speech, Media, and Ethics: The Limits of Free Expression* (Houndmills and New York: Palgrave, 2005), p. xiii.

5 For further discussion on the concept of rights, see Ronald Dworkin, *Taking Rights Seriously* (London: Duckworth, 1977); Roland J. Pennock and John W. Chapman (eds.), *Human Rights* (New York: New York University Press, 1981); L. W. Sumner, *The Moral Foundation of Rights* (Oxford: Clarendon Press, 1989); Alan Gewirth, *The Community of Rights* (Chicago: University of Chicago Press, 1996);

The chapter argues that free expression does not include the right to do unjustifiable harm to others.[6] Indeed, one of the four key principles of Sigma Delta Chi, the Society of Professional Journalists' Code of Ethics, is to minimize harm. It says, "ethical journalists treat sources, subjects and colleagues as human beings deserving of respect." The Code further instructs journalists to show compassion for those who may be affected adversely by news coverage and to avoid pandering to lurid curiosity, maintaining that the "pursuit of the news is not a license for arrogance."[7]

Privacy

Marshall McLuhan saw changes in the dominant medium of communication as the main determinant of major changes in society, culture and the individual. Print created individualism, mass production and privacy.[8] But the telephone, in turn, evicted people from the privacy

---

Annabel S. Brett, *Liberty, Right and Nature* (Cambridge: Cambridge University Press, 1997); Samuel Walker, *The Rights Revolution* (New York: Oxford University Press, 1998); Michael J. Perry, *The Idea of Human Rights: Four Inquiries* (New York: Oxford University Press, 1998); John R. Rowan, *Conflicts of Rights* (Boulder, Col.: Westview Press, 1999); Michael Ignatieff, *The Rights Revolution* (Toronto: House of Anansi Press, 2000); R.G. Frey, "Privacy, Control and Talk of Rights," *Social Philosophy and Policy,* Vol. 17 (2000): 45–67; William A. Edmundson, *Introduction to Rights* (Cambridge: Cambridge University Press, 2004).

6   Canadian Charter of Rights and Freedoms, section 1; *R. v. Keegstra* [1990] S.C.J. No. 131, 3 S.C.R. 870; *Canadian Human Rights Commission et al. v. Taylor et al.* [1990] 3 S.C.R. 892, 75 D.L.R. (4th); *R. v. Butler* [1992] 1 S.C.R. 452.

7   Founded in 1909 as Sigma Delta Chi, the Society of Professional Journalists is the US's largest and most broad-based journalism organization. SPJ is a not-for-profit organization made up of more than 10,000 members dedicated to encouraging the free practice of journalism; stimulating high standards of ethical behavior; and perpetuating a free press. Sigma Delta Chi's first Code of Ethics was borrowed from the American Society of Newspaper Editors in 1926. In 1973, Sigma Delta Chi wrote its own code, which was revised in 1984 and 1987. The present version of the Society of Professional Journalists' Code of Ethics was adopted in September 1996. http://spj.org/awards/SDX98/rules.htm#society; http://spj.org/ethics/ethics. pdf. See also Ontario Press Council, *24th Annual Report* (Toronto, Ontario, 1996), p. 79.

8   http://www.aber.ac.uk/media/Documents/tecdet/tdet12.html. For further discussion,

of their homes as barrages of phone calls offering anything you can imagine, from creative ways to decorate your home to fantastic cruises to not-so-isolated islands, interfere with our tranquility at all hours of the day, including the weekends.[9] As modes of communication developed, our privacy has been eroding. Large segments of the media have shifted to entertainment, and the sensational media prefer to intrude on private matters at the expense of analyzing social, cultural, scientific and political matters.[10] We witness far more gossip and a tendency to popularize the news, and the tabloids around the globe have specialized in character assassinations and incidents of intrusion on privacy. The large sensational narratives are taking so much space that they drive out discussion about politics.

According to the Angus Reid polling firm, two out of three Canadians think the media are guilty of sensationalizing scandals, and more than one-third (35 per cent) have actually boycotted certain media because of their extensive intrusive reporting. Almost two-thirds (65 per cent) feel reporting delves too deeply into the personal lives of public figures.[11]

This phenomenon, of course, is not uniquely Canadian. We are living in an age when news is becoming infotainment and intruding on private lives is a widespread phenomenon. One of the characteristics of the modern media is their intrusiveness. In today's world the leaders of democracies and celebrities are continuously watched, even hounded. Political leaders and public figures live in a media bubble where their every move is likely to be observed. Their public faces can almost never be taken off, and their private lives can be mercilessly exposed to the glaring spotlight of unwanted publicity. The willingness of public figures to have themselves aired demonstrates both the seductiveness and the reach of the media.[12]

---

see Harold A. Innis, "The Bias of Communication," in *The Bias of Communication* (Toronto: University of Toronto Press, 1964), pp. 33–60.

9 Paul Levinson, *Digital McLuhan* (London: Routledge, 1999), p. 134.

10 See the critique of H. A. Innis, *The Press* (Toronto and London: Oxford University Press, 1949).

11 "Most of us feel reporters pry too much into lives of public figures," *Globe and Mail* (October 10, 1998), p. C3.

12 David Taras, *The Newsmakers: The Media's Influence on Canadian Politics* (Ontario, Canada: Nelson Canada, 1990), p. 235.

In a public lecture delivered at Columbia University in 1995, The Right Honorable Brian Mulroney said that the personal abuse by the media that leaders suffer nowadays has become an unfortunately high – but necessary – price for them to pay for the privilege of service in democracies. He maintained that politicians are not the only ones tracked by the media, or by individuals masquerading as journalists: they are only the most numerous and the most visible. Prime Minister Mulroney called for responsibility and accountability by the media as they fulfill their "indispensable roles as vigorous critics and faithful chroniclers of our lives and times."[13]

Public figures v. ordinary individuals

In this context it is important to distinguish between public figures and ordinary citizens. Public figures are more susceptible to media invasion of their privacy. Justices L'Heureux-Dube and Bastarache of the Canadian Supreme Court said that "It is generally recognized that certain aspects of the private life of a person who is engaged in a public activity or has acquired a certain notoriety can become matters of public interest. This is true, in particular, of artists and politicians, but also, more generally, of all those whose professional success depends on public opinion."[14]

Ordinary citizens are usually of no interest to the public and therefore do not, generally speaking, attract media attention. For instance, ordinary people attending a funeral are not, generally speaking, photographed. In the first instance, there should be a very good reason to send a photographer to a funeral to take such pictures (for instance, when covering a funeral of a hostage killed by terrorists), and the photographer is obliged to ask for permission prior to taking the photos.[15] Celebrities

13 The Right Honourable Brian Mulroney, public speech delivered at Columbia University, New York (March 20, 1995).
14 *Les Editions Vice-Versa Inc. v. Aubry* [1998] 1 S.C.R. 591, Section IV of their judgement, at 616.
15 Death as a result of war is a very different matter. In the United States, the debate over privacy, secrecy, and the public's right to know has flared up at the Pentagon over a very sensitive subject: the photographing of soldiers' coffins as they are shipped home. See Cbsnews.com (April 23, 2004).

and politicians who attend funerals might be photographed and usually this conduct does not raise any controversy. Politicians attend those funerals as part of their public responsibilities, and celebrities not only do not mind the presence of the camera; often they welcome it.

Having said that, some standards of decency should be kept. For many years some organs of the media have exhibited poor taste by speculating that some dead celebrities are alive (the most notable examples being Elvis Presley and Marilyn Monroe). They excelled themselves by grossly claiming that one known celebrity, alive and kicking, had actually died. They repeatedly alleged that Paul McCartney died long ago. It does not matter that McCartney continues to produce songs and to hold concerts. The tale has become one of the cult stories associated with the Beatles. I always wondered, what does McCartney himself think about this? How does he feel about the allegations that he actually died, and that an imitator (he himself) took his place and exploits McCartney's reputation? In the summer of 1997 I had contacted a senior editor in the British press and through him asked Sir Paul for a response. After a while the editor returned to me, saying that Sir Paul has no interest in commenting on the issue. Maybe the story is for his advantage, making him some sort of a legend during his lifetime, literally greater than life. Apparently, he does not take offence being described as a phony imitator. Other celebrities might regard such an innovation differently.

In any event, public figures have experience in dealing with the media, and could gain access to present their side of the story, to voice their content or discontent, and to respond to allegations and gossip. Now let us turn to another interesting question: Whether the media are entitled to intrude on private matters of public officials when these matters do not directly concern their work and office.

If, for instance, a public figure known and respected for preaching family values, decency among couples and honesty in marriage, is found to be betraying his wife, the media have a right to break the news and bring the issue to public attention. The public is entitled to know that the person who spoke so eloquently about family values does not espouse those values at home. The issue is different when the public figure has made his reputation in other spheres, unrelated to his family life, and the conduct in his private life does not affect his public duties. Most broadsheet papers would not cover the infidelity story, while most of the popular press would probably publish the story in the name of the public's right to know. Most broadsheet papers don't consider as valid the argument that if a person is betraying the closest person to him or her, i.e., the spouse, then that person might cheat also on other matters in which he or she is less personally involved. Interestingly, the Israeli media have hardly ever exposed infidelity stories. They believe that the confines of the bedroom should remain intact. At most, they hint about such affairs without specifically identifying the adulterer. The only infidelity affair that became public during the 1990s was connected with Bibi Netanyahu, and the details of this episode were revealed by Netanyahu himself in a public television broadcast.[16]

What about sexual orientations of public officials? Many of us believe that sexual orientation is both immaterial and irrelevant to virtually all public sectors. Still, for a significant proportion of the population having a homosexual or bisexual orientation is immoral. Some would see the "right" and "normal" sexual orientation as a necessary qualification for holding public office. Personally, I do not conceive this view as persuasive enough to intrude on one's privacy. I am not aware of one single study that substantiates the claim that homosexuals are less capable than heterosexuals to carry out public responsibilities. However, others would resort to practical reasoning and argue that a homosexual candidate should disclose his or her sexual orientation because otherwise he or she might subject him or herself to blackmailing and to other pressures that might compromise the candidate's performance. The same argument can also be made about infidelity. Lies might necessitate coverups and misconduct. Information that some parts of the public – even a small part – deem relevant should be made available. The person who wishes to have information about a candidate's marital infidelity can be understood as saying that, in a democracy, the determination of the nature of a public office and its qualifications are as important to him or her as this personal preference is important to the adulterer.[17]

---

16 See Anat Balint, "Directing Itself: The Netanyahu Family and the Papparazzi," *The Seventh Eye*, Vol. 11 (October 1997): 6–11 (Hebrew).

17 Cf. Frederick Schauer, "Can Public Figures Have Private Lives?" in Ellen Frankel Paul, Fred D. Miller, Jr. and Jeffrey Paul (eds.), *The Right to Privacy* (New York: Cambridge University Press, 2000), pp. 293–309.

For this reason I cannot agree with Dennis Thompson who argues that citizens do not need to know about the drinking habits of an official because the alleged effects can be discovered by observing his actions on the job.[18] Alcohol, like drugs, might affect one's judgement and people should be aware that their representative has a soft spot for certain drinks and/or drugs that might cloud one's ability to make delicate decisions. Furthermore, some people would like to know about such a habit before electing or nominating someone for a responsible position. Many people don't have the time and energy to inquire about such habits themselves and they trust the media to disclose this information, upon obtaining it, to the public. Many people would not like to take the risk and discover that their representative is drunk at a moment of crisis. Then it might be too late. In this context, former president of Israel, Ezer Weizman, disclosed many years after the 1967 Six Day War that the Chief of Staff at that time, Yitzhak Rabin, collapsed on the eve of the war and asked Weizman to replace him. Weizman was his deputy at the time. He refused, Rabin collected himself and led the Israeli army to victory. Later it also became public that Yitzhak Rabin had a drinking problem.[19] The Israeli public deserved to know all this before the outbreak of the 1967 fateful war and before Rabin was elected to further high positions.

Yet, I wish to refrain from the sweeping generalization that **everything** is relevant. Some boundaries need to be introduced. A major consideration in coming to decide the confines of privacy is the consequences of the official's action on the political/social process. In all the examples pointed *supra*, infidelity, hidden sexual preferences, addiction problems, those kinds of behavior might affect the official's performances and his or her ability to function. But, is this the only consideration?

Suppose a public figure beats his wife in bed as part of their sexual foreplay. If this is done with the wife's consent, then this fact should

18 Dennis F. Thompson, "Privacy, Politics, and the Press," in John R. Rowan and Samuel Zinaich, Jr. (eds.), *Ethics for the Professions* (Belmont, Cal.: Wadsworth, 2003), p. 395.

19 Weizman told all this in public and specifically to me in a private discussion we had in 1986.

not be revealed to the public. I don't think that consenting violence might affect his public behavior. The case is different if the wife does not consent to the beating. Then it is just another version of domestic violence. Should this be revealed to the public? Now, if you focus all attention to the effect this behavior might have on the official's public conduct, it might be argued quite persuasively that domestic violence has no bearing on performing one's duties. The wife can complain to the police, and then there will be repercussions against the beater. But it is difficult to argue that this repugnant behavior might instigate coverups, commonly in use to hide infidelity stories that might have an effect on one's conduct.

It might be argued that if a certain behavior goes against the majority's norm, then that behavior needs to be exposed. I don't find the argument of majorities and minorities convincing. The majority may hold a norm which at another point of time may seem to be repugnant. Such, for instance, was slavery in North America. Nowadays, the majority may think homosexuality is repugnant. At another point of time homosexuality may be conceived as normal. Indeed, in Greek and Roman times homosexuality was conceived differently.[20] Majority opinion should not be considered as grounds for invasion of privacy.

My argument is that domestic violence should be exposed in public because the public needs to be aware of such a behavior, whether or not it has a bearing on one's public duties. One of the basic foundations of liberal democracy is not to harm others. Any action that causes physical harm to individuals or groups, for any reason other than self-protection, ought to be curtailed.[21] When this underpinning is broken, the public has the right to know. Violence against women is vile, goes against the underlying values of democracy, and should be fought against and curtailed. Violence against weak parties is something wrong. It is wrong *qua* unjustified violence, even if no one is aware of its existence.

20 Cf. Craig A. Williams, *Homosexuality: Ideologies of Masculinity in Classical Antiquity* (New York: Oxford University Press, 1999).
21 Cf. R. Cohen-Almagor, *Speech, Media, and Ethics: The Limits of Free Expression*, esp. chap. 1.

Public figures v. ordinary citizens who stumble into the public forum

Another pertinent distinction is between public figures who choose to live in the spotlights, and ordinary citizens who stumble into the public forum. On occasion, people stumble unintentionally into the spotlight, under circumstances that are not under their control. They, for instance, commit a significant public act, like saving a family from a fire, or rescuing a public figure from danger. The media should publish the heroic deed of the individual but should refrain from intruding into his or her private life that is of no importance to the public. A good example in this context is the Oliver Sipple story. Sipple was the ex-marine who knocked a gun out of the hands of a would-be assassin of then American President Gerald Ford. Shortly after the incident, it was revealed by the media that Sipple was active in the San Francisco gay community, a fact that had not been known to Sipple's family, who thereupon broke off relationship with him. His entire life was shattered as result of this publication. The good deed he had done brought about extremely harmful consequences for Sipple.[22] If the person who had stumbled into the public forum would prefer to remain in the public eye and to harvest more attention by further deeds or expressions, then he or she is no longer a private citizen and should accept the pros and cons involved in public life. But many of those who stumbled may wish to regain their privacy and return to normal life. With regard to these people, the media should refrain from intruding into their private lives and should respect their privacy, especially when exposure of certain details could harm one or more of the people involved.[23]

Look, for instance, at the painful story of the massacre of fourteen women in Montreal in December 1989. During the days that followed, there was what one writer describes as "a savage hunt" for gossip from

22 See R. Cohen-Almagor, *The Boundaries of Liberty and Tolerance* (Gainesville, Flo.: The University Press of Florida, 1994), pp. 113–115.

23 Section IIB(b) of the Quebec Press Council's *The Rights and Responsibilities of the Press* (second edition, 1987) holds: "Media and journalists should distinguish between matters of public interest and public curiosity. The publication of information concerning the private life of individuals is acceptable only to the extent that it is in the public interest."

neighbors and friends, and the ravaged faces of mourners. Information on the victims was gleaned from every possible source, invading people's privacy in the pursuit of a story. The killer's mother had to go into hiding, and her private life was reported in minute details taken from divorce papers.[24] The fact that her son was a killer legitimized crossing all ethical borders. In another case, a Canadian woman and her child were killed during a skyjacking in Malta in November 1985. When the husband returned to Canada, a "milling crowd of reporters, photographers and TV cameramen" met him at the airport. The man told them that they were not invited to the funeral.[25] After this episode, it was said that the encounter prompted soul searching in the newsrooms as editors weighed the news value of the event against the human grief and pain involved.

In this context it should be noted that the CBC's *Journalistic Standards and Practices* holds: "An individual's right to privacy is cherished in Canada... The invasion of an individual's privacy is repugnant. Privacy in its broadest sense means being left alone. It means protecting an individual's personal and private life from intrusion or exposure to the public view."[26] Democracy has an interest in protecting the privacy and tranquility of the home. That interest was recognized by the Israeli[27] and

---

24 Ronald D. Crelinsten, "Victims' Perspectives," in David L. Paletz and Alex P. Schmid (eds.), *Terrorism and the Media* (Newbury Park, Cal.: Sage, 1992), p. 217.

25 *Ibid.* p. 219.

26 See also Section VI of the Statement of Principles for Canadian Daily Newspapers, Canadian Daily Newspapers Publishers Association, adopted in April 1977: "Every person has a right to privacy. There are inevitable conflicts between the right to privacy and the public good or the right to know about the conduct of public affairs. Each case should be judged in the light of common sense and humanity." Quoted in Nick Russell, *Morals and the Media* (Vancouver: UBC Press, 1995), pp. 123, 199. For further discussion, see Sandra L. Borden and Michael S. Pritchard, "Conflict of Interest in Journalism," in Michael Davis and Andrew Stark, *Conflict of Interest in the Professions* (New York: Oxford University Press, 2001), pp. 73–91; Judith Lichtenberg, "Truth, Neutrality, and Conflict of Interest," in John R. Rowan and Samuel Zinaich, Jr. (eds.), *Ethics for the Professions* (Belmont, Cal.: Wadsworth, 2003), pp. 379–386.

27 H.C. (High Court of Justice) 456/73. *Rabbi Kahane v. Southern District Police Commander* (was not published); Shamgar J'.s judgement in F.H. 9/83. *Military Court of Appeals v. Vaaknin*, P.D. 42 (iii), 837, 851.

the American[28] Supreme Courts in several decisions. Justice Frankfurter wrote in one of his prominent rulings: "Homes are sanctuaries from intrusions upon privacy and of opportunities for leading lives in health and safety."[29] Similar reasoning was enunciated by Justices Black and Brennan. Justice Black held that a person's home is "the sacred retreat to which families repair for their privacy and their daily way of living," "sometimes the last citadel of the tired, the weary, and the sick," wherein people "can escape the hurly-burly of the outside business and political world."[30] In turn, Justice Brennan said:

> Preserving the sanctity of the home, the one retreat to which men and women can repair to escape from the tribulations of their daily pursuits, is surely an important value. Our decisions reflect no lack of solicitude for the right of an individual "to be let alone" in the privacy of the home.[31]

Here Brennan echoed what Warren and Brandeis had written in a classic article where they spoke of the right to be let alone and of privacy, referring to the "precincts of private and domestic life" as sacred.[32]

---

28 Cf. Justice Douglas in *Public Utilities Commission v. Pollack* 343 U.S. 451, 467 (1952). See also *Stanley v. Georgia*, 394 U.S. 557, 89 S. Ct. 1243, 22 L.Ed.2d 542 (1969); *City of Wauwatosa v. King* 182 N.W. 2d 530, 537 (1971). See also West's Legal News, "Supreme Court Denied Certiorari in Anti-Abortion Demonstrators' Picketing Case," *West's Legal News* 3061, 1995 WL 910586 (October 19, 1995).

29 *Martin v. City of Struthers* 319 U.S. 141, 153 (1943).

30 *Gregory v. City of Chicago*, 394 U.S. 111, 125, 118, 89 S.Ct. 946, 953–954, 950, 22 L.Ed.2d 134 (1969).

31 *Carey v. Brown* 447 U.S. 455, 471 (1980). In *Rowan v. United States Post Office Department*, 397 U.S. 728, 737, 90 S.Ct. 1484, 25 L.Ed.2d 736 (1970), Chief Justice Burger stated that the concept that "a man's home is his castle" into which not even the king may enter, has lost none of its vitality. For further discussion, see R. Cohen-Almagor, *Speech, Media, and Ethics: The Limits of Free Expression*, chap. 2; Richard J. Arneson, "Egalitarian Justice v. the Right to Privacy?" in Ellen Frankel Pail, Fred D. Miller, Jr. and Jeffrey Paul (eds.), *The Right to Privacy*, pp. 91–119.

32 Samuel Warren and Louis D. Brandeis, "The Right to Privacy," *Harvard L. Rev.,* Vol. 4 (1890), 289–320.

Intruding into the private life of previously well-known people

William James Sidis was a famous child prodigy in 1910. His name and prowess were well-known due to the efforts of his father who developed complex ideas on child training. When young Sidis was 3.5 year-old he could use a typewriter. By the time he was 5, Sidis was able to read, write and speak English, was an expert accountant, and had begun to study French and Latin. He wrote a textbook on anatomy and another on English grammar. At the age of 8 Sidis entered high school and in six weeks he had completed the mathematical course and had begun writing an astronomy book. Then he also plunged into the studies of German and Russian. Boris, the proud father, took care to issue bulletins to the press detailing all these (and other) achievements. The press complied and followed William and praised Boris for the so-called "successful" implementation of his "advanced" theories. At the age of 11 Sidis lectured to distinguished mathematicians on Four-Dimensional Bodies at Harvard. At 16 he graduated from Harvard College, amid considerable public attention. He was declared to be, according to the *New York Times*, "the most learned undergraduate that has ever entered the Cambridge institution."[33] Since then, however, his name appeared in the press only sporadically as Sidis sought to live as unobtrusively as possible, until *The New Yorker* published quite an unflattering article about him in 1937.

The New Yorker did features on past personalities under the title "Where are they now." The article on Sidis was printed with the subtitle "April fool," playing on the fact that William was born on April 1. The reporter described Sidis' early accomplishments and the wide attention he received, then recounted his general breakdown and the revulsion that Sidis felt for his former life of fame. The article described how Sidis tried to conceal his identity, his chosen career as an insignificant clerk, his enthusiasm for collecting streetcar transfers and for studying the history of a certain American-Indian tribe, and his proficiency with an adding machine. The untidiness of Sidis' room, his curious gasping laugh, his manner of speech, his wary eyes and other personal habits

---

33   "Sidis could read at two years old," *New York Times* (October 18, 1909), p. 7.

were commented upon at length. The article portrays William's lodgings, "a hall bedroom of Boston's shabby south end" and the man at the age of thirty-nine, "large, heavy… with a prominent jaw, a thickish neck, and a reddish mustache."[34] The article ends by saying that the little boy who lectured in 1910 on the fourth dimension to a gathering of learned men was expected to grow up to be a great mathematician, a famous leader in the world of science but, in the words of Sidis himself, "I was born on April Fools' Day."[35]

Sidis sued for violation of privacy. The issue at hand was not whether the article was true. Sidis who so desperately wanted to be let alone and to live his life away from the public eye was exposed in a cruel fashion. The court recognized that, saying "the article is merciless in its dissection of intimate details of its subject's personal life," maintaining that the article may be fairly described as "a ruthless exposure of a once public character, who has since sought and has now been deprived of the seclusion of private life."[36]

However, despite the sympathy for Sidis Judge Clark found for the defendant, saying that "Everyone will agree that at some point the public interest in obtaining information becomes dominant over the individual's desire for privacy."[37] Notice the language: Clark is recruiting "everyone" for this assignment of trumping the plaintiff's privacy. I hasten to think that there would be quite differences of opinion among "everyone" regarding the exact point at which public interest in obtaining information becomes dominant. This point is not clarified in the judgement. Clark maintained, "At least we would permit limited scrutiny of the 'private' life of any person who has achieved, or has had thrust upon him, the questionable and indefinable status of a 'public figure.'"[38] Indeed, "thrust upon him" is the correct phrase, as William was a child, incapable of independent, autonomous decision making, when he became a public figure due to the endless efforts of his father to push him to the spotlights. When he was able to break free and to stand

---

34 Jared L. Manly, "Where are they now?, April fool!" *The New Yorker* (August 14, 1937), pp. 22–26, at 25–26.

35 *Ibid.*, p. 26.

36 *Sidis v. F-R Publishing*, 113 F2d 806 (2nd Cir., July 22, 1940), at 807–808.

37 *Ibid.*, at 809.

38 *Ibid.*

on his own, Sidis opted for anonymity. The court essentially says that once a public figure, always a public figure. There is no escape. Even if you would like to be forgotten, you cannot. You owe to the public the right to inform them about major developments in your life, however tragic and personal those might be. The fact that Sidis never made a decision to become a public figure, and when he was able to control his life he chose the exact opposite of being one, was insignificant for the court.

In 1937, Sidis was no longer a public figure for some time. He was not a retired public official who may be still held accountable for past actions. He was not a celebrity who relishes the limelight. Quite the opposite. Sidis did whatever he could to sink into oblivion. Intruding into his privacy in the name of popular curiosity is unjustified and unethical. Granted that there is public interest in Sidis. The public is interested in many things, including state's security, official secrets, capturing Osama Bin-Laden, sexual behavior of supermodels and politicians, and how much money one's neighbor earns. This does not mean that the media should provide all data of interest. The court's decision was erroneous and damaging. Four years after the court decision Sidis died unemployed and destitute.[39]

Privacy is intimately associated with our most profound values, our understanding of what it means to be an autonomous moral agent capable of self-reflection and choice. Its violation is demeaning to individuality and an affront to personal dignity.[40] Jean Cohen contended that a constitutionally protected right to personal privacy is indispensable to any modern conception of freedom,[41] whereas Avishai Margalit asserted that the institutions of a decent society must not encroach upon personal privacy.[42] However, when one opens today's newspapers, especially the tabloids, one could read many details that concern very private aspects

39 Anthony Lewis, "The Right to Be Let Alone," in Craig L. LaMay (ed.), *Journalism and the Debate Over Privacy* (Mahwah, N.J.: Lawrence Erlbaum, 2003), p. 64.

40 Amitai Etzioni, *The Limits of Privacy* (New York: Basic Books, 1999), p. 191.

41 Jean L. Cohen, "Rethinking Privacy: The Abortion Controversy," in Jeff Weintraub and Krishan Kumar (eds.), *Public and Private in Thought and Practice: Perspectives on Grand Dichotomy* (Chicago: University of Chicago Press, 1997), p. 137.

42 Avishai Margalit, *The Decent Society* (Cambridge, Mass.: Harvard University Press, 1996), p. 201.

of the other. One of the most intrusive forms of reporting is media gossip.

Yellow Entertainment

By yellow entertainment I refer to gossip about events that are of little social value but are of interest to the public. Reporting of these events feeds the voyeuristic needs of many of us, to various extents. Many of us enjoy learning the details of what is thought to be unattainable by the common people. If I cannot be like the "beautiful people," at least I would like to know about their lifestyle: what living in a castle with servants is like; the pros and cons of living with three wives; what it is like to be an idolized rock star; what a famous basketball player eats for breakfast; why he chose to divorce his wife. Many of these gossip events can be quite banal. For instance, millions of women are pregnant around the globe at any given time. The media usually do not regard this as newsworthy. But it might attract public interest if the concerned woman is a soap opera star or a leading actress in one of the commercial comedy series. Many viewers of "Melrose Place" would be very interested in knowing that their favorite character is actually pregnant in her private life. They would begin to ponder and speculate about various questions: Will the character she acts out in the series become pregnant as well? Will the series' producers try to conceal her pregnancy? Will the star finally get married? Will a replacement be found in case the pregnancy does not fit the producers' plans? Will they decide, God forbid, to terminate the filming of the series during the advanced months of pregnancy? These are top priority questions for the captive followers of the series.[43]

In Israel, the gossip columns adopted some ethical standards in reporting about celebrities and public figures. They never report about their children, believing children should be left out of the public scene and their privacy should be maintained. Gossip reporters never do outing of homosexuals who prefer to remain "in the closet," and they would never publish material that might bring about the breakdown of families. Consequently, they may say that a minister, or a senior public

---

43 For further discussion, see R. Cohen-Almagor, *Speech, Media, and Ethics,* chap. 5.

official, or a famous singer is having extramarital affair, but they will keep his or her name anonymous.

The British press has been constantly under public scrutiny during the past two decades. At the end of the 1980s there was a growing uneasiness with regard to the functioning of the press. It was decided to set up an inquiry committee to consider the behavior of the press and to suggest remedies. In particular, the issue of privacy was in the forefront of concern. The first report of June 1990 concluded with the view that "the press should be given one last chance to demonstrate that non-statutory self-regulation can be made to work effectively. This is a stiff test for the press. If it fails, we recommend that a statutory system for handling complaints should be introduced."[44] However, both the 1990 Calcutt Report and the earlier Younger Report[45] recommended that no general tort of invasion of privacy be introduced.[46]

The press failed the test and in January 1993 a second report was issued by Sir David Calcutt QC, arguing that the Press Complaints Commission (PCC) was not an effective regulator of the press. Sir David maintained that the PCC did not "hold the balance fairly between the press and individual. It is not the truly independent body which it should be. As constituted, it is, in essence, a body set up by the industry, and operating a code of practice devised by the industry and which is over-favorable to the industry."[47] Accordingly the report recommended the replacement of the self-regulatory body of the press with a statutory regime designed to ensure that privacy "is protected from unjustifiable intrusion, and protected by a body in which the public, as well as the press, has confidence."[48]

---

44 Home Office, *Report of the Committee on Privacy and Related Matters* (London: Her Majesty's Stationary Office, June 1990), Cm 1102, at 73. Sir David Calcutt Report.

45 Younger Report, Cmnd 5012 (1972), para. 659.

46 Privacy is protected in Art. 12 of the UN Declaration of Human Rights and Art. 17 of the International Covenant on Civil and Political Rights as well as in Art.8 of the European Convention on Human Rights. Cf. Michael J. Beloff, "Politicians and the Press," in Jack Beatson and Yvonne Cripps (eds.), *Freedom of Expression and Freedom of Information* (Oxford: Oxford University Press, 2002), p. 76.

47 Sir David Calcutt QC (January 1993) *Review of Press Self-Regulation* (London: Her Majesty's Stationary Office), Cm 2135, at xi.

48 Calcutt, 1993, at xiv.

Sir David thought that his recommendations were "designed to make a positive contribution to the development of the highest standards of journalism, to enable the press to operate freely and responsibly, and to give it the backing which is needed, in a fiercely competitive market, to resist the wildest excesses."[49] The government, however, did not accept his recommendations. The feeling was that the formation of a statutory regime might hinder freedom of expression and the right of the public to know. However, the proprietors who formed the PCC out of necessity, fearing a possible governmental intervention, understand after Princess Diana's death that it is up to them to make the necessary accommodations, otherwise voices for governmental regulations might be reheard, possibly with greater public support.

The London press is arguably the most competitive market in the print industry worldwide. Soon enough the tabloids had realized that Princess Diana was their best sales promoter. Her picture on the front page may prompt people to buy their journal instead of another. Diana became the most photographed person in the world. The tabloids were willing to pay enterprising and shameless photographers millions of dollars for capturing Diana in her private moments. The more private, the better. Tapes of Dianna's intimate phone conversations were leaked to the media, she was watched by spy agencies, and journalists dissected her every move. Ex-lover James Hewitt betrayed her trust and published a humiliatingly juicy and detailed account of their affair for a very nice sum of money. According to one report, the widely circulated photo of Diana embracing boyfriend Dodi al-Fayed netted the photographer more than $3.2 million, an incentive that drove paparazzi to break any ethical boundary on the book in search for a quick fortune.[50]

On August 31, 1997, the Princess of Wales was killed in a shocking road accident in Paris. Princess Diana and Dodi al-Fayed were trying to escape some paparazzi photographers who raced after their car. Princess Diana was exceptional among celebrities because she insisted

49 Calcutt, 1993, at 63. I asked Sir David to grant me an interview during the summer of 1997 but he refused, saying that he had shifted his interests to other spheres.
50 Charles J. Sykes, *The End of Privacy* (New York: St. Martin's Press, 1999), p. 190. For discussion on ways to combat paparazzi journalism, see Rodney A. Smolla, "Privacy and the First Amendment Right to Gather News," *George Washington L. Rev.*, Vol. 67 (1999): 1097.

upon continuing to live as normal a life as possible despite the constant surveillance to which she was subjected. Princess Diana understood the power of the media and frequently used them and manipulated them for her own advantage. One can say that Diana confused public interest with public prurience. Although the paparazzi made her life very difficult in her last years, Princess Diana never filed a complaint against newspapers (under Section 8, Harassment, of the Code of Practice).[51] Even after her pictures were taken in a gym and subsequently published in the *Daily Mirror* (November 7, 1993), she chose not to complain and to resolve the matter through conciliation.[52] The court was therefore denied an opportunity to consider the limits of publicity when it comes to photos taken in a private place, without the public figure's consent.[53]

To a large extent Diana's image was built by the media that, in turn, used her to sell newspapers. You need two to tango, and the two – Princess Diana and the media – were eager to dance. Starting in 1991, she began recording the story of her life and her troubled marriage for journalist Andrew Morton, who took pains to conceal Diana's actual involvement until after her death. Largely as the result of her own revelation, the

51 The Oxford English Dictionary defines harassment as to trouble, worry, make repeated attacks on.
52 In August 1996, the Princess of Wales obtained an injunction restraining a named freelance press photographer from coming within 300 meters of her, wherever she might be, because of fear of harassment; and there have been cases where injunctions have been obtained to restrain publication of photographs taken of the Princess and other members of the Royal family in intimate settings, by means of telephoto lenses, etc. The general rule is that the taking of photographs cannot in itself be controlled (except where it is likely to cause a breach of the peace), unless the interference with the subject's life is so significant that it amounts to serious and probably intentional harassment. See Helen Fenwick and Gavin Phillipson, "Confidence and Privacy: A Re-examination," *Cambridge Law Journal,* Vol. 55, No. 3 (November 1996): 447–455, at 448–450. In *Hellewell v. Chief Constable of South Yorkshire* [1995] 1 WLR 804 Laws J. said that if someone with a telephoto lens were to take from a distance and with no authority a picture of another engaged in some private act, his subsequent disclosure of the photograph would amount to a breach of confidence and the law would protect a right of privacy, although the name accorded to the cause of action would be breach of confidence (at 807).
53 For further discussion concerning newspaper publishing photographs of the claimant taken without his consent in a brothel, see *Jamie Theakston v. MGN Ltd.* [2002] EWHC 137 (QB) QBD (Ouseley J) 14/2/2002.

public came to know what drugs she took, which psychologists and spiritualists she consulted, the size of her waist, the frequency of her vomiting, her 1982 attempt at suicide by throwing herself down a flight of steps, her therapies, and her various emotional turmoil.[54] Throughout her final years, she confided details of her married life and her romances to close journalists, often with the expectation that the stories would be published across the front pages of the newspapers. And as she came to resent the press, she went on BBC *Panorama* program to discuss her failing marriage. The program was watched by 21 million people in Britain and millions more around the world.[55] Princess Diana admitted her affair with James Hewitt, opening virtually every aspect of her life to scrutiny. Diana even publicly portrayed how she told her sons that she and Charles were splitting up and about how she and her sons discussed their father's relationship with her rival, Camilla Parker-Bowles, who was the third wheel in her marriage to Charles.[56]

Princess Diana was struggling against a far superior opponent, the Royal Court, and soon enough realized that her main, perhaps only, asset were the media. This was the only sphere in which she was able to compete against the court, and win. She knew what a good picture was and supplied those photos that were printed all over the world and helped newspapers to increase their sales. She attracted wide public attention and provided endless numbers of stories for the reporters and photographers who followed her. What she did not understand is that she could not choose which pictures should be taken, and which not; which photographers could accompany her during her trips, and which should not follow her. Princess Diana was disgusted and appalled by the behavior of the unscrupulous paparazzi photographers who made their living by recording her private moments. The famous British dictum, My Home is My Castle, was transformed when Diana was concerned to Her Castle Is Our Golden Peepshow. Apparently, Diana failed to recognize until her very last day that when you open the door for the media they would enter in force, to make the most of this opportunity to make some profit.[57]

---

54 Andrew Morton, *Diana: Her True Story* (NY: Simon and Schuster, 1992).

55 Karen Sanders, *Ethics and Journalism* (London: Sage, 2003), p. 79.

56 Charles J. Sykes, *The End of Privacy*, p. 191.

57 Mr. Robin Esser, Consultant Editor of *The Daily Mail,* argued that Princess Diana was obsessive about her image. It was not rare for her to phone our Royal reporter

Following Princess Diana's tragic death, many people in England called for a re-examination of the tension between the right to freedom of expression and the right to privacy. Lord Wakeham, Chairperson of the Press Complaints Committee declared immediately after Princess Diana's funeral (September 6, 1997) that the PCC will need to ponder ways to protect the privacy of Princes William and Harry so that they will not have to go through the agonizing experiences that their mother lived almost daily after she became the Princess of Wales. Lord Wakeham said he was "extremely concerned" about what will happen as the Princes reach the age of 16,[58] conceding that the PCC's Code of Practice might change after consultation with editors.[59] Lord Wakeham's statement followed the pledge made by Earl Spencer, Princess Diana's brother, during her funeral. The outraged Earl committed himself to protect her children from the media, not allowing them "to suffer the anguish that used regularly to drive you [Diana] to tearful despair."[60] Of course, all people concerned realize that it is not enough to join the Press Council and to subscribe to its Code of Practice. Although almost all newspapers in England subscribe to the Code, this is more of a lip service.[61]

---

a few times a week, sometimes a few times a day. Princess Diana was on the phone with him regularly every week for the past 2–3 years. Interview with Mr. Esser (October 20, 1997). Mr. Charles Moore, Editor of the *Daily Telegraph*, said that Princess Diana was regularly in touch with senior people in the paper, like himself, the Royal affairs reporter, and another senior member who is close to the Royal family. Interview with Mr. Moore on October 21, 1997.

58 Clause 12 of the PCC Code of Practice holds that "children under sixteen should not be interviewed or photographed on subjects involving their personal welfare without the consent of a parent or other adult responsible for them." For further discussion see Lord Wakeham's speech at St. Bride's Institute (August 23, 1995), in *Moving Ahead* (Press Complaints Commission, 1995).

59 Alison Boshoff, "Curbs on Press to Protect Princes," *The Daily Telegraph* (September 8, 1997), p. 1.

60 "Earl Spencer's Funeral Address," *The Sunday Telegraph* (September 7, 1997), p. 2. The most recent controversy regarding Diana concerned the CBS News program "48 Hours Investigates" which showed two pictures taken by paparazzi at the scene of the August 31, 1997, accident in Paris. It was the first time a major media outlet has published pictures of the injured princess. See "Anger At CBS Use Of Diana Photos," CBS News (April 23, 2004).

61 For further discussion, see Lawrence M. Friedman, "The One Way Mirror: Law,

There have been some interesting cases about the scope of privacy under the UK Human Rights Act 1998 (came into effect on October 2, 2000) which incorporates the European Convention on Human Rights (ECHR).[62] Article 8 of the ECHR has been used in a whole range of contexts, from phone tapping to the use of medical records in court; from the rights of children whose parents are deported to the right to have records altered.[63] It was held in a case brought by the ex-news anchor Anna Ford who had been photographed through a long distance lens on a beach that she had no reasonable expectation of privacy in a public place, and that if she wore a bikini in public she could not object to being photographed. [64] It was also used to restrain a magazine from publishing unauthorized photographs of Michael Douglas and Catherine Zeta-Jones taken at their wedding.[65]

Privacy and the Media," *Stanford Public Law and Legal Theory Working Paper Series,* Research Paper No. 89 (March 2004).

62 Article 8 of the ECHR provides: "1. Everyone has the right to respect for his private and family life, his home and his correspondence. 2. There shall be no interference by a public authority with the exercise of this right except such as is in accordance with the law and is necessary in a democratic society in the interests of national security, public safety or the economic well-being of the country, for the prevention of disorder or crime, for the protection of health or morals, or for the protection of the rights and freedoms of others."

63 Michael J. Beloff, "Politicians and the Press," in Jack Beatson and Yvonne Cripps (eds.), *Freedom of Expression and Freedom of Information*, p. 82.

64 I am grateful to Geoffrey Marshall for this piece of information. For further discussion on privacy and English law, see Sir Brian Neill, "Privacy: A Challenge for the Next Century," in Basil S. Markesinis (ed.), *Protecting Privacy* (Oxford: Oxford University Press, 1999), pp. 1–28. See also *Naomi Campbell v Mirror Group Newspapers Ltd.* where it was held that the media to conform with Art. 8 European Convention on Human Rights should respect information about aspects or details of the private lives of celebrities and public figures that they legitimately chose to keep private, certainly "sensitive personal data" under the 1998 Act, unless. there was an overriding public interest duty to publish consistent with Art. 10(2) of the Convention. Striking the balance between Art. 8 and Art. 10 of the Convention and having full regard to s. 12(4) of the 1998 Act, the court held that Campbell was entitled to the remedy of damages and/or compensation. Cf. *Campbell v Mirror* [2002] EWHC 499 (QB) QBD (Morland J) 27/3/2002. http://www.cs.mdx.ac.uk/staffpages/cgeorge/PrivacyIssues.doc.

65 *Michael Douglas, Catherine Zeta-Jones and Northern & Shell PLC v. Hello! Ltd.* CA (Brooke LJ, Sedley LJ, Keene LJ) 21/12/2000.

Les Editions Vice-Versa Inc. v. Aubry

Quebec is the only province in Canada to have enacted quasi-constitutional provisions[66] about privacy for the private sector.[67] The Quebec *Charter of Human Rights and Freedoms* holds that "Every person has a right to the safeguard of his dignity, honour and reputation," and that "Every person has a right to respect for his private life."[68] In turn, Chapter III of the *Civil Code of Quebec [1994]* holds:

35. Every person has a right to the respect of his reputation and privacy.

No one may invade the privacy of a person without the consent of the person or his heirs unless authorized by law.

36. The following acts, in particular, may be considered as invasions of the privacy of a person:

(1) entering or taking anything in his dwelling;

(2) intentionally intercepting or using his private communications;

(3) appropriating or using his image or voice while he is in private premises;

(4) keeping his private life under observation by any means;

(5) using his name, image, likeness or voice for a purpose other than the legitimate information of the public;

(6) using his correspondence, manuscripts or other personal documents.[69]

---

66 Rod MacDonald notes in his comments that it is accurate to characterize these two documents as "quasi" constitutional because, even though they take precedence over other legislation unless excluded, they are in no way entrenched as against subsequent Parliamentary activity. Personal communication on February 19, 2002.

67 The first legislation designed to protect privacy in the private sector was enacted in 1993 with the *Loi de protection des renseignements personnels dans le secteur privé*. For examination of existing legislation, international laws and initiatives relating to privacy and freedom of information as well as voluntary codes of conduct for Canadian businesses to ensure the safety of their clients' personal information see Media Awareness Network: Media Issues – Privacy, http://www.media-awareness. ca; http://www.screen.com/mnet/eng/issues/priv/laws/laws.htm

68 Quebec *Charter of Human Rights and Freedoms*, R.S.Q., c C–12.

69 Chapter III, "Respect of Reputation and Privacy," *Civil Code of Quebec [1994]*. It is argued that the Quebec privacy laws are too broad, having unintended effects on historical research because they impede the development of access to archival holdings. See Joanne Burgess, "The Right to Privacy in the Private Sector: What is at Stake for Historians and Historical Research," Canadian Historical Association (Summer 1998), pp. 26–27. See also http://www.cam.orga/~ihaf.

Both statutory provisions were invoked in a recent Supreme Court case, *Les Editions Vice-Versa Inc. v. Aubry.*[70] The case was concerned with Ms. Aubry who brought an action in civil liability against a photographer and the publisher of a magazine dedicated to the arts, for taking and publishing a photograph showing her, then aged 17, sitting on the steps of a building. The photograph was published without her knowledge and consent. *Les Editions Vice-Versa* sold 722 copies and the photograph was drawn to Aubry's attention by a friend who bought a copy of the magazine. Aubry sued for damages in the amount of $10,000, half as compensatory damages and the other half as exemplary damages. The trial judge recognized that the unauthorized publication constituted a fault and ordered the *Vice-Versa* magazine to pay her $2,000. The majority of the Court of Appeal for Quebec affirmed this decision, saying that the unauthorized publication of the photograph constituted an encroachment of her anonymity, which is an essential element of the right to privacy. Even in the absence of bad faith, the dissemination of Aubry's photo without her knowledge and consent was wrongful. Then the magazine appealed to the Supreme Court.

The majority of the Court, *per* L'Heureux-Dube, Gonthier, Cory, Iacobucci and Bastarache JJ., dismissed the appeal, holding that the right to one's image is an element of the right to privacy under the Quebec *Charter.* One of the purposes of the *Charter* is to protect people from compulsion or restraint. If the purpose of the right to privacy is to protect a sphere of individual autonomy, it must include the ability to control the use made of one's image. In this case, the appellants are liable *a priori,* because the photograph was published when the respondent was identifiable. The artistic expression of the photograph cannot justify the infringement of the right to privacy it entails. The majority of the Court maintained:

> An artist's right to publish his or her work is not absolute and cannot include the right to infringe, without any justification, a fundamental right of the subject whose image appears in the work. It has not been shown that the public's interest in seeing this photograph is predominant. In these circumstances, the respondent's right to protection of her image is more important

70 *Les Editions Vice-Versa Inc. v. Aubry* [1998] 1 S.C.R. 591.

than the appellant's right to publish the photograph of the respondent without first obtaining her permission.[71]

The minority of the Court, *per* Lamer CJ. and Major J., accepted the appeal. Lamer CJ. wrote that mere infringement of a right or freedom does not necessarily constitute fault. This case cannot be resolved "merely by relying upon the respondent's right to her image or the appellant's freedom of expression; the rights concerned must also be balanced."[72] Lamer CJ. acknowledged that the right to privacy "certainly includes a person's right to his or her image," and he agreed with his colleagues that the right to one's image is "primarily a personality right, an interest of an extrapatrimonial nature."[73] Consequently, the dissemination of Aubry's image constituted a violation of her privacy and of her right to her image. Lamer CJ. said that "in the abstract" to appropriate another person's image without her consent to include in a publication constitutes a fault. He also thought, and I concur, a reasonable person would have been more diligent and would at least have tried to obtain Aubry's consent to publish her photograph. Furthermore, Lamer CJ. said, and I agree, that the appellant did not do everything necessary to avoid infringing the respondent's rights.[74]

So why did Lamer CJ. and Major J. accept the appeal? Because, in their opinion, there was no evidence of damage. The respondent's statement that her classmates laughed at her did not in itself constitute sufficient evidence of prejudice, as it did not provide any information about how she felt. Nor was there any evidence that Ms. Aubry had

71 *Les Editions Vice-Versa Inc. v. Aubry* [1998] 1 S.C.R. 591. In his comments on this essay, Joe Magnet argues that *Aubry* is a property type case following a well-established property law doctrine in Canada as to the ownership of the image. Magnet thinks that the privacy aspect in this case, while interesting, is a side issue. Rod MacDonald elucidates the point by commenting that there is a famous 1973 court case involving a comedian Yvon Deschamps whose image was used by an automobile company in an advertising campaign without his consent. Cf. judgement of Rothman J. in *Deschamps v. Renault Motors* (1977), Cahiers de droit 937 (Quebec Superior Court, 1972). For a brief description of the case, see J.E.C. Brierley and R.A. Macdonald, et al. *Quebec Civil Law* (Toronto: Emond Montgomery, 1993), pp. 156–157.

72 *Les Editions Vice-Versa Inc. v. Aubry* [1998] 1 S.C.R. 591, at 604.

73 *Ibid.*, at 605.

74 *Ibid.*, at 605.

become a "well-known figure" or that the instant proceedings and the media coverage they received increased her notoriety.

I side with the majority in this case. The majority court also resorted to the balancing method, weighing one against the other the right to information and the right to privacy. They acknowledged that a photograph of a single person can be "socially useful" because it serves to illustrate a theme. But that does not make it acceptable if it infringes on the right to privacy. The majority did not consider it appropriate to adopt the notion of "socially useful" for the purposes of legal analysis. The artistic expression of the photograph, which was alleged to illustrate contemporary urban life, cannot justify the infringement of the right to privacy it entails.[75] As the justices said, since the right to one's image is included in the right to respect for one's private life, it is manifest that every person possesses a protected right to her image. This right arises when the subject is recognizable. Consequently there is a breach of the person's right to her image, and therefore fault when the image is published without permission. In the name of the public's right to know, magazines should not send photographers to the streets to take photos of people to decorate their covers without the people's consent. It is one thing to publish a group photograph, when none of the faces is identifiable, and quite another to zoom in on one person and circulate his or her photo. It is one thing to take a photo of a public place where people are depicted *en masse* and quite another to use a public place as a background for showing a person who is the true subject of the photo. Justices L'Heureux-Dube and Bastarache have noted these differences in their judgement. They wrote that public interest prevails when a person appears in an incidental manner in a photograph of a public place. An image taken then can be regarded as an anonymous element of the scenery, even if it is technically possible to identify certain individuals. Since "the unforeseen observer's attention will normally be directed elsewhere, the person 'snapped without warning' cannot complain. The same is true of a person in a group photographed in a public place."[76] Such a person cannot object to the photograph's publication if she is not the principal subject.

75 *Ibid.*, at 618.
76 *Ibid.*, at 617.

In the case at hand, I do not see any reasonable justification or legitimate purpose in invading anyone's privacy without his or her consent. The arguments for freedom of expression and freedom of information in this context are simply not persuasive. No harm would be done if the photo of Aubry were to be replaced with a photograph of another young, beautiful woman who consented, or even was paid to appear on the magazine's cover. There are enough women who would be delighted to appear on a cover. The issue of prior knowledge and consent of those photographed are not immaterial. Of course, if consent is granted then no problem arises. But people should enjoy the freedom to remain anonymous if they so desire. For Aubry, this was not an abstract issue but a concrete contravention of her right to privacy. Her friends and peers at school teased her, and she felt humiliated. I side with the majority who thought that a teenager's damages are the logical, direct and immediate consequence of the fault, and that Aubry's sensitivity and the possibility of "being teased by her friends are eminently foreseeable."[77]

Furthermore, young Ms. Aubry did not do anything that is of public interest. She was just sitting in a shopping mall. There is a difference between a person who does something of public significance, and a person who, say, strolls the streets. If someone, for instance, is polishing a new public sign, or symbol, that person who is totally unknown to the public might be photographed not because of who he is, but rather because of what he does. In December 2001 newspapers around the world showed workers cleaning and shining the Euro signs, posted in order to promote awareness of the new currency in Europe. Even in this instance I would urge photographers to ask the workers whether they mind that their faces will be shown in public newspapers while they polish the shining yellow Euro signposts.

Chief Justice Lamer argued in his dissent that Ms. Aubry's statement, "people laughed at me," does not in itself constitute sufficient evidence of damage, because it did not provide any information about how she felt.[78] But surely no one would like to be laughed at. This statement shows that Ms. Aubry felt that the dissemination of her photo was wrong, and that it did cause her moral prejudice. As the Court of Quebec

---

77 *Ibid.,* at 620.
78 *Les Editions Vice-Versa Inc. v. Aubry,* para. 32 in Lamer CJ.'s judgement.

held, to learn through teasing by friends that Aubry's picture had been published in a prestigious, large-circulation magazine without her even knowing that her picture had been taken and without her authorization merits compensation for the humiliation, discomfort and upset suffered as a result of the invasion of her privacy. The majority of the Supreme Court adopted this opinion thinking that there was sufficient evidence regarding the discomfort and upset felt by Aubry as a result of the publication.[79]

Another issue concerns the commercial aspect of this affair. The magazine had used Aubry's photo because its editors thought that her looks would attract people's eye and the magazine's sales would be increased. It is only fair that Aubry should have her share in the business.

Cases like *Aubry* are different from cases involving public officials and celebrities. Diana had no say in taking her photograph and published it when appearing in public places. This is a price she had to pay for being "Queen of Hearts," and one should bear in mind that Diana had gained a lot in terms of publicity and fame. She protested against taking unauthorized private photos. Thus, consent is required to publish photos of ordinary citizens that were taken either in public or in private spheres, whereas when public officials and celebrities are concerned consent is required when photos are taken only in the private sphere.

Conclusion

Marshall McLuhan said that as we transfer our whole being to the data bank, privacy will become a ghost or echo of its former self and what remains of community will disappear.[80] While this vision may have been

---

79 *Les Editions Vice-Versa Inc. v. Aubry,* paras. 614–618, 621–622 of the majority judgement delivered by L'Heureux-Dube and Bastarache JJ. MacDonald added that the flaw in Lamer's argument is that it implicitly denies that the invasion of privacy can be a tort *per se*, like trespass to land. MacDonald maintained that to date the private law has been much more solicitous of protecting the integrity of land, than it has the integrity of people. For further discussion on privacy law in Canada, see http://www.privacyinfo.ca/

80 http://scholar.google.com/scholar?hl=en&lr=&q=cache:hRZqgP8A8EcJ:www. foothill.edu/~kmanske/Lecture_notes/PDF/Media_Culture.pdf+Marshall+McLuha n+privacy

exaggerated, we undoubtedly pay a price for developing the advanced technology we have today. Privacy has been eroding.

People are constantly gaining information about us. They see what we do, what we buy, what we look at, and the like. If they know who we are, and if they have enough financial incentive, they can record this information. If we engage in computerized transactions with them, such recording becomes very easy, as does combining this information with still other information tied to our names. If the transactions are personalized—if we voluntarily turn over information about ourselves that facilitates our business arrangement—then they will have even more information to record. And once they've recorded this information, they can easily communicate it to others.[81]

Jeffrey Rosen notes that privacy is a form of opacity, and opacity has its values. We need more shades, more blinds and more virtual curtains. By respecting the boundaries between public and private speech and conduct, a liberal state can provide sanctuaries from the invasions of privacy that are inevitable in social interactions.[82] The right of the ordinary people to protection of their image is more important than the right to publish photographs without obtaining permission.

An American case that comes to mind is *De Gregorio v. CBS*.[83] It concerned a news broadcast entitled "Couples in Love in New York" showing briefly the plaintiff, a married man, walking hand-in-hand with an unmarried female co-worker on a city street. When De Gregorio noticed that he was filmed he demanded the TV crew to destroy the film, advising the production manager that he was married and that his female friend was engaged to be married. Therefore, it would not "look good" to have a film of this hand-holding episode shown on television. The manager ignored his plea, a five-second segment of the plaintiff and his friend was included in the footage and, subsequently, De

---

81 Eugene Volokh, "Personalization and Privacy," *Communications of the ACM*, Vol. 43, Number 8 (2000), pp 84–88, available at http://delivery.acm.org/10.1145/350000/345155/p84-volokh.html?key1=345155&key2=8521300211&coll=GUID E&dl=ACM&CFID=48608443&CFTOKEN=41371649

82 Jeffrey Rosen, *The Unwanted Gaze* (New York: Random House, 2000), pp. 223–224. For critique of Rosen, see Robert C. Post, "Three Concepts of Privacy," *Georgetown Law Journal*, Vol. 89 (June 2001): 2087.

83 *Carl De Gregorio v. CBS Inc.*, 473 N.Y.S.2d 922, Supreme Court of New York (March 14, 1984).

Gregorio sued CBS alleging invasion of privacy, intentional infliction of emotional distress, *prima facie* tort and defamation.

The court ruled that plaintiff's five-second appearance on the broadcast without speaking or being identified by name was merely an incidental use and, thus, cannot form the basis for liability under the civil rights statute; the fact that the defendant may have earned a profit from the broadcast does not alter its right to depict matters of public interest. Moreover, since there was no false representation in the broadcast, constitutional principles of freedom of the press preclude any redress for the film clip.

As a matter of law, the court judgement may be the right one. However, the behavior of the TV crew is ethically flawed. The broadcast included numerous shots of couples walking down Fifth Avenue holding hands, romantically walking through Central Park, or embracing in other public places. Upon the explicit request of De Gregorio not to include him in the film, the film manager should have complied with the request. There was enough material without this specific scene. Furthermore, showing the plaintiff and his friend was not a crucial news item. It was no news at all. In the name of free speech, free press and the public's right to know, the CBS crew had no qualms to potentially harm two individuals for no good cause or reason.

The two fundamental background rights underlining every democracy are respect for others and not harming others.[84] They should not be held secondary to considerations of profit and personal prestige of journalists and newspapers. Media freedom does not entail, nor does it protect, the taking of unlimited measures designed to increase the sales of a newspaper or promoting the ratings for certain broadcasts.

Journalists should see people as ends and not as means – a Kantian deontological approach.[85] This view implies the ability to control the

---

84 Ronald Dworkin, "Liberalism," in *A Matter of Principle* (Oxford: Clarendon Press, 1985), pp. 181–204; *idem, Taking Rights Seriously* (London: Duckworth, 1976); R. Cohen-Almagor, "Between Neutrality and Perfectionism," *Canadian J. of Law and Jurisprudence,* Vol. VII, No. 2 (1994): 217–236.

85 See Immanuel Kant, *Foundations of the Metaphysics of Morals* (Indianapolis, Ind.: Bobbs-Merrill Educational Publishers, 1969). For further discussion, see Joseph Raz, *Value, Respect, and Attachment* (Cambridge: Cambridge University Press, 2001), esp. pp. 140–151. For elaborated analysis of the right to privacy v. public's

power that lies in the hands of media professionals when reporting in the name of the people's right to know might cause unjustified harm to others. These instances should be distinguished from incidents when the harm is justified. For instance, when a person acts corruptly, and there is evidence to prove it, the media are allowed, and even obliged, to look into the issue and bring it to public scrutiny. This is what is meant when calling the media "the watchdog of democracy."

---

right to know, see R. Cohen-Almagor, *The Scope of Tolerance* (London: Routledge, 2006), chaps. 2 and 3.

LIMOR SHIFMAN AND MENAHEM BLONDHEIM

13. From the Spider to the Web: Innis' Ecological Approach to the Evolution of Communication Technologies

Harold Adams Innis is widely considered a founding proponent of a technological deterministic approach to communication studies. One of the fundamental notions usually ascribed to such an approach is that technology is an autonomous, powerful force, emerging independently of social expectations. Technology, according to this view, is the independent stimulus, social change the dependent response (Bijker, 1997; MacKenzie & Wajcman, 1990; Smith & Marx, 1996). In this sense, at least, we fail to detect symptoms of technological determinism in Innis' writings about communications (Blondheim, 2003; Innis, 1951; 1972). Far from it: Innis, rather than considering communication technologies to emerge out of the blue unattached to social expectations, understood them to be engineered and launched in response to society's perceived needs, through purposeful social choices.

In a different sense, however, Innis the social constructivist cannot be easily exonerated from the onus of technological determinism. He shared with the technological deterministic straw man a notion elemental to the approach, namely, that once new technologies are launched they are destined to have a most significant impact on society. Focusing on communications, Innis averred that once a society develops, adopts, and applies a certain technology (or a set of technologies) affecting knowledge and its transfer, great effects on political, social, economic, and cultural processes within that society may be expected to follow.

The fundamental criterion Innis used to analyze media technologies and their effects was their location on a theoretical time-space axis he constructed. He found that some media were more effective in passing knowledge over time, whereas others were more effective in spreading knowledge across space. Moreover, he suggested that there was a trade-off between these variables; that the play of time and space was a zero-sum game. To illustrate: stone tablets are durable and effective in preserving the message they carry across time, but they are not easily transportable and therefore ineffective in distributing the message chiseled on them widely. In contrast, papyri are light and easy to transport, but they rot, burn, and blow away. Hence they are effective in spreading knowledge in space but not in maintaining it over time.

For Innis, the history of communication technologies, and given their potentially tremendous impact, human history generally, is a story of purposeful shifts between the poles of time and space. When society recognizes a bias towards either time or space in its media complex, it produces a counter bias in order to achieve equilibrium. For instance, when the media of a sociopolitical system are shaped to enhance its control over space, it has a problem with continuity, with control over time. Once that society becomes aware of the problem, it will strive to develop time-binding media. And of course, the more severe the imbalance, the more radical the process of change will be. In fact, we see the core of Innis' writings on communication as the description and analysis of the broader implications of bias versus balance in the communication environment and, ergo, in social conditions.

When Innis passed away, in 1952, television was in a primordial state, and global networks of computerized communications were at most elements of imaginative science fiction. Nevertheless, a half-century of deep-going change in the communication environment does not seem to have diminished the relevance of his analysis of media technologies. *Au contraire*: as communication environments become more and more complex, Innis' big-picture approach to their description and to the analysis of their evolution appears more relevant than ever.

In this article we attempt to verify what we understand as Innis' core proposition, namely, that societies introduce and adopt new communication technologies in an attempt to eradicate bias and achieve balance in their media environment and social arrangements. In order to test the validity of this proposition, we find it necessary to extend Innis' historical analysis in two different ways. Firstly, we elaborate his analytical framework, originally construed of the overall dimensions of time and space, by breaking the time-space axis to a framework of six dimensions, a meta-dimension, and a sub-dimension. These dimensions are what we have identified as basic attributes of all communication technology systems – from oral communication to the

Internet. Secondly, we extend Innis' analysis over time, by continuing the historical analysis beyond the time he passed away and all the way to the present. In other words, we will observe the play of the six dimensions of communication technologies from time immemorial to the near future.

In doing so, we will test Innis' proposition by juxtaposing it with an alternative approach to media development, which we tag the progressive theory of communication technology. The roots of the notion of progress in relation to technology can be traced back to the legacy of the Industrial Revolution, itself influenced by the ideas of the Enlightenment. The progressive approach was applied to the thinking on communication technologies and elaborated by members of the Chicago School, among them Dewey, Mead, Park and Cooley, individuals who were shaped by, as well as advocates of, the American Progressive Movement (Peters, 1999; Simonson, 2001). More broadly, the premise that change in communication technologies follows a path of continuous progress reflected and reinforced the deterministic notion of technological development as a force that can't move backwards. It inevitably points to the future, ushering in new and improved epochs.

In many ways, this conception of technology spelling inevitable progress is congruent with the prevalent contemporary rhetoric of a purported "communication revolution" sweeping the 21st century world to new frontiers. A series of charismatic, self-appointed apostles of an "information revolution" and "digital age," from Barlow to Bill Gates and from George Gilder to Gore and Gingrich, have effectively promoted a vision of global change ushered in by new, cutting-edge technologies as applied to communications. Alvin Toffler, for instance, describes in his popular books waves of human progress that culminate in the third wave of an information revolution, which is supposed to bring about dramatic and benign change in the lives of individuals, as well as to their societies and cultures, and the human family generally.

This approach found its way into academia too, launching serious and solid interpretations of media development on a continuous-progress trajectory. Thus, early on Schement and Stout (1988) argued that over time media shifted in the direction of greater speed, wider reach and greater flexibility. More recently Paul Levinson, in his insightful *The Soft Edge* (1997), described a process he entitles "human replay," by which "all media eventually become more and more human in their performance – that is, they facilitate communication that is increasingly like the ways human process information 'naturally,' or prior to the advent of given media" (xvi).

Two complementary propositions form the basis of the progress theory of media: that media development proceeds consistently along a single path, and that that path is positive in its nature. In this article we don't address the second proposition concerning the normative implications of media technologies. We are, however, interested in the first proposition regarding the direction of media evolution – a fundamental element of the progress approach. Innis, as noted, was opposed to the view of the development of communications as a march of progress. He argued instead that media evolution was characterized by a constant quest for equilibrium. In what follows, we put these contending notions to the test.

We pose the "directionality" quandary, a fundamental question of media evolution: Is the history of communication a story of technology-driven progress, of continuous improvement in communication (and hence in social conditions) paced by technological advances, as theories of modernity would lead us to believe? Or is it as Innis held – pointing to post-modern sensibilities – a story of a constant back and forth movement between dysfunctional bias and healthy balance?

As we have seen, Innis buttressed his approach by way of demonstrating the shifting emphasis on technologies of space and technologies of time in the *longue duree* of communication history. In what follows, we too put the competing approaches to the historical test, but a much more detailed one. We break down the attributes of communication technologies to a larger number of elements, or dimensions, and trace the direction of historical change on each of these dimensions. Our intent in doing so is to verify either the unidirectional assumption of the progressive approach or the proposition of vicissitudes in the quest of balance, which follows from Innis' theory of communication.

Taxonomies of Media Technology

The detailed framework for analyzing communication technologies proposed below is universal in nature, making possible the comparison of media from different eras and environments. It is not, however, the first attempt at shaping an effective taxonomy of communication technologies. Among the earliest was a systematic Charles Horton Cooley (1998) proposed, comprising of four basic dimensions for characterizing communication technologies. It included permanence (i.e., "the overcoming of time"), swiftness (i.e., "the overcoming of space"), diffusion (a space-oriented measure of the size of the audience), and expressiveness (an aspect of the messages enabled by the medium). Cooley's taxonomy was followed by Innis' time-space dimension, and later yet by McLuhan's (1964) cognitive test of "hot" and "cold" media.

The rapid and thoroughgoing changes in communication environments during past decades brought about new attempts to characterize fundamental dimensions of media technologies. One group of studies responded to the expanding new universe of communication technologies by focusing on sub-spheres within the larger communication milieu. Thus, for instance, Steuer (1995) investigated the virtual reality sphere, Durlak (1987) analyzed interactive communications, and Schramm (1977) focused on media as tools for education. Our analysis is broader in its outlook, aimed at creating a universal typology that can be used to analyze the communication environment as a whole.

In this sense, our framework is closer to those suggested by Lievrouw and Finn (1990), Finn and Lane (1998), Finn (2002) and Van Dijk (1999) – all focusing on constructing universal media typologies. However, it differs from those models in three major ways: Firstly, we don't deal, as some of these models do, with technological features that effect aspects of the communicative process which are below the threshold of human sensual perception. Secondly, some of these frameworks include in their range of analysis social or psychological factors, whereas our framework focuses solely on communicative-technological dimensions, i.e., dimensions that stem from technology and have direct and substantial implications for the communication circuit of messenger–message–receiver. Finally, we use this framework not only as a static tool to describe specific media environments, as the above and other models do (usually with reference to contemporary media ecologies), but mainly as a tool for analyzing processes of long-term change.

The six dimensions framework

The framework here proposed consists of six basic dimensions, one meta-dimension, and one sub-dimension. Some of these dimensions form part of previous models, others are unique to the present model. These latter elements were found to be necessary components of a comprehensive analytical tool, applicable to any technology, in any era of communications history.

Morphology: The form of communicated information. While the most basic morphological divide is between the aural and the visual, we here consider voice, script, picture, and moving picture as basic forms. Another possible differential is the division between analogue and digital representations. However, digital is a secondary coding system imperceptible to human senses, and since the present taxonomy does not go beyond what meets the human eye or ear, it is not considered here a fundamental morphology. The divide between digital and analogue is, however, relevant to this analysis in the effects of digital representation on modulation, transformation, and convergence of different morphologies (Lunefeld, 1998).

Scalability: The scale and scope of audiences. This variable identifies the constituency for receiving communicated messages, taking into account the dimensions of both time and space. It features a basic division between one-to-one communications, what we call pointcast transmission (e.g., fax, telephone) and one-to-many communications, which may be divided into three types, or levels:

Narrowcast – for instance a newsgroup or a local cable channel;

Broadcast – generally a transmission on a national scale, for instance NBC, BBC, or newspapers of national circulation;

Globecast – A transmission that reaches international or global audiences, such as CNN, MTV via satellite or the Internet.

Scalability, as has been noted, is determined not only by the space dimension, but also by time. Thus, a televized news broadcast may expose a very large audience to a single message simultaneously, but a book can accumulate readers over the course of many years. Scalability is therefore affected by the next dimension: Synchronicity.

Synchronicity: The time plan for completing the communication circuit. The most salient division on this temporal dimension is between communication in real-time and communications in which sender and receiver are separated in time. An example of the former is a live television broadcast; an email message is an example for the latter. However, this dimension is not as dichotomous as it might appear: even in communications that are considered to take place in real-time, like a radio show, a certain interval separates the sending and receiving of signals, an interval we cannot sense.

Directionality: The direction of the flow of information. The basic division of media by this variable yields three clusters of media technologies:

One-way technologies – technologies that can only be used for communications in one way, for instance print or microphone.

Two-way technologies – technologies that are designed to enable communications between two or more parties, such as the telephone.

Neutral technologies – technologies that enable both one-way and two-way communications, and the users decide how to apply them. For example, a satellite transponder can be employed for either one-way broadcast or two-way telecommunications.

A further division between media emerges from the combination of this dimension with synchronicity: via some media messages can flow up- and downstream simultaneously, but via others only intermittently. Directionality, however, should not be confused with symmetry: some technological systems, such as telephony, allow for symmetry of both ends, while others, such as a two-way cable plant, feature a dramatic asymmetry between upstream and downstream communications.

Nodality: The spatial and accessibility attributes of the node, or terminal. This variable, which incorporates the man-machine interface (Golding, 1998; Meyrowitz, 1986; Rice, 2001), highlights the difference between stationary and moving nodes, and in addressability, a feature in which there is a salient division between station-to-station and person-to-person architectures of the node. This latter variable also reflects accessibility and user-friendliness of the terminal.

Mode: The attributes of the device, which reflect or determine the relationship of sender and receiver with regard to the information transmitted. This parameter encompasses differences between push plans, in which the information and the initative is on one side (e.g., TV, fax), and pull plans, which are based on the receiver's active initiative (e.g., a Web homepage, the act of buying a book) (Brodewijk & Van Kaam, 1982).

In addition to these six fundamental dimensions, and although not essential criteria, a meta-dimension and a sub-dimension improve the usefulness of this matrix as a heuristic tool:

Connectivity: Connectivity is proposed as a meta-dimension due to its powerful grouping of the six fundamental ones. Connectivity refers to the existence of a direct connection between senders and receivers through a technological channel. The basic division here is between networked media (for example, telephone, television, the Internet) and standalones, such as a books or a CD player (Kittler, 1997).

Throughput: While only a second-degree characteristic, throughput, which incorporates the co-variables of volume of information, velocity of its transmission, and the bandwidth of the carrier, is useful as an aggregative shorthand.

Patterns of Historical Development

In what follows, we apply the six-dimension framework to a historical review of media technologies. This analysis addresses the "directionality problem" in the evolution of communication technologies. It attempts to find support for either the notion of progress along a single trajectory, or the notion of a pendulum movement of bias and counter-bias in the cause of balance in the media environment. In this analysis, the overall pattern of media evolution is broken down into six composite-problems, according to the foregoing six-dimension framework.

Morphology: The story of morphology begins with script, which we consider the first communication technology, as it came into competition with primordial orality, namely, voice. Script dominated the media environment for a very long period, spanning the use of tablets and manuscripts, then books, newspapers and telegrams. From the middle of the 19th century the script bias was challenged by two new communication technologies: photography, which represented a new form of realistic visual communication, and the telephone, which enabled the transmission of voice over distance in real time. Whereas the significance of photography in this analysis is mainly as the seed of the moving realistic picture, which would become dominant only half a century later, the telephone brought about an immediate and marked change in the communication environment. It signaled the accelerated development of voice-based media such as phonograph and radio.

These two media increased the bias towards voice, but this state of affairs changed again with the invention of cinema and television, then coaxial cable and satellites – four media combining moving pictures with sound, and creating a strong bias towards this particular combination of morphologies. This bias was corrected in the 70s and 80s with media such as fax and telex – which were based on script, and by the DVD and cellular telephones in the voice department. The Internet, which combines all four morphologies: voice, script, picture and moving picture, can be seen as a "meta-correction" creating a new equilibrium on this dimension.

The pattern of change in the Morphology dimension, as illustrated in Chart 1, is thus a pattern of biases and balances, rather than a pattern of development in a single direction. Even when a single morphology, such as print, is dominant for a long period, it would eventually be balanced by media that operates on other morphologies.

Chart 1: Morphology

	orality	script	book	newspaper	photo	telegraph	phone	phonograph	silent movies	radio	tape recorder	cinema	TV	CATV	satellite	telex	fax	VCR	cellular	CD	DVD	internet
moving picture									■			■	■	■	■			■			■	■
picture				▓	▓																	▓
script		▓	▓	▓		▓										▓	▓					▓
voice	▓						▓	▓		▓	▓	▓	▓	▓	▓				▓	▓	▓	▓

Scalability: Here, again, we can detect fluctuations from pointcast to broader forms and vice versa, as illustrated in Chart 2. In its oral era, communication was limited to relatively short distances (delivering oral messages over the long-haul corrupted them). Script, and to a larger extent print made it possible to increase the communicative reach, up to mass-scales of books and newspapers. At the same time, script and print improved the preservation of massages over long periods of time. This enabled more readers to be exposed to the same products over time, increasing the scale of audiences.

In the age of electricity the telegraph was used on both pointcast and broadcast plans. While the point-to-point application of telegraphy is well known and intuitive, its application as a broadcast medium was at least as important. It affected the sending of single messages such as news or stock reports simultaneously over regional and national circuits, to numerous receivers (Blondheim, 1994; 2000). Point-to-point and broadcast schedules continued to develop side by side in the early days of wireless, until radio and then television biased the ecology towards broadcast. This bias persisted in the 50s and the 60s, but in the 70s and 80s it was balanced by the emergence of global satellite networks and by cable TV. The expanded bandwidth allowed for narrowcast applications, and systems could be established to serve relatively small areas and audiences. Another corrective to the bias of broadcast was brought about by fax and telex, pointcast media par excellence.

Thus, just like on the dimension of morphology, media evolution on the scalability dimension followed a back-and-forth, to and fro course. Contrary to the constant progress approach, which would lead us to expect continuous increases in reach of media and scales of audiences, stopping only at the global communication, the history of media is characterized by vicissitudes of broadening and narrowing of communication spheres. Processes tending to globalization and to localization appear to overlap and complement each other sequentially. These overlapping processes become especially salient when we consider the Internet, which combines point-to-point communications such as email, narrowcast communications such as MUDs, MOOs and newsgroups, and internationally available data sources, let alone globecasts.

Chart 2: Scalability

	orality	script	book	newspaper	photo	telegraph 1	telegraph 2	phone	phonograph	silent movies	radio 1	radio 2	tape record.	inema	TV	CATV	satellite	telex	fax	VCR	cellular	CD	DVD	internet
global																								
broad																								
narrow																								
point																								

The next three dimensions to be considered: Synchronicity, Directionality and Mode, are reflected, to a considerable extent, by the meta-dimension of connectivity, and therefore can be seen to follow a similar pattern of change.

Synchronicity – The watershed transformation from the synchronous oral to asynchronous script was followed by a long period of relative stability in this dimension of communications. It was ended abruptly on the day the telegraph was born. Chart 3, in describing subsequent historical movement on the synchronicity dimension might remind one (hopefully, none of our readers), of the electrocardiogram (ECG) of a person suffering a heart attack. And indeed, the launching of practically every new synchronous technology was followed by the emergence of an asynchronous one.

These radical changes can be partly explained by the fact that standalones are asynchronous in nature (first the sender produces the message, and only then is it duplicated and distributed), whereas networked media tend to facilitate simultaneity. Since the invention of telegraph, almost every synchronous medium has been followed by an asynchronous one, balancing it in the communication environment. For example: immediately after the asynchronous silent film, synchronous radio was developed, then came asynchronous talkies, subsequently synchronous television, and so on.

The fluctuations of the synchronicity dimension reinforce the pattern that emerged in the analysis of the previous dimensions, a pattern of biases, counter bias, and overall balance. Once again, the survey yields the Innisian dynamic rather than the plan of progress along one, single, trajectory.

Chart 3: Synchronicity

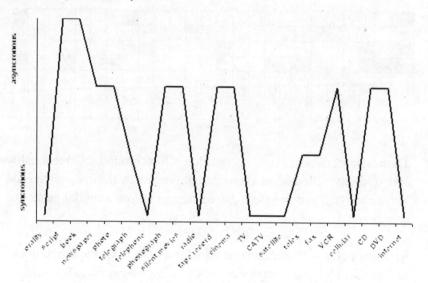

Directionality – The fluctuations on this dimension may be ascribed to a triple distinction between standalone media (usually used for one-way communication), networked interpersonal communications (usually used for two-way communication) and networked mass communication. Until the 80s, networked mass communication was mainly used in a one-way plan, but cable and satellite TV opened the option of two-way applications. The mosaic created from the gradual evolution within and between those media families – networked and standalones – is one of intermittent movement and reciprocity between one- and two-way media.

Mode – In this dimension, likewise, we can distinguish between the standalones, which are based on active pulling by receivers, and networked media, which enable greater diversify of push and pull plans. Similar to the pattern characterizing synchronicity, we find recurring fluctuations on the mode dimension between push and pull technologies.

The last dimension, **Nodality**, follows a slightly different course from that found in the previous dimensions. When analyzing the development of each discrete technology, we find that over time they tend to become cheaper, more friendly to users, and more accessible. For instance, in its beginnings, radio was a large and cumbersome appliance, that was difficult to operate, but over the years it became smaller and simpler, ultimately taking the shape of a tiny pocket item or headset.

In this sense, Nodality comes closest to the progressive notion of communication technologies. However, the constant progress pattern only fits the historical development of each medium separately. Once the perspective shifts from single media to developments within the broader communication environments, one finds that every new medium shifts the nodality dimension dramatically, creating new accessibility problems. Hence, this dimension too, which at first sight may appear exceptional, follows the by now familiar pattern of continuous vicissitudes from balance to bias and back again.

Conspectus and Conclusion

Seldom do investigations of competing scholarly propositions, such as the forgoing evaluation of the Innisian and progressive approaches to the development of communication technologies, reach such a decisive, one-sided conclusion. It would appear that the particular topos of the controversy – communication technology – may account, in a significant way, for this unusual outcome.

Communication, viewed as the process of linking minds through the transference of information, is essentially a single phenomenon; nevertheless, the process can be carried out in a myriad ways, and take on a great variety of forms. Technologies enable some of these forms, and enhance others, but once they are launched they promote particular plans of communication, and inevitably retard others. Innis viewed the shifting combinations of various forms of communication as an ecology seeking equilibrium. The application of a new technology to enhance a certain dimension of the process, he realized, both reflected and effected a state of imbalance in the ecology of communications.

With a certain plan enhanced by effective technologies, the imbalance would tend to develop into a general bias towards the privileged form of communications, swamping as it were other forms of communicating. This would make room for a corrective by way of technologically empowering the repressed forms, so as to restore balance to the system.

However, given the emphasis society had placed on the technologically enhanced set of communicative options, the resurgence of the repressed features, as well as the restoration of balance to the communication environment as a whole, would appear to represent a revolutionary departure.

This recurrent notion of revolutionary change, so characteristic of the reception of new communication technologies, may well be the origin of the progressive theory. The perceived historical sequence of dramatic change in communications could understandably be misread as a march of progress. Yet as this study shows, the notion of novelty and revolution with regard to communication technologies could well be a chimera, one that Innis and very few other observers did not fall for.

To illustrate, the telegraph was extremely effective in facilitating written communications on a one-way, asynchronous plan. Its ascendance in the mid-19th century both represented and affected an extreme imbalance in the communication environment. This bias retarded the development of alternative plans of communicating, but once voice and two-way synchronous emerged with the phonograph and telephone, their diffusion was dramatic. So much so that the consequent dominance of synchronous voice (and later video) with the telephone and phonograph, later radio and TV, at first seriously handicapped, but then made inevitable, the resurgence of written asynchronous with the telex, fax, email and other such media.

Similarly, the dominance of radio and TV underscored an imbalance towards the real-time, one-to-many forms. The dramatic shrinking of network TV's share in the media market over the past decade underscores the vengeance with which two-way communication and narrowcasting, as unleashed by increased bandwidth, alternative infrastructures and as performed over Internet, small satellite dish, and microwave transmissions technologies, have been filling in the void and eradicating the bias.

These media, we have seen, the Internet in particular, have generated a lavish rhetoric of a communication/information/digital revolution. Digital communications indeed represent a major reshuffling of forms and plans of communication – a new deal – made possible by a new technological concept, in response to individual and social needs. Digital processing which enables the rapid and smooth modulation of morphologies ("multimedia") works to converge communication systems that were formerly differentiated by morphologies of the delivered contents. At the same time, compression of digital packages and streams, accompanied by the conquest of previously unused ranges of the spectrum and the laying of new infrastructures (e.g., fiberoptic) dramatically increase throughputs. This, in turn, would have significant implications on scalability and directionality in making possible at the same time a greater reach for given content as well as more programming, inevitably diversified and specialized. The packet-switching architecture of digital content is at the core of the new-found flexibilites in synchronicity and scalability.

At first, the development of digital communications was severely restricted by limitations of nodality and mode. Digital communications developed in a telephone network dominated environment, with computers (first terminals, then PCs) as the default endware. Telephone-like plans of communication therefore dominated the modes of message-flow, and computers constrained the vision of the man-machine interface. These circumstances were the source of a bias which inhibited broadcast-like distribution of data, and also limited the potential variety of nodes. Due to this latter constraint, the problem of data-gap – of populations disunited by the criterion of their computer literacy – have emerged. However, with the migration of digital applications to broadcast infrastructures these biases are in the process of eradication, enabling data broadcast (to the extent of interactive programming), and convergence of nodes (e.g., Internet on TV, cellular). Thus, digital came to encompass the full spectrum of historical communicative applications.

Their realignment in the context of a changed world-order, transformed economy, and redefined social structures serves to highlight the way a major process of rebalancing can be understood as revolution, a step on an imagined ladder of progress. Innis would have understood the process for what it is – a major act of balancing. He had never thought of the possibility, however, that a major new technology can not only correct biases, but possibly also prevent the appearance of any new ones.

References

Bijker, W. E. (1997). *Of Bicycles, Bakelites, and Bulbs: Toward a Theory of Sociotechnical Change.* Cambridge: MIT Press.

Blondheim, M. (1994). *News over the Wires: The Telegraph and the Flow of Public Information in America, 1844–1897.* Cambridge: Harvard University Press.

Blondheim, M. (2003). Harold Adams Innis and his Bias of Communication. In: Katz, E., et al. (Eds.). *Canonic Texts in Communication Research*, London: Polity Press, 2002, pp. 156–190.

Blondheim, M. (2000). The Click: Telegraphic Technology, the Press, and the Transformations of the Associated Press. *American Journalism* 17 (Fall 2000): 27–52.

Brodewijk, J. L., & Van Kaam, B. (1986). Towards a Classification of New Tele-Information Sevices. *Intermedia* 14(1): 16–21.

Cooley, C. H. (1998). The Significance of Communication. In: Schubert, H.J. (Ed.). *On Self and Social Organization*, Chicago: University of Chicago Press, pp. 100–109.

Durlak, J. T. (1987). A Typology for Interactive Media. In: McLaughlin, M.L. (Ed). *Communication Yearbook* 10: 743–56. Newbury Park, Cal.: Sage.

Finn, T. A., & Lane, D. R. (1998). *A Conceptual Framework for Organizing Communication and Information Systems.* Paper presented at the International Communication Association Conference, Jerusalem.

Finn, T. A. (2002) *Communication and Information Technology (CIT) Model.* http://mason.gmu.edu/~afinn/

Golding, P. (1998). Worldwide Wedge: Division and Contradiction in the Global Information Interface In: Tussu, D.K. (Ed.). *Electronic Empires: Global Media and Local Resistance.* London: Arnold.

Innis, H. A. (1951). *The Bias of Communication.* Toronto: University of Toronto Press.

Innis, H. A. (1972). *Empire and Communication.* Toronto: University of Toronto Press.

Kittler, F. A. (1997). Gramophone, Film, Typewriter. In: Kittler, F. A. (Ed.). *Literature, Media, Information Systems.* Amsterdam: Overseas Publishers Association.

Levinson, P. (1997). *The Soft Edge.* London & New York: Routledge.

Lievrouw, L. A., & Finn, T. A. (1990). Identifying the Common Dimensions of Communication: The Communication Systems Model. In: Liverouw, L. A., & Ruben, B. D. (Eds.). *Mediation, Information, and Communication.* New Brunswick and London: Transaction Publishers.

Lunefeld, P. (1998). Screen Grabs: The Digital Dialectic and New Media Theory. In: Lunefeld, P. (Ed). *New Essays on New Media.* Cambridge & London: MIT Press, pp. 14–21.

MacKenzie, D., & Wajcman, J. (1990). *The Social Shaping of Technology: How the Refrigerator Got its Hum.* Buckingham: Open University Press.

McLuhan, M. (1964). *Understanding Media: The Extension of Man.* New York: McGraw Hill .

Meyrowitz, J. (1986). *No Sense of Place.* New York: Oxford University Press.

Peters, J. D. (1999). *Speaking into the Air: A History of the Idea of Communication.* Chicago: University of Chicago Press.

Rice, R. (2001). Primary Issues in Internet Use: Access, Civic and Community Involvement, and Social Interaction and Expression. In: Liverouw, L. A., & Livingstone, S. (Eds.). *Handbook of New Media.* London: Sage, pp. 105–130.

Schement, J., & Stout, D. A. (1988). A Time Line of Information Innovation. In: Ruben, B. D. (Ed.). *Information and Behavior*, vol III Rutgers: Transaction Books, pp. 395–423.

Schramm, W. (1977). *Big Media, Little Media: Tools and Technologies for Instruction.* Beverly Hills: Sage.

Simonson, P. (2001). Varieties of Pragmatism and Communication: Visions and Revisions from Peirce to Peters. In: Perry, D. (Ed.). *Pragmatism and Communication Research.* Mahway, NJ: Lawrence Erlbaum, pp. 1–26.

Smith, M.R., & Marx, L. (1996). *Does Technology Drive History? The Dilemma of Technological Determinism.* Cambridge: MIT Press.

Steuer, J. (1995). Defining Virtual Reality: Dimensions Determining Telepresence. In: Biocca, F., & Levi, M. (Eds.). *Communication in the Age of Virtual Reality.* Hillsdale: Lawrence Erlbaum Associations.

Van Dijk, J. (1999). *The Network Society: Social Aspects of New Media.* London: Sage.

Afterword

DAVID R. OLSON,

Whatever Happened to the Toronto School?

The excitement that greeted the publication of McLuhan's *The Gutenburg Galaxy* in 1962 and in *Understanding Media* two years later is now difficult to imagine. Indeed, in Canada, McLuhan remains a revered icon frequently mentioned in the popular press. The enthusiasm for McLuhan brought with it a renewed interest in Harold Innis' *The Bias of Communication* (1951) and in Eric Havelock's *Preface to Plato* (1963). These three along with a few acolytes including myself were first labeled the "Toronto School" by Jack Goody, himself a leading theorist of culture and communication (Goody, 1986; 1987). Walter Ong, who was deeply influenced by McLuhan, developed perhaps the most coherent account of the impact of literate practices on culture and mentality in his book *Orality and Literacy* (1982). The best account of the background of the formation of the theory linking communication and culture, written from a first-person perspective and written only months before his death in 1990, is Havelock's "The oral-written equation: a formula for the modern mind" (Havelock, 1991).[1] Derrick DeKerckhove (1986) and Robert Logan (2004) have done much to keep McLuhanism, the more literal readings of McLuhan, alive.

Current scholarship owes two large debts to these formative documents of the Toronto School. First, they essentially created a new field of research and study. Although the "media" were studied

---

1   Havelock presented his paper orally at the University of Toronto with a clear and steady voice despite of his obvious frailty. When his voice faltered part way through his lecture, he retrieved a glass of rum mixed with honey from under the podium and took a long draft adding "I wish I could share this with you but I assure you my need is greater."

in terms of their content at least since the time of Lazarsfeld and other students of popular culture, the Toronto School denied that new media simply spread the same information as earlier media, insisting rather that the media themselves put an indelible stamp on the structure of knowledge and on the "mentality" of their users. Admittedly, it has not succeeded in convincing the intellectual world of the truth of its central claims, but they do remain as lively perspectives on current research. And secondly, these volumes remain monuments of erudition. Almost any page of McLuhan's writings can cause a modern reader to pause and wonder. "Print created individualism and nationalism in the 16th century" (McLuhan, 2003, p. 33) or "Typography ended parochialism and tribalism" (p. 233) or "typography... brought in nationalism, industrialism, mass markets, and universal literacy and education" (p. 235). Properly contextualized and nuanced, the pronouncements are among the most remarkable conjectures of the century.

So why have Innis and McLuhan not held the respect they once garnered? In my view it is because the theories that were suggested to explain these changes were too ambitious. Innis tried to explain the properties of empire in terms of communication, Egypt "binding time" through lapidary monuments, Rome "binding space" through paper. McLuhan, not to be outdone, summarized Innis' view thus: "The Roman road was a paper route" (McLuhan, 2003, p. 126). Time and space may be not carry the explanatory power that Innis attributed to them. For example, writing preserves information through time and across space and, thus, may have been as important to the formation of law and bureaucracies working through time as to the distribution of information across space. While the hypostatized variables, time and space, adopted by Innis to explain the impact of the media seem inadequate, it does not follow that the historical epochs to be explained are not affected in important ways by the media.

McLuhan's explanations also appear unequal to the task. He tied his explanations of the effects of the media to the "bias" of the senses. He contrasted oral and written cultures in terms of the ear versus the eye, the bias of visual media was said to articulate, to analyze, to develop fixed perspective. In one of his dazzling apercus he linked the rise of printing to the development of perspective in Western art. In later years he tried to attach these apparently perceptual effects to the specialized cerebral hemisphere, the so-called "right-brain" versus "left-brain." Indeed, it is not inconceivable that given the new enthusiasm for the brain sciences that the sensory and cognitive aspects of McLuhan's theory will have a revival. But I believe this would be a step backward. It may be argued, as Goody (1987) and I (Olson, 1994) have done, that McLuhan was largely correct about the relation between media and mentality – there is indeed such a thing as a literate mentality which differs in important ways from an oral mentality – but it is to be explained, not by appeal to the bias of the senses, but by appeal to the "technologies of the intellect" that the media make available. These technologies include such straightforward devices as dictionaries, logics, tables, formularies, lists, recipes, formulas, algorithms and ultimately computer programs and bureaucracies.

Exploring culture and consciousness from this later perspective has turned out to be extraordinarily productive. Elizabeth Eisenstein's monumental *The Printing Press as an Agent of Change* (1979) and Brian Stock (who Goody included as a member of the Toronto school), author of *The Implications of Literacy* (1983), showed that substantial social and cognitive change was bound up with the availability of fixed texts and private silent reading. My own attempt, in *The World on Paper* (1994), was to show how the cultural conception of knowledge changed from that of the wise man to that of the archival source with the rise of literacy. Not only did knowledge change, the conceptual categories for operating on that knowledge changed as well to include distinctions between theory and evidence, on one hand, and truth and validity, on the other. Inculcating these and other such epistemological distinctions through formalized schooling is what creates what we now refer to as a literate mentality.

I will conclude by describing two recent books by historians that demonstrate that the study of culture can no longer ignore the transformative role of written documents in social and mental life in both antique cultures and in contemporary modernizing ones. One of them, by Cambridge historian Simon Franklin (2002), shows how documentary practices and bureaucratic social organization spread through the land of the Rus beginning in 10th century. These practices had been imported from Byzantium with the adoption of the Christian religion and were then to spread over a period of three centuries into many aspects of government, economic and social life. The other, by University of Toronto historian Sean Hawkins (2002), shows how the documentary practices of the colonial British power were imposed on the traditional practices of the LoDagaa of Ghana. Both show in precise detail how "power came to reside in writing" (p. 328) and how "writing was a necessary condition and component part of, a crucial enabling device... [for] the changes in social and cultural life," including the economy, the structures of authority, international politics, and political ideology, as well as "for the urban environment, for aesthetic standards, for public and private behavior" (Franklin, 2002, p. 279).

Both books take as indicative of written culture the enterprise of turning social practices into explicit categories, rules and laws. Hawkins gives a fascinating portrayal of how the British, in attempting to impose colonial power systematically misread traditional LoDagaa cultural practices by trying to impose their well-defined bureaucratic categories on them. For example, in regard to marriage, the British were first baffled by social practices that allowed a woman to change partners and for children to be unconcerned about biological paternity. The British formal categories of "married" and "father" rendered a large part of local practice as deviant. The law courts attempted to "shape the identities of LoDagaa women as wives, to define their relationships with men as marriage, and to use the concept of adultery to punish younger and less powerful men and so prevent them from eloping with the wives of older men and chiefs. However, the courts' use of concepts such as wife, marriage, and adultery was highly problematic because of the lack of commensurability between indigenous practices and these categories of colonial control" (Hawkins, 2002, p. 229).

Similarly, in imposing the rule of law the British were appalled to find, as one colonial officer claimed, that "there are no criminal laws among these pagans" (Hawkins, 2002, p. 161). Conflicts were resolved, not by appealing to a rule or law, but by dispute: "The ensuing discussion is confusing, it is laborious, and [yet] it generally ends in agreement" (p. 240). Hawkins argues that the problem arose from the descriptive dilemma facing observers. They are torn between the actual social practices of the indigenous people or the written categories brought by the British occupiers: "The use of writing has resulted in a series of misrepresentations:... culture became ethnicity, paths became roads, memory became history, scarification patterns became clothes, Earth priests became chiefs, god became God, noumenal knowledge became political power, arrows became summonses, cowries became coins, speech became writing, actions became words, practices became rules, conjugal payments became blood, and women became wives only" (Hawkins, 2002, pp. 323-324). The LoDagaa now live under the jurisdiction of writing, of formal categories, rules, norms and laws. Yet, as Hawkins points out, this newly-arrived document culture penetrates only peripherally into the daily lives of the people. Franklin analyzes the form, content and function of every piece of writing surviving in the "land of the Rus" from the earliest times up to the Mongol invasions of the 13th century. He shows how writing came to serve not only a communicative convenience but as a formal record or document and as a part of official procedure. In the 10th century the Rus adopted a Cyrillic writing system, an alphabetic system developed by St. Cyril, along with the bureaucratic structures of the Eastern Catholic Church. While monastic life was ordered by written rules and the acceptance of written codes was essential to the Christian identity, the rest of social and economic life was not. How the formation of rules, laws, norms and standards spread to become part of social life more generally is examined in detail. Franklin points out that the Primary Chronicle for 1051 set out the Rules for "how to sing the monastic offices, how to make prostrations, how to read the lessons, and standing in church, and all the church rites, and sitting at table, and what to eat on which days, all according to regulation" (Franklin, 2002, p. 144). This attitude to rules diffused through the society so that written rules came to have authority. Over the 11th and 12th centuries rule-lists expanded to cover a range of social activities beginning with rules on homicide, injury, theft, penalties for killing the prince's stable master, for the theft of a boat, a dove, a dog, a goat, or hay" (pp. 156–157). In the period examined, this rule-list "mentality" spread widely but never became a part of a pervasive cultural pattern. Local activities continued relatively unfazed by this writing revolution.

Both writers insist that this social change is not merely the transcription of custom into written form. In the case of the LoDagaa, the written was borrowed and superimposed on local practice. For the Rus, where this development was more indigenous, writing turned a precedent into a norm or rule. At first it is unclear whether procedures are adopted because they follow the rule or if the rule is derivative from the procedure but by the late 13th century the written "did acquire a kind of 'constitutional' aura as a unitary written rule-code which was formed and maintained in a land without a unitary structure of authority" (Franklin, 2002, p. 158).

Both books emphasize the importance of documentary practices in the "scripting" of social relations, in the formalization of concepts and categories and in the realignment of authority between the oral practices and the written record. Thus, even if such histories frame their analysis neither in terms of space and time nor in terms of the bias of the senses, they nonetheless advance the more basic agenda of the Toronto School, namely, the role that the media of representation and communication play both in the form and structure of social systems and of the mentalities of those who participate in them.

References

DeKerckhove, D. (1986). Alphabetic literacy and brain processes. *Visible language, XX,* 27–293.

Eisenstein, E. (1979). *The printing press as an agent of change.* Cambridge: Cambridge University Press.

Franklin, S. (2002). *Writing, society and culture in early Rus, c. 950–1300.* Cambridge: Cambridge University Press.

Goody, J. (1986). *The logic of writing and the organization of society.* Cambridge: Cambridge University Press.

Goody, J. (1987). *The interface between the oral and the written.* Cambridge: Cambridge University Press.

Hawkins, S. (2002). *Writing and colonialism in Northern Ghana: The encounter between the LoDagaa and "the world on paper."* Toronto: University of Toronto Press.

Havelock, E. (1963). *Preface to Plato.* Cambridge: Cambridge University Press.

Havelock, E. (1991). The oral-literate equation: A formula for the modern mind. In D. R. Olson & N. G. Torrance, Eds., *Literacy and orality.* Cambridge: Cambridge University Press.

Innis, H. (1951). *The bias of communication.* Toronto: University of Toronto Press.

Logan, R. (2004). *The alphabet effect: A media ecology understanding of the making of western civilization.* New York: Hampton Press.

McLuhan, M. (1962). *The Gutenberg galaxy: The making of typographic man.* Toronto: University of Toronto Press.

McLuhan, M. (2003). *Understanding media: The extensions of man.* Critical edition edited by W. T. Gordon. Corte Madera, Cal.: Ginko Press. Original edition published in 1964. (Unlike the original the critical edition contains a helpful index.)

Olson, D. R. (1994). *The world on paper: The conceptual and cognitive implications of writing and reading.* Cambridge: Cambridge University Press.

Ong, W. (1982). *Orality and literacy: The technologizing of the word.* London: Methuen.

Stock, B. (1983). *The implications of literacy.* Princeton: Princeton University Press.

List of Contributors

Hanna Adoni

is Associate Professor of Communication and Information Studies at the Hebrew University of Jerusalem. She is a former Chair of the Department of Communication and Journalism at the Hebrew University, a former director of the Smart Family Institute for Communications and former editor of *Devarim Achadim: The Israel Journal of Communication, Culture and Society*. Since the year 2000 Hanna Adoni is incumbent of the Danny Arnold Chair in Communication at the Hebrew University of Jerusalem. Her research interests are in the area of mass communication and cultural behavior, with special emphasis on media technologies and their effect on different types of literacy and the construction of social identities. She has published extensively on these subjects and she is a co-author of *Social Conflict and Television News* (1990), and *Twenty Years of Communication and Culture*.

Gene Allen

is Associate Professor in the School of Journalism at Ryerson University in Toronto. Before joining Ryerson's faculty in 2001, he worked for more than 20 years as a newspaper editor and reporter (mostly at the Toronto Globe and Mail) and as a producer of news and documentaries for CBC Television. He first became interested in the work of Harold Innis while a graduate student in Canadian history at the University of Toronto, with an emphasis on historical geography, economic and business history and the history of transportation. Since returning to academic work, he has begun researching subjects in the history of journalism and in this context has developed a greater interest in Innis' later work on communications. Allen is currently working on a history of the Canadian Press news agency.

Menahem Blondheim

is Associate Professor in Communications and American studies at the Hebrew University of Jerusalem, and serves as the director of the university's Smart Family Institute of Communications. He holds a BA degree from the Hebrew University, and MA and PhD degrees from

Harvard University. A major focus of his research work is the study
of the history of communications and communications in history. A
former entrepreneur and executive in the communication technology
sector of Israel's high-tech industry, he also studies the development
of communication technologies, old and new. His publications include
*News over the Wires: The Telegraph and the Flow of Public Information
in America, 1844–1897* (1994), and "Harold Adams Innis and His Bias
of Communication," in: Elihu Katz, Tamar Liebes, John D. Peters and
Avril Orloff (Eds.) *Canonic Texts in Communication Research* (2003).

James W. Carey (1934–2006)
was CBS Professor of International Journalism and chair of the
Interdepartmental Committee on Communications at Columbia
University. He held degrees from Rhode Island and Illinois Universities
and had held numerous academic posts, including Director of the
Institute of Communications Research at the University of Illinois,
George H. Gallup Professor at the University of Iowa; Dean, College
of Communications at the University of Illinois; President of the
Association for Education in Journalism; President of the American
Association of Schools and Departments of Journalism. He was
a Fellow of the National Endowment for the Humanities and of the
Gannett Center for Media Studies. He was a member of the advisory
board of the Poynter Institute for Media Studies, a member of the Board
of Directors of the Public Broadcasting System, and a board member of
the Peabody Awards for Broadcasting. He was the author of numerous
academic articles, book chapters and books, among them *Television and
the Press* (1988), *Communication as Culture* (1989) and *James Carey:
A Critical Reader* (1997).

Raphael Cohen-Almagor
D. Phil. (Oxon., 1991), is Assoc. Professor at the Department of
Communication, and Library and Information Studies, and founder and
director of the Center for Democratic Studies, Haifa University. He has
served on the Israel Press Council, and has been a Fulbright Visiting
Professor at the UCLA School of Law and Dept. of Communication
and a Senior Fellow at the Institute for Policy Studies, Johns Hopkins
University. His published works include *The Boundaries of Liberty and
Tolerance* (1994), *The Right to Die in Dignity* (2001), *Speech, Media*

and Ethics (2001, 2005) and *Euthanasia in the Netherlands* (2004); and (as editor) *Liberal Democracy and the Limits of Tolerance: Essays in Honor and Memory of Yitzhak Rabin* (2000), and *Challenges to Democracy: Essays in Honour and Memory of Isaiah Berlin* (2000); and he has authored two poetry books: *Middle Eastern Shores* (1993), and *Travels* (forthcoming).

Nava Cohen-Avigdor
is an Instructor in the Department of Political Studies (Public Communications Program) at Bar-Ilan University, Israel, where she has recently completed her doctoral dissertation that forms the basis of her article in this volume. She was formerly a senior editor at Israel's largest woman's magazine, *La'Isha*. Her article *The Natural Life Cycle of New Media Evolution* recently appeared in *New Media & Society* (2004).

Ronald J. Deibert
is Associate Professor of Political Science at the University of Toronto and Director of the Citizen Lab. He has been a Ford Foundation Research Scholar of Information and Communication Technologies (2002–4) and has been awarded the Northrop Frye Distinguished Teaching and Research Award (2002). He is the Author of *Parchment, Printing and Hypermedia: Communications and World Order Transformations* (1997), has published in *International Organization, The Review of International Studies*, and *Journal of Social Issues*, and is on the editorial board of *International Studies Perspectives* and *Explorations in Media Ecology*. He has been consultant to the Canadian Department of Foreign Affairs and International Trade on issues relating to the Internet and international relations, and has been a guest on CBC, CTv and Fox news networks. He is currently working on a book on the politics of internet security, entitled *Code Wars: Internet Security and Global Civic Networks*.

Paul Frosh
is a Lecturer in the Department of Communication and Journalism at the Hebrew University of Jerusalem. His research interests include consumer culture, cultural production, visual culture, the political economy of media and new media technologies. An unexpected congruence of the last three fields led to an interest in Innis' work. He is

the author of *The Image Factory: Consumer Culture, Photography and the Visual Content Industry (2004)*.

Elihu Katz
is Professor and founder of the School of Communication at the Hebrew University of Jerusalem, and Professor at the Annenberg School of Communications at the University of Pennsylvania. He obtained his PhD at Columbia where he worked with Paul Lazarsfeld. He has held positions at the University of Chicago and the Israel Institute of Applied Social Research, and headed the task force to introduce television broadcasting in Israel in the late 1960s. He is the author of many papers, book chapters and author and editor of numerous books, including (with J. J. Strange) *The future of fact: Special Issue of the Annals of the American Academy of Political and Social Science* (1998); (with Daniel Dayan) *Media Events: The Live Broadcasting of History* (1992) and *Canonic Texts in Media Research: Are there any? Should there be? How about these?* (2003).

Hillel Nossek
is the Academic Director of the Teaching and Research Authority of the College of Management and Academic Studies in Tel Aviv, Israel, and Associate Professor at the School of Media Studies in the College. His research and publications focus on the social implications of the new media technologies and multi-channel media environments, specifically their impact on individuals and families, broader ethnic communities and the nation state. A primary concern is contrasting the Toronto School perspective with a sociological framework in the analysis of effects of new media technologies in Israel.

David R. Olson
is Professor Emeritus at the Ontario Institute for Studies in Education, University of Toronto. He is a graduate of the University of Saskatchewan and the University of Alberta, and was Post-Doctoral Fellow at the Harvard Center for Cognitive Studies, where he worked with Jerome Bruner. He has been a Fellow at the Stanford Center for the Behavioral Sciences, the Netherlands Institute for Advance Studies and, most recently, at the Wissenschaftskolleg zu Berlin. He is a Fellow of the Royal Society of Canada and holds honorary degrees from Gothenburg

University (Sweden) and the University of Saskatchewan. He is former Director of the McLuhan Program in Culture and Technology at the University of Toronto and was named University Professor in 1998. He is author of some 300 articles and book chapters, and author or editor of 16 books, most recently *The World on Paper* (1994), *Psychological Theory and Educational Reform* (2003) and (with Nancy Torrance) *The Handbook of Education and Human Development* (1996). He is currently editing, with Michael Cole, a Festschrift entitled *Culture, technology and history: Implications of the work of Jack Goody* and (with Nancy Torrance) *The Cambridge Handbook of Literacy*.

Limor Shifman

is research fellow at the Oxford Internet Institute, University of Oxford. She completed a PhD dissertation in the Department of Communications at the Hebrew University of Jerusalem. Her work focuses on the interrelationship between humor, media, and social processes. In the last few years she has taught in the OII, the Department of Communications at the Hebrew University of Jerusalem and in the Israeli Open University. Until recently she served as head of research for a ten-chapter documentary series on the history of Israeli humor, produced for the IBA, and has worked as writer, producer, and on-camera anchor in the Children and Youth Division of Israel Public Television. As a research Fellow at the OII she is investigating various aspects of Internet-based humor.

Arthur Siegel

is Professor of Communications and Social Science at York University in Toronto. His research focuses on political communications, differences and similarities in French language and English language media content in Canada, and propaganda. Recent publications include the books, *Radio Canada International* and *Politics and the Media in Canada (2nd edition)*. His interest in the Toronto School dates from the 1970s when he was involved with Northrop Frye and Roderique Chiasson in a CRTC inquiry into national broadcasting in Canada.

Rita Watson

has held a tenured Associate Professorship in Educational Psychology at the University of British Columbia, Canada and currently holds the Abraham Shiffman Chair in Secondary Education at the Hebrew University School of Education. She has a PhD degree from the University of Toronto (OISE) and was Social Sciences and Humanities Research Council of Canada Post-doctoral Fellow for two years at the Department of Psychology, New School for Social Research in New York City. Her primary research interests are language and literacy and their relation to human cognitive development. Recent publications include articles in the *Journal of Child Language,* and book chapters: *Cognition and the lexicon in the environment of texts*, in J. W. Astington (Ed.) *Minds in the making* (2000); and *Literacy and oral language: Implications for early literacy acquisition,* in Dickenson and Neuman (Eds.) *Handbook of research on early literacy* (2001).

Sam Lehman-Wilzig

is currently Chairman of the Department of Political Studies and Head of the Public Communications Program at Bar-Ilan University in Israel. He has served as Chairman of the Israeli Political Science Association and is the founder and editor of *Patuakh*, Israel's academic journal for Mass Communications. His fields of expertise include Political Communication as well as the New Media. His recent publications include articles in *New Media & Society*, *The European Journal of Communications*, and *Journalism*.

Xiaoquan Zhao

holds a PhD from the University of Pennsylvania (2005) and is an instructor in the Department of Communication at George Mason University. His research examines the social and psychological effects of mass communication. One area in which he is particularly interested is the effects of the structural features of mass media on audience members' attitudes and behaviors (i.e., how *the medium* per se can function as *the message*). His research has been published in journals such as the *Journal of Communication, Communication Research*, and *Health Communication*.